BEYOND ECONOMIC MI

Beyond Economic Migration

Social, Historical, and Political Factors in US Immigration

Edited by

Min Zhou *and* Hasan Mahmud

NEW YORK UNIVERSITY PRESS
New York

جــامـعـة جـورجـتـاون قـطـر
GEORGETOWN UNIVERSITY QATAR

Center *for* **International** *and* **Regional Studies**

New York University Press gratefully acknowledges the support of the Center for International and Regional Studies, Georgetown University in Qatar, for this book.

NEW YORK UNIVERSITY PRESS
New York
www.nyupress.org

References to Internet websites (URLs) were accurate at the time of writing. Neither the author nor New York University Press is responsible for URLs that may have expired or changed since the manuscript was prepared.

Please contact the Library of Congress for Cataloging-in-Publication data.
ISBN: 9781479818532 (hardback)
ISBN: 9781479818549 (paperback)
ISBN: 9781479818570 (library ebook)
ISBN: 9781479818556 (consumer ebook)

New York University Press books are printed on acid-free paper, and their binding materials are chosen for strength and durability. We strive to use environmentally responsible suppliers and materials to the greatest extent possible in publishing our books.

Manufactured in the United States of America

10 9 8 7 6 5 4 3 2 1

Also available as an ebook

From Min Zhou: To Sam N. Guo, my loving husband of 40 years.

From Hasan Mahmud: To my mother, Azizunnahar, who has raised me to be who I am today.

CONTENTS

LIST OF FIGURES

LIST OF TABLES

Understanding Economic Migration to the United States

An Introduction

MIN ZHOU AND HASAN MAHMUD

The world has entered a new phase of hyperglobalization since the 1990s.[1] The turn of the twenty-first century has also been a period of rapid population movements across national borders, with the number of international migrants worldwide increasing from 153 million in 1990 to nearly 272 million in 2019.[2] The United States took the lion's share, receiving one-fifth of the world's international migrants, mostly from the developing countries. The foreign-born population in the United States reached a record number of 44.8 million as of 2018, accounting for nearly 14 percent of the total population.[3] This newer wave of immigrants quadrupled since 1970, when the number stood at 9.7 million, or 4.8 percent of the total population. More than three-quarters (77 percent) entered the country legally and nearly half (45 percent) were naturalized US citizens.

Contemporary immigrants are extremely diverse across a variety of categories—economic and political, temporary and permanent, legal and undocumented, low-skilled and high-skilled, single and family, and refugees or asylees—as well as by individual attributes—age, gender, race/ethnicity, religion, and socioeconomic backgrounds. These contemporary immigrants have hailed from diverse origins. Mexicans, as the largest immigrant group, comprised 25 percent of the total influx. About 28 percent came from different countries in Asia, 10 percent from the Caribbean, 8 percent from Central America, 7 percent from South America, 4 percent from the Middle East and North Africa, 5 percent from sub-Saharan Africa, and only about 13 percent from Europe and Canada. The number of arrivals from Asia had surpassed that from Latin America since 2015.[4] Added to this influx were nearly three million refugees from diverse origins. In 2019, the total number of refugees resettled in the United States was 30,000, with the largest groups coming from the Democratic Republic of the Congo, followed by Myanmar, Ukraine, Eritrea, and Afghanistan, with Christians constituting 79 percent and Muslims, 16 percent.[5]

Contemporary immigrants to the United States are also tremendously diverse in socioeconomic characteristics. While immigrants were equally as likely as their US-born counterparts to have a bachelor's degree or more (32 percent and 33 percent, respectively), there were wide variations in the educational selectivity by national origin. For instance, 71 percent of the immigrants from South Asia and 50 percent of those from the Middle East and North Africa had a bachelor's degree or more, whereas only 7 percent of those from Mexico, 11 percent of those from Central America, and 22 percent of those from the Caribbean had a bachelor's or advanced degree. Immigrants from Mexico and Central America were also significantly less likely than other immigrants and the US-born to have a high school diploma. More than half (54 percent) of Mexican immigrants and nearly half (47 percent) of Central American immigrants, as compared to 8 percent of the US-born, have not completed high school.

Scholarly research conducted in the United States often divides international migrations into two broad categories: political and economic. A closer look at the way this demarcation is accomplished reveals a significant problem: While a detectable immediate threat to life of an individual in her/his country of origin defines political migration, a lack thereof puts everyone else in the category of economic migration. Underlying the political category is a moral call for helping refugees and asylees based on the Declaration of Universal Human Rights of the United Nations that is enshrined in international legal systems.[6] The economic category, in contrast, makes a general assumption that all other migrants are motivated by economic interests, implying that an individual migrant's voluntary choice can be accomplished in the open market. Claire Alexander and her colleagues argue that the conceptualization of economic migration, as opposed to political, or "forced" migration, is arbitrary and theoretically fallacious.[7] Putting all migrants, except for refugees and asylees, into a single category makes it analytically difficult to distinguish between—for instance—those motivated by actual economic opportunities and those driven by varieties of noneconomic motives (such as marriage, retirement, military deployment abroad, and so forth).[8] Moreover, such conceptualization leads to a normative differentiation between economic migrants—those with desirable skills migrating through legal channels, and refugees/asylees—those deemed liabilities or burdens for the host country despite the moral urgency in assisting them with their resettlement.

In this volume, we focus on economic migration but critically engage it in conceptual discussions and empirical analyses from a multidisciplinary perspective. We argue that contemporary immigrants cannot simply be categorized as "economic" migrants. Although many contemporary migrants in the United States may have been driven by the economic interests of seeking better employment opportunities and life chances, the processes of their immigration and integration are shaped by the intersection of a range of noneconomic factors, including migration histories, cultures, networks, and state policies in both sending and receiving countries. Drawing insights from Payal Banerjee's rigorous analysis in chapter 1, we argue further that the making of immigrant labor involves multilevel processes in which migration histories, family ties, diasporic networks, homeland politico-economic circumstances, immigration regimes, and other institutional mechanisms interact with individual motivations and socioeconomic characteristics to determine immigrants' social positioning and outcomes of their economic incorporation and social mobility in the host society.[9]

Framing Economic Migration

The idea that individuals decide to migrate on the basis of their self-interest in maximizing economic gains or enhancing material success constitutes the core of understanding economic migration.[10] The classical theoretical understanding of migration has been dominated by functional models derived from neoclassical development economics.[11] Microeconomic theories consider migration as an aggregation of individual decision-making to move abroad for economic betterment. According to this theoretical perspective, migration is viewed as a means of transferring surplus labor from an agricultural economy to an urban economy of manufacturing employment to stimulate economic development in the destination and a psychosocial reorientation of the migrant in the process. Another microeconomic model is the new economics of labor migration (NELM) approach, which assumes that individual members of a migrant household seek to minimize risks to aggregate family incomes or overcome capital constraints on the family's productive activities by finding employment abroad.

Scholars with a structural orientation, by contrast, focus on the macroeconomic processes that produce sociospatial inequalities and constrain the life chances of individual migrants as members of specific social classes in particular places.[12] Macroeconomic theories conceptualize migration not merely as the result of the aggregation of individual decisions and actions, but also as the product of objective social and spatial structures that produce the necessary conditions for labor migration. Macroeconomic theories are founded on three general assumptions. First, the economy consists of two sectors: a primary sector with capital-intensive and high-wage jobs and a secondary sector with labor-intensive and low-wage jobs. The behavior of firms and individuals in these two sectors requires different theoretical explanations. Second, the distinction between good and bad jobs is of greater importance for analysis than that between skilled and unskilled workers. Third, workers in the secondary sector tend to be transient and unstable, moving frequently between jobs, or in and out of unemployment and labor force participation.[13] Thus, international wage differentials are neither sufficient nor necessary for migration to occur.

One such macroeconomic theory is the dual labor market theory, which examines how the structural conditions of modern industrial economies cause migration.[14] This theory postulates that international migration is largely driven by the labor demand in developed countries. According to this theory, the labor market in developed societies is bifurcated by social and institutional mechanisms whereby dirty, dangerous, and demeaning jobs, popularly known as three-D jobs, are demarcated for immigrants in the secondary/informal labor market or economies, while better jobs (both in terms of pay and status) in the primary/formal labor market are reserved for natives or locals.

Another influential macroeconomic theory is the world system theory, which considers migration as an inevitable consequence of economic globalization and market penetration across national boundaries.

It posits that the expansion of capitalism from advanced industrial countries at the core of the world system leads to the destruction of local systems of production, often in agrarian communities, in underdeveloped or developing countries in the periphery. Consequently, people begin to migrate to industrial centers from rural areas to cities and to industrialized countries in search of viable livelihood.[15] From this perspective, the expansion of the capitalist market in noncapitalist peripheries and past colonies drives internal and international migrations. Moreover, the international flow of labor follows the international flow of capital and goods, but in the opposite direction. Furthermore, receiving-country governments influence immigration rates by regulating overseas investment activities of corporations and controlling international flows of capital and goods. Finally, international migration follows the dynamics of the global economy as well as political and military interventions by the governments of the countries at the core to protect investments abroad and support foreign governments sympathetic to the expansion of the global market.[16]

The neoclassical economic theories of migration continue to dominate migration studies. However, scholars identify a number of limitations, such as a commitment to methodological individualism, a uniform conception of rationality, an assumption of the individual as a utility-maximizing being, and the neglect of the impact of structural inequalities, all of which render these theories insufficient to predict migration.[17] Moreover, there is a growing call for incorporating the various social, economic, and political phenomena within which migratory flows are embedded.[18]

Beyond the Economic Frame

Neoclassical economic theories explain how individuals or families respond to changing circumstances in their home societies caused by drastic structural transformations and economic globalization and how they utilize migration as a strategy to raise incomes, accumulate capital, manage risks, and, ultimately, improve standards of living. Moving beyond the limitations of the economic frame, migration scholars have formulated new theoretical approaches that address various noneconomic forces influencing migration.

Douglas Massey and his colleagues advance a social network theory.[19] They note that migration flows, even when initially driven by economic necessities, tend to become self-sustaining once set in motion. Each act of migration contributes to the expansion of migrant networks based on family and friendship ties and sets off a process of social capital accumulation that makes additional movement more likely. Moreover, the spread of migratory behavior within sending communities sparks other structural changes, such as shifting distributions of income and land, and transforming local cultures in ways that promote additional and continual migration.

The social network theory considers the intersection of economic and noneconomic factors in the following six postulations.[20] First, migration abroad begins only if a number of complementary structural changes occur in both the labor-sending and labor-receiving countries. Second, subsequent migration from a migrant's hometown creates and expands local relations between migrants and those left behind, resulting in a migration infrastructure in the hometown in which social networks are embedded. Third, the adaptation of local-migrant relations to the requisites of migration prompts more emigration from that hometown, hence further strengthening the migrant infrastructure and expanding the network. Fourth, migration becomes self-sustaining once network resources are widely available, in spite of the changes in the structural conditions at home that triggered outmigration in the first place or unfavorable policy changes in receiving countries. Fifth, when some migrants are resettled in a receiving country and form diasporic communities, these diasporic structures stabilize the migration network and facilitate transnational contacts with compatriots back home. Last, migration networks expand further whenever migrants return home to share news about their migratory process and experiences and present themselves as successful role models for compatriots to emulate, all of which further stimulate the aspiration to emigrate.

While migratory flows connect migrants with those left behind in sending communities, social institutions supporting migration also gradually emerge to form an ecosystem that perpetuates ongoing migration. Calling this process "cumulative causation" of migration, scholars recognize how each instance of migration transforms the social context in ways that enhance the likelihood of further migration.[21] First, the contextual transformations in both sending and receiving countries set off a momentum by taking migration regulation out of the state's capacity, which results in the continuation of cross-border movements. Second, changing valuation of jobs—whereby local workers would shun "immigrant" jobs and refuse to take those positions even in times of high unemployment—leads industries to put pressure on the government to import foreign labor, despite widespread anti-immigrant nativism on the ground. Third, once a particular job sector recruits a significant number of migrant workers, it would be labeled as an "immigrant" niche, which would dissuade local workers from taking jobs from that niche, thereby consolidating the contextual basis of continued migration.[22]

Relevant to cumulative causation is the transmission of migration desire or aspiration between immigrants in destination societies and nonimmigrants in sending communities, which occurs over generations. Growing support for outmigration and frequent transnational flows lead to the development of a migration culture.[23] Once the migration culture develops, individuals become less likely to invest in their socioeconomic mobility in the community of origin and aspire to build their future in the destination country, and they often do so without much knowledge about the costs involved in their migration. As a result, migration becomes more of a habitual practice than a rationally planned economic action.[24]

Much of the scholarship on international migration at present recognizes the existence and role of family and friendship ties among the migrants who constitute the core of a migrant network, embedded in a migrant infrastructure, ecosystem, and/or culture. Such networks activate cumulative causation. Improved transportation and information and communication technology (ICT) have enabled migrants to maintain continued relations with family and community members back in their countries of origin as well as diasporas founded in other countries of destination outside their country of origin. As such, most of the migrant communities have established and maintained transnational connections that sustain stable flows of money, information, and other material and symbolic resources along with people across nation-state borders.[25] Contrary to the basic assumption of economic theories about migration being motivated primarily by economic interests, an increasing number of scholars are beginning to pay attention to the combination and interaction of both economic and noneconomic factors, such as family and migration histories, social networks, bilateral relations between sending and receiving countries, and natural as well as man-made crises in the sending countries, all of which lead to population exodus, transnational movements, and immigrant incorporation all over the world.

Immigration Regimes from the Receiving-Country Perspective

Neoliberal Globalization

Since the late 1980s, accelerated globalization has come to define the contemporary world. It is marked by an increasing interdependence among countries in terms of their economies, cultures, and populations through exchanges of labor and capital, goods and services, technologies and information, and natural resources. A central feature of this world order is the neoliberal economic system, which embodies "a belief in the efficacy of markets, export-oriented manufacturing, and a liberalized trade regime in bringing about the greatest good for the greatest number of people."[26] Since its inception as a policy strategy adopted by many countries in both the Global North and South, neoliberalism has resulted in a fundamental restructuring of the world's economy through the workings of major multinational corporations (MNC) as well as the World Bank, the International Monetary Fund (IMF), and the World Trade Organization (WTO).[27] This policy shift has allowed MNCs to counteract falling profit margins in domestic economies by relocating production to countries in the Global South—endowed with abundant cheap labor and natural resources—and exporting manufactured goods to a wider global market. Many countries sustain economic growth at great expense to the working class throughout the world. As David Harvey argues, capital is gained through "accumulation by dispossession" under neoliberalism.[28] Contrary to the popular expectation of extended individual freedom, such capital gain has led to increasing monopolization of global production, finance, services, and commerce, along with intensifying labor exploitation and environmental degradation.[29]

One of the principal mechanisms of restructuring the contemporary world is known as the structural adjustment programs (SAPs) of the IMF and World Bank, which aim at rebalancing public accounts by reducing government expenditure, relaxing institutional constraints to stimulate business development, and lifting protectionist barriers to boost trade balances.[30] As a result of several rounds of innovations and strategic re-orientations of SAPs, a new international division of labor has emerged in which the exploitation of the workforce is achieved through international migration. Saskia Sassen outlined this process in her seminal work *The Global City*, demonstrating how globalization—particularly the flows of foreign direct investments (FDI) to underdeveloped or developing countries—generated counterflows of people (migrants) toward the global cities in the developed world.[31] Gerardo Otero confirms this pattern through a case study of the impact of the North American Free Trade Agreement (NAFTA) on Mexico's north-bound migration.[32] Other scholars recognize similar consequences of globalization in developing countries around the world.[33]

With unprecedented development in transportation and ICT, neoliberal globalization has indeed made international migration easier and faster than at any time in the past. This, however, should not lead us to assume that the nation-state—the only sovereign authority over international borders—has lost its control over immigration. Although some scholars have shifted their attention to post-national conceptions of citizenship, or citizenship that transcends the confines of the nation-state,[34] many others maintain that the role of the nation-state in migration control and regulation, both at the origin and destination, is ever present and significant. On the one hand, countries of origin in the developing world actively engage in managing international migration, primarily motivated by economic interests of earning foreign currencies in remittances as well as reducing the problem of unemployment and the risk of political unrest.[35] On the other hand, countries of destination, even those of liberal immigration regimes, continue to play a decisive role through various regulatory mechanisms at the border and within their territorial boundaries.[36] Despite greater freedom in border crossing, more expansive migration networks, and more developed migration industry, countries of destination are tightening, not loosening, their grip on immigration. Moreover, the receiving country's immigration and integration policies shape immigrant selectivity and the context of reception,[37] hence affecting migrants' experiences of adaptation or incorporation in their host countries.

Regime Types and Changes

The most direct role of the receiving nation-state in shaping migration is found in visa/entry policies. Some of the largest flows of economic migration since World War II (WWII) involved what was known as "guest worker" programs. In the United States, for example, hundreds of thousands of low-skilled workers from Mexico entered the country under the Bracero program in 1942. These workers were brought in on short-term visas as seasonal labor to meet the demand of the expanding US economy. Despite the explicit economic motives of both migrants and the US state at the beginning of the program, a number of developments—including flattening of labor demand and supply, emergence of large immigration communities, and rising anti-immigration nativism—eventually led the United States to end this migration program. In the 1950s and 1960s, West Germany signed bilateral recruitment agreements with other countries, including Italy, Spain, Portugal, Turkey, Greece, Yugoslavia, Morocco, Tunisia, and South Korea, to recruit thousands of guest workers to fill jobs in industrial sectors that required few qualifications.[38]

The United States, as well as other liberal regimes in the West, has to maintain a certain level of border openness to allow international migrants to enter, find employment, and raise families. One way receiving nation-states exercise control over migration is by conferring on migrants different legal statuses upon their arrival. Through immigration and border control policies, countries of destination define migrants within a variety of categories, including "permanent residents," who are granted immigrant visas to resettle in the country; "temporary workers" and short-term "visitors," who are allowed to stay for a certain period; and "undocumented" immigrants, who either evade the legal procedures upon entry or overstay their nonimmigrant visas.[39] Receiving countries also regulate the adjustment of migrants' legal status once they have already reached their destination. For example, in the United States, international students may adjust their student visas to different work visas and eventually to permanent residency and citizenship.[40]

The history of immigration regulation in the United States offers important insights about the role of receiving countries in shaping international migration.[41] Prior to WWII, US immigration policy and practices had been heavily tilted toward Western and Northern Europeans and against immigrants from other regions. For example, the 1875 Page Act banned the immigration of Chinese women, and the 1882 Chinese Exclusion Act was the first—and remains the only—law enacted to exclude members of an entire national origin group from immigrating to the country. These two laws effectively curbed Chinese immigration and stifled the natural growth and social integration of the diasporic Chinese community in the United States.[42] The 1924 Immigration Act, known as the Johnson-Reed Act, was to regulate the number of immigrants allowed to enter the United States through a national origins quota system, which disproportionately targeted immigrants from Southern and Eastern Europe.[43]

US immigration law was drastically reformed during the civil rights movement. In 1965, the US Congress passed the Immigration and Nationality Act, known as the Hart-Celler Act, which abolished the national origins quota system laid down in the 1924 Immigration Act and legislated an arguably more liberal system of immigration control. The Hart-Celler Act had a humanitarian goal of reuniting family members and an economic goal of bringing in skilled labor. Each country of origin would have the same annual numerical cap of 20,000, while immediate family members—spouses, minor children, and parents—were not subject to the per-country cap.[44] In 1990, US immigration law was reformed further. It maintained the dual goals in policy orientation, while creating a new immigration category, the Diversity Immigrant Visa Program.[45] As the reformed law stipulated, immigration from Europe was, for the first time, restricted, and immigration from countries in the Western hemisphere, including Mexico, was also curbed. But the door was reopened to Asian immigration.[46] One unintended consequence of the policy reform was obviously the exponential growth in Asian immigration. Asians, except for Southeast Asian refugees, have been admitted to the United States either as family-sponsored or employer-sponsored migrants. The employer-sponsored migrants include predominantly highly educated and highly skilled workers, which creates a new phenomenon termed "hyperselectivity" with significant consequences for socioeconomic integration.[47] Another unintended consequence is a highly visible population of undocumented immigrants who are gainfully employed but lack viable paths to legal status and citizenship. This is partly due to policy provisions that leave little room for the immigration of "unskilled" workers in sectors like agriculture, construction, and domestic service.

Racialized Immigration Control

Despite the popular belief that the United States has one of the most liberal immigration systems in the world, racism has been embedded in immigration policymaking from the very beginning. The Chinese Exclusion Act of 1882 is known to mark a turning point in US history, and its conceptualization as "a nation of immigrants," by setting the stage for race-based admission and exclusion, or racialized immigrant control.[48] The US Congress passed a series of immigration laws after the Chinese Exclusion Act that would racially discriminate against all but white immigrants from Northwestern Europe, including the Asiatic Barred Zone Act of 1917 and the Immigration Act of 1924. Most of these laws were in effect until the Hart-Celler Act of 1965.[49] As noted above, the hyperselectivity of some Asian origin groups and a steady increase in the number of undocumented immigrants in the United States were unintended but direct consequences of the Hart-Celler Act of 1965.[50] The unintended consequences and policy feedback suggest that US immigration policy is shaped by prevailing economic circumstances and political ideologies that are hardly random. Race was built into restrictive immigration lawmaking. Up until the 1960s, US immigration laws targeted Asians, and later Southern and Eastern Europeans, but not those from Latin America and the Caribbean.[51] Both Asians and Southern and Eastern Europeans were perceived not merely as an economic threat, taking jobs away from natives and depressing wages, but also as a cultural threat of un-Americanizing Americans, as they were considered nonwhite and culturally inferior.

Between 1942 and when it was discontinued in 1964, the temporary low-skilled worker program (known as the Bracero program) brought millions of migrant workers mainly to the US agricultural sectors. For more than two decades, this program resulted in extensive migrant networks between the communities of origin in Mexico and their US destinations. The Bracero workers toiled in agricultural fields on American soil, making tremendous contributions to the US economy, but the program was discontinued partly due to a growing civil rights concern about severe labor exploitation as well to a heightened fear of a "Latino threat."[52] However, the Bracero program transformed socioeconomic contexts that set in motion the processes of cumulative causation and the development of a migration culture.

Protracted political battles between interest groups defending immigration and conservatives doubting the contributions of immigrants over time transformed the policy regimes in the United States. Daniel Tichenor traces the history of US immigration from vibrant nineteenth-century politics that opened up expansive admissions of Southern and Eastern Europeans to the draconian restrictions on non-European nations that had taken hold by the early 1920s, including racist quotas that severely hampered the rescue of Jews from the Holocaust.[53] The changing domestic politics and international geopolitical stance of the United States, with its ascendency to global leadership after WWII, resulted in an unexpected expansion of immigration opportunities, with the passage of the 1965 Hart-Celler Act, the 1986 Immigration Reform and Control Act (IRCA), and the 1990 Immigration Act being the most notable.

However, a surge of nativist fervor spurred the political mobilization for immigration restriction since the beginning of the 1990s. The federal government, as well as a number of states, passed various exclusionary laws to curb undocumented immigration and expel those who were already in theUnited States without authorization.[54] Yet, immigration law enforcement measures along the US-Mexico border and inside the United States were ineffective. Amuedo-Dorantes and Pozo found that those measures had no impact on the deportee's intent to re-enter the United States in the future, but increased the expenditure of the US government significantly.[55]

In fact, receiving-country governments vary widely in their approaches to immigration regulation, but show a common tendency of adopting increasingly restrictive measures at the present time. Some of the most restrictive immigration regimes exist in the countries of destination in the Middle East and East Asia, including Singapore, where nation-state governments use immigration laws to keep immigrants in certain labor market sectors by linking their visas closely to a particular employer or job (e.g., the *kafala* in the Middle East), housing them in workers' colonies, and limiting their labor market mobility, while rigid law enforcement, such as frequent raids and strict security checks, prevent them from overstaying their visas.[56] Liberal democracies like the United States cannot openly adopt such draconian immigration policies due to their official subscription to universal norms and values. For instance, on humanitarian grounds, the Universal Declaration of Human Rights limits the ability of liberal democratic governments to deny entry to refugees and political asylees. Moreover, the US government has to respond to the demands of some pro-immigration domestic interest groups—e.g., organized agro-industry sectors or workers' unions in some service sectors—that play important roles in shaping the final outcomes of immigration policy debates and the enforcement of restrictive immigration laws.[57]

Thus, the role of destination states in the contemporary era of globalization is more, not less, significant. Hollifield introduces the idea of the "migration state," arguing that international trade and migration are two sides of the same coin and that the states are involved in regulating both. In other words, destination states need to be prepared to accept higher levels of migration in order to take full advantage of economic prosperity through globalization. However, this would put liberal states into what Hollifield calls the "liberal paradox," whereby destination states must strike a balance between maintaining a competitive advantage by keeping their economy and society open to trade and migration and managing potentially great political risks domestically. This paradox often plays out explicitly in US presidential campaigns. As the 2020 election showed, for instance, while liberal and left-leaning politicians (mostly Democrats) advocated for immigration reform, highlighting the needs for economic prosperity and humanitarian leadership of the United States, conservative right-wing politicians (mostly Republicans) championed an overtly anti-immigration and populist xenophobic position. The organized interest groups—such as capitalists, labor unionists, feminists—also demonstrated their respective positions with regard to the immigration question. This was evident in the opposition of big-tech companies to restrictive immigration policies of the Trump administration.[58]

Economic Incorporation of Immigrants

The idea of the "American Dream" offers an attractive image of the United States as a promised land with opportunities for permanent resettlement and socioeconomic betterment. Many immigrants hold a positive view of their host country, believing that through grit and hard work they can earn prosperity and achieve upward mobility. Empirical research shows that, despite commonly shared experiences of downward occupational mobility upon arrival, a great majority of immigrants managed to eventually catch up over time with their native counterparts on key measures of socioeconomic status (SES), including education, occupation, and income.[59]

Immigrants' levels of educational achievement and job skills are often country-specific. Upon arrival, immigrants encounter a range of disadvantages associated with immigrant status that negatively affect their entry into the host labor market. Ivan Light and Carolyn Rosenstein differentiate between resource disadvantage and labor market disadvantage.[60] Resource disadvantage occurs when an immigrant group attempts to enter the labor market with fewer human capital resources, whereas labor market disadvantage is a result of race, gender, or nativity discrimination that is not intrinsic to the productivity of the group. The common labor market disadvantages unique to immigrants are the lack of fluency in the host language, limited information about the labor market and its functioning, lack of social networks and experience in the host society, differences in work-related culture and practices, and few transferable job skills and work experiences.[61] Even for the highly educated and highly skilled, it takes time to adapt to the receiving labor market and society, often because of problems getting their educational and occupational credentials validated and valued.[62]

Observing how immigrants fare in the American workplace informs us about their modes of economic incorporation. In general, immigrants are more strongly attached to the labor force than native-born workers, and their rate of unemployment is no higher than that of natives. While the US labor market offers ample work opportunities for immigrants, many often find themselves in low-wage and low-status jobs with little access to the social safety net. This is indicative of the presence of a dual-labor market in which "immigrant jobs" are associated with low wages, few fringe benefits, poor working conditions, limited job security, and low social value. These jobs undervalue immigrants' skills and technical knowledge, and are perceived as mundane or unappealing by native-born workers.[63]

Three main structural features of the labor market segmentation in the United States have profound impacts on how well immigrants fare. First, there is a prevalence of small and micro firms, mostly in the secondary sector of the economy, in which labor regulations are either not enforced or only partially enforced, or are circumvented. Immigrants are disproportionately employed in these firms. Second, there is a massive use of more flexible temporary contract labor—even in the primary sector of the economy, such as specialists and engineers in high-tech industries—to respond to the rigidities stemming from state regulations for the purpose of protecting the permanent and core positions within firms. Increasingly, age, rather than education or job skills, structures the cleavage between the insiders—those who hold better-protected positions—and the outsiders—new entrants in the labor market with unstable and less-protected positions within firms. Immigrants, especially the new arrivals, are more likely than natives to be in temporary contract work.[64] Third, irregular arrangements and practices are widespread in secondary labor market employment and in the informal economy. Immigrants are more likely than natives to be involved in low-skilled jobs, such as within small firms in traditional sectors of retail and service, or domestic and care work in the secondary and informal economies.[65]

Because of their concentration in the secondary labor market and poor ethnic enclaves, many immigrants are likely to be trapped in the ranks of the working poor.[66] Failing to achieve earnings parity with natives seems to disprove the general expectation about upward mobility embodied in the idea of the American Dream. Once popular among scholars of migration studies, the theory of assimilation predicts that immigrants are initially held back by their lack of fluency in English, US-specific education and skills, as well as familiarity with the US labor market, but that with time and in succeeding generations, they should be able to close their economic gap with natives. Past studies of immigrants' job market integration, based on the 1970 US census data, found that immigrants generally earned less than natives upon initial arrival but were able to catch up rapidly, and that in some cases they overtook natives after spending 15–20 years in the United States. This, however, is conditional upon their ability to "pass" as natives, for instance, by changing their name or losing their accent.[67] Recent studies found that the closing of the immigrant-native earnings gap varied by national origin and that the gap remained significant for some groups even after controlling for age, duration of stay in the United States, and country of origin.[68]

The persistent gaps in economic incorporation across national origin groups and generational cohorts are explained by immigrant selectivity, which is measured by levels of education (in years) of the immigrant group vis-à-vis those of compatriots in the countries of origin. Positive selectivity means that, on average, the immigrant groups had more years of education than the population in origin.[69] The level and type of immigrant selectivity is related to the characteristics of their places of origin and destination, the historical relationship between origin and destination, and entry barriers at destination.[70] The earlier immigrants to the United States hailed from Northern and Western Europe, but such transatlantic migration was prohibitively costly for the aspirants, which constrained migration flows. Revolutions in shipping technology (i.e., a shift from sail to steam technology), intersecting migration networks, significantly reduced migration costs, led to a sustained age of mass migration from Northwestern Europe until 1850 and then from Southern and East Europe at the turn of the twentieth century. The imposition of a literacy test for entry in 1917 and the strict immigration quotas established in the 1924 Immigration Act ended the massive European migration. Much later, a modification—although not elimination—of such restrictive measures in 1965 and relaxation of immigration quotas allowed for a period of constrained mass migration, primarily from Asia and Latin America. These historical trends showed that the intersection of immigration regimes on top and migrants' access to networks and ethnic resources on the ground played a decisive role in immigrant selectivity.

Historians of migration studies recognize that immigration to the United States involved a mixed selectivity at the beginning,[71] but gradually leaned toward positive selectivity, as seen in the widening income disparity between the United States and the origin countries of the immigrants.[72] Immigrants from Latin American countries to the United States also demonstrated similar patterns of initially negative selectivity toward increasingly positive selectivity in terms of access to migrant networks, level of education, and asset ownership.[73] In fact, almost all immigrant groups now demonstrate a highly positive selectivity in terms of education and other observable skills.[74]

While positive educational selectivity is also found to positively affect the economic mobility of immigrants, their labor market experience and occupational mobility is more complex than the generally held positive trends suggest.[75] An adequate understanding of immigrants' modes of economic incorporation involves the questions of not only whether immigrants were positively or negatively received by their host countries, but also whether they are positively or negatively selected from their origin countries.[76] Jennifer Lee and Min Zhou propose a more refined concept of immigrant selectivity. Instead of using average years of education of an immigrant group via-à-vis its compatriots in the country of origin, they measured selectivity in terms of hyperselectivity, high selectivity, and hypo-selectivity based on the percentage of college graduates of an immigrant group in contrast not only to compatriots back home but also to natives in the countries of destination.[77] While most of the immigrant groups are highly selected, only a limited number of them are hyper- and hypo-selected. While immigrant selectivity is generally consequential for group members, Lee and Zhou showed how hyperselectivity is particularly conducive to upward social mobility. The obvious effects include a favorable starting point for the ethnic group; an ethnic-specific success frame to ensure upward economic mobility; the creation of ethnic capital in tangible and intangible forms to support that success frame, which benefits not only middle-class coethnics but also coethnics of relatively low SES backgrounds; and a unique stereotype promise, the promise of being positively viewed by others as successful and high-achieving. Lee and Zhou's study suggests that the reason some immigrant groups fare better than others has a lot to do with the way in which they are initially selected. And as we have discussed, immigrant selectivity is impacted by immigration regimes and networks and is consequential for the economic incorporation of immigrants.

Immigrant Transnationalism

Immigrants' economic incorporation, and ultimately assimilation, into the mainstream of their destination country was regarded as a norm in migration studies until anthropologists called attention to the concept of transnationalism in the early 1990s. Since then, the study of transnationalism has gained popularity as an important subfield of international migration in anthropology, sociology, geography, economics, political science, and cultural studies.[78] The proponents of transnationalism posit that contemporary immigrants do not always aim at complete assimilation and that not all countries of destination offer immigrants unproblematic and easy paths to permanent resettlement and citizenship. This nascent anthropological approach to migration recognizes that immigrants are capable of exercising their agency and become transnational beings by establishing a new kind of life across national borders between their origin and destination societies.[79]

The original conceptualization of transnationalism sees the nation-state—the only sovereign authority in the contemporary world order—in decline and losing control over its borders, inhabitants, and territories. Neoliberal globalization has restructured the world economy so much so that all countries are functionally dependent on one another, leading to increased immigration, not only to countries of the Global North but also to countries of the Global South, as well as to frequent back-and-forth movements between countries of origin and destination. As a result, countries of destination have been inevitably transformed into multicultural societies characterized by more mobile but less assimilated immigrant populations who maintain sustained contact with their cultures of origin. With increased global mobility and access to instantaneous ICTs worldwide, existing international borders are assumed to have dissolved, rendering the role of the nation-state either weakening or irrelevant.

Transnationalism is not new, but modern transportation and ICT development have qualitatively changed the immigrant experience since the 1990s.[80] As the literature well documents, immigrants in the United States have always maintained cross-border connections.[81] Adopting a transnationalism perspective, sociologists and anthropologists emphasize how migrants either adapt themselves to their country of destination, or are excluded from their country of origin, but also how they take advantage of their movements between here in the host country and there in the home countries to benefit themselves and their families *here* and those left behind *there*. When looking at migrants' transnationalism, some anthropologists explore how migration shapes an individual's subjectivity and the perception of migration,[82] whereas sociologists are interested in exploring how the social fields that stretch between a specific community of origin and a specific place of destination enable immigrants to exchange economic and social resources.[83]

Immigrants do not come randomly from any part of their country of origin, nor do they settle randomly anywhere in their country of destination. The transnationalism approach recognizes how immigrants from a certain locality in the country of origin interact with local structural barriers and opportunities in an immigrant neighborhood of a particular city in the country of destination to create a unique lifestyle characterized by selectively accumulating and synthesizing social and cultural elements from both communities. A transnationalism lens allows us to observe—as the chapters in this volume demonstrate—the diversities among immigrants beyond their legally established national identities and to explore how places of origin and destination, social class, gender, educational credentials, and professional experiences interact with the larger and seemingly overpowering forces of US immigration to shape the lived experiences of both immigrants and native-born people in the United States.

Understanding migration within the context of global capitalism, the transnationalism approach—articulated by anthropologists—recognizes how the structures of global capitalism shape migration. However, the tendency among some transnational scholars to emphasize the fluidity of transnational social fields as a routine practice and lifestyle,[84] and transmigrant identities as a form of resistance to "the global political and economic situations that engulf them,"[85] leads to the idea of migrants' emancipation from nation-state control and capitalist exploitation. Combined with the neoliberal conception of the individual as "an unattached, self-responsible market player,"[86] the idea of migrants' freedom in transnationalism runs the risk of overlooking how immigrants are embedded in the legal and social structures of their origin and destination societies, which inevitably shape their lived experiences here and there. Yet, transnationalism can be seen as migrants' response to the structural barriers in the destination countries. For instance, Min Zhou recounts the history of Chinese exclusion in the late nineteenth century, which resulted in the development of Chinatowns across the United States and formed the bedrock of adaptation and transnationalism among Chinese immigrants.[87]

Other scholars also note similar responses from immigrants against structural barriers—such as denial of citizenship/legalization and limited opportunities of upward social mobility in the host society—through establishing what are known as hometown associations,[88] or engaging in remittances.[89] Moreover, gender shapes immigrants' transnationalism in important ways. For example, immigrant women are centrally involved in creating and sustaining affective and emotional bridges through return travels.[90] Furthermore, rather than seeing immigrant transnationalism as an opposition to the restrictions imposed by nation-states, scholars recognize how nation-states, especially sending states, actively promote migrants' transnational practices to advance their own interests.[91] In fact—as Roger Waldinger shows—nation-states play a singularly consequential role in determining migratory flows, including regulating or facilitating migrants' back and forth movement and return migration.[92]

In sum, we recognize transnationalism as a useful theoretical lens to explore immigrants' lived experiences. However, we argue that transnationalism is not just a way of life that immigrants experience across borders, but a pragmatic strategy that these immigrants adopt to overcome challenges as they get themselves resettled in their country of destination. Hence, our focus in this book is on how immigration and the lives of immigrants in the United States are shaped by structural mechanisms and the strategies immigrants adopt to achieve the best possible outcomes of their migration.[93]

Chapters at a Glance

The book is organized as follows. Chapter 1, "The Making of Immigrant Labor: Inequality, Digital Capitalism, and Racialized Enforcement" by Payal Banerjee, problematizes the conceptualization of the immigrant as a predominantly *economic* entity by moving beyond framing based primarily in terms of livelihoods, skills, and sector-specific employment. Banerjee argues that the making of immigrant labor is a sociohistorical process in which structural mechanisms intersect with gender-race discourses to arbitrate the construction of immigrants' social positioning and govern the goals, means, nature, and outcomes of their economic incorporation. She argues further that a principal focus on livelihoods, skills, and jobs serves to divert attention away from crucial issues, such as racial formation, capital-labor relations, inequality, and a host of closely integrated social, legal, and discursive arrangements that produce the economic aspects associated with migration. This chapter brings the matter of jobs and immigrant employment in conversation with adjacent scholarship on socioeconomic inequality in late globalization, digital capitalism, and racialized surveillance and immigration enforcement in the United States to bridge scholarships between international migration and neoliberal globalization.

Chapter 2, "Evolving Trends of Latin American Immigration in the United States: Challenges for the Integration of Skilled Immigrants" by René Zenteno, presents an overview of immigration from Latin America to the United States from 1990 to 2019. Analyzing data from a variety of sources, Zenteno points to significant changes in the characteristics and qualities of Latino immigrants as the overall magnitude of Latin American migration is decreasing. He also shows that the contemporary flow has become more diverse in terms of countries of origin and more selective with respect to education, especially since the Great Recession in 2008. He argues that these trends are not driven merely by classic push-pull factors, but by a combination of demographic changes and economic development in sending countries, as well as racialized immigration control in the United States. The descriptive analysis reveals that larger supplies of high-skilled immigrants contribute to enhancing the economic integration of Latino immigrants. However, despite changes in cohort quality, the successful integration of Latino immigrants into US society is still hindered by the large presence of unskilled workers and undocumented migrants, whose path to legalization is blocked, as they face low rates of naturalization among legal immigrants and are subjected to ethno-racial profiling of US immigration enforcement.

Chapter 3, "East Asian Immigration: Historical Trends and Contemporary Issues in Movement to the United States" by Min Zhou, focuses on Americans of Chinese, Japanese, and Korean descent. The three major ethnonational groups under study arrived in the United States at different historical times, dating back to the mid-nineteenth century, from diverse socioeconomic backgrounds, and with varied patterns of resettlement and integration, but have shared similar lived experience of racialization in the host society. Zhou addresses the question of why and how earlier immigrants reached the other shores of the Pacific Ocean and formed diasporic communities and analyzes how changes in the contexts of immigration and emigration over the past half century shape contemporary trends of cross-border movements, socioeconomic characteristics of immigrants, and patterns of social mobility. She also tackles the issues of racialization facing East Asian immigrants and their offspring who have arguably made it into the American mainstream, explaining, in particular, how the old and new stereotypes have interacted to affect the life chances of Asian Americans. She concludes with a discussion on the prospects of panethnicity.

Chapter 4, "The US Visa System: Growing Complexity and Difference without Legislative Change" by Katharine M. Donato and Catalina Amuedo-Dorantes, offers an overview of the US visa system created by the Immigration Act of 1990. The chapter examines whether and how the numbers and types of visas vary by national origin characteristics, US presidential administrations, and the Great Recession. Based on a review of prior studies and analysis of data broadly covering the 2002 through 2017 period, the authors show that, although the visa system itself has remained unchanged, it increasingly reflects policies and practices embedded in executive orders and actions implemented by different presidential administrations. The findings reveal a sizeable increase in temporary visas issued to foreign nationals, including increases in low-skilled temporary work visas among Mexicans, high-skilled temporary work visas among Indians, and high-skilled temporary work, student, exchange, and tourist visas among Chinese. Moreover, visa issuance varies significantly across presidential administrations, but less so with the Great Recession and specific country-of-origin traits. The authors conclude that the substantial shifts in visa issuances—in the absence of legislative reforms—are symptomatic of differential types of visa access, which ultimately creates hardships for many immigrants already in the United States and those hoping to enter in the future, and has varying impacts on the US economy.

Chapter 5, "Preferential Hiring: US Earnings of Skilled Temporary Foreign Workers" by B. Lindsay Lowell, takes a close look at the phenomenon of the increasing number of temporary skilled workers on H-1B visas, addressing the debate on whether the H-1B visa scheme supplies US employers with much needed foreign workers to fill labor shortages or whether it fosters employer dependence on and exploitation of skilled temporary foreign workers. Combining data on actual H-1Bs with the American Community Survey of the US population, Lowell finds that skilled temporary foreign workers earn significantly less than local workers, with the exception of H-1B workers from Africa, and that their earnings vary by industrial sector, age, and national origins. For example, the youngest Indian-born H-1Bs, concentrated in the IT sector, earn substantially less than local workers, which reinforces the expectation of sector-specific preferential demand. He concludes that temporary programs can incentivize some employers to pursue preferential hiring that undercuts working conditions and constrains foreign workers' bargaining power and mobility.

Chapter 6, "Elusive Permanent Residency: Democratic Deficit of Skilled Temporary Foreign Workers" by Sangay K. Mishra, looks at how a restrictive temporary visa program has produced precarious conditions for skilled foreign workers who are generally not associated with the experiences of precariousness and marginality. Mishra suggests that a part of precarity comes from a flexible labor market that relies not only on a lean workforce but also on outsourcing to "body shop" companies, known for their exploitative practices, both inside the United States and outside. The other part of precarity comes from the nature of visas. Temporary foreign workers are dependent on their employers and face multiple restrictions and bureaucratic hurdles. In the case of H-1B workers from India, a large part of precarity produced by temporary work visas also involves a long wait time for visa status adjustment to permanent residency. The long wait time for permanent residency creates intended as well as unintended consequences for skilled workers and adversely impacts their professional and family lives. This chapter suggests that durational time is a political good and thus wait time should be approached through the lens of justice, equality, and fairness. The increased inequality for Indian skilled workers in terms of their wait time denies them the right to equality and justice. Such a racialized devaluation of time deprives certain populations of fairness and equal treatment integral to the experience of living in a liberal democracy.

Chapter 7, "International Students: Mobility and Resettlement" by Terry Wotherspoon, presents a nuanced understanding of international student migration, which debunks a number of commonly held assumptions about highly skilled labor migration. Many international students regard the opportunity to study in another country as a gateway to potential migration and resettlement. This gateway is increasingly feasible and effective as nation-states come to regard international students as important sources of highly skilled labor. However, despite a range of policy innovations to facilitate post-graduation employment and resettlement, the proportion of students who remain are well below those who leave, making shortages of highly skilled labor major concerns for many employers. Wotherspoon explores the key factors that influence diverse pathways international students experience in the course of outcomes associated with remaining in or leaving the countries in which they studied. He shows that, while the discussion is focused predominantly on developments in the United States, it is informed by consideration of comparative and global trends that are crucial for understanding these issues.

Chapter 8, "Highly Skilled African Immigrants: Field of Study, Education-Occupation Matching, and Earnings in the US Labor Market" by Kevin J. A. Thomas, calls attention to the varied effects of fields of study on the economic incorporation of highly skilled immigrants from Africa. Using data from the American Community Survey, Thomas investigates whether the variations are associated with inequalities in two outcomes: education-occupation mismatches and weekly earnings. The analysis shows that African immigrants with STEM degrees have lower risks of experiencing education-occupation mismatches and have higher earnings compared to their counterparts with non-STEM degrees. However, this STEM earnings premium disappears among graduates who are overeducated for their jobs. These findings suggest that highly skilled Africans have the highest risks of being mismatched for their jobs among graduates with degrees in STEM, business, social science, arts and humanities, and other fields compared to other, similarly educated immigrants. Furthermore, among highly skilled individuals, Africans are among the least able to earn a wage premium for their field-specific human capital. The chapter concludes by pointing out that the labor force integration of highly skilled African immigrants remains a work in progress because it lags behind that of similarly educated immigrants in the US labor market.

Chapter 9, "Highly Skilled Female Pakistani Immigrants: Devalued Credentials" by Misba Bhatti, looks at the issue of devalued credentials among highly skilled female immigrants from Pakistan. Bhatti examines the experiences of these highly skilled women migrants and details the issues they face in the United States with regard to the devaluation of their foreign earned degrees. She finds that, while most migrant professionals from developing countries face devaluation and denigration of their prior education and work experience in the United States, highly skilled female immigrants from Pakistan face systematic dual disadvantages, based on their gender and country of origin, when it comes to their foreign earned credential recognition in the United States.

Chapter 10, "Transnationalism and Gender among Immigrants: Economic, Political, and Social Challenges" by Silvia Pedraza, offers a critical review of existing research on migration, assimilation, and transnationalism through a gender lens. As international migrants are getting resettled in their host countries, they typically develop subjectivities, engage in communication, take actions, and live many aspects of their social lives across two or more nation-states. Pedraza argues that while immigrants have always been transnational, the advent of modern communications has qualitatively changed the immigrant experience since the 1990s. Transnationalism has a threefold impact: on the societies of origin, the societies of destination, and on the immigrants themselves. Pedraza demonstrates three major types of transnationalism—economic, political, and social—through myriad examples from the history of many immigrant groups to the United States and highlights the role that gender plays in all three. She also discusses the positive and negative consequences of transnationalism for immigrants and raises questions for further research.

Last but not least, chapter 11, "Remittances as Transnationalism: The Case of Bangladeshi Immigrants in Los Angeles" by Hasan Mahmud, goes beyond both the conventional migration-development nexus that overemphasizes the perceived economic impacts of remittances in migrant origin countries and the transnationalism perspective that underemphasizes the financial implications of remittances when focusing on migrants' social and personal experiences. Mahmud argues that migrant agency should be placed at the center of the analysis of migrant remittances as an important form of transnational practice. Focusing on migrant life trajectories, the chapter details how the structural conditions and the migrants' own evaluation of those conditions interact to shape decision-making about their remittances. The study analyzes migrants' perspectives about whether to send remittances, to whom, how much, and when—questions that allow us to recognize migrants' agential capacity as they exhibit it in remittances. Mahmud concludes by highlighting how his findings complement both the economic and transnationalism perspectives in studying migrant remittances and disentangle migrants' agency, demonstrating their ability to interact with the structural opportunities and constraints in the transnational social field.

* * *

Overall, the chapters in this book examine the persistent and evolving phenomenon of economic migration to the United States. However, as we have discussed, the descriptor "economic" may be misleading. Trends, patterns, causes, and consequences of cross-border mobility, transnationalism, and integration are indeed impacted by multilayered historical, cultural, and politico-economic processes beyond economic logic. Various noneconomic factors in both sending and receiving countries have been found to shape the entire terrain of migration, from the decision to leave the homeland, to resettlement and integration in the country of destination, to transnationalism. We thus reiterate the need for paying close attention to the sociocultural forces and politico-institutional contexts in the study of economic migration. Furthermore, we highlight the need for analyzing immigrant labor as a sociohistorical construct in which immigrants' individual attributes interact with institutional mechanisms and social processes in affecting how immigrants navigate through structural constraints to achieve their socioculturally defined goals through migration.

For future research, one of the most urgent but understudied areas in migration studies, which coincides with our emphasis on noneconomic factors in understanding migration, is climate migration. Global warming exacerbates climate hazards and increases the risk of extreme weather disasters, leading to the destruction of livelihood, food supply, and livable habitats and hence climate migration. Earlier research on climate migration involved security concerns as severe climate conditions and natural disasters led to mass exodus of refugees from affected areas and caused anxiety, tension, and even violent conflict in receiving societies.[94] Recently, more systematic studies of large-scale data have revealed an increasing trend and widespread scope of climate-induced migration. While some scholars recognize the possibility of huge population shifts due to climate change,[95] others are skeptical about such a conclusion due to a lack of adequate data and conclusive analysis.[96] Nonetheless, as millions of people around the world have been driven from their homes by floods, droughts, storms, and other weather-related disasters in recent decades, climate change has been recognized as a decisive factor shaping both internal and international migrations. Although this volume does not include a chapter on climate migration, we do think that further research should pay attention to how climate change shapes the direction and scale of migration, how it interacts with other non-economic factors to affect human mobilities across nation-state borders, and how receiving nations can be better prepared for the resettlement and integration of climate migrants in the coming years.

In sum, the studies included in this book demonstrate that international migration is affected not merely by supply and demand at work in labor markets, nor by rationally calculated economic action of the individual, but by the complex interplay of migration histories, cultures, networks, and state policies and politico-economic circumstances in the countries of origin and destination, as well as capital flows in a globalized world. Moreover, motivations and actions of individual migrants do not occur in a vacuum. The making of immigrant labor is shaped by dynamic relations and interactions in histories, families, diasporic communities, immigration regimes, and other institutional settings beyond individual demographic and socioeconomic characteristics, leading to divergent destinies.

NOTES

1   Arvind Subramanian and Martin Kessler, "The Hyperglobalization of Trade and
    its Future," The Peterson Institute for International Economics Working Paper
    Series 13–6 (July 2013), www.piie.com.
2   United Nations Department of Economic and Social Affairs, "International
    Migration 2019 Report," 2019, www.un.org.
3   Abby Budiman, "Key Findings about U.S. Immigrants," Pew Research Center,
    August 20, 2020, www.pewresearch.org.
4   Budiman, "Key Findings about U.S. Immigrants."
5   Budiman, "Key Findings about U.S. Immigrants."
6   United Nations, "Universal Declaration of Human Rights: The Foundation of
    International Human Rights Law," www.un.org.
7   Claire Alexander, Joya Chaterji, and Annu Jalais, The Bengal Diaspora: Rethinking
    Muslim Migration (New York: Routledge, 2015).
8   For more in-depth discussions of noneconomic motivations for migrants and the
    mischaracterization of migrants as economic migrants, see chapter 1 by Banerjee,
    chapter 3 by Zhou, chapter 7 by Wotherspoon, and chapter 9 by Bhatti in this volume.
9   This argument, and the book's subtitle, draw on Payal Banerjee's insightful con-
    ceptualization. For details, see chapter 1 by Banerjee in this volume.
10 Jonathan Portes, "The Economics of Migration," Contexts 18, no. 2 (2019): 12–17.
11 Douglas S. Massey, Joaquin Arango, Graeme Hugo, Ali Kouaouci, Adela Pel-
    legrino, and J. Edward Taylor, "Theories of International Migration: A Review and
    Appraisal," Population and Development Review 19 (1993): 431–466.
12 Jon Goss and Bruce Lindquist, "Conceptualizing International Labor Migration:
    A Structuration Perspective," International Migration Review 28 (1995): 317–351.
13 Michael M. Wachter, "Primary and Secondary Labor Markets: A Critique of the
    Dual Approach," Brookings Papers on Economic Activity 3 (1974): 637–680.
14 Michael J. Piore, Birds of Passage: Migrant Labor and Industrial Societies
    (Cambridge: Cambridge University Press, 1979).
15 Immanuel Wallerstein, The Modern World System I: Capitalist Agriculture and
    the Origins of the European World-Economy in the Sixteenth Century (New York:
    Academic Press, 1974).
16 Massey et al., "Theories of International Migration."
17 Christina Boswell, "Combining Economics and Sociology in Migration Theory,"
    Journal of Ethnic and Migration Studies 34, no. 4 (2008): 549–566; Hein De Haas,
    "Migration Theory: Quo Vadis?" International Migration Institute Working Paper
    Series no. 100 (2014), www.migrationinstitute.org.
18 Darren P. Smith and Russell King, "Editorial Introduction: Re-Making Migration
    Theory," Population, Space and Place 18, no. 2 (2012): 127–133.
19 Douglas S. Massey, "Understanding Mexican Migration to the United States,"
    American Journal of Sociology 92, no. 6 (1987): 1372–1403; Massey et al., "Theories
    of International Migration."

20 Massey et al., "Theories of International Migration."

21 Gunnar Myrdal, "The Principle of Circular and Cumulative Causation," in *Rich Lands and Poor: The Road to World Prosperity*, ed. Gunnar Myrdal (New York: Harper, 1957), 11–22; Douglas S. Massey, "Social Structure, Household Strategies, and the Cumulative Causation of Migration," *Population Index* 56 (1990): 3–26; Massey et al., "Theories of International Migration."

22 Massey et al., "Theories of International Migration."

23 William Kandel and Douglas S. Massey, "The Culture of Mexican Migration: A Theoretical and Empirical Analysis," *Social Forces* 80, no. 3 (2002): 981–1004.

24 Christiane Timmerman, "Marriage in a 'Culture of Migration'. Emirdag Marrying into Flanders," *European Review* 16, no. 4 (2008): 585–594.

25 See also chapter 10 by Pedraza and chapter 11 by Mahmud in this volume.

26 Jeff Popke, "Latino Migration and Neoliberalism in the U.S. South: Notes Toward a Rural Cosmopolitanism," *Southeastern Geographer* 51, no. 2 (2011): 246.

27 David Harvey, *A Brief History of Neoliberalism* (Oxford: Oxford University Press, 2005); Leyla Dakhli and Vincent B. Bonnecase, "Introduction: Interpreting the Global Economy through Local Anger," *International Review of Social History* 66 (2021): 1–21; Raúl Delgado Wise and Humberto Márquez, "Neoliberal Globalization and Migration," in *The Encyclopedia of Global Human Migration*, ed. Immanuel Ness (2013). Wiley Online Library, https://onlinelibrary.wiley.com /doi/10.1002/9781444351071.wbeghm389.

28 Harvey, *A Brief History of Neoliberalism*, 159.

29 Wise and Márquez, "Neoliberal Globalization and Migration."

30 Dakhli and Bonnecase, "Introduction."

31 Saskia Sassen, *The Global City: New York, London, Tokyo* (Princeton, NJ: Princeton University Press, 1991).

32 Gerardo Otero, "Neoliberal Globalization, NAFTA, and Migration: Mexico's Loss of Food and Labor Sovereignty," *Journal of Poverty* 15 (2011): 384–402.

33 Layna Mosley and David A. Singer, "Migration, Labor, and the International Political Economy," *Annual Review of Political Science* 18 (2015): 283–301; Nicola Phillips, "Migration as Development Strategy? The New Political Economy of Dispossession and Inequality in the Americas," *Review of International Political Economy* 16, no. 2 (2009): 231–259.

34 Yasmin Soysal, *Limits of Citizenship: Migrants and Post-National Citizenship in Europe* (Chicago: University of Chicago Press, 1996).

35 Laurie A. Brand, *Citizens Abroad: Emigration and the State in the Middle East and North Africa* (Cambridge: Cambridge: Cambridge University Press, 2006); Robyn M. Rodriguez, *Migrants for Export: How the Philippine State Brokers Labor to the World* (Minneapolis: University of Minnesota Press, 2010).

36 Stephen Castles, "Migration, Crisis, and the Global Labour Market," *Globalizations* 8, no. 3 (2011): 311–324; James Hollifield, "The Emerging Migration State," *International Migration Review* 38, no. 3 (2004): 885–912; Hasan Mahmud, "Impact of the Destination State on Migrants' Remittances: A Study of Remitting

among Bangladeshi Migrants in the USA, the UAE and Japan," *Migration and Development* 5, no.1 (2016): 79–98; Aristide R. Zolberg, "The Politics of Immigration Policy: An Externalist Perspective," *American Behavioral Scientist* 42, no. 9 (1999): 1276–1279. See, in this volume, chapter 1 by Banerjee, chapter 4 by Donato and Amuedo-Dorantes, chapter 5 by Lowell, chapter 6 by Mishra, and chapter 8 by Thomas.

37   The context of reception involves a range of factors in the country of origin, including nation-state policy, labor market conditions, and public attitude pertaining to the national origin group, as well as the strength of the preexisting ethnic community. See Alejandro Portes and Min Zhou, "The New Second Generation: Segmented Assimilation and Its Variants," *The Annals of the American Academy of Political and Social Science* 530, no. 1 (1993): 74–96; Alejandro Portes and Rubén G. Rumbout, *Immigrant America: A Portrait* (Berkeley: University of California Press, 2014).

38   Deniz Göktürk, David Gramling, and Anton Kaes, *Germany in Transit: Nation and Migration 1955–2005* (Berkeley: University of California Press, 2007).

39   Castles, "Migration, Crisis, and the Global Labour Market"; Ronaldo Munck, "Globalisation, Governance and Migration: An Introduction," *Third World Quarterly* 29, no. 7 (2008): 1227–1246; Eric Neumayer, "Unequal Access to Foreign Spaces: How States Use Visa Restrictions to Regulate Mobility in a Globalized World," *Transactions of the Institute of British Geographers* 31, no. 1 (2006): 72–84. Also see chapter 4 in this volume.

40   See chapter 7 in this volume.

41   See chapter 3 in this volume.

42   Erika Lee, *At America's Gates: Chinese Immigration During the Exclusion Era, 1882–1943* (Chapel Hill: University of North Carolina Press, 2003). Also see chapter 3 in this volume.

43   See chapter 3 in this volume.

44   See chapter 4 in this volume.

45   See chapters 4, 9, and 11 in this volume.

46   Douglas Massey and Karen A. Pren, "Unintended Consequences of US Immigration Policy: Explaining the Post-1965 Surge from Latin America," *Population and Development Review* 38, no. 1 (2012): 1–29.

47   Hyperselectivity refers to the situation in which an immigrant group arrives with average levels of education that are higher than both their compatriots back home and natives in the United States. See Jennifer Lee and Min Zhou, *The Asian American Achievement Paradox* (New York: Russell Sage Foundation, 2015).

48   Lee, *At America's Gate*; also see chapter 3 in this volume.

49   The Chinese Exclusion Act was repealed in 1943 when the United States and China became allies during World War II.

50   Julia G. Young, "Making America 1920 Again? Nativism and US Immigration, Past and Present," *Journal of Migration and Human Security* 5, no. 1 (2017): 217–235.

51 However, there were some significant qualitative restrictions out of concern for the assimilability of Black and Latinx immigrants into the American mainstream. See Massey and Pren, "Unintended Consequences of US Immigration Policy."

52 Massey and Pren, "Unintended Consequences of US Immigration Policy."

53 Daniel J. Tichenor, *Dividing Lines: The Politics of Immigration Control in America* (Princeton, NJ: Princeton University Press, 2002).

54 Massey and Pren, "Unintended Consequences of US Immigration Policy"; Catalina Amuedo-Dorantes and Susan Pozo, "On the Intended and Unintended Consequences of Enhanced U.S. Border and Interior Immigration Enforcement: Evidence from Mexican Deportees," *Demography* 51, no. 6 (2014): 2255–2279.

55 Amuedo-Dorantes and Pozo, "On the Intended and Unintended Consequences of Enhanced U.S. Border and Interior Immigration Enforcement."

56 Abdulhadi Khalaf, Omar AlShehabi, and Adam Hanieh, eds., *Transit States: Labour, Migration and Citizenship in the Gulf* (London: Pluto Press, 2014); Dong-Hoon Seol and John D. Skrentny, "Why Is There So Little Migrant Settlement in East Asia?" *International Migration Review* 43 (2009): 578–620; Apichai W. Shipper, "The Political Construction of Foreign Workers in Japan," *Critical Asian Studies* 34, no. 1 (2002): 41–68; Yen-fen Tseng and Hong-zen Wang, "Governing Migrant Workers at a Distance: Managing the Temporary Status of Guestworkers in Taiwan," *International Migration* 51, no. 4 (2011): 1–19; Brenda Yeoh and Weiqiang Lin, "Rapid Growth in Singapore's Immigrant Population Brings Policy Challenges," Migration Information Source (April 3, 2012), www.migra tionpolicy.org.

57 Tichenor, *Dividing Lines.*

58 Greg Bensinger and Rachael King, "Tech CEOs Take a Stand Against Donald Trump's Immigration Order," *The Wall Street Journal*, February 6, 2017, www.wsj .com; Ted Hesson, "Tech Giants Back Legal Challenge to Trump's Foreign Worker Restrictions," August 10, 2020, *Reuters*, www.reuters.com.

59 Ran Abramitzky and Leah Boustan, "Immigration in American Economic History," *Journal of Economic Literature* 55, no. 4 (2017): 1311–1345; Min Zhou and Carl L. Bankston, *The Rise of the New Second Generation* (Cambridge, UK: Polity, 2016).

60 Ivan Light and Carolyn N. Rosenstein, *Race, Ethnicity, and Entrepreneurship in Urban America* (Hawthorne, NY: Aldine de Gruyter, 1995).

61 Sibylle Heilbrunna, Nonna Kushnirovichb, and Aviva Zeltzer-Zubida, "Barriers to Immigrants' Integration into the Labor Market: Modes and Coping," *International Journal of Intercultural Relations* 34 (2010): 244–252.

62 For details, see chapters 2, 5, 8, and 9 in this volume.

63 Aaron Terrazas, "The Economic Integration of Immigrants in the United States: Long- and Short-Term Perspectives," Migration Policy Institute (July 2011), www .migrationpolicy.org.

64 See chapter 5 in this volume.

65 Ivana Fellini and Raffaele Guetto, "A 'U-Shaped' Pattern of Immigrants' Occupational Careers? A Comparative Analysis of Italy, Spain, and France," *International Migration Review* 53, no. 1 (2019), 26–58.
66 Paul A. Jargowsky, "Immigrants and Neighbourhoods of Concentrated Poverty: Assimilation or Stagnation?" *Journal of Ethnic and Migration Studies* 35, no. 7 (2009): 1129–1151.
67 Abramitzky and Boustan, "Immigration in American Economic History."
68 George J. Borjas, "The Slowdown in the Economic Assimilation of Immigrants: Aging and Cohort Effects Revisited Again," *Journal of Human Capital* 9, no. 4 (2016): 483–517; Zadia M. Feliciano, "The Skill and Economic Performance of Mexican Immigrants from 1910 to 1990," *Explorations in Economic History* 38, no. 3 (2001): 386–409; Darren Lubotsky, "The Effect of Changes in the U.S. Wage Structure on Recent Immigrants' Earnings," *Review of Economics and Statistics* 93, no. 1 (2011): 59–71; Pablo Ibarraran and Darren Lubotsky, "Mexican Immigration and Self-Selection: New Evidence from the 2000 Mexican Census," in *Mexican Immigration to the United States*, ed. George J. Borjas (Chicago: University of Chicago Press, 2007), 159–192; Jargowsky, "Immigrants and Neighbourhoods of Concentrated Poverty."
69 Cynthia Feliciano, "Educational Selectivity in U.S. Immigration: How Do Immigrants Compare to Those Left Behind?" *Demography* 42, no. 1 (2005): 131–152; Steven Kennedy, James Ted McDonald, and Nicholas Biddle, "The Healthy Immigrant Effect and Immigrant Selection: Evidence from Four Countries," Social and Economic Dimensions of an Aging Population, *SEDAP Research Paper* no. 164 (2006), https://socialsciences.mcmaster.ca; Jeffrey Grogger and Gordon H. Hanson, "Income Maximization and the Selection and Sorting of International Migrants," *Journal of Development Economics* 95, no. 1 (2011): 42–57.
70 David P. Lindstrom and Adriana López Ramírez, "Pioneers and Followers: Migrant Selectivity and the Development of U.S. Migration Streams in Latin America," *The ANNALS of the American Academy of Political and Social Science* 630, no. 1 (2010): 53–77.
71 Timothy Hatton and Jeffrey G. Williamson, "International Migration in the Long Run: Positive Selection, Negative Selection and Policy," Institute for Economic Research, Harvard University, Working Paper No. 2038 (September 2004), http://ftp.iza.org.
72 Abramitzky and Boustan, "Immigration in American Economic History." Also see chapter 2 in this volume.
73 Lindstrom and Ramírez, "Pioneers and Followers." Also see chapter 2 in this volume.
74 Feliciano, "Educational Selectivity in U.S. Immigration"; Kennedy, McDonald, and Biddle, "The Healthy Immigrant Effect and Immigrant Selection"; Grogger and Hanson, "Income Maximization and the Selection and Sorting of International Migrants."

75 Barry R. Chiswick and Paul W. Miller, "The International Transferability of Immigrants' Human Capital," *Economics of Education Review* 28, no. 2 (2009): 162–169.

76 Abramitzky and Boustan, "Immigration in American Economic History."

77 Hyperselectivity refers to a national origin group whose percentage of college graduates is higher than compatriots in the countries of origin and natives in the countries of destination, whereas hypo-selectivity refers to the exact opposite. High selectivity is defined the same as positive selectivity except using percentage of college graduations rather than years of education in comparison with compatriots back home. See Lee and Zhou, *The Asian American Achievement Paradox.*

78 Linda Basch, Nina Glick Schiller, and Cristina Szanton Blanc, *Nations Unbound: Transnational Projects, Postcolonial Predicaments and Deterritorialized Nation-States* (Amsterdam: Overseas Publishers Association, 1994); Stephen Castles, Hein de Haas, and Mark J. Miller, eds., *The Age of Migration: International Population Movements in the Modern World* (Basingstoke, UK: Palgrave MacMillan, 2014); Nina Glick Schiller, Linda Basch, and Cristina Blanc-Szanton, eds., *Toward a Transnational Perspective on Migration* (New York: New York Academy of Sciences, 1992); Steven Vertovec, "Transnationalism and Identity," *Journal of Ethnic and Migration Studies* 27, no. 4 (2001): 573–582.

79 Basch et al., *Nations Unbound*; Schiller et al., *Toward a Transnational Perspective on Migration*; Patricia Landolt, "Salvadoran Economic Transnationalism: Embedded Strategies for Household Maintenance, Immigrant Incorporation, and Entrepreneurial Expansion," *Global Networks* 1 (2001): 217–242; Peggy Levitt, *The Transnational Villagers* (Berkeley: University of California Press, 2001); Vertovec, "Transnationalism and Identity."

80 See chapter 10 in this volume.

81 William I. Thomas and Florian Znaniecki, *The Polish Peasant in Europe and America* (Chicago: University of Chicago Press, 1918).

82 Nina Glick Schiller, Linda Basch, and Cristina Szanton Blanc, "From Immigrant to Transmigrant: Theorizing Transnational Migration," *Anthropological Quarterly* 68, no. 1 (1995): 48–63; Ann Miles, *From Cuenca to Queens: An Anthropological Story of Transnational Migration* (Austin: University of Texas Press, 2004).

83 Levitt, *The Transnational Villagers*; Robert C. Smith, *Mexican New York: Transnational Lives of New Immigrants* (Berkeley and Los Angeles: University of California Press, 2005).

84 Hannerz Ulf, 2003. "Being There . . . and There . . . and There!: Reflections on Multi-Site Ethnography," *Ethnography* 4(2): 201–216; Jonathan Sullivan, Yupei Zhao, Simon Chadwick, and Michael Gow, "Chinese Fans' Engagement with Football: Transnationalism, Authenticity and Identity," *Journal of Global Sport Management* (2021), DOI: 10.1080/24704067.2021.1871855; Magdalena Nowicka, "(Dis)Connecting Migration: Transnationalism and Nationalism beyond Connectivity," *Comparative Migration Studies* 8, no. 20 (2020), https://doi.org/10.1186/s40878-020-00175.

85   Schiller, Basch, and Blanc, eds., *Toward a Transnational Perspective on Migration*, 11; Tom Brocket, "From 'In-Betweenness' to 'Positioned Belongings': Second-Generation Palestinian-Americans Negotiate the Tensions of Assimilation and Transnationalism," *Ethnic and Racial Studies* 43, no.16 (2020): 135–154; Mabel Teye-Kau and Amal Madibbo, "Transnational Migration as a Strategy of Resistance among Refugees: The South Sudanese Diaspora in Canada," *Canadian Ethnic Studies* 52, no. 3 (2020): 27–45.

86   Massimo Pendenza and Vanessa Lamattina, "Rethinking Self-Responsibility: An Alternative Vision to the Neoliberal Concept of Freedom," *American Behavioral Scientist* 63, no. 1 (2019): 100–115.

87   See chapter 3 in this volume.

88   Smith, *Mexican New York*.

89   See chapter 11 in this volume.

90   Elizabeth M. Aranda, *Emotional Bridges to Puerto Rico: Migration, Return Migration, and the Struggles of Incorporation* (Lanham, MD: Rowman & Littlefield, 2006); See chapter 10 in this volume.

91   Mark I. Choate, *Emigrant Nation: The Making of Italy Abroad* (Cambridge, MA: Harvard University Press, 2008); David Fitzgerald, *A Nation of Emigrants: How Mexico Manages Its Migration* (Berkeley: University of California Press, 2009).

92   Roger Waldinger, "The Bounded Community: Turning Foreigners into Americans in Twenty-First Century Los Angeles," *Ethnic and Racial Studies* 30 (2007): 343; Roger Waldinger and David Fitzgerald, "Transnationalism in Question," *American Journal of Sociology* 109 (2004): 1177–1195.

93   See chapters 10 and 11 in this volume.

94   Ingrid Boas, *Climate Migration and Security: Securitisation as a Strategy in Climate Change Politics* (New York: Routledge, 2017).

95   Abrahm Lustgarten, "The Great Climate Migration Has Begun," *New York Times Magazine* (July 23, 2020).

96   Ingrid Boas and associates, "Climate Migration Myths," *Nature Climate Change* 9 (2019): 901–903.

1

The Making of Immigrant Labor

Inequality, Digital Capitalism, and Racialized Enforcement

PAYAL BANERJEE

As is widely known, scholarly work on economic migration has centered, directly or indirectly, around the idea of migration for employment.[1] An immense body of research along these lines has provided key insights on income/wages for livelihoods, jobs to support families, employment for improved economic prospects, ranging from concerns around basic survival to sense of professional advancement. In response to the idea of economic migration, this chapter seeks to formulate more expansively the prefix "economic" in ways that can account for the social and political mechanisms vital to the making of immigrant labor and the terms of its incorporation. It is undeniable that immigrants are individuals. They are the protagonists of their lives and carry aspirations, effort, love and affection, adversities, pride, hope, and dreams—and much else that is elemental, and maybe even eternal, about the human condition. However, they also occupy a social configuration, produced by historical, structural, and political circumstances that govern their life chances and contributions. In this regard, the immigrant worker is not a timeless being who reappears in different market settings for economic advancement or survival. Rather, immigrant workers are made and remade by the spectrum of social parameters and relationships. The ongoing iterations of race, gender, and other categorical hierarchies enunciate in sharp relief migrants' lives, as well as their social positioning in relation to the state, capital, and polity.[2] In short, the migrant being is a social one. The "economic" aspects of migrants' lives are not reducible to their employment, nor are these aspects external to the social field that determines migrants' status, incorporation, and discourses about their usefulness and value. Any prefix—such as "economic"—qualifying the migrant needs to account for the political economy of legal mandates and disciplinary systems that reproduce migrants as a particular historically specific category of people rendered accessible as "economic" beings. In addition, the terms that shape the incorporation of migrants as "economic" beings are as much about labor market matters as they are about the social field of migrants' legal status, racialized surveillance and exclusions, and immigration enforcement, which have direct implications for the manner in which migrants' labor is made accessible.

This accounting sees the transformation of an ordinary "foreign-born" into an "immigrant worker" as an extraordinary one: It takes place in relation to the historical and structural contingencies of the relations among the state, capital, and labor on a transnational scale (global capitalism). The state's immigration laws and capital's labor needs interlock with shifting public cultures and ongoing contestations about who is entitled to work, who can belong, or who may represent the nation. These processes, in turn, reproduce the legal and social systems that demarcate, classify, and evaluate migrants (of any description), determine the various requirements for their legal and employment status, and mitigate their life chances, prospects, and sociocultural membership. In this matrix, gender, race, and legal status marginalization cut through the tangible experiences of criminalization, deportability, and dependence, which then govern the substance of migrants' economic incorporation and life course as human beings.

The legal and sociocultural specificities that thread through immigrant lives are thus indications of the varied cross-currents of US Homeland Security laws, the need for flexible workers, and the highly racialized and gendered social anxieties associated with immigrants (risk, criminality, and unfair apportionments of jobs or other common goods). Far from being illiberal lapses or inadvertent oversights that compromise equality, immigration policies in race-gender systems are designed specifically to maintain immigrants' subordination to the state and capital, produce dependence by legal means, confer inclusion in fragments, and subject this constituency to recurring scrutiny of immigrant labor's worth and value.[3]

Thus, the category "economic migrant" stands for much more than a terminology for people in search of, or placed in, jobs in a foreign country while being subjected to specific immigration status categories.[4]

The prefix "economic" needs to stretch beyond predominant associations made on the basis of immigration groups' employment, skills and occupational categories, credentials and wages, or the ups and downs of sector-specific labor demands in the United States.[5] These units of examination in the study of economic migration are important and offer relevant insights into immigrants' labor-force participation and experiences. Nevertheless, they do not adequately address economic migration and immigrant labor as historical and social configurations. Instead, they reproduce a functionalist understanding of the dynamics between labor market needs and the employment of immigrants.

Rather than construe economic migration primarily in terms of employment tracks or sector-specific labor demands, this chapter underscores the proposition that the prefix "economic" should be redefined to account for the systems of racial formation, capital-labor relations, and legal status classifications integral to the production, accessibility, and incorporation of immigrants as economic beings.[6] To address how this process has been at work in recent years, the chapter brings the matter of jobs and immigrant employment in conversation with adjacent scholarship on late globalization, specifically with regard to inequality, data and digital technology, racialized surveillance, and immigration enforcement in the United States.[7]

The first section of the chapter provides a brief overview of recent trends in immigrant labor-force participation in the United States and key contributions from the economic migration perspective. Relatedly, it suggests that researchers still need to demand more, say more, and do more with immigrants' labor-force participation research in ways that might provide an expansive and critical accounting of global capital's emerging configurations and the place of US labor in these processes. The second section takes a look at how data-driven reorganizations of capital's profit-making systems and growing socioeconomic inequality—two intertwined and highly significant features of our times—have interacted with the systems of immigrant labor incorporation as well as immigration control. This analysis underscores racialized and technology-mediated surveillance, criminalization, and immigration enforcement as being crucial processes that "produce" migrants by determining the basis of their *relationship* to the state and capital. In this vein, the analysis addresses how the simultaneous formations of rising socioeconomic inequality and digital capitalism in late globalization have rebooted racialized migration management and contributed to increasing status precarity and the criminalization of migration.[8]

Economic Migration and Immigrants' Labor-Force Participation

Research on foreign-born workers in the United States has offered substantial data and a highly informative profile of immigrant labor in the US economy.[9] The US Bureau of Labor Statistics estimated that in 2019 there were 28.4 million foreign-born workers, representing 17.4 percent of the people in the US labor force.[10] Foreign-born workers maintained their larger employment share in service occupations overall at 22.5 percent compared to the native-born at 16 percent in 2019. The percentages analyzed by sector are as follows: in natural resources, construction, and maintenance occupations (13.4 percent foreign-born and 8.2 percent native-born); and, in production, transportation, and material moving occupations (14.7 percent foreign-born and 11.2 percent native-born). As may be expected, foreign-born workers were less likely than native-born workers to be employed in management, professional, and related occupations (33.9 percent compared with 42.2 percent), with the gap being even larger in sales and office occupations (15.5 percent compared with 22.4 percent). Healthcare occupations in recent years have seen foreign-born workers overrepresented in certain jobs. While immigrants represented 17 percent of the overall US civilian workforce in 2018, they constituted 28 percent of physicians, 24 percent of dentists, as well as 38 percent of home health aides—in both the high-wage and low-wage segments of this sector. Healthcare employment data also shows that immigrant men are concentrated in better-paid, high-status positions (physicians and surgeons) compared to the overrepresentation of immigrant women in the lower-paid segments (e.g., as nurses, nursing aide, home healthcare aides).[11]

As is well known, scholarly research from the perspective of economic migration has sustained a tight focus on immigrants' labor-force participation trends and on how specific labor market sectors have relied on immigrant labor: for example, healthcare, IT and STEM fields, construction, hospitality, or care work, to list a few across the skills and wage spectrum. Important assessments have thus become available on immigrants' skills, education, as well as the impact of skilled immigrants on a variety of measures, such as innovation, entrepreneurship, economic activity, consumption, and demand for goods and services.[12]

Furthermore, prior research has provided important evidence of socioeconomic inequality and other constraints experienced by immigrants; for example, in terms of the impact of legal status variations on labor outcomes and income for documented and undocumented workers.[13] The research on gender, migration, and employment has offered additional data and analysis on the subject.[14] Overall, this body of work had pieced together larger socioeconomic patterns, thus offering a fuller picture of immigrants' employment, sector-specific distribution, and differences in terms of legal status and gender. Studies have also noted how the so-called unskilled labor migrants are seen as plentiful and generally less desirable, while skilled immigrants tend to be appraised more favorably in comparison.[15]

Yet, it should be underscored that immigration is an articulation of transnational capital and labor within the structures of a geopolitical economic system.[16] The so-called US economy that immigrant labor steps into occupies a predominant position in the world political economy constituted by a dense circuitry of trade, foreign investments, labor incorporation, and capital accumulation. Each one of the sectors that employs immigrants—IT, financial services, medicine, hospitality, or construction—is a member constituency of global capital and finance, their circulation stock-indexed internationally, and investments and trade interlinked across nation-states. And further, the globalized US economy that immigrants step into has also been intertwined historically with a succession of racialized immigration policies, designed to regulate this workforce in ways that can further facilitate labor flexibilization while reproducing a range of socioeconomic insecurities structured around immigrants' legal status and race-gender designations.[17]

This being so, the *economic* aspects of immigrant life—as enumerated in economic terms in the matrix of occupational profiles, income/wages, and work trajectories—enunciate, if examined closely, the co-exigencies of race, gender, the state's immigration system, and global capital; or, what can be called the social configurations of economic migration. In this analytical context, this chapter's call for situating the figure of the migrant in these social and historical terms is not new, but is one that marks the need for renewed attention to better understand two emerging, highly interrelated developments: worsening inequality in wealth and income, and advanced capital's reorganization based on digital data-centric systems (algorithms, AI, automation, and biometrics). In conjunction, these two developments are transforming the mechanisms of capital accumulation, employment, and systems of transnational mobility, that is, areas that represent some of the core constituents of the "economic" in economic migration. The following section takes this up in more detail.

The Social Habitat of the Prefix "Economic" and the Making of Immigrant Labor

The scholarship that covers globalization's impact on labor, particularly on women in the Global South and immigrants of color in advanced economies, had, by the early 1990s, sounded the alarm on several troubling trends: uneven distribution of gains, socioeconomic displacements, labor flexibilization, and the racial feminization of labor in a rapidly restructuring economy.[18] Subsequently, over the last decades, a growing body of research built on this work has further parsed out the impact of neoliberal restructuring and cuts in public welfare on increasing labor exploitation and control, social insecurities, poverty, and inequality in the United States for racial minorities and immigrants.[19]

This section outlines how this line of research enquiry on existing race, gender, and immigration status–based inequalities has expanded its scope to account for the extensive convergences between two interlinked areas of concern: The first is the growing wealth and income inequality and livelihood insecurity in finance- and technology-dominated late globalization; and the second is the concomitant emphasis on managing low-income people and immigrants through state-enforced surveillance and criminalization.[20] In this context, the proliferation of data-based algorithms and automation technology in late globalization has become highly consequential: It provides a significant basis for high financial returns for those with invested capital, particularly in the highly profitable data- and technology-oriented markets; relatedly, it heightens preexisting income inequality and employment precarity; and it offers the surveillance and enforcement technologies that drive the management of socioeconomically displaced people, immigrants, and people of color.

Rising Inequality

Thomas Piketty's analysis, as a vital addition to an extensive literature on inequality in the United States, links the question of income inequality in the country's "hyperinegalitarian society" not only to very large incomes from labor at the uppermost echelons of the labor hierarchy (e.g., "super managers"), but just as potently to the concentration of wealth ownership—and the income, therefore, from this capital:[21]

> [W]hat primarily characterizes the United States at the moment is a re-cord level of inequality of income from labor (probably higher than in any other society at any time in the past, anywhere in the world, including societies in which skill disparities were extremely large) together with a level of inequality of wealth less extreme than the levels observed in traditional societies or in Europe in the period 1900–1910.[22]

Financial investments and a prioritization of shareholder value orientation contributed to an intensification of this wealth's growth and ownership concentration since the 1980s. In the wake of neoliberal globalization and deregulation, the portion of national income going to "rentiers"—financial institutions and owners of financial assets—has been increasingly in OECD countries since the 1980s and 1990s.[23]

As the share of finance capital became concentrated in private ownership and the share of income from this capital increased manifold for large corporations and the wealthy, a set of profound economic and social consequences unfolded. These included an exacerbation of existing income distribution and income inequality,[24] corporate downsizing,[25] and financial instability, accompanied by a steady decline in labor conditions and the share of labor income. While the labor of educated professionals and experts is valued and highly paid, the wages and labor conditions of workers with less specialization and less education have declined in sharp contrast. Furthermore, given that the capital-rich today also tend to be labor-rich—i.e., employed in advanced education-oriented professional fields—those endowed with capital income are at the same time able to increase their wealth by commanding very high incomes for their specialization.[26]

In this context, existing class and racial disparities in wealth and income distribution have worsened within wealthy, immigrant-receiving nations and regions in the Global North.[27] The COVID-19 pandemic has unleashed further evidence of alarming consequences stemming from preexisting levels of inequality in wealthy nations: low-income and working-class people of color have suffered astoundingly higher rates of infection, illness, and death in comparison to others in white-collar professional jobs that could be carried out remotely. Simultaneously, despite the sharp economic fallout as seen in GDP contractions and high levels of unemployment during the pandemic, people in higher-income professional occupations (the "labor-rich") encountered lower rates of job loss compared to the high rates of unemployment experienced among those in lower-income service and blue-collar jobs. Individuals with invested assets and capital have seen a remarkable increase in their financial holdings from historically high market returns, especially since mid-2020.[28]

Migration scholars need to reckon with the overall conditions, consequences, and policies surrounding persistent socioeconomic inequality in the United States (and the Global North in general), which have had a direct relationship with discourses and policies that govern the so-called management of migration and immigrants, especially in terms of immigrants' racial criminalization, surveillance, detention, and overall marginalization. As mentioned above, neoliberal economic restructuring and globalization produced vast wealth for the "rentier" class, while causing a decline in earnings for people dependent on wage incomes (often the hourly minimum). Employment in this latter category, primarily in the low-wage service sector, has been stamped with increasing precarity: short-term contracts without benefits, part-time work, irregular hours, and unpredictable schedules have become the predominant labor condition, alongside economic displacement and dispossession amidst neoliberalization, privatization, and the state's steady retreat from social services.

A raft of terms—such as working poor, the new poor, informal proletariat, the global poor, unprotected workers, the neo-proletariat, the non-employed, the precariat, and surplus humanity—have sought to

THE MAKING OF IMMIGRANT LABOR | 45

capture the dynamics of accumulation and dispossession in which people, particularly women, racial minorities, and immigrants, try to make ends meet in irregular, insecure, informal, and temporary forms of employment.[29] While the consequences of rising inequality and precarious employment have been dire, as seen in food, health, and housing insecurity, chronic underemployment and unemployment, and poverty, the post-Keynesian US state's response approaches have prioritized policies designed to "select, eject, and immobilize" what it views to be "problem populations."[30] In other words, these policies deploy systems of state control that seek to isolate, punish, and further marginalize people caught at the vortex of multiple forms of human insecurity. The merger between the prison industrial complex and immigration enforcement enacted through the expansion of surveillance, detention, and criminalization of racial minorities, immigrants, and low-income people—citizen and non-citizen—draws attention to an increasingly militarized approach toward managing people's existential insecurity.[31]

The mechanisms of racial criminalization of poverty have become inseparable from the racial criminalization of immigration—both operationalized through common technologies of surveillance, securitization, and incarceration targeted at the so-viewed "problem populations."[32] In this context, devoting a sustained focus on the management of socioeconomic inequality overall has become imperative for critical migration studies. New innovations applied in technology-mediated immigration control—embedded within and driving the larger apparatus of militarized management of poverty—signal an augmentation of existing state processes that reproduce immigrants' racialization and subordination across the occupational spectrum. Mainstream formulations of the "economic" in economic migration do not appraise these ongoing reconstitutions of immigrants' *relationship* to the state and capital, despite the salient role this dynamic plays in shaping the kind of "economic" entities that migrants would be constructed as within the nation and its labor market.

Digital Globalization, Digital Capitalism

The "old globalization," the argument goes, of "global value chains reliant on labor cost competitiveness, [and] the salience of transnational distribution of manufacturing based on lower labor and operational costs, have reached a ceiling."[33] Key processes, like foreign acquisition of equities and bonds, loans, and foreign direct investments, which had grown rapidly from the early 1990s, have been on the decline since the financial crisis of 2008; likewise, cross-border financial transactions have slowed down. While the trade in services has continued to grow, its growth rate has been sluggish. And yet, rather than any turn toward de-globalization, a reconfiguring of the pathways of capital's circulation has appeared in the form of an unprecedented "surge in the movement of data" or "digital globalization" across national boundaries.[34] This includes data flow, video streaming, file-sharing, emails, and the world of Internet of Things, in which everyday "smart" objects—from cars, to home security, to household electronics like watches and TV sets, and even immigration documents—have become linked with data processes. Together, data technologies and AI are also changing the traditional rules of business and competition, as elaborated in the following terms:

> the advent of the cloud and new technologies . . . allow firms to quickly process and make sense of vast amounts of data. Internet-connected products and services can now directly collect information on customers, including their personal details, search behavior, choices of content, communications, social media posts, GPS location, and usage patterns. After machine-learning algorithms analyze this "digital exhaust," a company's offerings can be automatically adjusted to reflect the findings and even tailored to individuals.[35]

The predominance of algorithms placed deep within the fabric of firms' operations and digital networks has not only eliminated the limits to scale, the new rules of competition based on AI advantage have also altered how companies operate—from management strategies and service delivery to hiring.[36] The work of data processing or making sense of complex "digital exhaust" harvested from vast sources, for example, has been relegated to what has been termed the "AI Factory," i.e., a company's data- and algorithms-based decision hub at the core of the firm, run nearly exclusively by software, such that "humans are moved to the edge."[37] This new form of company, "built on a digital core," tends to have no workers in its "'critical path' of operating activities. AI runs the show."[38]

The emerging suite of technological innovations and the use of robotics technology to replace workers, as is known from economic and employment analysis reports, is on course to accelerate the disappearance of certain jobs, causing job replacements and unemployment.[39] Furthermore, new trends in algorithms- and data-driven hiring processes show that the work of identifying and evaluating job candidates has changed in ways that raise new questions about automation and employment access. Consider the following description of these changes:

> [The old model of HR-oriented] recruiting and hiring function has been eviscerated. Many U.S. companies—about 40%, according to research by Korn Ferry—have outsourced much if not all of the hiring process to familiar organizations such as Randstad, Manpower, and Adecco, which in turn use subcontractors, typically in India and the Philippines . . . To hire programmers . . . these subcontractors can scan websites that programmers might visit, trace their "digital exhaust" from cookies and other user-tracking measures to identify who they are, and then examine their curricula vitae.[40]

In late globalization's onward path, data algorithms have been rapidly transforming the *social dimensions* of work and inequality in general. As this system expands and unfolds, further changing the social dynamics of hiring, questions about unemployment, access, and the substance of work itself will linger at the core of untidy equations between job creation and job loss at technology's present juncture. Immigrant workers, nevertheless, cannot be treated as an add-on constituency that will navigate this whirlwind of change like most others. The commercial aspects of innovations in business administrations—such as the elimination of the various limits from capital's path or AI-driven companies outstripping traditional ones—represents key changes in those aspects of economic and employment reorganization that are linked with the incorporation of immigrant labor. Given that immigrants' labor and economic relations with capital are tied to their socio-legal status equations with the state, technology-mediated shifts in business practices not only impact immigrants' employment choices but also *alter* their relationship to employment-based visas and overall migration and legal status prospects.

It therefore becomes necessary to ask how data technology mediated shifts in capitalism, and the concurrent advent of surveillance capitalism will not only change the question of immigrants' work opportunities (i.e., the more mainstream understanding of "economic" migration), but also reassemble the social and legal constituents of all that produces the immigrant. In this vein, scholars studying the race and gender politics of immigration and labor have turned their attention to study the applications of data analytics and biometrics in immigration control, manifested in terms of the securitization of immigration and criminalization of immigrants and people of color.[41] To carry the discussion forward, it will be instructive to review Shoshana Zuboff's summary definition of the term surveillance capitalism:

> 1. A new economic order that claims human experience as free raw material for hidden commercial practices of extraction, prediction, and sales; 2. A parasitic economic logic in which the production of goods and services is subordinated to a new global architecture of behavioral modification; 3. A rogue mutation of capitalism marked by concentrations of wealth, knowledge, and power unprecedented in human history.[42]

Unlike the benign connotations of terms such as "digital globalization" or globalization's reboot being tied to unprecedented surges in the "flow of data," Zuboff's assessment of data-centric corporate capitalism places at its center urgent concerns about the methods and ramifications of digital surveillance, behavior modification, and their co-implications for market democracy and people's sovereignty.[43] Data technologies have increased the traffic and mutual reliance between commerce and surveillance. This nexus, rendered accessible to both capital and the state, carries us to the crux of economic migration; specifically, to the question of accounting for the historical making of immigrant labor presently at the overlap of digital capitalism, biometrics and big data, surveillance, and racialized immigration enforcement.

Surveillance, Big Data, and the Penal Turn in Immigration Enforcement

With the rising significance of data-analytics, the mechanisms of integration and convergences among US immigration, national security, and economic security have been enhanced even further:

> The worlds of security and economy do not so much as "melt together" as they become elements across which the imagination of future possibilities resonates, vibrates, and intensifies. . . . Thus it is that there is an intensifying resonance across spheres of economy and security, an infiltration of each one into the other, such that a moving complex emerges—a complex of the governing of emergent, uncertain, possible futures. The point of resonance on the horizon . . . is precisely a horizon of possible futures, arrayed in such a way as to govern, to decide, or to act in the present. Economy, one might say, is always and inescapably concerned with the unfolding of future possibilities.[44]

Panels of consumer data and everyday browsing information can now be accessed and cross-referenced with other data caches and measures, including, for example, threat indicator calculations, immigrant biometrics, visa forms, migration maps, and refugee GPS routes. This corpus of data—or what can be called for our interests "bio-analytics"—can be recorded from nearly every pore of lived life and processed just as seamlessly for marketing, financial and investment decisions, and production processes, or marshaled for security reasons. Further, the quantity of this data store expands cumulatively over time.

Data collected from digital spaces or people's activities online, for example, purchases made at websites, internet browsing and streaming history, social media contacts, in-flight meal selections, smartphone apps, subscriptions, any number of smart household gadgets, or CCTV footage at commercial spaces are not conventionally associated with the purview of the state. And yet, these forms of digital matter have been amalgamated within the state's domain of operations.[45] Digital information collected online or from other forms of electronic monitoring have become increasingly accessible to the state, by means of partnership triangulation between government agencies and private corporations, ranging from commercial entities to firms with government security contracts.[46] Accumulated over decades, any aspect of this stored data can be activated to extract patterns, to map associations, and to forecast likely probabilities concerning practically any aspect of human life, from behavior predictions and personal choice to political beliefs and mental tendencies. Gathered from what might be seen as non-state sites of life, this system of networked information has intensified and extended the state's "forensic gaze," fortifying its monitoring powers as needed to enforce "smart walls" for immigration control and border security, to punish, exclude, or filter immigrants and racial minorities in ways that can be difficult to predict or know in advance. This data history has become constitutive of an increasingly overlapping, shared domain of state and corporate surveillance.

The proliferation of data technologies and biometrics-driven processes—both in private commerce and in the state's border/security enforcement practices—has unfolded alongside inequality and employment insecurity, a troubling pattern of intensified surveillance, policing, and criminalization for immigrants, particularly the undocumented in low-income areas.[47] Documented workers in white-collar occupations, e.g., those on work visas such as the H-1B, have also come to encounter somewhat different but related features of the same immigration enforcement system's penal logics, manifested in the expansion of disciplinary control, legal precarity, and status subordination.[48] Work visas activate a field of disciplinary technologies to control immigrants: these visas confer upon employers the power over an immigrant's legal status—and thus ensure an immediate corollary, the power to produce the conditions of an immigrant's deportability. Given that the continuation of their employment-based dependent status is the primary safeguard against deportability, immigrants on work visas make many accommodations in deference to their employers' priorities, rather than their own, in matters that bear heavily on their lives and careers.[49] For this immigrant workforce then, the ever-present specter of status loss and deportability, encoded within the legal parameters of the visa, enable employer dependence and surveillance, economic marginalization, and labor flexibilization.

While working-class immigrants of color have become the most immediate, visible targets of immigration control and criminalization, the core logics of racialized exclusion and immigration enforcement also govern related means of exploitation and subordination for documented immigrants placed in white-collar occupations.[50] Unfolding with and melded into existing arrangements of racialized surveillance and immigration enforcement, digital capitalism will do more than transform work and access to employment across occupational sectors. By resetting the nature and scale of disciplinary technologies that constitute the interlinked forensic gaze of the state and capital, surveillance capitalism stands to increasingly transform the socio-legal and cultural processes that produce migrants as a historically situated category, including those aspects of the social positioning of migrants that govern their lives as economic beings.

Reflections for the Road

As this chapter has outlined, the bedrock of social systems that scholars study has been undergoing important transformations: Advanced globalization and capitalism have reproduced unprecedented socioeconomic inequality, while engendering and incorporating into this mix an updated *brave new* world of data analytics. And yet, conventional measures of skill and education, supply and demand of the labor market, and economic contributions have continued to arbitrate perceptions of immigrants' desirability, thus placing these enumerations at the center of public opinion and policy debates about US immigration, border control, and national security.

The view privileged herein, more or less across the Global North, is that "market-oriented policies designed to attract skilled migrants are likely to yield economic and social benefits," and that "attitudes towards migrants and consequently their success in the hosting society are strongly correlated with immigrants' success in the labour market."[51] Long endorsed by the US state (and some academics alike), this line of thinking has reached a canonical status, as evidenced in the state's reiterations, time and again, emphasizing a clear preference for well-managed "legal" migration as opposed to "illegal" migration. Here is a more recent installment of such a proclamation from the US Department of State:

> The illegal movement of people across international borders threatens national security and public safety, suppresses wages and strains public resources, and leaves immigrants themselves vulnerable to exploitation and abuse. It also undermines the rule of law by reducing citizens' faith in the ability of government to enforce the law. But well-managed, legal immigration can support national economic competitiveness and promote financial success and assimilation for newcomers.[52]

This official statement represents a multiplex of verdicts: "Illegal" migration is regarded as an economic and social burden, in addition to being a source of national insecurity, law and order threat, and public distress. In contrast, carefully calibrated and well-selected "legal migration" is associated with economic advantages and American competitiveness, as well as the added benefit accrued from a relatively trouble-free assimilation of undemanding newcomers, kept busy and satisfied with the task of making a success of their migration. This distinction represents an optic and disciplinary divide—namely, between one set of people who are collocated with chaos and catastrophe ("floods, waves, and surge") and another category of individuals seen as well-behaved contributors suitably ready to propel the nation forward by winning victory from global economic competitions. Furthermore, this distinction insists on demarcating undocumented migrants, irrespective of skill or education, as a mass of bodies with little individuality, while conferring conditional approval to documented ones, whose members, when necessary, are described as the "best and the brightest" and are seen as worthy individuals (owing to a recognition of their credentials and financial success).

This bifurcation produces chilling consequences: On one hand, it manufactures consent to disparage and disenfranchise one group of immigrants and makes them targets of wars on crime or terror, and therefore subject to deportation and incarceration; and, on the other, this bifurcation renders it difficult, and even confounding, to address the range of marginalization and legal status precarity that documented immigrants encounter day to day. This facet of the immigration canon is reproduced in migration studies, in the form of conventional immigration categories used to render immigrants legible: skilled and unskilled migration, economic migrants versus refugees or asylum seekers, and documented and undocumented (or irregular and unauthorized, or, worse, "illegal" immigrants).[53] The convention in the field for classificatory order serves as a deputy for reproducing a system of rank-ordering immigrant desirability.

But more complex than that, this narrow focus on the classifications and bisections between the desired and the undesirable—laid out on the basis of skill, safety/security, legality, and economic productivity pervasive in the economic migration framework—diverts attention away from what data analytics, biometrics, AI, and algorithms can do, will do, and have already done to bolster immigration enforcement and exclusion practices. The traditional approaches in economic migration—skills, jobs, sector-specific employment—obfuscate a scrutiny of these systems and their unequivocal role in *remaking* the immigrant *worker* in historically situated ways.

As this chapter has discussed, the socio-legal terms of employment—status-based exploitation, the passageways of capital accumulation, and the state's forensic gaze that emplaces immigrants under various enactments of surveillance, dependence, and precarity—each coalesce, often in untidy ways, to direct the terms in which immigrant labor and life will be incorporated. In this assessment, the economic aspects of migration are analyzed as being irrevocably co-constituted and mediated by a larger constituency of social relations that inform the making of the migrant as a particular social category. These include racial and gendered hierarchies within the specific structural context of the United States as an advanced capitalist economy in late-stage globalization with a congenital history of racial formation and immigration exclusions as a settler nation. Economic migration, in this framing, cannot be confined to a point of convergence for, or absence of, the double coincidence of wants between economic demand-pull and labor supply-push factors from immigrant receiving and sending countries, and immigrants' employment somewhere in between.

Immigrants' extraordinary passage—not by land or air, but from where one is *foreign-born* to occupy the figure of a migrant—is both a personal story and a potent accounting of social-historical processes:

legislation (immigration laws); gendered and racial discourses (language about "waves of aliens," "job-stealers," and "security risks"); cultural and social prejudices (around race, or, sending countries' poverty/unemployment); scrutiny of value (determination of immigrants' skills and balance sheets of their impact on jobs or public welfare); and tangible evidence of economic disentitlements (anti-immigrant discrimination, wage gaps between citizens and immigrants). In conversation with recent literature on inequality, surveillance, and immigration enforcement, this chapter had called attention to the need to rework our formulation of the "economic" metrics of immigrants' employment in ways that can address more substantially the impact that the unfolding iterations of socioeconomic polarization and surveillance capitalism will continue to have on immigrants' relationship to advanced capital and the state, and the terms of their incorporation and exclusion therein.

NOTES

1 Alexandre Abreu, "The New Economics of Labor Migration: Beware of Neoclassicals Bearing Gifts," *Forum for Social Economics* 41, no. 1 (2012): 46–67; Joaquín Arango, "Explaining Migration: A Critical View," *International Social Science Journal* 52, no. 165 (2000): 283–296; International Labor Organization (ILO), *ILO Global Estimates on International Migrant Workers: Results and Methodology* (Geneva International Labour Office, 2018); Douglas Massey and Fernando Riosmena, "Undocumented Migration from Latin America in an Era of Rising U.S. Enforcement," *Annals of the American Academy of Political and Social Science* 630, no. 1 (2010): 294–321; Emily Ryo, "Deciding to Cross: Norms and Economics of Unauthorized Migration," *American Sociological Review* 78, no. 4 (2013): 574–603; Nicholas Van Hear, Oliver Bakewell, and Katy Long, "Push-Pull Plus: Reconsidering the Drivers of Migration," *Journal of Ethnic and Migration Studies* 44, no. 6 (2018): 927–944.

2 This method of historicization is not the same as the project of assessing ups and downs of economic sectors, market expansion or contraction, related impact on employment opportunities, or mapping out what sorts of jobs are about to decline or rise in significance.

3 Payal Banerjee, "Indian Information Technology Workers in the United States: The H-1B Visa, Flexible Production, and the Racialization of Labor," *Critical Sociology* 32, nos. 2–3 (2006): 427–445. For a historical analysis of race, legal status, and US immigration laws, see Mae M. Ngai, "The Architecture of Race in American Immigration Law: A Reexamination of the Immigration Act of 1924," *Journal of American History* 86, no. 1 (1999): 67–92; and Mae M. Ngai, *Impossible*

Subjects: Illegal Aliens and the Making of Modern America (Princeton, NJ: Princeton University Press, 2004).

4 The many categories used to classify migrants—skilled and unskilled migrants, refugees, asylum seekers, documented and undocumented workers—draw from neoclassical approaches to migration in general, and methodological individualism therein, in particular. In this framing, the various legal, entry, and occupational *categories* employed to classify and distinguish migrants are: (one) taken as real and objective indicators able to cogently sort immigrants by skills, demographic details, or method of arrival at the destination country; and (two) not as historically specific socio-legal constructs that signal the state's race-gender systems embedded in nation-building and the organization of capital's access to flexible labor ensured through racialized immigration legislation. This conventional approach of holding immigration/migration categories as self-evident and natural has been challenged in recent years. Given this volume's emphasis on *economic* migration, this chapter limits its deliberations to the prefix "economic" and will not address other classificatory categories, for which a cognate theoretical critique and substantive political economic analysis apply. For more on the scholarship that examines the socio-legal construction of visa and migration categories, see Payal Banerjee, "The Production of Noncitizen Exclusions under H-1B and L-1 Visas," in *Immigration Policy in the Age of Punishment: Detention, Deportation, and Border Control*, ed. David C. Brotherton and Philip Kretsedemas (New York: Columbia University Press, 2017), 276–291; and Sandro Mezzadra and Brett Neilson, *Border as Method, or, the Multiplication of Labor* (Durham, NC: Duke University Press, 2013).

5 Based on neoclassical approaches to migration, the predominant take on economic migration has been characterized by methodological individualism (rational choice, skills) and a focus on themes such as economic outcome optimization, capital-labor ratios, jobs and wage differentials, demand-supply equilibrium, etc. For more details, see Abreu, "The New Economics of Labor Migration"; Arango, "Explaining Migration."

6 This formulation of historical and structural construction of immigration, race, gender, and legal status draws from a long line of scholarship on the subject, specifically from Critical Race Theory and Asian American critique of US immigration. The following scholars' works are most relevant to this chapter's conceptualization of the migrant/immigrant—across the spectrum of classification and categories—as a historically specific, social category. See Eduardo Bonilla-Silva, "'This Is a White Country': The Racial Ideology of the Western Nations of the World-System," *Sociological Inquiry* 70 no. 2 (2000): 188–214; Ngai, *Impossible Subjects*; Evelyn Nakano Glenn, *Unequal Freedom: How Race and Gender Shaped American Citizenship and Labor* (Cambridge, MA: Harvard University Press, 2002); Ian Haney López, *White by Law: The Legal Construction of Race* (New York: New York University Press, 2006); Lisa Lowe, *Immigrant Acts:*

On Asian American Cultural Politics (Durham, NC: Duke University Press, 1996); Mary Romero, "Crossing the Immigration and Race Border: A Critical Race Theory Approach to Immigration Studies," *Contemporary Justice Review* 11, no. 1 (2008): 23–37; and Aristide R. Zolberg, *A Nation by Design: Immigration Policy in the Fashioning of America* (New York: Russell Sage Foundation, 2006).

7 In reference to this chapter's emphasis on the intersections among migration, inequality, and technology, it is worth mentioning here that the United Nations Department of Social and Economic Affairs' (UNDESA) most recent report, *World Social Report 2020: Inequality in a Rapidly Changing World* (2020), on global inequality has also included these themes. This report identifies four mega-trends—namely, technological innovation, international migration, climate change, and urbanization—to represent the four thematic areas of focus on this subject. See the full report: www.un.org.

8 It must be stated that the relationship between international migration and climate change is critically important and relevant to this discussion. Nevertheless, in the interest of space, this chapter will focus on rising inequality and advances in technology as they relate to migration. For a recent analysis that includes the relevance of climate change in this vein, especially in terms of global inequality's intersections with migration, technology, and urbanization, see UNDESA's *World Social Report 2020*.

9 The US Bureau of Labor defines foreign-born in the following terms: "The foreign born are persons residing in the United States who were not U.S. citizens at birth. That is, they were born outside the United States or one of its outlying areas such as Puerto Rico or Guam, to parents neither of whom was a U.S. citizen. The foreign-born population includes legally admitted immigrants, refugees, temporary residents such as students and temporary workers, and undocumented immigrants. The survey data, however, do not separately identify the number of persons in these categories." See US Department of Labor, Bureau of Labor Statistics, "Foreign-Born Workers: Labor Force Characteristics—2019," May 15, 2020, www.bls.gov.

10 US Department of Labor, "Foreign-Born Workers."

11 See Jeanne Batalova, "Immigrant Health-Care Workers in the United States," Migration Policy Institute, May 14, 2020. The breakdown is as follows: "Regardless of nativity status, women were more likely to be employed as RNs and in health-care support occupations and less likely to be physicians and surgeons than men. Both immigrant men and women employed in health-care occupations in 2018 were more likely than their U.S.-born counterparts to work as physicians and surgeons: 25 percent and 5 percent of foreign-born men and women employed in health care, respectively, worked in these professions, compared to 17 percent and 3 percent of native-born men and women. Foreign-born health-care workers overall were also more likely than their native-born peers to work as nursing assistants, personal care aides, and home health aides: For the foreign born, 38

percent of women and 19 percent of men worked in these occupations, compared
to 22 percent and 14 percent of U.S.-born women and men, respectively."

12 For an overview of these mainstream approaches, see: Anna Boucher and Lucie
Cerna, "Current Policy Trends in Skilled Immigration Policy," *International
Migration* 52, no. 3 (2014): 21–25; John Bound, Breno Braga, Joseph M.
Golden, and Gaurav Khanna, "Recruitment of Foreigners in the Market for Computer
Scientists in the United States," *Journal of Labor Economics* 33, no. S1, part 2 (2015):
S187–S223; William R. Kerr and Sarah E. Turner, "Introduction: US High-Skilled
Immigration in the Global Economy," *Journal of Labor Economics* 33, no. 3, part
2 (2015): S1–S4; Jennifer Hunt, "Which Immigrants Are Most Innovative and
Entrepreneurial? Distinctions by Entry Visa," *Journal of Labor Economics* 29, no.
3 (2011): 417–457; Jennifer Hunt, "Are Immigrants the Most Skilled US Computer
and Engineering Workers?," *Journal of Labor Economics* 33, no. S1 (2015): S39–S77;
Jennifer Hunt and Marjolaine Gauthier-Loiselle, "How Much Does Immigration
Boost Innovation?," *American Economic Journal: Macroeconomics* 2, no. 2 (2010):
31–56; Giovanni Peri, Kevin Shih, and Chad Sparber, "STEM Workers, H-1B Visas,
and Productivity in US Cities," *Journal of Labor Economics* 33, no. S1, part 2 (2015):
S225–S255; Jonathan Portes, "The Economics of Migration," *Contexts* 18, no. 2
(2019): 12–17; Stuart Anderson and Michaela Platzer, *American Made: The Impact
of Immigrant Entrepreneurs and Professionals on U.S. Competitiveness* (Arlington,
VA: National Venture Capital Association, 2006).

13 Peter B. Brownell, "Wages Differences Between Temporary and Permanent Im-
migrants," *International Migration Review* 44, no. 3 (2010): 593–614; B. Lindsay
Lowell and Johanna Avato, "The Wages of Skilled Temporary Migrants: Effects of
Visa Pathways and Job Portability," *International Migration* 52, no. 3 (2014): 85–98;
Stan Malos, "Employment Discrimination Based on Immigration Status: Recent
Cases Involving H-1Bs," *Employee Responsibilities and Rights Journal* 24, no. 1
(2011): 23–36.

14 Katharine M. Donato and Donna Gabaccia, *Gender and International Migration:
From the Slavery Era to the Global Age* (New York: Russell Sage Foundation, 2015).

15 Anna Boucher, *Gender, Migration and the Global Race for Talent* (Manchester:
Manchester University Press, 2016); Boucher and Cerna, "Current Policy Trends
in Skilled Immigration Policy."

16 For an elaboration of this point and related details concerning the structural links
among imperialism, globalization, circulation of capital and foreign investments,
international migration, and immigration policy, see: Edna Bonacich and Lucie
Cheng, "Introduction: A Theoretical Orientation to International Labor Migration," in *Labor Immigration under Capitalism: Asian Workers in the United States
before World War II*, ed. Lucie Cheng and Edna Bonacich (Berkeley: University
of California Press, 1984), 1–56; Saskia Sassen, *The Mobility of Labor and Capital:
A Study in International Investment and Labor Flow* (Cambridge, UK: Cambridge
University Press, 1988).

17 Banerjee, "Indian Information Technology Workers in the United States";
    Banerjee, "The Production of Noncitizen Exclusions under H-1B and L-1 Visas";
    Glenn, *Unequal Freedom*; Tanya Maria Golash-Boza, *Immigration Nation: Raids,
    Detentions, and Deportations in Post-9/11 America* (New York: Routledge, 2012);
    Ngai, *Impossible Subjects*; Romero, "Crossing the Immigration and Race Border."

18 Lourdes Beneria, Günseli Berik, and Maria Floro, *Gender, Development, and
    Globalization: Economics as If All People Mattered* (New York: Routledge, 2003);
    Grace Chang, *Disposable Domestics: Immigrant Women Workers in the Global
    Economy* (Boston, MA: South End Press, 2000); Marianne H. Marchand and
    Anne Sisson Runyan, "Introduction: Feminist Sightings of Global Restructuring:
    Old and New Conceptualizations," in *Gender and Global Restructuring: Sighting,
    Sites, and Resistances*, ed. Marianne H. Marchand and Anne Sisson Runyan (New
    York: Routledge, 2000), 1–22; Valentine M. Moghadam, "Gender and Globaliza-
    tion: Female Labor and Women's Mobilization," *Journal of World-Systems Research*
    5, no. 2 (1999): 367–388; Aihwa Ong, "The Gender and Labor Politics of Postmo-
    dernity," *Annual Review of Anthropology* 20, no. 1 (1991): 279–309.

19 Golash-Boza, *Immigration Nation*; William L. Conwill, "Neoliberal Policy as
    Structural Violence: Its Links to Domestic Violence in Black Communities in the
    United States," in *The Gender of Globalization: Women Navigating Cultural and
    Economic Marginalities*, ed. Nandini Gunewardena and Ann Kingsolver (Santa Fe,
    NM: School for Advanced Research Press, 2007), 127–146; Ruth Wilson Gilmore,
    Golden Gulag: Prisons, Surplus, Crisis, and Opposition in Globalizing California
    (Berkeley: University of California Press, 2007); Sandy Smith-Nonini, "Sticking to
    the Union: Anthropologists and 'Union Maids' in San Francisco," in *The Gender
    of Globalization: Women Navigating Cultural and Economic Marginalities*, ed.
    Nandini Gunewardena and Ann Kingsolver (Santa Fe, NM: School for Advanced
    Research Press, 2007), 197–214.

20 A growing body of scholarship has provided compelling evidence concerning
    dense convergences and mutual enhancement between immigration and the
    criminalization of poverty, manifested in hyper-policing, monitoring, surveil-
    lance, and incarceration of low-income and immigrant communities of color. To
    conceptualize the significance of these patterns of securitization and control on
    reproducing the field of meaning and material consequences surrounding im-
    migrant labor—rendered disposable, dependent, precarious, and subjected to sur-
    veillance, detention, and deportation—this chapter has specifically drawn from
    the work of the following scholars: Gilmore, *Golden Gulag*; Gerald P. López, "Re-
    belling against the War on Low-Income, of Color, and Immigrant Communities,"
    in *After the War on Crime: Race, Democracy, and a New Reconstruction*, ed. Mary
    Louise Frampton, Ian Haney López, and Jonathan Simon (New York: New York
    University Press, 2008), 151–165; Tanya Maria Golash-Boza, *Deported: Immigrant
    Policing, Disposable Labor, and Global Capitalism* (New York: New York Univer-
    sity Press, 2015); Patrisia Macias-Rojas, *From Deportation to Prison: The Politics
    of Immigration Enforcement in Post-Civil Rights America* (New York: New York

University Press, 2016); Sunaina Marr Maira, *The 9/11 Generation: Youth, Rights, and Solidarity in the War on Terror* (New York: New York University Press, 2016); Ana Muñiz, "Bordering Circuitry: Crossjurisdictional Immigration Surveillance," *UCLA Law Review* 66 (2019): 1636–1680; Julia Sudbury, *Global Lockdown: Race, Gender, and the Prison-Industrial Complex* (New York: Routledge, 2005).

21 Thomas Piketty, *Capital in the Twenty-First Century*, trans. Arthur Goldhammer (Cambridge, MA and London: The Belknap Press of Harvard University Press, 2017), 323.

22 Piketty, *Capital in the Twenty-First Century*, 330–332.

23 Petra Duenhaupt, "Financialization and the Rentier Income Share: Evidence from the USA and Germany," *International Review of Applied Economics* 26, no. 4 (2012): 465–487; Gerald A. Epstein, ed., *Financialization and the World Economy* (Northampton, MA: Edward Elgar, 2005); Gerald Epstein and Dorothy Power, "Rentier Incomes and Financial Crises: An Empirical Examination of Trends and Cycles in Some OECD Countries," *Canadian Journal of Development Studies* 24, no. 2 (2003): 229–248; Shampa Roy-Mukherjee and Ejike Udeogu, "Neo-liberal Globalization and Income Inequality: Panel Data Evidence from OECD and Western Balkan Countries," *Journal of Balkan and Near Eastern Studies* 23, no. 1 (2021): 15–39.

24 Ozgür Orhangazi, "Financialization of the U.S. Economy and Its Effects on Capital Accumulation: A Theoretical and Empirical Investigation," PhD diss., University of Massachusetts Amherst, 2006.

25 William Lazonick and Mary O'Sullivan, "Maximizing Shareholder Value: A New Ideology for Corporate Governance," *Economy and Society* 29, no. 1 (2000): 13–35.

26 Piketty, *Capital in the Twenty-First Century*; Branko Milanovic, "The Clash of Capitalisms: The Real Fight for the Global Economy's Future," *Foreign Affairs* 99, no. 1 (January/February 2020), 10–21.

27 Karen E. Fields and Barbara J. Fields, *Racecraft: The Soul of Inequality in American Life* (London and New York: Verso Books, 2012); International Labour Organization (ILO), *Work Employment and Social Outlook: The Changing Nature of Jobs* (Geneva: International Labour Organization, 2015); UNDESA, *World Social Report 2020*.

28 Patricia Buckley and Akrur Barua, "COVID-19's Impact on US Income Inequality: It's Going To Get Worse Before It Gets Better," *Deloitte Insights*, July 23, 2020, www2.deloitte.com; Eduardo Porter and Karl Russell, "How the American Unemployment System Failed," *New York Times*, January 21, 2021, www.nytimes.com.

29 Randy Albelda, Aimee Bell-Pasht, and Charalampos Konstantinidi, "Gender and Precarious Work in the United States: Evidence from the Contingent Work Supplement 1995–2017," *Review of Radical Political Economics* 52, no. 3 (2020): 542–563; Joshua Greenstein, "The Precariat Class Structure and Income Inequality among US Workers: 1980–2018," *Review of Radical Political Economics* 52, no. 3 (2020): 447–469; Victor L. Shammas, "Superfluity and Insecurity: Disciplin-

ing Surplus Populations in the Global North," *Capital & Class* 42, no. 3 (2018): 411–418; Tamar Diana Wilson, "Precarization, Informalization, and Marx," *Review of Radical Political Economics* 52, no. 3 (2020): 470–486.

30 Leanne Weber and Benjamin Bowling, "Valiant Beggars and Global Vagabonds: Select, Eject, Immobilize," *Theoretical Criminology* 12, no. 3 (2008): 355–375; Shammas, "Superfluity and Insecurity," 411.

31 Overall, existential insecurity refers to the multifaceted dispossession that people, especially immigrants and low-income communities of color, encounter in a neo-liberal, penal state: limited employment opportunities characterized by flexible, precarious, temporary, and low-income jobs in a restructured economy; systemic deskilling; and lack of adequate housing, health care, family care, and public wel-fare services. For a detailed elaboration, see Loïc Wacquant's *Punishing the Poor: The Neoliberal Government of Social Insecurity* (Durham, NC: Duke University Press, 2009); and Golash-Boza, *Deported*.

32 Julie A. Dowling and Jonathan Xavier Inda, *Governing Immigration through Crime: A Reader* (Stanford, CA: Stanford University Press, 2013).

33 Susan Lund and Laura Tyson, "Globalization Is Not in Retreat: Digital Technol-ogy and the Future of Trade," *Foreign Affairs* 97, no. 3 (May–June 2018): 130–140.

34 Lund and Tyson, "Globalization Is Not in Retreat," 132.

35 Andrei Hagiu and Julian Wright, "When Data Creates Competitive Advantage . . . and When It Doesn't," *Harvard Business Review* (January–February 2020): 96.

36 Peter Cappelli, "Your Approach to Hiring Is All Wrong: Outsourcing and Algo-rithms Won't Get You the People You Need," *Harvard Business Review* (May–June 2019): 50–58; Marco Iansiti and Karim R. Lakhani, "Competing in the Age of AI: How Machine Intelligence Changes the Rules of Business," *Harvard Business Review* (January–February 2020): 62.

37 Iansiti and Lakhani, "Competing in the Age of AI," 63.

38 Iansiti and Lakhani, "Competing in the Age of AI," 62.

39 Richard Baldwin, *The Globotics Upheaval: Globalization, Robotics, and the Future of Work* (New York: Oxford University Press, 2020); Lund and Tyson, "Globaliza-tion Is Not in Retreat"; World Economic Forum, *The Future of Jobs: Employment, Skills and Workforce Strategy for the Fourth Industrial Revolution* (Geneva: World Economic Forum, 2016).

40 Cappelli, "Your Approach to Hiring Is All Wrong," 50.

41 Louise Amoore, *The Politics of Possibility: Risk and Security Beyond Probability* (Durham, NC: Duke University Press, 2013); Ruha Benjamin, *Race After Technol-ogy: Abolitionist Tools for the New Jim Code* (Cambridge, UK: Polity Press, 2019); Simone Browne, *Dark Matters: On the Surveillance of Blackness* (Durham, NC and London: Duke University Press, 2015); Joseph Pugliese, *Biometrics: Bodies, Technologies, Biopolitics* (New York: Routledge, 2010).

42 Shoshana Zuboff, *The Age of Surveillance Capitalism: The Fight for a Human Future at the New Frontier of Power* (New York: Public Affairs, 2019), v.

43 Data-driven economic reorganization led by state governments has been associated, in certain cases, with political authoritarianism; i.e., systems of rule in
which a government sees itself as a technocratic bureaucracy with commitments
primarily to delivering high economic growth in order to legitimize its increasing
authoritarianism. A singular focus on economic growth necessitates a growing need to be freed from legal requirements and regulations, which are seen as
constraints in the way of the promised economic growth, making the applications
of laws arbitrary, unequal, and repressive; i.e., undemocratic. See Milanovic, "The
Clash of Capitalisms"; and Zuboff, *The Age of Surveillance Capitalism.*
44 Amoore, *The Politics of Possibility,* 4–5.
45 Amoore, *The Politics of Possibility.*
46 Louise Amoore, "Biometric Borders: Governing Mobilities in the War on Terror,"
Political Geography 25, no. 3 (2006): 336–351; Amoore, *The Politics of Possibility.*
47 Browne, *Dark Matters*; Golash-Boza, *Immigration Nation*; Philip Kretedemas and
David C. Brotherton, "Open Markets, Militarized Borders?: Immigration Enforcement Today," in *Keeping Out the Other: A Critical Introduction to Immigration
Enforcement Today,* ed. David C. Brotherton and Philip Kretsedemas (New York:
Columbia University Press, 2008), 1–25.
48 Payal Banerjee, "The Production of Noncitizen Exclusions under H-1B and L-1
Visas."
49 Payal Banerjee, "Flexible Hiring, Immigration, and Indian IT Workers' Experi-
ences of Contract Work in the United States," in *People at Work: Life, Power, and
Social Inclusion in the New Economy,* ed. Marjorie L. DeVault (New York: New
York University Press, 2008), 97–111.
50 Banerjee, "The Production of Noncitizen Exclusions under H-1B and L-1 Visas."
See also Sangay Mishra's chapter in this volume.
51 Anna Rosso, "The Economics of Migration: Introduction," *National Institute
Economic Review* 229, no. 1 (2014): R1.
52 See the US Department of State, Bureau of Population, Refugees, and Migration,
"International Migration," www.state.gov.
53 Payal Banerjee, "Skilled Migration's Unmarked Subject: Notes on Reformulating
Typological Thinking," paper presented at the Highly Skilled Migrants: The Gulf
and Global Perspectives Workshop, Center for Regional and International Studies, Georgetown University in Qatar, June 1–2, 2016, Doha, Qatar.

2

Evolving Trends of Latin American Immigration in the United States

Challenges for the Integration of Skilled Immigrants

RENÉ ZENTENO

By its size, concentration, and duration, immigration from Latin America to the United States stands as an extraordinary event in the annals of contemporary migrations worldwide and unprecedented in the long history of economic immigration to the United States. In 1970, only 1.7 million Latino immigrants lived in the United States. That number soared to 20.9 million by 2019. During the same period, the percentage of the foreign-born population from Latin America grew from 17.2 to 46.8.[1]

This vigorous migration phenomenon has exerted a strong influence on the transformation of the demography and the ethnoracial composition of the United States.[2] The Latino population constitutes the largest racial minority group in the United States, representing 18 percent of the population and accounting for half of the country's population growth between 2010 and 2019.[3]

Yet, the available evidence suggests that the large-scale migration from Latin America declined drastically with the onset of the Great Recession. With the bursting of the housing bubble in the United States that precipitated a global financial crisis, the US economy lost almost 8 million jobs and sent the unemployment rate to 10.1 percent from May 2007 to October 2009.[4] The number of migrants coming north, particularly from Mexico, started to decrease, coinciding with a slowdown in the construction industry.[5] However, even after employment in the US labor market recovered and rose to historic levels in the second half of the 2010s, migration flows from Latin America did not recover to pre-recession levels. As a result, the Latin American migrant stock in the United States has experienced its lowest annual growth rate since the 1960s, and Asian immigration has accelerated and exceeded those arriving from Latin America in recent years.

Most of our understanding of migration from Latin America derives from the unique experience of Mexican and Central American migrants. There is relatively little research on immigration from Latin America, as a region, to the United States, and less so on skilled migration from the region. This chapter combines data from a variety of sources to construct an up-to-date demographic and socioeconomic profile of Latin American migration to the United States. It underscores recent changes in the size and composition of the Latin American immigrant population to reflect upon two critical aspects for their integration into US society: educational selectivity and immigration status.[6] The chapter is organized in three sections. The first section examines the evolution of Latin American immigration to the United States from 1970 to 2019 by presenting evidence on the continuities and changes in Latino immigrants' demographic and socioeconomic characteristics since 1990. The second section analyzes variations in the skill selectivity of immigrants from Latin America, and a third section addresses current challenges concerning the immigration status of this population. The chapter concludes by noting gaps in understanding recent migration trends and patterns, highlighting implications and proposing suggestions for future research.

Contemporary Immigration from Latin America to the United States

During the last fifty years of the twentieth century, Latin America turned from an immigrant-receiving region into a region of emigration.[7] The United States became by far the world's largest destination for Latino immigrants.[8] Prior to the passage of the Immigration and Nationality Act of 1965, there was significant immigration from Mexico, Cuba, Dominican Republic, and Colombia to the United States.[9] However, in 1960, fewer than one million Latino immigrants lived in the United States.[10]

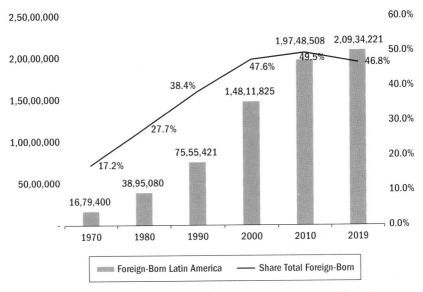

Figure 2.1: Foreign-Born Population from Latin America and the Caribbean Region, 1970–2019. Source: Author's calculations based on weighted 1-year American Community Survey (ACS) Public Use Microdata (PUMS): Steven Ruggles, et al., "IPUMS USA: Version 10.0 [dataset]," 2020, https://doi.org/10.18128/D010.V11.0.

Changing Trends

The data in figure 2.1 fully capture the upsurge of northbound flows from Latin America. Between 1970 and 2019, the number of Latino immigrants in the United States multiplied twelve times, passing from an estimated 1.7 million in 1970 to almost 21 million in 2019. The inflow from Latin America increased sharply from 1970 to 2000, when it doubled every ten years and became the primary driver of the foreign-born population in the United States.[11] This period saw an unprecedented Latin American migration to the United States that was mainly driven by economic, demographic, rich social networks, and family-reunification motives, and, to a lesser extent, by US immigration policies, civil wars, and violence in Central America and the Caribbean.[12]

The era of large-scale migration from Latin America came to a slowdown in the 2000s and almost to a halt since the Great Recession.

Between 2000 and 2010, the number of Latino immigrants increased only by 33 percent to reach 19.7 million in 2010. Yet, despite a slower growth rate than in the previous three decades, Latino immigrants accounted for 49.5 percent of the foreign-born population in 2010.

The 2008 US financial crisis exposed a fundamental reality about Latin America–US migration: its strong ties to labor demand in the US economy.[13] By the time the US economy hit bottom years later, migration appeared to have collapsed. An enforcement campaign by the Obama administration that produced more than 2 million removals contributed, as did conditions in countries like Mexico, including an easing of demographic pressures due to low birth rates and the reduction of family size, relative macroeconomic stability, and violence along trafficking routes. The result is a new era of reduced northbound flows, reduced circularity, and an increase in the number of former migrants returning to Latin America. Between 2010 and 2019, the Latin American migrant stock in the United States rose by only 1.2 million, its lowest growth in the last sixty years. As new immigrant arrivals from Asia rapidly increased at a faster rate during this time,[14] Latin America saw its share of the nation's migrant stock fall from 49.5 percent in 2010 to 46.8 percent in 2019.

The 2010–2019 period has been characterized by a setback of historical migration patterns from Latin America. In addition to the Great Recession and a significant decline in low-skilled employment in the US economy, other demographic, social, and economic developments in Latin America and enhanced immigration enforcement efforts and controls at all levels of government in the United States contributed to the decline of immigration from Latin America.[15]

Numerous factors in both the United States and Latin America contribute to shaping the size and characteristics of migration flows, and it is difficult to draw clear, simple lines of causality between events and migration trends. However, in recent years, dramatic changes in the US economy appear to have exercised a dominant influence.

Changing Profiles

The new reality of Latin American immigration has shaped the character of the Latino immigrant population in the United States. Table 2.1

TABLE 2.1: Selected Demographic and Socioeconomic Characteristics of
Latino Immigrants to the United States, 1990–2019

	1990	2000	2010	2019
Distribution by Country of Origin[a]				
Mexico	56.4	61.9	59.5	51.9
El Salvador	6.2	5.5	6.1	6.9
Cuba	9.8	5.9	5.6	6.5
Dominican Republic	4.6	4.6	4.5	5.6
Guatemala	2.9	3.2	4.0	5.3
Colombia	3.8	3.5	3.3	3.8
Honduras	1.4	1.9	2.6	3.6
Haiti	2.9	2.9	3.0	3.4
Other Countries	12.1	10.6	11.4	13.1
Sex Ratio[b]				
Immigrants from Latin America	109.2	112.0	106.6	99.7
Immigrants Other Countries	87.9	88.5	86.8	87.5
Natives	95.0	95.7	96.7	97.6
Median Age (years)				
Immigrants from Latin America	32	33	38	44
Immigrants Other Countries	41	41	44	47
Natives	32	35	35	36
Percentage Long-Term Residents[c]				
Immigrants from Latin America	49.3	54.0	63.9	77.6
Immigrants Other Countries	60.5	60.8	66.6	69.3
Percentage US Citizens				
Immigrants from Latin America	26.2	28.2	30.0	40.4
Immigrants Other Countries	49.4	51.2	57.3	61.4
Percentage Poor				
Immigrants from Latin America	25.2	23.1	24.1	16.3
Immigrants Other Countries	13.2	12.6	13.2	11.3
Natives	12.6	11.7	14.9	12.2

Source: Author's calculations based on Steven Ruggles, Sarah Flood, Ronald Goeken, Josiah Grover, Erin
Meyer, Jose Pacas and Matthew Sobek. IPUMS USA: Version 10.0 [dataset]. Minneapolis, MN: IPUMS, 2020.
[a]Descending order according to the distribution of 2019.
[b]Number of males per one hundred females.
[c]More than ten years residing in the United States.

presents information on demographic and socioeconomic characteristics of Latino immigrants to the United States from 1990 to 2019.

Historically, migration from Latin America in the United States has
been largely the movement of Mexican workers. As can be seen, Mexico
has remained the major contributor to the stock of Latino immigrants

over the last thirty years. However, as fewer Mexicans attempted to cross since the Great Recession, the proportion of immigrants arriving from Mexico fell from a peak of 61.9 percent in 2000 to a low of 51.9 percent in 2019. Mexico is followed by El Salvador (6.9 percent), Cuba (6.5 percent), and Dominican Republic (5.6 percent) as the top source countries among Latino immigrants. The country composition of Latino immigrants shifted away from Mexico toward Central American countries during the last two decades. Three countries from Central America, El Salvador, Guatemala, and Honduras, increased their share of total Latino immigrants from 10.5 percent in 2000 to 15.7 percent in 2019. A similar but more modest increase can be seen in other countries from Latin America.

Until recently, migration streams from Latin America occurred predominantly for economic reasons. However, recent trends show large segments of the population being forced to migrate because of violence and human rights violations. Although migration from Central America to the United States is not a new phenomenon, high crime rates and violence combined with stagnant economic growth have led many Salvadorians, Guatemalans, and Hondurans to head north, including thousands of families and unaccompanied migrant children seeking asylum in the United States.[16] Furthermore, the humanitarian crises in Central America, Mexico, and the United States–Mexico border have escalated in recent years in response to the absence of adequate policies to halt the economic decline and civil violence in Central America.

Table 2.1 shows that the demographic characteristics of Latino immigrants shifted somewhat from the traditional pattern of male migration. Unlike the female-dominated pattern of migration from other countries, immigrants from Latin America have been highly selective of males. For example, in 2000, there were 112 males per every 100 females among the foreign-born population from Latin America. The most recent data available indicate a more balanced gender mix among Latino immigrants. In contrast, the sex ratio appears to be relatively stable for the rest of the immigrants, about 87 or 88 men per 100 women.

Two tangible trends in key characteristics of Latino immigrants that emerge from the data are their aging and longevity as migrants. At the peak of Latin American immigration at the end of the twentieth century, large waves of young people looking for better economic opportunities in the United States kept the Latino immigrant population young and with no significant differences in the shares of recently arrived and long-term immigrant residents. Thus, migrants in 1990 and 2000 were considerably younger and more likely to have arrived recently to the United States than those in the most recent years.

In general, the overall immigrant population is aging fast. Whereas the median age of Latino and non-Latino immigrant populations living in the United States in 1990 was 32 and 41 years old, respectively, in 2019, the corresponding figures were 44 and 47 years. The shift in the age composition of the Latino immigrant population does not derive from any secular trend in the age of departure but from the fact that fewer young Latinos are entering the United States since the Great Recession. The trend of the age distribution becoming progressively older over time is similar among immigrants from other countries.

The percentage of long-term residents shows a parallel upward trend. In 1990, nearly half of all migrants from Latin America had lived in the United States for more than ten years, and immigrants from other countries were more likely to be long-term residents (60.5 percent). As the influx of immigrants drastically decreased in the last fifteen years, the percentage of new immigrant residents from Latin America reached only 22.4 percent in 2019, down from 50.7 in 1990. Until recently, immigrants from other regions of the world, mainly Asia, showed a larger share of newcomers than Latinos. However, the presence of long-term residents in both immigrant groups is much higher today than at the end of the twentieth century.

The significant increase in age and length of stay has coincided with an increase in the proportion of naturalized citizens among all immigrants. From 1990 to 2010, less than one-third of the foreign-born population from Latin America were naturalized citizens. During the last ten years, the proportion of US citizens among Latino immigrants rose to 40.4 percent—an important step toward their political membership and socioeconomic integration. Still, there exists a significant variation in the propensity to become a US citizen by region of birth. In part due to their much higher levels of unauthorized migration, the proportion of naturalized citizens is lower among Latino than non-Latino migrants.

Poverty rates among the foreign-born in the United States tend to be higher than those of natives, a phenomenon attributable to immigrants' high levels of unskilled and unauthorized migration. Table 2.1 confirms this fact for Latino migrants in the United States. Latino immigrants were roughly twice as likely to be poorer than natives and immigrants from other countries in 1990 and 2000. At the end of the Great Recession, in 2010, poverty rates were higher for both natives and immigrants than in 2000. The poverty rate was still close to one-quarter among Latin American migrants in 2010, an incidence 62 percent higher than for natives. However, for the first time, immigrants from other countries had a lower poverty rate than natives.

Just before the COVID-19 pandemic, the US population reached its lowest poverty rate since 1959: 10.5 percent in 2019.[17] The decline is notable for Latino immigrants. The share of Latino immigrants in poverty dropped to only 16.3 percent in 2019, its lowest level in many decades. Yet the poverty rate for the rest of the immigrants is only 70 percent of that for Latinos. Lower levels of poverty among immigrants in the United States, including Latinos, coincide with the intensification of highly skilled migration.

Selection and the Emergence of Highly Skilled Migration

Migrants are not a random sample of the source population. Since migration decisions depend on the predicted benefits and the cost of migration, neoclassical economic theory predicts that migration is more likely to be undertaken by individuals who can produce the highest payoff to their investment.[18] Expected benefits and income for potential migrants increase with education and skills, and highly skilled workers are then more responsive to an income maximization opportunity. The positive self-selection of migrants is reinforced by the presence of the out-of-pocket costs of migration.[19] A significant body of literature has found support for the positive-selection hypothesis among international migrants.[20]

The US population census and the American Community Survey offer snapshots of the share of recently arrived immigrants, ages 25–64, with low (less than high school) and high (bachelor's degree or more) levels of educational attainment for the years 1990, 2000, 2010, and 2019.

As we can see in table 2.2, recent immigrants from countries other than Latin America show notable skill levels. In 1990, 35.1 percent of them had earned at least a college degree. The share of highly educated individuals among immigrants from other countries systematically expanded to a remarkable 58.9 percent in 2019. The presence of unskilled people in this immigrant group dropped from 23.8 percent in 1990 to a mere 10.0 percent in 2019.

Northbound flows from Latin America have historically been characterized by their abundant social capital (networks of friends and family relationships) and scarce human capital (skills and education).[21] From the 1970s to the mid-2000s, immigrants in the United States were dominated by waves of low-skilled persons from Latin America, particularly from Mexico.[22] However, significant variations exist within this group in terms of skill levels as migrants from the Caribbean and South America have proven to be more selective in terms of education.[23] Differences also exist in terms of legal status. Clark, Hatton, and Williamson show that authorized Latino immigrants have higher levels of education than the populations in the source countries.[24]

As seen in table 2.2, the educational level of Latino immigrants lags far behind the levels of immigrants from other countries. At the end of the twentieth century, semiskilled and unskilled migrants were heavily overrepresented in the skill distribution of new Latino immigrants: 62.4 percent and 59.7 percent in 1990 and 2000, respectively, never completed high school. In 1990, only 157,383, or 8.0 percent of the immigrant population from Latin America, had a college or advanced degree. The number of highly skilled migrants in the United States rose to 335,906, or one-tenth of the foreign-born Latinos in 2000. Differences in highly skilled flows of migrants from Latin America and other migrants were striking twenty years ago: fewer than 20 highly educated Latinos for every 100 migrants from other countries with at least a college degree (last row in table 2.2).

In order to understand the presence of a large number of unskilled migrants from Latin America in the United States, George Borjas refined the neoclassical economic model. He attached the educational selectivity of migrants to the income inequality of the home and destination countries.[25] At the aggregate level, Borjas suggests that differences

TABLE 2.2: Educational Characteristics of Recent Latino Immigrants 25–64 Years Old, 1990–2019

	1990	2000	2010	2019
Percentage with Less than High School				
Immigrants from Latin America	62.4	59.7	47.8	32.0
Mexico and Central America	71.6	69.1	58.3	46.6
Caribbean and South America	41.8	33.0	20.6	13.5
Immigrants Other Countries	23.8	16.4	11.4	10.0
Percentage with Bachelor's Degree or More				
Immigrants from Latin America	8.0	9.7	12.1	24.5
Mexico and Central America	5.2	5.4	6.4	14.4
Caribbean and South America	14.4	22.1	26.7	37.2
Immigrants Other Countries	35.1	45.3	52.0	58.8
Population with a Bachelor's Degree or More				
Immigrants from Latin America (A)	157,383	335,906	532,713	712,602
Immigrants Other Countries (B)	1,039,277	1,806,315	2,254,616	2,851,641
Ratio (A/B) × 100	15	19	24	25

Source: Author's calculations based on Steven Ruggles, Sarah Flood, Ronald Goeken, Josiah Grover, Erin Meyer, Jose Pacas and Matthew Sobek. IPUMS USA: Version 10.0 [dataset]. Minneapolis, MN: IPUMS, 2020.
Note: Table refers to Latino immigrants who have lived in the United States 0–10 years.

in the return (wages) to skills across countries hold the key to selecting migrants from different parts of the skill distribution.[26] Advancing the theory of immigrants' selection and Roy's model,[27] Borjas challenged the assumption of positive selection by formalizing the analysis of self-selection mechanisms to predict that income dispersion in both the country of origin and the country of destination determines migration movements (flows) and immigrants' selection patterns with respect to unobservable and observable characteristics. According to Borjas, if income dispersion is more unequal in the sending than in the host country, like the Latin American-US case, migrants will be chosen from the lower tail of the income distribution in the sending country and they will enjoy below-average earnings in the country of destination as well.[28] Highly educated individuals will find it more attractive to stay in Latin American countries with high inequality to seek the highest reward for their skills.

Most of the empirical work on Borjas's self-selection model has been done in relation to Mexican migration to the United States. Studies of the skill composition of Mexican immigrants have produced mixed evidence. Initial studies underscored the existence of intermediate or positive selection for Mexican immigrants; however, more recent research either finds negative selection aligning with Borjas's model or confirms the intermediate selection.[29]

Low levels of education and skills among Mexican and Central American migrants in the United States have also been facilitated by the existence of strong social networks, proximity, and history. Table 2.2 shows that the low-skilled levels of Latin American migrants are driven by the flows from Mexico and Central America. The proportion of the foreign-born population from this Latin America subregion, ages 25–64, with less than a high school diploma, is much higher than among the Caribbean and South American immigrant population. At the turn of the twenty-first century, 69.1 percent and 33.0 percent of recently arrived migrants from the former and latter nationalities, respectively, had educational levels below high school completion. College education levels by region of birth in Latin America also present significant variations. While slightly more than one-fifth of migrants from the Caribbean and South America had completed a college or advanced degree in 2000, the proportion was only one-twentieth among migrants born in Mexico and Central America.

Although low levels of education and skills among Latino migrants in the United States have been significant throughout the modern immigration history of the United States, the last three decades have witnessed the emergence of highly skilled migration, thus aligning more closely with the positive self-selection of migrants worldwide. The proportion of Latino immigrant workers with professional skills has been rising sharply in recent years, reaching a peak of 24.5 percent in 2019. In 1990, only 8.0 percent of recently arrived migrants from Latin America had a college degree or more. The relative number of college graduates increased faster among immigrants from the Caribbean and South America than those from Mexico and Central America. The American Community Survey reports that 37.2 percent of Latinos from the Caribbean and South America had a bachelor's or advance degree in 2019, while only 14.4 percent of migrants from Mexico and Central America were identified with a similar educational attainment.

The last year in which the United States experienced an increase in the number of unskilled migrants was 2007,[30] which was, coincidentally, the last time that the number of Mexican immigrants grew in this country.[31] The rapid decline of the share of unskilled migrants in the United States is evident in the data. Indeed, the educational progress among Latinos is even more striking when looking at the reduction of the proportion of migrants with educational levels below high school completion, which was cut by half between 2000 and 2019 (from 59.7 percent to 32.0 percent). As shown in table 2.2, the incidence of low-skilled migrants among newly arrived Latino migrants was reduced from two-thirds to one-third in a period of 29 years.

The size of the college-educated immigrant population from Latin America who recently arrived in the United States doubled this century. Latino immigrants show substantial gains in educational attainment since the Great Recession. The stock of highly skilled Latino immigrants ages 25–64 totaled 532,000 persons in 2010, and it grew to 713,000 in 2019, an increase of 34 percent from nine years before. Higher rates of skilled migrants from Latin America entering the United States are likely to be explained by the combination of many events, including the political, economic, and social instability of the region in recent years.

Despite the faster growth of highly educated new arrivals among Latinos than migrants from other regions of the world, the ratio of Latino to non-Latino immigrants with a college or advanced degree was only 25 per 100 in 2019. The data shown in the bottom panel of table 2.2 indicate the progressive increase in the education of migrants from other regions. The highly skilled population that recently arrived from countries other than Latin America is about 2.9 million (eight out of every ten immigrant college graduates who arrived in this country in the decade before 2019). The hyperselectivity of international migrants in the United States has become a reality in the case of East Asian immigrants.[32]

In sum, the growth of skilled migrants in the United States has been substantial, and migrants from Latin America have followed this pattern.[33] Overall, the foreign-born population in the United States has shown notable increases in skill levels since the Great Recession. The increase of highly skilled immigrants, including those from Latin America, is related to the rising educational levels around the globe and the expansion of permanent and temporary visa programs in the United States.[34] Information on the educational characteristics of recently arrived Latino immigrants confirms that the volume of highly skilled migrants from Latin America has soared to unprecedented levels. However, they are still behind immigrants from other regions in terms of skill levels. Although current immigrants from Latin America are more selective with respect to education, the proportion of immigrants with low levels of schooling is still higher. The bifurcation of Latino immigrants into extremely low or relatively high levels of formal educational attainment represents the new reality of Latin America-US migration.

Challenges for Integration

Conventional theory would suggest that successful integration of immigrants depends on economic success and access to rights, which in turn are a function of migrants' education, legal status, and racial/ethnic discrimination.[35] Education is a strong predictor of social and economic well-being.[36] On the one hand, human capital facilitates economic integration through access to high-paying jobs and occupation mobility. On the other, education is related to intergenerational educational and economic mobility, better health outcomes, and greater civic engagement.[37]

Less negative selection among Latino immigrants is encouraging, as larger supplies of highly skilled immigrants would enhance their economic success and integration. In general, skilled immigrants tend to integrate rapidly in terms of language proficiency, intermarriage, political participation, and civic engagement. The impact of skills in the integration of immigrants is facilitated by their English language fluency, and the ability of migrants and their children to attend college, obtain better jobs, become US citizens, marry outside their ethnic group, and have better residential options.

Increasing highly skilled immigration will accelerate the integration of immigrants in the United States; however, their economic incorporation can be affected by their ability to transfer professional skills and credentials across countries. Employers and professional associations are

reluctant to recognize the value of educational and professional credentials of immigrants belonging to certain ethnic minorities and countries.

Highly skilled immigrants not only experience difficulties in converting education, skills, and experience into economic success in the
United States; they also face discrimination in the labor market based
on characteristics of their country of origin, race, and ethnicity. Without
a doubt, for many Latin American immigrants, incorporation into the
US labor market has more to do with socioracial segregation than with
skills. A recent study demonstrates that Mexican immigrants see Anglo-
Americans as the main perpetrators of anti-immigrant discrimination.[38] Discrimination in the workplace is one of the most significant
challenges for skilled Latino workers. For example, using survey ex-
periments, a recent study found that Americans' favoritism for highly
skilled immigrants decreases when a Hispanic descriptor is added to
the highly skilled qualification.[39] An analysis by Gandini and Lozano
finds that skilled migrants from Latin America are more discriminated
against in the labor market than other migrants. Their results show that
highly educated Latino immigrants are underrepresented in professional occupations, and women are significantly affected by labor market discrimination.[40]

The most serious structural problem related to the social integration
of Latino immigrants is the lack of legal status, low rates of naturalization, and the racialization of immigration enforcement. Table 2.3 shows
the top ten countries of origin of the foreign-born population in the
United States and the same population ranked by several immigration
status categories around 2018.

Half of the top ten birthplaces of the foreign-born population in
the United States are from Latin America. Immigration from Mexico
amounted to a little over 11 million in 2018, or one-quarter of the total
immigrant population in the United States. The immigrant population
from El Salvador, Cuba, Dominican Republic, and Guatemala represented 11 percent.

The major obstacle for the integration of Latino immigrants is the
unsolved situation of millions of people living without proper legal
status. As seen in the top center column in table 2.3, only 16 percent
of naturalized citizens are from Mexico. Immigrants from Cuba and
the Dominican Republic show a higher or equal representation than

TABLE 2.3: Immigration, Immigration Status, Enforcement Categories: Top Ten Countries, 2017–2018

Total Immigrants[a]			Total Naturalized Immigrants[a]			LPRs Eligible to Naturalize[b]		
2018			2018			2018		
Mexico	11,182,111	25%	Mexico	3,600,786	16%	Mexico	2,500,000	28%
India	2,634,871	6%	Philippines	1,422,743	6%	China	470,000	5%
China	2,228,730	5%	India	1,188,908	5%	Philippines	360,000	4%
Philippines	2,008,074	4%	China	1,103,966	5%	Cuba	320,000	4%
El Salvador	1,420,399	3%	Vietnam	1,035,739	5%	Dominican R.	320,000	4%
Cuba	1,340,670	3%	Cuba	799,513	4%	India	290,000	3%
Vietnam	1,322,684	3%	Korea	690,981	3%	Canada	250,000	3%
Dominican R.	1,174,729	3%	Dominican R.	636,245	3%	El Salvador	220,000	2%
Korea	1,057,487	2%	Jamaica	512,891	2%	United K.	220,000	2%
Guatemala	1,003,841	2%	El Salvador	500,924	2%	Vietnam	220,000	2%
Other Countries	19,344,027	43%	Other Countries	11,161,729	49%	Other Countries	3,780,000	42%
Total	44,717,623	100%	Total	22,654,425	100%	Total	8,950,000	100%
Unauthorized Immigrants[c]			DACA Recipients[d]			Apprehensions[e]		
2017			2018			2018 FY		
Mexico	4,950,000	47%	Mexico	561,420	80%	Mexico	252,267	44%
El Salvador	750,000	7%	El Salvador	26,630	4%	Guatemala	135,354	24%
Guatemala	600,000	6%	Honduras	18,220	3%	Honduras	91,141	16%
India	525,000	5%	Peru	16,730	2%	El Salvador	42,132	7%
Honduras	400,000	4%	South Korea	7,240	1%	India	9,953	2%
China	375,000	4%	Brazil	7,170	1%	Nicaragua	4,014	1%
Dominican R.	240,000	2%	Ecuador	5,810	1%	Brazil	2,810	0%
Brazil	160,000	2%	Colombia	5,390	1%	Ecuador	2,708	0%
Philippines	160,000	2%	Argentina	4,920	1%	Dominican R.	2,628	0%
South Korea	150,000	1%	Philippines	3,920	1%	China	2,322	0%
Other Countries	2,190,000	21%	Other Countries	46,440	7%	Other Countries	27,237	5%
Total	10,500,000	100%	Total	703,890	100%	Total	572,566	100%

Notes: [a]Author's calculations based on weighted 2018 1-year American Community Survey (ACS) Public Use Microdata (PUMS): Steven Ruggles et al., "IPUMS USA: Version 10.0 [dataset]," 2020, https://doi.org/10.18128/D010.V11.0.
[b]Bryan Baker, "Estimates of the Lawful Permanent Resident Population in the United States and the Subpopulation Eligible to Naturalize: 2015–2019," US Department of Homeland Security, Office of Immigration Statistics, *Population Estimates* (September 2019), www.dhs.govwww.dhs.gov
[c]Jeffrey S. Passel and D'vera Cohn, "Mexicans Decline to Less than Half the US Unauthorized Immigrant Population for the First Time," Pew Research Center, June 12, 2019, www.pewresearch.org
[d]US Citizenship and Immigration Services, Deferred Action for Childhood Arrivals (DACA), "Approximate Active DACA Recipients: Country of Birth, As of July 31, 2018," 2018, www.uscis.gov
[e]Mike Guo and Ryan Baugh, "Immigration Enforcement Actions: 2018," *Annual Flow Report* (October 2019), US Department of Homeland Security, Office of Immigration Statistics,www.dhs.gov

in the overall immigrant population. El Salvador and Guatemala, like Mexico, are underrepresented among the naturalized citizen population of the United States.

The low numbers of naturalized citizens among the foreign-born population from Mexico and Central America are attributable to many factors. Of utmost importance is the large segment of the Latino immigrant population illegally residing in the United States. As late as 2017, the Pew Research Center estimated that 10.5 million, or about one of every four immigrants, have unauthorized status in the United States (bottom left column in table 2.3). Mexicans make up 47 percent of the unauthorized population, followed by El Salvador (7 percent), Guatemala (6 percent), India (5 percent), and Honduras (4 percent). For Latino immigrants and their children, the challenge of moving up the socioeconomic ladder is, for the most part, the challenge of acquiring legal status in the United States.[41]

Prospects of labor market incorporation and potential pathways for social mobility depend on legal status and labor market opportunities for Latino immigrants. Although the undocumented population is more prominent among low-skilled or semi-skilled migrants, a recent study shows that 25 percent of recent arrivals who are undocumented immigrants are college graduates.[42] Balatova and Fix put the number of college graduates without legal documents in the United States at one million.[43] The importance of legal permanent residence is highlighted by the fact that for visa-holder immigrants with a college education, access to a green card leads to an annual wage increase of almost $12,000.[44]

The Deferred Action for Childhood Arrivals Program (DACA) constitutes one of the most critical instruments today to provide legal status to undocumented migrants who were brought to the United States as children. The DACA executive action, signed by President Obama in 2012, has provided 703,890 recipients temporary protection from deportation based on humanitarian concerns. DACA beneficiaries, 80 percent of whom were born in Mexico, have had a positive effect on the transition to adulthood of this highly educated population.[45]

Although access to legal status can significantly improve the life chances of millions of Latino immigrants in the United States, increasing their naturalization rates is necessary to fully participate in the nation's political life and welfare system. For Latino immigrants without citizenship, the alternative means for support during retirement are limited due to the lack of Social Security pensions. According to the population estimates of the Department of Homeland Security, almost 9.0 million legal permanent residents were eligible to become US citizens in 2018. Mexican natives represent 28 percent of the eligible immigrant population to naturalize, while Cuba, Dominican Republic, and El Salvador constitute another 10 percent. The low naturalization rates of Latino immigrants have been documented elsewhere.[46]

Racialization of immigration policies has a long history in the United States.[47] The selective enforcement of US immigration is evident in the data. Mexico, Guatemala, Honduras, and El Salvador make up 91 percent of the 572,566 immigrants apprehended by US immigration authorities in the 2018 fiscal year, while immigrants from these countries represented roughly six out of every ten unauthorized migrants in 2017. The ethnoracial profiling of immigration enforcement represents a serious barrier to the safety and integration of Latino migrants and their families in the United States.

Conclusions

The 1960–2019 period saw the rise and sudden decline of the major immigration stream in US history: outmigration from Latin America. The effects of the influx of massive numbers of Latin American immigrants in the demography of the United States are visible and permanent. However, during the past thirteen years, Latin American migration to the United States has endured a significant transformation. Gone is the large-scale migration that had characterized this phenomenon. The beginning of the Great Recession led to an era of limited migration. Flows today are at a much lower level, and yet the migratory framework that placed millions of Latin Americans in the United States appears to have weathered the Great Recession and is now in an extended convalescence.

As argued in this book, immigrant labor from Latin America is the product of a sociohistorical process in which multiple causal factors, including demographic changes, social networks, economic trends, immigration policies, federal deportation campaigns aimed at Latino immigrant communities, and the enactment of laws by various state and local governments, designed to produce attrition through enforcement. The transformation of a rising trend into a declining one seems to be a stable new reality for economic migration from Latin America.

The new reality in the Americas has fundamentally altered the flows and characteristics of Latino immigrants in the United States. A review of data from 1990 to 2019 shows that Latin American migration has shifted away from past male-dominated flows. Migrants from Latin America are also older and more settled today than at the turn of the twenty-first century. The American Community Survey also provides evidence of the diversification of the Latin American outflows in light of the decline of Mexicans entering the United States. Outflows from the rest of Latin America have risen, mainly from Central America—a region with severe conditions of crime, violence, and economic stagnation. Over the same period, as Latino immigrants have become older and long-term residents, the proportion of naturalized citizens from Latin America has shown a remarkable increase; and as Latino immigrants have become more selective with respect to education, poverty has decreased to historically low levels—at least until the most recent world pandemic.

Today, we are seeing remarkably high levels of skilled immigrant workers in the United States, and the highly skilled population is growing faster in the immigrant than the native population. The migration of highly skilled Latin Americans was a rare phenomenon in the twentieth century, but now, in the third decade of this century, the shift in the volume and characteristics of recent migrants from the region have impacted the composition of Latino immigrants in terms of enhancing educational attainment. The migration of highly skilled Latin Americans will significantly impact the way Latinos experience the process of assimilation into the US mainstream.

Many who migrate today from Latin America have earned a college degree. Despite changes in cohort quality, Latino immigrants lag behind immigrants from other regions in educational attainment and skills. Latin American migrants have been questioned for their low skill levels and their alleged resistance to assimilate into the culture of the United States. Still, the truth is that the US economy has a strong dependency on Latin American workers. Moreover, significant segments of the Latino population integrate into US society across generations despite racial and class barriers.

The challenge is that millions of the most vulnerable people living in the United States are from Latin America. Although many Latino immigrants contribute to the US economy with their skills and hard work, they face increasing integration challenges because of labor market, poverty, and legal status conditions. The big picture regarding the economic integration of Latino immigrants will be difficult to discern without considering the role racial stereotypes play in US society. In contrast to the detrimental effect of the "model minority" stereotype of Asian Americans discussed in Zhou's chapter in this volume, immigrants from Latin America are incorporated into a structure of socioracial stratification in which they are portrayed as inferior and as a threat to Anglo-American culture. The structural racism in the United States will impose serious constraints on Latinos' economic incorporation in the country, despite growing investments in their human capital. The still prominent presence of unskilled undocumented workers, the ethnoracial profiling of immigration enforcement, and the low naturalization rates hinder the process of assimilation of Latino immigrants. Paths to legal status and citizenship are probably the most important steps to facilitate the integration of Latin Americans.

The scholarship in this book engages with the argument that institutional mechanisms intersect with individuals' socioeconomic and demographic characteristics to define the social positioning and incorporation of migrants. One of the conclusions evident from a review of recent research and data on skilled workers in the United States is that we know little about their incorporation into the US labor market and society and almost nothing about highly educated Latino immigrants. From this perspective, much more needs to be done to understand immigrant skill underutilization and how highly educated immigrants experience difficulties in converting education, professional credentials, and skills into economic success in the United States, particularly if they belong to certain countries or ethnic minorities.

The most critical gap in understanding the integration of highly skilled migration from Latin American countries is the lack of research on the effects of legal status. We also need to sharpen our understanding of how patterns of labor market incorporation vary by country of origin, ethnic group, and race. In this context, we need to draw more attention to unauthorized immigrants who entered the United States as children, also known as Dreamers, a particular group of skilled immigrants who have been placed in legal limbo. Sociologists must also consider gender as an essential dimension of the changing profile of Latino immigrants in terms of their skills, especially among more recent migrants.

NOTES

1   Author's calculations based on weighted 2019 1-year American Community Survey (ACS) Public Use Microdata (PUMS): Steven Ruggles et al., "IPUMS USA: Version 10.0 [dataset]," 2020, https://doi.org/10.18128/D010.V11.0. See figure 2.1.

2   For more on this topic, see Jorge del Pinal, "Demographic Patterns: Age Structure, Fertility, Mortality, and Population Growth," in *Latinas/os in the United States: Changing the Face of América*, ed. Havidán Rodríguez, Rogelio Sáenz, and Cecilia Menjívar (New York: Springer, 2008), 57–71; Douglas S. Massey, "The New Immigration and Ethnicity in the United States," *Population and Development Review* 21, no. 3 (1995): 631–652; Douglas S. Massey and Karen Pren, "Unintended Consequences of US Immigration Policy: Explaining the Post-1965 Surge from Latin America," *Population & Development Review* 38, no. 1 (2012): 1–29.

3   Numbers based on US Census Bureau reported in an analysis by Luis Noe-Bustamante, Mark Hugo Lopez, and Jens Manuel Krogstad, "U.S. Hispanic Population Surpassed 60 Million in 2019, but Growth has Slowed," Pew Research Center July 7, 2020, www.pewresearch.org. See also Matt Barreto and Gary M. Segura, *Latino America: How America's Most Dynamic Population Is Poised to Transform the Politics of the Nation* (New York: Public Affairs, 2014).

4   David B. Grusky, Bruce Western, and Christopher Wimer, "The Consequences of the Great Recession," in *The Great Recession*, ed. David B. Grusky, Bruce Western, and Christopher Wimer (New York: Russell Sage Foundation, 2011), 4.

5   See Gordon Hanson, Chen Liu, and Craig McIntosh, "The Rise and Fall of U.S. Low-Skilled Immigration," *Brookings Papers on Economic Activity* 48, no. 1 (Spring 2017): 83–168; Andrés Villarreal, "Explaining the Decline in Mexico-U.S. Migration: The Effect of the Great Recession," *Demography* 51, no. 6 (2014): 2203–2228; René Zenteno and Roberto Suro, "Recession Versus Removals, Which Finished Mexican Unauthorized Migration?" in *The Trump Paradox: Migration, Trade, and Racial Politics in US-Mexico Integration*, ed. Raúl Hinojosa-Ojeda and Edward Telles (Berkeley: University of California Press, 2021), 63–77.

6   For this chapter, the Latin American region encompasses twenty countries: Argentina, Bolivia, Brazil, Chile, Colombia, Costa Rica, Cuba, Dominican Republic, Ecuador, El Salvador, Guatemala, Haiti, Honduras, Mexico, Nicaragua, Panama, Paraguay, Peru, Uruguay, and Venezuela. These countries accounted for 93 percent of the immigrant population in the United States from the Latin American and Caribbean regions in 2018.

7 Adela Pellegrino, "Trends in Latin American Skilled Migration: 'Brain Drain' or 'Brain Exchange'?," *International Migration* 39, no. 5 (2001): 113.

8 Phillip Connor and Douglas S. Massey, "Economic Outcomes among Latino Migrants to Spain and the United States: Differences by Source Region and Legal Status," *International Migration Review* 44, no. 4 (2010): 802.

9 Massey, "The New Immigration," 637.

10 Campbell Gibson and Kay Jung, "Historical Census Statistics on the Foreign-Born Population of the United States: 1850 to 2000," US Census Bureau, *Population Division Working Paper* no. 81 (2006): 104.

11 Marta Tienda and Susana M. Sánchez, "Latin American Immigration to the United States," *Daedalus* 142, no. 3 (2013): 48.

12 See Ximena Clark, Timothy J. Hatton, and Jeffrey G. Williamson, "What Explains Emigration Out of Latin America?," *World Development* 32, no. 11 (2004): 1871–1890; Douglas S. Massey and Fernando Riosmena, "Undocumented Migration from Latin America in an Era of Rising U.S. Enforcement," *ANNALS of the American Academy of Political and Social Science* 630, no. 1 (2010): 294–321; Douglas S. Massey, "The Real Crisis at the Mexico-U.S. Border: A Humanitarian and Not an Immigration Emergency," *Sociological Forum* 35, no. 3 (2020): 787–805.

13 Douglas S. Massey, Jorge Durand, and Karen A. Pren, "Explaining Undocumented Migration to the U.S.," *International Migration Review* 48, no. 4 (December 1, 2014): 1053.

14 Jie Zong and Jeanne Batalova, "Immigrants from New Origin Countries in the United States," Migration Policy Institute, January 16, 2019, www.migrationpolicy.org.

15 Zenteno and Suro, "Recession Versus Removals," 73.

16 See José Miguel Cruz, "Central American *Maras*: From Youth Street Gangs to Transnational Protection Rackets," *Global Crime* 11, no. 4 (2010): 379–398; Douglas S. Massey, "Creating the Exclusionist Society: From the War on Poverty to the War on Immigrants," *Ethnic & Racial Studies* 43, no. 1, Special Issue on "Children of Immigrants in the Age of Deportation" (January 2020): 18–37; Nestor Rodriguez, Ximena Urrutia-Rojas, and Luis Raul Gonzalez, "Unaccompanied Minors from the Northern Central American Countries in the Migrant Stream: Social Differentials and Institutional Contexts," *Journal of Ethnic and Migration Studies* 45, no. 2, Special Issue on "Undocumented & Unaccompanied: Children of Migration in the European Union and the United States" (2019): 218–234.

17 John Creamer, "Inequalities Persist Despite Decline in Poverty for all Major Race and Hispanic Origin Groups," US Census Bureau, September 15, 2020, www.census.gov.

18 Larry A. Sjaastad, "The Costs and Returns of Human Migration," *Journal of Political Economy* 70, no. 5 (1962): 85; Jeffrey Grogger and Gordon H. Hanson, "Income Maximization and the Selection and Sorting of International Migrants," *Journal of Development Economics* 95 (2011): 44.

19 Barry R. Chiswick, "Are Immigrants Favorably Self-Selected?" *American Economic Review* 89, no. 2 (1999): 81.

20 See Randall Akee, "Who Leaves? Deciphering Immigrant Self-Selection from a Developing Country," *Economic Development and Cultural Change* 58, no. 2 (2010): 323–344; Mariya Aleksynska and Ahmed Tritah, "Occupation–Education Mismatch of Immigrant Workers in Europe: Context and Policies," *Economics of Education Review* 36 (2013): 229–244; Michèle V. K. Belot and Timothy J. Hatton, "Immigrant Selection in the OECD," *Scandinavian Journal of Economics* 114, no. 4 (2012): 1105–1128; Cynthia Feliciano, "Educational Selectivity in U.S. Immigration: How Do Immigrants Compare to Those Left Behind?," *Demography* 42, no. 1 (2005): 131–152; Grogger and Hanson, "Income Maximization"; Thomas Liebig and Alfonso Sousa-Poza, "Migration, Self-Selection and Income Inequality: An International Analysis," *Kyklos* 57, no. 1 (2004): 125–146.

21 Connor and Massey, "Economic Outcomes," 807.

22 Hanson et al., "The Rise and Fall," 109.

23 See Çağlar Özden, "Brain Gain in Latin America," Expert Group Meeting in International Migration and Development in Latin America and the Caribbean, United Nations Secretariat, February 5, 2006. www.un.org.

24 Clark et al., "What Explains Emigration Out of Latin America?," 1877.

25 See George J. Borjas, "Self-Selection and the Earnings of Immigrants," *American Economic Review* 77, no. 4 (1987): 531–553; George J. Borjas, "Immigration and Self-Selection," in *Immigration, Trade, and the Labor Market*, ed. John M. Abowd and Richard B. Freeman (Chicago: University of Chicago Press, 1991), 29–76.

26 Borjas, "Self-Selection," 536.

27 A. D. Roy, "Some Thoughts on the Distribution of Earnings," *Oxford Economic Papers* 3, no. 2 (1951): 135–146.

28 Borjas, "Self-Selection," 534.

29 Mexico seems to be a special case of immigrant selection. For a review of the Mexican case, see René Zenteno, "Is Mexican Migration to the United States an Issue of Economic Inequality?" Mission Foods Texas-Mexico Center Research 6 (2019), https://scholar.smu.edu.

30 Hanson et al., "The Rise and Fall," 96.

31 Zenteno and Suro, "Recession Versus Removals," 65.

32 See Min Zhou's chapter in this volume.

33 According to data from the America Community Survey not shown here, one out of every two immigrants who arrived in this country after 2010 had a university degree or higher. Immigrants from almost all regions have shown substantial gains in educational attainment since the Great Recession. Immigrants from Asia and Europe have driven the recent arrival of immigrants with greater levels of education: about 62–65 percent of recent immigrants from these two regions are college graduates.

34 See Andrew Kennedy, "The Politics of Skilled Immigration: Explaining the Ups and Downs of the US H-1B Visa Program," *International Migration Review* 53, no.

2 (2019): 346–370; Gabriela León-Pérez, "An Analysis of High Skilled and Low Skilled Migration from Mexico to the US, 1970–2010," Paper presented at the annual meeting of the American Sociological Association, New York, August 10–13, 2019; B. Lindsay Lowell, "Skilled Temporary and Permanent Immigrants in the United States," *Population Research and Policy Review* 20 (2001): 33–58; Connor and Massey, "Economic Outcomes."

35 See Engineering National Academies of Sciences and Medicine et al., *The Integration of Immigrants into American Society* (Washington, DC: National Academies Press, 2016); Min Zhou, "Segmented Assimilation: Issues, Controversies, and Recent Research on the New Second Generation," *International Migration Review* 31, no. 4 (1997): 975–1008.

36 See Edward E. Telles and Vilma Ortiz, *Generations of Exclusion: Mexican Americans, Assimilation, and Race* (New York: Russell Sage Foundation, 2008).

37 See Richard Alba and Victor Nee, *Remaking the American Mainstream: Assimilation and Contemporary Immigration* (Cambridge, MA: Harvard University Press, 2005).

38 Sylvia Zamora, "Mexican Illegality, Black Citizenship, and White Power: Immigrant Perceptions of the U.S. Socioracial Hierarchy," *Journal of Ethnic and Migration Studies* 44, no. 11 (2018): 1910.

39 Annabella España-Nájera and David Vera, "Attitudes Toward Immigration: Ethnicity Trumps Skills But Not Legality?" *Social Science Quarterly* 101, no. 2 (March 2020): 555.

40 Luciana Gandini and Fernando Lozano-Ascencio, "The Effects of the Crisis on Occupational Segregation of Skilled Migrants from Latin America and the Caribbean in the United States, 2006–2012," *Population, Space and Place* 22, no. 5 (2016): 448.

41 See Frank D. Bean, Susan K. Brown, and James D. Bachmeier, *Parents Without Papers: The Progress and Pitfalls of Mexican American Integration* (New York: Russell Sage Foundation, 2015), 185–186.

42 Jeanne Batalova and Michael Fix, "New Brain Gain: Rising Human Capital among Recent Immigrants to the United States," Migration Policy Institute (2017): 6.

43 Batalova and Fix, "New Brain Gain," 6.

44 Sankar Mukhopadhyay and David Oxborrow, "The Value of an Employment-Based Green Card," *Demography* 49, no. 1 (2012): 234.

45 See Roberto G. Gonzales, Basia Ellis, Sarah A. Rendón-García, and Kristina Brant, "(Un)Authorized Transitions: Illegality, DACA, and the Life Course," *Research in Human Development* 15, nos. 3–4 (2018): 345–359.

46 See Francesca Mazzolari, "Determinants of Naturalization: The Role of Dual Citizenship Laws," The Center for Comparative Immigration Studies, Working Paper 117 (April 2005), https://ccis.ucsd.edu.

47 See Mae M. Ngai, *Impossible Subjects: Illegal Aliens and the Making of Modern America* (Princeton, NJ: Princeton University Press, 2004).

3

East Asian Immigration

Historical Trends and Contemporary Issues in Movement
to the United States

MIN ZHOU

This chapter examines the trends, patterns, and issues of immigration
to the United States (US) from East Asia from historical and comparative perspectives. The three major ethnonational groups under
study—Chinese, Japanese, and Korean—arrived in the United States at
different historical periods, from diverse cultural and socioeconomic
backgrounds, and with varied patterns of resettlement and integration,
but have shared similar experiences of racialization in the host society.
In this chapter, I analyze how race/ethnicity and class intersect larger
structural forces to shape patterns of immigration and diasporic formation and how these patterns influence the life chances of Americans of
East Asian descent. I organize my analysis in three sections. The first
section provides a historical overview of immigration trends, addressing the question of why and how earlier immigrants reached the other
shores of the Pacific Ocean and formed diasporic communities. The
second section analyzes how changes in the contexts of immigration
and emigration since passage of the Immigration and Nationality Act of
1965 (also known as the Hart-Celler Act) affect contemporary trends of
cross-border movements, socioeconomic characteristics of immigrants,
and patterns of social mobility. The third section tackles the issues of
racialization facing East Asian immigrants and their offspring who
arguably have made it into the American mainstream. I conclude with
a discussion on changing immigration dynamics and the prospects of
panethnicity.

Immigration from East Asia: A Historical Overview

Chinese, Japanese, and Koreans comprise three of the largest ethno-national groups from Asia in the United States, and each group had surpassed the one-million mark by the turn of the twenty-first century.[1] In the eyes of the broader American public, these "Orientals" all look alike and share similar demographic characteristics, cultural traits, and behavioral patterns. However, the three ethnonational groups under study hail from different origins and have different histories of immigration and patterns of adaptation to the United States, which shaped their contemporary demographics, diasporic development, and identity formation. The Chinese were the earliest Asian group to have arrived in the United States in the mid-nineteenth century, earlier than the mass immigration of the Southern and Eastern Europeans such as the Italians and Poles. The Japanese came next, reaching the American shores nearly half a century later. Comparatively, earlier Korean immigration to the United States occurred on a much smaller scale and remained insignificant until after the passage of the Hart-Celler Act of 1965.

Pre-1965 Chinese Immigration

Chinese immigration dates back to the late 1840s, beginning with the arrival of male laborers of rural and uneducated backgrounds from China. Although immigration at the time was unrestricted, Chinese laborers to the United States were not "free" labor in the true sense of the word.[2] Rather, they were highly controlled contract or indentured laborers, whose immigration was financed primarily by the Chinese credit ticket system, in which brokers advanced the cost of the trip to destinations and ensured their advances be repaid via control over laborers' employment.[3] While war, poverty, and lack of economic opportunities might be push factors, direct access to overseas migration networks largely accounted for nineteenth-century Chinese immigration to North America from one single region—the Pearl River Delta region—of South China. During the 1850s, some 35,000 Chinese entered the United States legally, and the number peaked in the 1870s (see figure 3.1).

The earlier Chinese immigrants worked initially in the plantation economy in Hawaii and in the mining industry on the West Coast, later

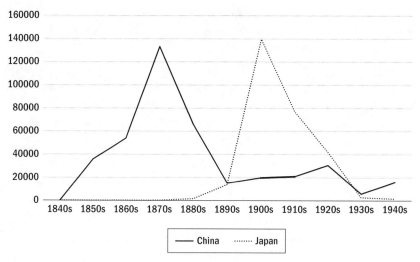

Figure 3.1: Immigration to the United States from China and Japan: 1840s–1940s.
Source: US Government, Department of Homeland Security, "Yearbook of Immigration Statistics 2018," 2018, www.dhs.gov.

on the transcontinental railroads west of the Rocky Mountains, and subsequently in select industries in major cities on the West and East coasts and in the Midwest.[4] In the first two decades of their arrival, most of the Chinese were contract laborers working for non-Chinese employers in the expanding US labor market.[5] During this time, a class of Chinese merchants evolved to take advantage of the new opportunities for profit, opening up businesses where their coethnic workers lived, including in work camps, to provide fellow countrymen with familiar and culturally specific goods, ranging from imported ethnic foods, clothing, herbal medicines, to tobacco and liquor. Over time, their businesses formed the basis of the diasporic community, serving as meeting places where socially isolated laborers gathered and engaged in nostalgia and personal interactions.[6]

Despite having different occupations, both Chinese laborers and merchants were sojourners, like "birds of passage." They came to America, alone without family, to make money; in their own words, to "dig gold in the gold mountain."[7] They considered themselves "gold mountain guests" (*gum san hak*), and their dream was to eventually return home to their families with "gold and glory."[8] Yet even as they themselves expected, and were expected by their families, to return home, many could not afford to go home after their labor contract ended, because their wages were barely enough for them to pay off debts or because their savings were too small to afford the much anticipated glorious return.[9] Circumstances changed when mines were depleted, the railroads completed, and a recession set in. Chinese laborers soon became scapegoats for economic distress. White workers perceived them as the "yellow peril," a threat to the American nation on both economic and cultural terms.[10] In the 1870s, the white workers who experienced labor market insecurities and exploitation channeled their frustrations into racist attacks on the Chinese, driving them out of the mines, farms, wool mills, and factories on the West Coast.[11] Under intense political pressure from organized labor against the Chinese, the US Congress passed the Chinese Exclusion Act in 1882.[12] The act prohibited immigration of Chinese labor for ten years and, subsequently, indefinitely until its repeal in 1943.[13] As a result, the number of new immigrants from China plunged from a peak of 133,000 in the 1870s to 15,000 in the 1890s, and to a historic low of 5,800 in the 1930s (see figure 3.1).

Under legal exclusion, the Chinese—laborers or merchants—were pushed into Chinatowns in major immigrant gateway cities, such as San Francisco, Los Angeles, New York, and Chicago. They had to further delay their return in hopes of fulfilling the gold dream. The structural changes in the US economy and society prolonged their sojourning and led to the development of a diasporic Chinese community, dominated by men.[14] The Chinese American community had highly skewed male-to-female ratios, 19:1 in 1900 and 14:1 in 1910.[15]

Paradoxically, exclusion strengthened and expanded the existing diasporic networks to facilitate Chinese immigration through illegal means. For example, some of the Chinese immigrants entered under "fictitious identities"—taking on the identities of individuals who were legally entitled to reside in the United States, including the "paper sons."[16] Others used "substitution," in which traveling Chinese in transit switched places with Chinese who were legal residents or US citizens.[17] Legal exclusion also fueled the growth of a self-sustaining ethnic economy and a range of social organizations lodged in Chinatowns, giving rise to a resilient pattern of adaption via ethnic entrepreneurship and wage employment within the ethnic enclave. Merchants used Chinatown as a platform to launch businesses, providing jobs and culturally specific goods and services for fellow Chinese, while making China-town an exotic place for a small non-Chinese clientele to satisfy the occasional curiosity. Laborers served as a loyal coethnic labor force to Chinatown's ethnic economy as well as coethnic consumers. Chinese-owned businesses and ethnic associations operated on a shared moral system, based on a patriarchal structure of rights and obligations, and a shared pool of resources, manifested in bounded solidarity and en-forceable trust.[18]

The repeal of the Chinese Exclusion Act in 1943, during World War II, in principle opened up Chinese immigration anew. However, few Chinese emigrated, owing to the national-origins quota system in effect since the implementation of the Johnson-Reed Act of 1924, which allot-ted China an annual quota of only 105 immigrant visas. One exception was the entry of war brides. About 10,000 Chinese women entered the United States immediately after World War II as facilitated by the War Brides Act of 1945.[19] Another exception was the refugee flight. Hundreds of thousands of refugees were driven out to Hong Kong, a British colony, by the Chinese Civil War between 1945 and 1949. Many more fled with the defeated Kuomintang (KMT) troops to Taiwan at the collapse of the Republic of China (RoC) and the founding of the People's Republic of China (PRC) in the late summer of 1949. In the 1950s, the United States admitted nearly 9,000 Chinese immigrants, most of whom were politi-cal refugees who had already fled to Hong Kong and Taiwan before the Communist takeover, or students who had been studying in the United States.

The arrival of Chinese women after WWII strengthened the Chinese immigrant family and began to transform an ethnic enclave of sojourn-ing "bachelors" into a family-based diasporic community. But the politi-cal refugees and students shared little in common with their coethnics who had migrated in earlier decades. They were mainly Mandarin- rather than Cantonese-speaking and of urban middle- and upper-class backgrounds. They held professional jobs in the larger labor market, residentially integrated into suburban white middle-class communities, and intentionally distanced themselves from coethnics who lived and worked in Chinatowns. Later, the 1952 McCarran-Walter Act enabled Chinese immigrants to become naturalized US citizens. The removal of legal barriers, along with a diminution of anti-Chinese sentiment, slowly opened up opportunities for the Chinese to participate in mainstream America.

However, when China turned into an enemy nation during the Cold War, Chinese Americans were only conditionally accepted by their host society as they were often suspected of being communists or communist sympathizers disloyal to their host nation. Meanwhile, immigration from China to the United States was at low tide, despite the US immigration reform in 1965. In the 1950s and 1960s, fewer than 23,000 Chinese immigrants arrived in the United States; most were China-born persons, students included, from Taiwan.[20] The political transformation at home shattered the sojourners' dream of ever returning to China, with or without "gold."

Pre-1965 Japanese Immigration

Japanese immigration to the United States dates back to the late 1860s when Japan began to open up from isolation following the Meiji Restoration of 1868 and particularly after Japan legalized emigration in 1886. However, large-scale emigration from Japan did not take place until the late 1890s. The US immigration statistics recorded 331 legal admissions of Japanese immigrants between 1860 and 1879, and 1,585 in the 1880s, which included a visible number of students.[21] The number of arrivals shot up to 13,998 in the 1890s, and to a historic record high of 139,712 in the 1900s. As shown in figure 3.1, Japanese immigration peaked during the time when Chinese immigration plummeted. Chinese exclusion led US agriculturalists and industrialists to turn to Japan as a source of cheap labor to replace Chinese labor.[22]

Earlier, Japanese immigrants hailed primarily from the Hiroshima and Yamaguchi prefectures in southwest Japan, as well as Kumamoto on the southern island of Kyushu and Okinawa prefecture on the Ryukyu islands.[23] Except for a small number of students, most of them migrated to escape poverty and unemployment.[24] The first group of 153 Japanese came to Hawaii in 1886 to work in sugarcane and pineapple fields. Hundreds of thousands more immigrants arrived in the following decades, including Okinawan laborers who began to arrive in Hawaii in large numbers in 1900 after Japan lifted its emigration ban on the Okinawa prefecture.[25] It was estimated that 87,932 Japanese entered Hawaii between 1901 and 1907, and more than 40 percent transmigrated to the Pacific Northwest of the US mainland.[26]

Like their Chinese counterparts, most of these "Pacific pioneers" were men. Some were sojourners with the intention to return to Japan. However, many of these men, particularly second or younger sons—who, by Japanese law, could not inherit family land—later sought to resettle in the United States and build a better life for themselves and their families. Many became small farmers and small business owners.[27] Prior to 1900, few Japanese women emigrated. The male-to-female ratios were highly skewed, 24:1 in 1900 (more skewed than the Chinese ratio of 19:1), but drastically declined to 7:1 in 1910 as more women arrived to join their families.[28]

At the turn of the twentieth century, anti-Asian agitation grew as the number of Japanese immigrants on the West Coast increased. Japanese immigrants largely took up occupations as independent farmers, fishermen, or small business owners.[29] Despite the fact that they did not compete with native white workers for the same jobs in the larger labor market, they were suspected of doing so. In 1905, the Japanese and Korean Exclusion League, later renamed the Asiatic Exclusion League, was established in San Francisco to promote immigration restriction of Japanese and other Asians and school segregation. In 1906, the San Francisco Board of Education passed a regulation that required Japanese children to attend schools separated from white children. Anti-Japanese nativism in California was met with strong protests from Japan, who rose to military power in defeating the Russian Empire in the Russo-Japanese War of 1904–1905. Japan did not want to see its own citizens subjected to inferior social status and to such legislation as the Chinese Exclusion Act. The Japanese government demanded equal rights and just treatment of its nationals and negotiated an informal agreement with the US government. Under the agreement, known as the Gentlemen's Agreement of 1907, Japan would restrict issuing passports to laborers intending to enter the US mainland while recognizing the United States' right to exclude Japanese holding passports originally issued for entering other countries. The United States would accept the presence of Japanese immigrants already residing there, permit the immigration of wives, children, and parents, and forbid legal discrimination against Japanese American children in California schools.[30]

One of the most significant impacts of the Gentlemen's Agreement was to enable Japanese immigrants already in the United States to send for their spouses and children left behind in Japan and to resettle them in the United States permanently, which did not happen to Chinese immigrants until after WWII. Because of the anti-miscegenation law in Western United States that prohibited Asians from marrying whites, those who wished to establish families had to turn to Japan to find their brides, hence the emergence of "picture brides."[31] According to US immigration statistics, more than 14,000 Japanese "picture brides" immigrated to Hawaii between the years 1907 and 1923, and about 10,000 entered the US mainland during the same period.[32]

In the process of their resettlement, the first generation, or *issei*, established their own social organizations in close-knit diasporic communities in both rural and urban areas.[33] The arrival of Japanese women transformed and stabilized the ethnic community while giving rise to a significant second generation, or *nisei*, US-born children of immigrant parentage in the 1930s.[34] By 1940, the Japanese population had grown to 126,000, with 44 percent women (increasing from 4 percent in 1900) and a majority *nisei* (60 percent). By comparison, the Chinese population had shrunk to 77,000, less than three-quarters of its 1890 peak, with 30 percent females and 50 percent US-born.[35]

The experience of the *nisei* was unique in that they grew up under Asian exclusion and in internment during WWII. During WWII, more than 120,000 Japanese Americans—two-thirds of whom were US citizens by birth—were forced out of their homes, lands, and businesses, to be incarcerated in military camps. President Franklin D. Roosevelt, in his Executive Order 9066, justified these actions as a "military necessity" vital to the national defense of the United States, despite overwhelming evidence confirming the loyalty of Japanese Americans. In contrast, no such categorical treatments were imposed on German Americans and Italian Americans. After WWII, Japanese American internees were set free but left to rebuild their lives on their own. The *issei* had to confront poverty due to their huge losses of homes, businesses, farms, occupations, and other material assets that they had worked so hard to earn, as well as their lost social status, dignity, self-respect, and sense of achievement. The *issei* did not protest their harsh treatment and kept quiet about their internment experience in order to protect their *nisei* children from being traumatized.[36] World War II discouraged the *nisei* internees from returning home to the West Coast where they had built communities through sheer hard work before the war while severing their diasporic ties to their homeland Japan. Many families moved away from the West Coast to intermountain West states such as Utah and other Midwestern states such as Illinois, Ohio, and Michigan, because they were blocked from returning home by anti-Japanese groups, such as the Remember the Pearl Harbor League and the Japanese Exclusion League in Seattle.[37] Since then, the Japanese American community gradually transitioned from a concentrated diasporic immigrant community on the West Coast to a more dispersed multigenerational ethnic community.[38]

Pre-1965 Korean Immigration

The US immigration statistics did not record immigration from Korea until the late 1940s.[39] In the first decade of the twentieth century, Chinese labor was legally excluded, and Japanese immigrants arrived in Hawaii to fill the labor shortage in the plantation economy. Harsh working conditions and low wages drove Japanese immigrant workers to strike. Korean labor was brought to Hawaii as strikebreakers by the Hawaiian planters.[40] It was estimated that about 7,500 workers came between 1903 and 1906.[41] Immediately upon arrival, thus, Koreans and Japanese were pitted against each other, and the Koreans were discriminated against not only by plantation owners, mostly whites, but also by Japanese immigrants.[42] Few Koreans migrated after 1910 when Japan annexed Korea and restricted Koreans from emigrating until 1945.[43] The US immigration statistics recorded only eighty-three Korean immigrants entering in the 1940s, and 4,845 in the 1950s, mostly war brides of US military personnel and orphans adopted by Americans.[44] Between 1946 and 1964, the total number of Korean immigrants admitted to the United States was fewer than 15,000.[45] By and large, Korean Americans were invisible on the American scene prior to 1965.

Changing Patterns of Contemporary Immigration from East Asia

Before High Tides Hit

Pre-1965 Chinese, Japanese, and Korean immigrants shared similar experiences of initial sojourning in Hawaii and the Pacific Northwest and anti-Asian racism and discrimination. However, their migration histories and resettlement patterns prior to World War II were quite different. First, they arrived at different points in time. Chinese immigrants arrived in the late 1840s, and their number declined as that of Japanese immigrants increased at the turn of the twentieth century. Korean immigrants appeared in insignificant numbers only in the 1900s.[46] Second, Chinese immigration was shunned by US law. Comparatively, Japanese immigration was also restricted, but was regulated through a bilateral gentlemen's agreement that reduced the number, yet balanced the sex ratio. Koreans, as colonial subjects of Japan between 1910 and 1945, were not allowed to emigrate. Third, the Japanese were geographically concentrated in the Pacific Northwest, with 74 percent in California, 15 percent in Washington and Oregon, and only 55 percent in urban areas by 1940. In contrast, the Chinese were more spread out and highly urban, being confined to Chinatowns in major cities, with about half living in California and nearly 90 percent in cities in 1940.[47] The Japanese made significant contributions to the agriculture in the western United States, particularly in California and Hawaii, while the Chinese contributed more to industrial development. Fourth, the Chinese Exclusion Act of 1882 stifled community development and natural growth because of the restriction of female Chinese immigration. Although the Chinese community was formed nearly half a century earlier than the Japanese community, it had remained a predominantly bachelors' society, with fewer women and fewer US-born children until WWII. Last but not least, US-China and US-Japan relations shaped the state of Chinese and Japanese America. A weak China failed to negotiate with the United States to protect the rights and interests of Chinese immigrants, while the rising power, Japan, managed to do so.

World War II marked a watershed for Chinese and Japanese Americans since their homelands, China and Japan, were in different positions. China became an ally with the United States, while Japan became an enemy. US Congress repealed the Chinese Exclusion Act in 1943 and other Asian exclusion acts during the war while passing the War Brides Act in 1945 to allow American GIs to reunite with their Asian wives in the United States.[48] In the wake of WWI, Japanese Americans were considered a national security threat and were incarcerated in internment camps, suffering from grave injustice. After WWII, Japanese Americans were dispersed elsewhere. They quietly rebuilt their communities and strove to assimilate into the American mainstream despite lingering discrimination. But Chinese Americans were once again perceived as suspects during the Cold War when China turned Communist. In either case, members of both ethnonational groups struggled to assimilate but found themselves living in the shadow of the "yellow peril," and being only conditionally accepted by American society. World War II defeated Japan and freed Korea from Japanese colonial control. The Korean War (1950–1953) brought South Korea closer to the United States, tightening bilateral military, political, and economic ties, while setting off the beginning of contemporary Korean immigration to the United States.

Changing Contexts in Contemporary Immigration and Emigration

The passage of the Hart-Celler Act of 1965, which favored family reunification and skilled migration, was a significant turning point in Asian immigration. This landmark piece of legislation, which prioritized family reunification and skilled migration, led to the exponential surge of Asian immigration. The tide has continued to remain high and forceful with little sign of subsiding for immigrants from China, but not for those from Korea or Japan.[49]

However, the main driving forces are beyond the scope of US immigration policy reform. Global economic restructuring, rapid economic development in Asia, and increasing US political, economic, and military involvement in Asia have all combined to perpetuate Asian immigration to the United States. The globalization of the US economy in the post-industrial era, particularly since WWII, has forged an extensive link of economic, cultural, and ideological ties between the United States and many developing countries in the Pacific Rim. Globalization has perpetuated emigration from East Asia in three important ways.

The first step was direct US capital investments in postwar Japan and Korea, and later in China after its economic reform. Industrial development caused domestic occupational structures to change in which skills and aspirations were unmatched by the jobs available, leading to underemployment and displacement of the domestic urban workforce and potential for emigration in sending countries.

Second, economic development following the American model stimulated consumerism and consumption and raised expectations regarding the standard of living. The widening gap between consumption expectations and the available standards of living within the structural constraints of the sending countries, combined with easy access to information and migration networks, in turn created tremendous pressure for emigration.[50] For example, economic ties between the United States and Korea, the continuous presence of American servicemen in Korea, and US TV networks all exerted strong American influence on Korean society, reinforcing the image of America as a country of affluence and prosperity, to which middle-class Koreans were inspired to emigrate.[51] Consequently, US foreign capital investments, political intervention, and cultural influence have resulted in the paradox of rapid economic growth and high emigration from sending countries in Asia to the United States.

The third point was the global integration of higher education and advanced training in the United States. The superior higher education system interacts with the constraints in the opportunity structure in the homelands, which has attracted international students from East Asia, thereby setting in motion highly skilled immigration. International students from Korea, Japan, Taiwan, Hong Kong, and mainland China constituted the main source of skilled migration, as significant numbers of students found employment in the US labor market upon completion of their studies, especially advanced graduate studies, in US universities. While China was consistently the country sending the most students to the United States to study in between 2000 and 2015, South Korea and Japan were among the top ten source countries. In 2015/16, Chinese students reached a record high of 328,547, comprising 32 percent of all international students in the United States and far exceeding those from any other country for the seventh consecutive year.[52]

Push factors in sending countries also matter. In South Korea, lack of economic and educational opportunities were major factors that pushed Koreans to emigrate to the United States in the 1970s and 1980s. Rapid industrialization took off in the 1970s, and the country quickly achieved high economic growth to become known as one of "Four Little Dragons" by 1990. Although South Korea's per capita income was $5,000 in 1990, which increased drastically from only $251 in 1970 to $1,355 in 1980, it was still only about one-fifth of the per capita income in the United States.[53] Moreover, the extremely competitive college entrance examinations for admission to prestigious universities, the value of a US college degree, and extraordinarily high costs of supplementary education pushed middle-class South Korean families to the United States. Furthermore, the lack of political freedom associated with military dictatorships between 1960 and 1987 and the fear of another war between North and South Korea also pushed many middle-class Koreans to find a safe haven for themselves and their families in the United States.[54]

In China, similar push factors were at work, such as the lack of employment and educational opportunities and political uncertainty at home. However, the long-standing diasporic networks and the subsequent development of the migration industry have played an important role. Most significantly, the drive for economic reform and modernization has not only opened the doors to unprecedented emigration—as families in China and international students studying in the United States benefit from the US Hart-Celler Act—but also has stimulated transnational engagement. Contemporary transnational engagements take on new forms, not only to support the basic needs of families left behind, but also to invest in business ventures and to remit for philanthropic purposes. This is quite different from the past, when transnational practices primarily consisted of monetary remittances to families. The Chinese central and local governments have also become transnational actors, proactively reaching out to the Chinese diaspora to promote national, regional, and local development programs. The reengagement of the Chinese diaspora with its homeland has revived transnational flows and long-established migration networks to further perpetuate emigration.[55]

In contrast, the push for emigration from Japan was not as strong. Japan quickly recovered from the ashes of WWII, partly due to the aid and assistance of the US Marshall Plan and partly due to Japanese government policy that focused on heavy industrialization.[56] By the late 1980s, Japan had risen to the status of a rich and developed country, becoming the third largest economy in the world. Economic prosperity, low unemployment, a lifetime employment system with a strong safety net, social harmony, and political stability eased pressures to emigrate. The unjust treatment of Japanese Americans disrupted the long-standing migration network and also shattered the American dream of potential emigrants.[57] Furthermore, unfavorable demographic trends of declining fertility and rapid aging created severe labor shortages in Japan's economy, putting pressure on the government to relax its immigration policy. Consequently, the pool of potential emigrants in Japan shrank. Even among international students and expats and their families on temporary nonimmigrant visas in the United States, the rate of return was high, and fewer chose to have their visas adjusted or to get resettled in the United States permanently.

Post-1965 Demographic Trends

Before the immigration surge in the late 1960s, the Asian American population was a tiny fraction of the total US population—about a third of 1 percent in 1900 and 0.7 percent in 1970. In 1970, Japanese, Chinese, and Filipinos made up 89 percent of the total Asian American population—Japanese formed the largest Asian-origin group, numbering 591,000 (38 percent), Chinese were second, at 436,000 (28 percent), Filipinos, third, at 343,000 (22 percent),[58] and Koreans, a distant fourth, 69,000 (4 percent). During this time, a sizeable US-born cohort, comprising mostly Japanese and Chinese Americans, came of age to form the core force of the Asian American movement at college campuses on the West Coast and in the Northeast in the 1960s.[59]

Since the late 1960s, the Asian American population has grown exponentially, from 1.5 million in 1970 to 22.4 million (or 6.5 percent of the US population) in 2017, along with the "big six" and many other fast-growing ethnonational groups, largely due to immigration.[60] The Chinese surpassed the Japanese as the largest Asian-origin group in 1980. Table 3.1 shows that the Chinese American population grew more than ten times, from 436,000 in 1970 to more than 5 million in 2017. The Korean American population also grew more than twenty-seven-fold, from 69,000 in 1970 to 1.9 million in 2017. In contrast, the Japanese American population grew at a much slower rate, from 591,000 in 1970

TABLE 3.1: US Ethnic Asian Population in Selected Time Points

Number	1970	1990	2010	2017
US Asian	1,538,721	6,808,638	17,320,856	22,408,464
Chinese	435,062	1,645,472	4,010,114	5,025,817
Korean	69,130	798,849	1,706,822	1,887,914
Japanese	591,000	848,000	1304,286	1,466,514

Source: Information gathered from the US Census Bureau, 1970, 1990, 2000; "American Community Survey," 2017. https://data.census.gov.

to 1.5 million in 2017, ranking sixth of the "big six." Nearly three-quarters of Japanese Americans are multigenerational US-born. Comparatively, only about a third of Chinese and Korean Americans are US-born and most are of foreign-born parentage.

Figure 3.2 displays different trends of immigration for Chinese, Koreans, and Japanese, as immigration accounts for much of the population growth. The Hart-Celler Act set an annual per-country numerical level of 20,000, but immediate family members and "special immigrants" were not subject to the numerical restriction. For the Chinese, the annual average of legal admissions was more than 30,000 between 1980 and 2000, and 65,000 since 2000, which far exceeds the per-country numerical limit. Koreans experienced a sharp increase in the 1970s and 1980s, but the trend flattened since 1990 when the annual number of new arrivals fluctuated slightly at the per-country numerical limit. The trend for immigration from Japan was low and flat, with the average number of new immigrants hovering around 4,000–8,000, far below the per-country numerical ceiling. Low emigration from Japan, intertwined with high integration of Japanese Americans into mainstream society, turned the *issei*-dominant community into a multi-generational US-born community of *nisei*, and *sansei* (third generation), and even *yonsei* (fourth generation).[61]

Socioeconomic Characteristics of Post-1965 East Asian Immigrants

In the post-1965 era, contemporary immigrants from East Asia have become socioeconomically more diverse than their earlier counterparts. No longer predominantly male sojourners from rural origins with

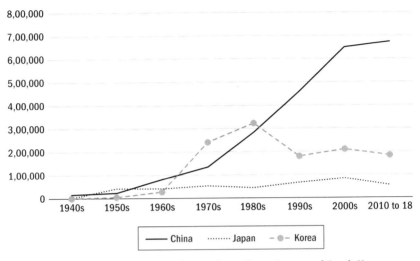

Figure 3.2: Immigration to the United States from China, Japan, and South Korea: 1940s–2018. Source: US Government, Department of Homeland Security, "Yearbook of Immigration Statistics 2018," 2018, www.dhs.gov/.

low levels of education, little English language ability, and few industrial job skills, contemporary immigrants are generally highly selected with a disproportionately large professional middle class. The majority of the post-1965 immigrants enter the United States through family or employer sponsorships.

Among post-1965 Chinese immigrants, nearly two-thirds were family-sponsored migrants, among which are significant intra-group differences. Those arriving between 1978 and 1990 were predominantly family migrants from rural areas of the original migrant-sending communities in South China. They had more lived experiences with the negative outcomes of the Communist regime, especially the Cultural Revolution, and fewer experiences with the positive outcomes of China's economic reform that began in 1978. In the earlier decades, they were subject to purges and stigmatization, being discriminated against as "suspects," anti-revolutionaries, or bourgeoisie. The migrant cohort of the 1980s, regardless of rural or urban origin, was generally of low socioeconomic status, had little English language ability, few economic resources, minimum education, and few job skills suitable for the US labor market, and was segregated in ethnic enclaves.[62] However, a smaller number of migrants in the 1980s were sponsored by the political refugees of the 1950s and were able to reproduce the social class statuses of their sponsors.[63] The Chinese family-sponsored migrants arriving after 1990 are more diverse than their earlier counterparts arriving in the 1980s. Post-1990 immigrants include not only those originated from the old hometowns in South China but also those student and professional migrants from other parts of China. Once they become naturalized US citizens, they sponsor family members from all over China rather than from traditional sending communities. Moreover, before immigration, many post-1990 immigrants have benefited from economic reform and achieved middle-class status, including nouveaux riches.

Among post-1965 Korean immigrants, the proportion of family-sponsored migrants is nearly as high as the Chinese. While many family sponsors are themselves immigrants who have attained permanent residency (PR) status or naturalized US citizenship, unique characteristics of Korean family sponsorship include the links to the Korean War, adoption, and contemporary immigration. Most Korean immigrants admitted to the United States between 1950 and 1964 were wives of US servicemen or war orphans adopted by Americans. The Korean adoptee phenomenon continued into the 1990s, and it was estimated that about 110,000 Korean children, two-thirds girls, were adopted by American families between 1976 and 2009.[64] The female spouses of US servicemen and Korean adoptees later sponsored the immigration of parents, siblings, and other relatives. However, the numbers of wives in cross-border mixed marriages and adoptees slowly decreased in the 1990s, which may be one of the factors contributing to the overall decline in Korean immigration since the late 1990s.[65]

Post-1965 Japanese immigration occurred on a much smaller scale, with family sponsorship not as high as those of Chinese and Koreans. This was due in part because the Japanese American community had long been a settled family community rather than a bachelor's society full of men in transnational split households. Because of the WWII traumatic disruption and the pressure to assimilate, Japanese Americans have lost social connections to Japan, and no longer consider Japan as their homeland.[66] By the late 1960s, many earlier *issei* were already aging, with few immediate relatives in Japan, quite unlike the Chinese. Thus, post-1965 family migrants from Japan were likely to be sponsored by their relatives who were also post-1965 immigrants like the Korean family migrants.

About a quarter of the post-1965 Chinese immigrants were employer-sponsored. Because of the unique cultural, economic, and political circumstances in China, very few Chinese could obtain employment in the United States to secure employer sponsorship. The only viable path was through student migration, where students found jobs in the US labor market after completing their studies and had their nonimmigrant student visas adjusted to H-1B visas, which allowed them to further adjust to immigrant PR status under their employers' sponsorship.[67] Since 1979, the Chinese government supported hundreds of thousands of students to study abroad, while many others studied abroad with private funding, first from their overseas relatives and later from their newly enriched families.

According to US Immigration statistics, 62,000 student visas were issued to the Chinese between the 1979 and 1987 fiscal years, slightly more than half were privately sponsored students who were on F-1 student visas, while others were on J-1 nonimmigrant status. For a variety of reasons, including better career opportunities, professional freedom of expression, higher income, and a more desirable lifestyle, many Chinese students found employment in the United States upon completion of their research or degree programs. Only about 15 percent of students prior to 2000 returned to China upon completion of their studies.[68] Since 2000, China has become the leading source of international students in the United States, with their number increasing from 127,628 in 2009/10 to 372,532 in 2019/20.[69] Despite higher return rates, the majority of these students do resettle in the United States.

However, a single historic event—namely, the Chinese government crackdown of the pro-democracy student movement in Tiananmen on June 4, 1989—allowed more than 60,000 Chinese students, scholars, and their families to adjust to immigrant PR status, or "June 4th green cards," as the Chinese call it, as beneficiaries of the Chinese Student Protection Act of 1992.[70] The Chinese student migrants graduated on time instead of prolonging their studies. Many have been willing to be retrained in more marketable fields in the US labor market, have succeeded in securing professional jobs in the mainstream US economy, and have resettled in either "ethnoburbs," multiethnic and Chinese immigrant-dominant suburbs,[71] or white middle-class suburbs. Unlike other political refugees, however, most of the student migrants holding June 4th green cards have favorable attitudes toward their homeland China, and are actively engaged in immigrant transnationalism when opportunities arise. Once they obtained PR status or naturalized citizenship and became resettled in the United States, they sent for their family members who were likely of urban middle-class status, thus contributing to further diversification of the immigrant population.[72] Those of highly educated middle-class status were not only able to resettle in white middle-class suburbs, but were also capable of building new ethnoburbs.

Like the Chinese student migrants, most of the employer-sponsored Korean migrants were also formerly international students. In the mid-1990s, some 45,000 students per year entered US universities from Korea, and that average annual number surged to 75,000 in 2008. A significant proportion of these students adjusted their status once they secured employment upon graduation. The visa adjustment rates for Koreans were relatively high at nearly 80 percent in 2009, many of whom were student migrants while others were short-term visitors.[73] However, the medical professionals, particularly nurses, were recruited directly from South Korea by US employers.[74]

Most of the post-1965 Japanese immigrants were initially sponsored by their US employers. After they had their nonimmigrant visas adjusted to immigrant visas or became naturalized, they would sponsor their own family members to migrate. Among Japanese immigrants, most were formerly student migrants. But a visible number of Japanese students, visitors, and others on short-term nonimmigrant visas residing in the United States obtained green cards through the Diversity Immigrant Visa Program,[75] known as the lottery system, without family or employer sponsorships.

Some post-1965 Chinese immigrants entered the United States as refugees or asylees. In the 1980s and 1990s, many Chinese applied for asylum protection on the basis of forced abortion or sterilization due to China's one-child-per-family policy, as well as political and religious persecution (e.g., Falun Gong). The asylum seekers were often trapped in a legal limbo as it took a long time for their applications to be processed, and they risked losing their status if their applications were denied.

Undocumented Chinese immigration is a post-1990 phenomenon. The undocumented Chinese immigrants, known as "snake people" by compatriots, have been smuggled to the United States by Chinese smugglers, known as "snakeheads." The smugglers are connected to long-standing migration networks that used to facilitate labor migration and undocumented migration in the Chinese diaspora.[76] The majority of the undocumented Chinese immigrants originated from the rural Fuzhou region in southeastern Fujian Province, a region with a long history of migration and easy access to "snakehead"-driven human smuggling networks that have stimulated and assisted the illegal entry of prospective migrants to the United States.[77] Most undocumented immigrants from Fuzhou are from rural villages and have few transferable job skills and little English proficiency. They are sojourners without legal status, clustering in ethnic enclaves (initially concentrated in New York's Chinatown and later branching out to suburbs and other parts of the United States), and working in Chinese-owned restaurants in Chinatown. They have a flexible plan: Their main goal is to make enough money to buy land and build homes in their places of origin and then return to "enjoy life" once they achieve this goal. However, they are also prepared to stay in the United States permanently if they are able to legalize through amnesty programs.

Patterns of Social Mobility

Historically, immigrants move ahead in their host society through three main routes. One is the time-honored path of starting from the bottom rungs of the mobility ladder and gradually climbing up through sheer will and hard work, like many earlier immigrants of Southern and Eastern European origins and those earlier Chinese railroad workers and Japanese plantation laborers. A second route, which is also long-standing and common among immigrants, is through the ethnic enclave either as business owners or workers of coethnic enterprises. Korean immigrants tend to be overrepresented in ethnic entrepreneurship, doing business either in their own ethnic enclaves like Koreatown or in poor urban neighborhoods of non-coethnic minorities, while Chinese

TABLE 3.2: Selected Socioeconomic Characteristics by Race: 2015

Number	Chinese	Korean	Japanese	Non-Hispanic Black	Hispanic	Non-Hispanic White
% US population	1.1	0.5	0.4	12.3	16.7	63.3
% Foreign born	63	62	27	—	33	—
% Bachelor's degree or higher	54	53	49	23	16	36
Median household income ($)	70,000	60,000	74,000	36,898	45,148	62,950

Source: "Key Facts about Asian Americans, a Diverse and Growing Population," Pew Research Center, April 29, 2021, www.pewresearch.org.

immigrants tend to be entrepreneurs and workers in their own ethnic economy.[78]

Still a third route is via educational achievement, which was closed off to earlier Asian immigrants and their *nisei* children because of prejudice and discrimination. The education route is well taken by all three ethno-national groups, especially among the children of immigrants, who would later enter the larger labor market as professionals. The relatively high proportions of employer-sponsored migrants among the ethno-national groups from East Asia suggest that these immigrants are generally highly selected and, for the Chinese and Koreans, hyperselected. Hyperselectivity is measured by the percentage of college graduates of an immigrant group that is not only higher than that in the sending country but also in the receiving country.[79] The obvious consequence of hyperselectivity is the reproduction of class at the individual or family level. As shown in table 3.2, East Asian Americans display average levels of education and income that are significantly higher than other racial minority groups as well as non-Hispanic whites. The higher proportions of foreign-born among Chinese and Koreans suggest that highly skilled immigrants would be at a more favorable starting point in their quest for upward social mobility; would have greater capacity in generating ethnic resources; and would be more positively perceived and received by the host society.[80] Immigrant selectivity profoundly affects ethnonational group members of lower socioeconomic status as well as societal racialization that transcends ethnicity.

Positionality and Racialization: "Oriental," "Honorary White," "Asian American"

In the mid-1960s, just before the surge of Asian immigration to the United States, Chinese and Japanese Americans "quietly" rose up, making remarkable inroads into mainstream America. Two articles in 1966—"Success Story, Japanese-American Style" by William Petersen in the *New York Times Magazine*, and "Success of One Minority Group in U.S." by the *US News and World Report* staff—marked a significant departure from how Asian immigrants and their offspring had been traditionally depicted in the media.[81] Both articles extolled the "Orientals"—Chinese and Japanese Americans—for their persistence in overcoming extreme hardships and discrimination to achieve success, unmatched even by US-born whites, with "their own almost totally unaided effort" and "no help from anyone else."[82] Is the shift from the unassimilable aliens to the honorary white, or the model minority an indication that Asian Americans have finally made it?

Positionality

Where do Asian Americans stand in the larger society? Both immigrants and their US-born children share the experience of being in America but not ever being fully a part of it. This lived experience suggests that Asian Americans, despite socioeconomic success as a group, are caught in the middle of the host society's racial hierarchy, held up high but not treated equally. However, the first and later generations respond quite differently to this positionality.

Members of the first generation of Asian immigrants are often perceived as the "Oriental," a term connoting the "Other." They tend to confront such social exclusion and unfair treatment with a dual frame of reference, comparing their current situation in the United States to the less favorable one they left behind in their homeland. As a reactive strategy to resist subjugation and discrimination, Asian immigrants retreated into their own ethnic enclaves, rebuilding ethnic institutions that resembled those found in the homeland and relying on one another for moral and practical support. Extreme adversity allowed them to develop a clearer sense of their position in the host society, even as "foreigners," and to maintain tangible ties to their diasporic communities and their ancestral homelands.

Because many East Asian immigrants *chose* to come to the United States to seek better lives, their shared experience of marginalization actually works to reinforce their determination to "make it" in material terms. To do so, they tend to take the path of least political resistance. Yet the very marginalization may also serve to politicize the hearts and minds of these immigrants and to mobilize their class consciousness. Some, though not all, fought actively for the rights of their fellow workers. As early as the 1930s and 1940s, for example, Ben Fee, who came to America at the age of thirteen, organized Chinese garment workers in New York and San Francisco, and founded the Chinese Workers Mutual Aid Association. Later, he was active in organizing the Alaskan Cannery Workers Association, which employed many Asian immigrant workers. Likewise, pre–WWII *issei* Japanese drew upon extensive ethnic resources in order to develop trade and business associations that interacted with the larger economy, thus providing for their offspring. *Issei* parents, traumatized during WWII, were reluctant to share wartime injustices with their *nisei* children and *sansei* grandchildren for fear of hurting the younger generations' chances of upward social mobility. Yet many of these same *issei* summoned the courage and voice to testify in Japanese, their native language, during the nationwide hearings for redress and reparations for Japanese Americans who were unfairly incarcerated in concentration camps during WWII. Their oral and written testimonies, together with the words and documentation of others, resulted in the Civil Liberties Act of 1988 and a congressional and presidential apology to Japanese Americans.

Members of the US-born generations, citizens by birth, fully embrace the ideals of personal freedom, equality, and civil liberties on which citizenship is based. They do not think of their parents' home country as a place to which they might return, nor do they use it as a point of reference by which to assess their progress in American society. Rather, their expectations are governed by the same standards to which other Americans aspire and by which they assess themselves and are assessed by others. However, American society is not color-blind, and the phenotypical characteristics of the "yellow race" subject the US-born generations to the same types of discrimination and injustice faced by an earlier generation, regardless of how long they have been in the United States. The forced incarceration of Japanese Americans, with two-thirds citizens by birth, is a historical case in point. The children and grand-children of Asian immigrants thus take the socially imposed "otherness" much harder than their immigrant counterparts. A second-generation Chinese American in her sixties explained her feelings:

> The truth is, no matter how American you think you are or try to be, you do not look "American." If you have almond-shaped eyes, straight black hair, and a yellow complexion, you are a foreigner by default. People will ask where you come from but won't be satisfied until they hear you name a foreign country. And they will naturally compliment your perfect English.[83]

The yearning to become unhyphenated "Americans" free of prejudice and discrimination and the demand from family and ethnic commu-nity to maintain their cultural heritage pose daunting challenges to East Asian immigrants and their offspring.

Pressured to Assimilate

US-born generations are particularly torn between their own ethnic cul-ture and the dominant American culture. A Chinese American youth said in an interview:

> We ABC [American-born Chinese] were ridiculed by the old immigrants as "bamboo stick" for not being able to speak Chinese and not being ac-cepted as "white people." We are not here. We are not there . . . We are different. Most of us are proud of the Chinese cultural heritage, but due to the pressure to assimilate and the lack of opportunity, we don't know much about the Chinese way.[84]

Growing up in an immigrant family can be taxing and stressful for US-born children. Parents often place multiple pressures on their chil-dren to "do and say the right things" or even to "act white" as a means of moving into the mainstream and accessing resources typically reserved for "insider" whites. When they fail to meet their parents' unusually high expectations, the children are often scolded for not trying hard enough or, conversely, for being too Americanized. As they are breaking into the American mainstream by way of extraordinary educational and occupational achievements, the children quickly become the objects of another stereotype, being held up as the "model minority." This new seemingly positive stereotype is detrimental to Asian Americans. It holds the group at higher than average standards, on the one hand, and justifies America's racialized social system, on the other hand, setting Asian Americans apart not only from other minorities but also from whites.

The pressure to assimilate takes a heavier toll on the second generation growing up in white middle-class suburbs than on those who live in segregated ethnic enclaves in central cities. Within the enclave, the homeland is transplanted; ancestral language, culture, and values are honored and practiced as a way of life; and ethnic pride is invigorated. Outside the enclave, ethnicity is subject to the rank order of the racial stratification system, operating under the assumption that ethnic traits should be abandoned in order to become "American," or "white." In fact, more than two-thirds of US-born Chinese, Japanese, and Koreans have lived all their lives amidst the white middle class, speak accentless English and English only, and consider themselves an indistinguishable part of white middle-class suburbia.[85] Particularly striking is their high rates of intermarriage, marriage outside of the ethnic community—64 percent among Japanese Americans, 39 percent among Korean Americans, and 35 percent among Chinese Americans as of 2015.[86]

From Ethnic to American and Back

For Americans of East Asian origin, ethnic identity formation is a process that relates and reacts to exclusion and racialization. Historically, Americans regarded people of Asian ancestry as "inferior races" and negatively portrayed them as the "yellow peril" that threatened to un-Americanize Americans. No matter how hard they tried to adapt to American ways, Asian immigrants, who looked different and spoke with little or heavily accented English, were considered undesirable and unassimilable aliens and were subject to injustices, as in the enactment of the Chinese Exclusion Act of 1882 and WWII Japanese American internment. Under racial exclusion, Chinese and Japanese immigrants had to rely on their own ethnic community for survival, and a strong ethnic identity was nurtured in the immigrant offspring. After WWII, when American society became relatively more open, the immigrants pushed their children to assimilate, to become American, by downplaying ethnicity and systemic racism.

Despite the fact that US-born Asian Americans have, since the 1960s, been highly integrated into mainstream America, their American identity is constantly questioned. Asian Americans often find that they lack a homeland or an immigrant culture on which they can fall back and an ethnic space in which they can express their fears and vent their frustrations. In the process of vacillating between the "Oriental" outsider and "American" insider, US-born Asian Americans, including mixed-race children of intermarriages, are increasingly ambivalent about their identities. Such an identity crisis is not uncommon among adolescents as they grow into adulthood, but it does imply an aversion to second-class or partial citizenship based on skin color or racial identity.[87]

Inspired by the civil rights movement of the 1960s, US-born children of East Asian immigrants rose to reclaim a place in American society under a panethnic banner: "Asian American." To adopt the Asian American identity proactively is to reject the imposed categorization of the "Oriental." This political identity is neither mainstream American nor associated with the immigrant generation. It is a hybrid form that has come to assume tremendous social significance among Asian Americans as a viable means of resistance and compromise within the existing power structure. This panethnic identity serves as an effective tool for Asian Americans to carve out a social and cultural space in which they can share their lived experiences that are uniquely Asian American while rebuilding a sense of self-worth and political empowerment.

Conclusion

East Asian immigrants in the United States started from humble origins. Their multifaceted lived experiences in the United States suggest that they are more than economic migrants, even though the majority of the earlier cohorts may have initially come with an economic goal. Over the course of more than one and a half centuries, they have encountered severe racism and discrimination, along with many cultural and structural barriers, and have nonetheless achieved remarkable socioeconomic success in American society. Yet, the positive outcomes of their social mobility cannot be explained merely by individual drives and hard work, nor by immigrant cultures or a more open societal reception, but by the intersection of these multilevel factors as well as changing immigration dynamics. As they are asserting themselves in American society, East Asian immigrants and their offspring find themselves going through the processes of being ethnic, becoming American, and currently reaffirming an ethnic identity that differs from the one their immigrant parents tried to retain or shed. This ethnic identity, panethnicity rather, takes a new form that is quintessentially American.

Is the Asian American identity truly significant or is it merely symbolic? Ethnic identity associated with a homeland has become blurred among the second or third generations, who have lost their ancestral languages, intermarried at rates far exceeding the national average, and no longer involve themselves with their ethnic communities on a daily basis, thus making their ethnicity "symbolic." Among the features of symbolic ethnicity is the fact that it does not carry with it material consequences and does not serve to enhance group solidarity, as exemplified by the experience of European ethnics who have now become indistinguishably white.

However, symbolic ethnicity may not apply well to Asian Americans. Asian Americans find it hard to be treated simply as an unmarked, nonethnic, unhyphenated American. They also find it hard to choose whether they want to be Asian, or how Asian they should be when they want to be. Their identity is very much conditioned by their look and the immigrant status of their parents. The outcry that "America does not include me, but only a part of me," is heard from many US-born, "well-assimilated" Asian Americans. This suggests that unless the whole racialized notion of who an American is changes into one that is more inclusive of all ethnic groups, panethnicity will continue to remain instrumental and consequential for Asian Americans and for other excluded social groups. Such an Asian American identity serves as a defense mechanism against racism and an empowering mechanism for self-determination and unity.

The construction of a panethnic Asian American identity is not simply a reaction to externally imposed dual stereotyping of the "model minority" and "forever foreigner." It also involves a complex process of internal socialization of Asian values, shared experiences of growing up Asian, and an Asian upbringing within the contexts of immigration, racialization, and US-Asian relations. However, diverse cultures, languages, religions, migration histories in the United States, and historical legacies of domination and colonization in Asia, as well as different socioeconomic backgrounds among the immigrant generation and diverse patterns of integration of that first generation, pose a serious challenge to the formation of a panethnic coalition. The success of Asian Americans' integration into American society as individuals can both enhance and weaken their ability to act collectively.

NOTES

1 Estimated by the 2019 American Community Survey, the "big six" Asian-origin groups in the United States are Chinese (5.2 million), Asian Indian (4.6 million), Filipino (4.2 million), Vietnamese (2.2 million), Korean (1.9 million), and Japanese (1.5 million). www.census.gov.

2 Min Zhou, "Intra-Diaspora Dynamics in Generational Formation: The Case of Chinese America," *Diaspora* 18, nos. 1–2 (2015): 89–116.

3 Roger Daniels, "Chinese and Japanese as Urban Americans, 1850–1940," *The History Teacher* 25, no. 4 (1992): 427–441.

4 Sucheng Chan, *This Bittersweet Soil: The Chinese in California Agriculture, 1860–1910* (Berkeley: University of California Press, 1989).

5 Zhou, "Intra-Diaspora Dynamics in Generational Formation."

6 Min Zhou and Rebecca Kim, "Formation, Consolidation, and Diversification of the Ethnic Elite: The Case of the Chinese Immigrant Community in the United States," *Journal of International Migration and Integration* 2, no. 2 (2001): 227–247.

7 Min Zhou, *Chinatown: The Socioeconomic Potential of an Urban Enclave* (Philadelphia, PA: Temple University Press, 1992), 19.

8 Madeline Hsu, *Dreaming of Gold, Dreaming of Home: Transnationalism and Migration between the United States and South China, 1882–1943* (Stanford, CA: Stanford University Press, 2000); Zhou, "Intra-Diaspora Dynamics in Generational Formation."

9 Zhou, *Chinatown*.

10 Alexander Saxton, *The Indispensable Enemy: Labor and the Anti-Chinese Movement in California* (Berkeley: University of California Press, 1975); Roger Daniels, *Asian America: Chinese and Japanese in the United States since 1850* (Seattle: University of Washington Press, 1988).

11 Erika Lee, *At America's Gates: Chinese Immigration during the Exclusion Era, 1882–1943* (Chapel Hill: University of North Carolina Press, 2003); Chan, *This Bittersweet Soil*.

12 Saxton, *The Indispensable Enemy*.

13 Chan, *This Bittersweet Soil*; Roger Daniels, "Immigration Policy in a Time of War: The United States, 1939–1945," *Journal of American Ethnic History* 25, nos. 2/3 (2006): 107–116.

14 Zhou, "Intra-Diaspora Dynamics in Generational Formation."

15 US Bureau of the Census, "Chinese and Japanese in the United States: 1910," Department of Commerce Bulletin 127 (Washington, DC: US Government Printing Office, 1914).

16 Estelle T. Lau, *Paper Families: Identity, Immigration Administration, and Chinese Exclusion* (Durham, NC: Duke University Press, 2007). The San Francisco earthquake of 1906 destroyed local public records, allowing many Chinese to claim that they were born in San Francisco. Having obtained birth-right citizenship, a Chinese American man was able to claim citizenship for offspring born in China. Following trips home, he would report the birth of a child, usually a son. Papers of the "children" of "U.S.-born" fathers were then sold to young men who wanted to migrate to the United States.

17 Robert Chao Romero, *The Chinese in Mexico, 1882–1940* (Tucson: University of Arizona Press, 2010).

18 Chia-ling Kuo, *Social and Political Change in New York's Chinatown: The Role of Voluntary Associations* (New York: Praeger, 1977); Bernard P. Wong, *Patronage, Brokerage, Entrepreneurship, and the Chinese Community of New York* (New York: AMS Press, 1988); Zhou and Kim, "Formation, Consolidation, and Diversification of the Ethnic Elite."

19 Daniels, "Immigration Policy in a Time of War."

20 US Government, Department of Homeland Security, "Yearbook of Immigration Statistics 2018," 2018, www.dhs.gov.

21 Yuji Ichioka, "Amerika Nadeshiko: Japanese Immigrant Women in the United States, 1900–1924," *Pacific Historical Review* 49, no. 2 (1980): 339–357.

22 Daniels, *Asian America*; Tetsuden Kashima, "Before Pearl Harbor," in *Personal Justice Denied: Report of the Commission on Wartime Relocation and Internment of Civilians*, ed. The Commission on Wartime Relocation and Internment (Seattle: University of Washington Press, 1997), 27–46.

23 Kazuo Ito, *Issei: A History of Japanese Immigrants in North America*, trans. Shinichiro Nakamura and Jean S. Gerard (Seattle, WA: Executive Committee for Publication of *Issei*, 1973).

24 Iwata Masakazu, "The Japanese Immigrants in California Agriculture," *Agricultural History* 36, no. 1 (1996): 25–27; Ichioka, "Amerika Nadeshiko"; Yuji Ichioka, *The Issei: The World of the First Generation Japanese Immigrants, 1885–1924* (New York: Collier Macmillan, 1988).

25 Scott Y. Matsumoto, "Okinawa Migrants to Hawaii," *Hawaiian Journal of History* 16 (1982): 125–133.

26 Daniels, *Asian America*; Hosok O, "Cultural Analysis of the Early Japanese Immigration to the United States during the Meiji to Taisho Era (1868–1926)," (PhD diss., Department of History, Oklahoma University, 2010).

27 Ichioka, "Amerika Nadeshiko"; Ito, *Issei*; John E. Van Sant, *Pacific Pioneers: Japanese Journeys to America and Hawaii, 1850–80* (Chicago: University of Illinois Press, 2000).

28 US Bureau of the Census, "Chinese and Japanese in the United States."

29 Iwata Masakazu, "The Japanese Immigrants in California Agriculture," *Agricultural History* 36, no. 1 (1996): 25–27.

30 Ichioka, *The Issei*.

31 A practice in the early twentieth century in the Japanese immigrant communities in Hawaii and the West Coast in which Japanese immigrant men selected their marriage partners by reviewing photos sent from Japan. Ichioka, "Amerika Nadeshiko"; Catherine Lee, *Prostitutes and Picture Brides: Chinese and Japanese Immigration, Settlement, and American Nation-Building, 1870–1920* (La Jolla: University of California San Diego Center for Comparative Immigration Studies, 2003); Kei Tanaka, "Japanese Picture Marriage and the Image of Immigrant Women in Early Twentieth-Century California," *Japanese Journal of American Studies* 15 (2004): 115–138.

32 Evelyn Nakano Glenn, *Issei, Nisei, Warbride: Three Generations of Japanese American Women in Domestic Service* (Philadelphia, PA: Temple University Press, 1986); Ichioka, "Amerika Nadeshiko"; O, *Cultural Analysis of the Early Japanese Immigration*.

33 Ichioka, *The Issei*; Valerie J. Matsumoto, *Farming the Home Place: A Japanese American Community in California, 1919–1982* (Ithaca, NY: Cornell University Press, 1993).

34 Glenn, *Issei, Nisei, Warbride*.

35 Daniels, "Chinese and Japanese as Urban Americans."

36 Glenn, *Issei, Nisei, Warbride*; Sandra C. Taylor, "Leaving the Concentration Camps: Japanese American Resettlement in Utah and the Intermountain West," *Pacific Historical Review* 60, no. 2 (1991): 169–194.

37 Miyako Inoue, "Japanese-Americans in St. Louis: From Internees to Professionals," *City & Society* 3, no. 2 (1989): 142–152; Thomas M. Linehan, "Japanese American Resettlement in Cleveland during and after World War II," *Journal of Urban History* 20, no. 1 (1993): 54–80; Taylor, "Leaving the Concentration Camps."

38 Takeyuki (Gaku) Tsuda, "Disconnected from the 'Diaspora': Japanese Americans and the Lack of Transnational Ethnic Networks," *Journal of Anthropological Research* 68, no. 1 (2012): 95–116.

39 Korea was colonized by Japan between 1910 and 1945.

40 David K. Yoo, *Contentious Spirits: Religion in Korean American History, 1903–1945* (Stanford, CA: Stanford University Press, 2010).

41 Daniels, *Asian America*.

42 Daniels, *Asian America*.

43 Wayne Patterson, *The Ilse: First-Generation Korean Immigrants in Hawaii, 1903–1973* (Honolulu: University of Hawaii Press, 2000); Yoo, *Contentious Spirits*.

44 Haeyun Juliana Kim, "Voices from the Shadows: The Lives of Korean War Brides," *Amerasia Journal* 17, no. 1 (1991): 15–30; Pyong Gap Min, "The Immigration of Koreans to the United States: A Review of 45 Year (1965–2009) Trends," *Development and Society* 40, no. 2 (2011): 195–223; Eui-Young Yu and Earl H. Phillips, *Korean Women in Transition: At Home and Abroad* (Center for Korean-American and Korean Studies, California State University, Los Angeles, 1987). Yu and Philips note that the number of Korean war brides during and immediately after the Korean War was estimated at 6,423.

45 Herbert Baringer, Robert W. Gardener, and Michael J Levin, *Asians and Pacific Islanders in the United States* (New York: Russell Sage Foundation, 1995), 24–25.

46 Yoo, *Contentious Spirits*.

47 Daniels, "Chinese and Japanese as Urban Americans."

48 Min Zhou, Anthony Ocampo, and J. V. Gatewood, "Contemporary Asian America: Immigration, Demographic Transformation, and Ethnic Formation," in *Contemporary Asian America: A Multidisciplinary Reader*, ed. Min Zhou and Anthony Ocampo (New York: New York University Press, 2016), 101–128.

49 Korean immigration since 2010 has flattened and experienced decline. Post-1965 Japanese immigration has remained relatively low in comparison to immigration from the rest of Asia. Also see Zhou et al., "Contemporary Asian America."

50 Alejandro Portes and Min Zhou, "Transnationalism and Development: Mexican and Chinese Immigrant Organizations in the United States," *Population and Development Review* 38, no. 2 (2012): 191–220; Zhou et al., "Contemporary Asian America."

51 Min, "The Immigration of Koreans to the United States."

52 Institute of International Education (IIE), "A World on the Move: Trends in Global Student Mobility," 2017, www.iie.org.

53 Min, "The Immigration of Koreans to the United States."

54 Min, "The Immigration of Koreans to the United States."

55 Portes and Zhou, "Transnationalism and Development."

56 Chalmers Johnson, *MITI and the Japanese Miracle: The Growth of Industrial Policy, 1925–1975* (Stanford, CA: Stanford University Press, 1982).

57 Tsuda, "Disconnected from the 'Diaspora.'"

58 Filipinos arrived in significant numbers in the late 1920s and 1930s as US nationals not subjected to immigration restriction.

59 Zhou et al., "Contemporary Asian America."

60 Other fast-growing Asia-origin groups include Cambodian, Laotian, Hmong, Thai, Burmese, Nepalese, Indonesian, Pakistani, and Bangladeshi, who arrived in the United States only after 1965, with numbers exceeding 100,000. See US Census Bureau, "Asian-American and Pacific Islander Heritage Month: May 2019," May 8, 2019, www.census.gov.

61 Tsuda, "Disconnected from the 'Diaspora.'"

62 Zhou, *Chinatown*.

63 Zhou, "Intra-Diaspora Dynamics in Generational Formation."

64 Min, "The Immigration of Koreans to the United States."

65 Min, "The Immigration of Koreans to the United States."

66 Tsuda, "Disconnected from the 'Diaspora.'"

67 Terry Wotherspoon, "International Students: Mobility and Resettlement," chapter 7 in this volume.

68 The return rate has been much higher since 2010, see Luke Kelly, "How China Is Winning back More Graduates from Foreign Universities than Ever Before," *Forbes*, January 25, 2018, www.forbes.com. Government-sponsored exchange students and visiting scholars are on J-1 visas. All J-1 visa holders are subject to a two-year home residence restriction before they can apply for immigration to the United States.

69 See "Number of College and University Students from China in the United States from Academic Year 2009/10 to 2019/20," *Statista*, April 12, 2021, www.statista .com/.

70 The US Senate passed the bill S1216 on May 21, 1992, and the House Judiciary Committee approved it on July 22, 1992. This legislation, known as the Chinese Student Protection Act of 1992 (CSPA), would allow Chinese nationals who were afraid of returning home after the 1989 Tiananmen Square massacre to convert their temporary protected status to PR status, www.govinfo.gov.

71 Wei Li, "Spatial Transformation of an Urban Ethnic Community from Chinatown to Chinese Ethnoburb in Los Angeles" (PhD diss., Department of Geography, University of Southern California, 1997).

72 Zhou, "Intra-Diaspora Dynamics in Generational Formation."

73 Min, "The Immigration of Koreans to the United States."

74 Min, "The Immigration of Koreans to the United States."

75 Each year, Citizenship and Immigration Services of the US Department of Homeland Security randomly selects up to 50,000 from a pool of persons from countries with low rates of immigration to the United States.

76 Ko-lin Chin, *Smuggled Chinese: Clandestine Immigration to the United States* (Philadelphia, PA: Temple University Press, 1999).

77 Chin, *Smuggled Chinese.*

78 Zhou, *Chinatown*; Min Zhou, "How Neighborhoods Matter for Immigrant Children: The Formation of Educational Resources in Chinatown, Koreatown, and Pico Union, Los Angeles," *Journal of Ethnic and Migration Studies* 35, no. 7 (2009): 1153–1179.

79 Jennifer Lee and Min Zhou, *The Asian American Achievement Paradox* (New York: Russell Sage Foundation, 2015).

80 Lee and Zhou, *The Asian American Achievement Paradox.*

81 William Peterson, "Success Story, Japanese-American Style," *New York Times Magazine*, January 9, 1966, www.dartmouth.edu; "Success of One Minority Group in U.S.," *US News and World Report*, December 26, 1966, www.dartmouth.edu.

82 Cited in Min Zhou, "Are Asian Americans Becoming White?" *Context* 3, no. 1 (2004): 32.

83 Cited in Zhou, "Are Asian Americans Becoming White?" 35.

84 Bernard P. Wong, *Chinatown: Economic Adaptation and Ethnic Identity of the Chinese* (New York: Holt, Rinehart, and Winston, 1982), 33.

85 Zhou, "Are Asian Americans Becoming White?"

86 Intermarriage between ethnic group members and whites was used as a measure of assimilation. See Richard D. Alba, "Intermarriage and Ethnicity among European Americans," *Contemporary Jewry* 12 (1991): 3–19; Gretchen Livingston and Anna Brown, "Trends and Patterns in Intermarriage," Pew Research Center, May 18, 2017, www.pewsocialtrends.org.

87 Zhou, "Are Asian Americans Becoming White?"

4

The US Visa System

Growing Complexity and Difference without Legislative Change

KATHARINE M. DONATO AND CATALINA AMUEDO-DORANTES

In 1981, the US Select Commission on Immigration and Refugee Policy recommended comprehensive reform of policies regulating undocumented and documented migration.[1] Following years of legislative debate, President Reagan signed the 1986 Immigration Reform and Control Act (IRCA) to reduce unauthorized migration, and President George H. W. Bush signed the 1990 Immigration Act to overhaul the legal immigration system. Since then, notwithstanding legislation passed by the US Congress aimed at curbing unauthorized migration in 1996, the legal visa system has remained largely unchanged. As a result, more than thirty years after its passage, the 1990 Immigration Act continues to define the ways in which immigrants legally enter the United States, despite its inability to address immigration demand.[2] During this same period, following the growth of the unauthorized migrant population during the 1990s, many prior studies focused on unauthorized migration in lieu of the visa system and legal immigration.

In this chapter, we build on a small set of existing studies that largely examine wage differences among immigrants with different visas, as well as between them and US natives. We examine patterns and trends in the US visa system and its supported legal migration. We begin by describing the various immigrant visa categories and the context that led to their regulation. Subsequently, we analyze trends in the number of visas issued in relation to country-specific political and macroeconomic factors. We conclude with a discussion of the implications of our findings for the future of legal immigration in the United States.

An Overview of the US Visa System

In a recently published introduction to a journal issue about the legal landscape of US immigration,[3] Donato and Amuedo-Dorantes describe the immigration laws and policies that created and shifted the US visa system since early in the twentieth century. They reveal that the current immigration system is anything but simple. Instead, it is a labyrinth of complex visa categories and subcategories, derived from the 1990 Immigration Act and from a growing reliance on presidential executive actions, which are used "more often and more broadly than in the past."[4]

Regular use of executive actions and orders by US presidents first appeared in the mid-twentieth century. For example, in 1945, President Truman issued an executive order that allocated the quotas on immigrant visas to persons displaced because of World War II. This action allowed those who entered to permanently live in the United States. Approximately ten years later, President Eisenhower used parole to permit the entry of thousands of Hungarian refugees. In the 1960s, President Kennedy set up the Cuban Refugee Emergency Center, which jumpstarted the Cuban Refugee Program. Presidents Ford and Carter used executive actions to open the United States to Southeast Asian refugees. The Carter administration also used executive action to parole approximately 150,000 Cuban and Haitian refugees who arrived as part of the Mariel boatlift. Presidents Reagan and G.H.W. Bush protected from deportation the immediate relatives of those who received amnesty as part of the 1986 Immigration Reform and Control Act. Presidents G.H.W. Bush and Clinton gave temporary protected status to various immigrant groups, including Salvadoran and Haitian refugees.

Since the start of the twenty-first century, presidents and their administrations have implemented more executive actions and regulatory orders related to immigration, and their scope and impact have broadened. During the first decade of the 2000s, the actions and orders were mostly related to enforcement, such as expanding the use of expedited removal of migrants caught within 100 miles of the US-Mexican border,[5] developing the Secure Border Initiative that allocated billions of dollars to reduce unauthorized migration and secure US borders, and spurring partnerships between federal and local agencies for internal enforcement through the 287(g) provision of the 1996 Illegal Immigration Reform and Immigrant Responsibility Act.[6] In 2012, the Obama administration used its executive power to create DACA, the Deferred Action for Childhood Arrivals program. In its first year, it gave approximately 800,000 young adults temporary status to live and work in the United States. President Trump further amplified the use of executive orders and actions. During the initial year of his administration, Trump issued hundreds of executive orders and actions that had broad, deep, and exclusionary impacts on the immigration system.[7]

In addition to executive actions and rule changes, the current US visa system derives from the 1990 Immigration Act. It expanded the visa system to "open the front door wider to skilled immigrants of a more diverse range of nationalities."[8] The legislation revised immigrant family-based and employment-based visas and created a diversity visa using a lottery system for those in countries with low levels of US immigration. It also expanded nonimmigrant visas for a wide variety of foreign nationals such as specialty workers, students, exchange visitors, tourists, business travelers, and crew members in transit.[9] In addition, it established Temporary Protective Status (TPS), invoked by various presidents to protect certain groups from deportation after 1990.

The current system contains more than 150 specific visa types, which can be classified into two broad categories: nonimmigrant and immigrant visas.

Nonimmigrant Visas

These visas permit foreign-born persons to temporarily enter the United States. The vast majority of nonimmigrant visas are for tourists or business travelers (B-1 and/or B-2), and for those entering the country under the Visa Waiver (VW) program. Those eligible for the VW program are foreigners planning to stay for ninety days or less from countries such as the UK, France, and Japan; citizens of Canada, Micronesia, Marshall Islands, and Palau; citizens of British Overseas Territory connected to Bermuda, Bahamas, British Virgin Islands, Cayman Islands, or Turks and Caicos Islands.[10]

Although temporary work visas for high- and low-skilled immigrants, as well as for foreign-born trainees, existed before 1990, the 1990

Act also added caps to the first two categories. In addition, it narrowed the H-1B professional worker definition by shifting those with extraordinary ability in the sciences, arts, education, business, athletics, and performing arts to new nonimmigrant visa categories. Specifically, the 1990 Act limited high-skilled H-1B visas to 65,000 and low-skilled H-2B visas to 66,000—even though initial and continuing H-1B visas have always exceeded their limits, usually more than doubling them.[11] H-1B visas for high-skilled immigrant workers also include free trade agreement visas for workers from Chile and Singapore (H-1B1), professionals working for the Department of Defense Cooperative Research and Development Program (H-1B2), and fashion models (H-1B3). Low-skilled worker visas are for agricultural workers (H-2A) and those in other temporary or seasonal jobs (H-2B). In addition, the North American Free Trade Agreement (NAFTA), which began in January 1994, created a nonimmigrant trade NAFTA (TN) visa that permits Canadian and Mexican accountants, engineers, lawyers, pharmacists, scientists, and teachers to work for US or foreign employers.

Foreign nationals may also enter temporarily with F-1 or M-1 visas to attend primary, secondary, university, and other academic institutions; J-1 visas go to exchange visitors such as au pairs, teachers, researchers, and interns; airline employees and those on cruise ships receive transit visas (C-1 and D visas); and temporary visas are available for spouses and children of lawful permanent residents (V).

Finally, the passage of the 2000 Victims of Trafficking and Violence Protection Act created the U visa for victims of criminal activity and the T visa for victims of trafficking. Unlike most nonimmigrant visas, U and T visas offer immigrants multiyear temporary residence that can lead to permanent residence.[12] To receive these visas, immigrant workers must work with law enforcement officers as they investigate or prosecute a crime.

Immigrant Visas

Foreign-born persons receive immigrant permanent residency visas based on family ties, diversity, employment, special immigrants, and humanitarian concerns.[13] Although it did not contain or change provisions about immigrant visas for refugees, the 1990 Immigration Act revised the system of family-sponsored and employment-based visas and created the diversity-based visas. It also set a numerical limit on total immigrants and for different visa categories, while increasing the per-country limit on visas to 26,000. However, because immediate family relatives of US citizens are exempt from numerical limitations, family-sponsored visas exceed the annual limit each year.

Among those with family ties are immediate relatives and those granted visas based on family preferences. Most immediate relatives are spouses, minor children, and parents of a US citizen (i.e., IR-1/CR-1, IR-2/CR-2, and IR-5, respectively). They are exempt from numerical visa limitations. Other immediate relatives include orphans adopted abroad or domestically by US citizens (i.e., IR-3 and IR-4, respectively). Each year, a limited number of visas are also available for relatives with less direct connections to US citizens and relatives of permanent residents (F1, F2A, F2B, F3, and F4).

In addition, the 1990 Act created five new employment-based (EB) preferences for permanent immigrant visas, intended to grow the population of foreign workers sponsored by employers, especially those with high levels of skill and education.[14] These visas include: EB-1 for priority workers with extraordinary ability in a variety of fields, outstanding professors and researchers with international recognition, and multinational managers and executives; EB-2 for professionals with advanced degrees or undergraduate degrees with at least five years of experience, and those with exceptional ability in the sciences, arts, or business; EB-3 for skilled workers with at least two years of experience, professionals with jobs requiring at least a college degree, and unskilled workers who fill jobs that require less than two years of training or experience; EB-4 for ministers and other religious workers, former employees who worked on the Panama Canal, certain foreign nationals who serve as interpreters-translators, retired workers of international organizations and their immediate family, and special immigrant juveniles who were abused, abandoned, or neglected by a parent; and EB-5 for investors in a commercial enterprise who create at least ten permanent full-time jobs for US workers.[15]

The Act also implemented a diversity visa (DV) program that offers up to 55,000 visas to foreign nationals, who have at least a high school degree, born in countries with low rates of immigration—e.g., those sending

TABLE 4.1: Visa Counts in 2017

Visa Category	Count	%	%
Total	**10,861,503**		
Total Temporary (Nonimmigrant)	**9,766,322**	**89.91**	**100**
Temporary Employment	746,859		7.65
High-Skilled Temporary Worker	441,077		4.52
Low Skilled Temporary Worker	245,777		2.52
Other Worker	60,005		0.61
Student	384,017		3.93
Exchange	310,893		3.18
Tourist	7,272,112		74.46
Spouse	303,555		3.11
Other Temporary	2,027		0.02
Total Permanent (Immigrant)	**1,095,181**	**10.09**	**100**
Permanent Family	724,451		66.15
Permanent Employment	134,385		12.27
Diversity	47,196		4.31
Refugee/Asylum	68,681		6.27
Cancellation of Removal	77,547		7.08
Other Permanent	42,921		3.92

Sources: US Department of State, Bureau of Consular Affairs, Nonimmigrant Visa Statistics, FY1997–2018 NIV Detail; US Department of Homeland Security, Office of Immigration Statistics, Office of Strategy, Policy & Plans, "Annual Flow Reports: Lawful Permanent Residents," August 2018.

fewer than 5,000 immigrants in the last five years. According to Wilson, the diversity visa program is responsible for the growth of African- and Asian-born immigrants to the United States since the late 1990s.[16]

In addition, in 2006, Congress enacted legislative provisions permitting some Iraqi and Afghan nationals to receive special immigrant visas (SIV) and become lawful permanent residents.[17] To be eligible, they had to have worked directly as translators or in other capacities for the US government for at least a year, beginning March 20, 2003. By the end of FY2018, approximately 79,000 Iraqis and Afghans received SIVs. The 1990 Act also established Special Immigrant Visas for Juveniles (SIJ), a status that subsequently could be adjusted to immigrant permanent residency.

Table 4.1 presents the number and distribution of most nonimmigrant and immigrant visas issued to foreign nationals in 2017. Most of the approximately 10.9 million visas were nonimmigrant temporary visas (90 percent). Tourists received the largest share (74.5 percent) of those visas. Of the remaining nonimmigrant visas, about 4.5 percent were issued to high-skilled workers, 2.5 percent issued to low-skilled workers, and 3.2 percent to students and participants in exchange programs.

In 2017, immigrant visas comprised just 10 percent or 1,095,181 of the 10.4 million visas issued. Relatives reuniting with family in the United States received 66 percent of immigrant visas. Another 12.3 percent were employment-related visas, and 6.3 percent were refugee and asylum visas. A non-negligible share (7.1 percent) were immigrant visas related to the cancellation of removal offered to those in deportation proceedings, whereas diversity visas represented 4.3 percent of immigrant visas.

Prior Studies

Much of the literature on authorized migration explores the economic and labor market impacts of employment under certain visa types. In this section, we review some of the studies in this extensive literature.

Economic Productivity of Immigrants on Family-Based Visas

One recurrent topic in this literature refers to the economic productivity of those receiving family-based visas when compared to their counterparts on employment-based visas. In this regard, Duleep and Regets show that earnings profiles of family-based visa immigrants are often comparable to, if not better than, those of immigrants with work-based visas. They also find that immigrant wage growth exceeds native wage growth, a finding that fails to be emphasized in much of the literature on immigrant economic assimilation.

For example, using 1980 census data matched to immigrant admission cohort information obtained from the Immigration and Naturalization Service, Duleep and Regets report that immigrants entering with family-based visas have lower occupational entry earnings.[18] However, they exhibit higher earnings growth than immigrants entering with work-based visas. As a result, the earnings for both groups tend to converge over time.[19]

Pooling data from the 1970, 1980, and 1990 decennial censuses, Duleep and Regets assess earnings differences between immigrant and native men.[20] They find that immigrants enjoy faster earnings growth than US natives, despite their initially lower earnings. Duleep and Regets then use 1960, 1970, and 1980 census data to show that the decline in immigrant earnings at entry resulted from the limited transferability of their human capital, as opposed to their lower ability.[21] To underscore this fact, they follow immigrant and native men across one year, using matched Current Population Survey data, and show how immigrant wage growth exceeded that of natives.[22]

In a recent paper, Gelatt considers whether employer-sponsored immigrants fare better in the labor market than family-sponsored immigrants.[23] Using the New Immigrant Survey (NIS) and following legal immigrants after they enter in 2003 over the subsequent 4–6 years, she finds that most permanent immigrants, after several years of residence, have high employment and self-employment rates compared to US natives. However, she also reports that employment-sponsored immigrants and spouses have the highest levels of education and English proficiency upon entry and work in the highest skilled occupations over time.

Wages of Temporary Immigrant Workers

Many studies have examined immigrants receiving H-1B and other temporary visas.[24] Some consider the earnings of workers with temporary employment-based visas, and how they differ from those of permanent US residents and natives. Using aggregate data, studies reveal no negative impacts of the temporary H-1B program on wages.[25] Yet, Hamm and Herbst describe abusive employer treatment of temporary workers, who often are paid less, lack healthcare benefits, are mandated to pay excessive fees, and/or are not paid in between successive projects.[26]

In a first attempt to reconcile these findings, Gass-Kandilov uses data from the 2003 NIS to compare immigrants' initial wages at entry to their wages after receiving permanent residency.[27] Consistent with Hamm and Herbst,[28] she reports immigrants enjoying a substantial (18–25 percent) wage gain between their first and most recent job—a gain attributed to migrants' green card acquisition. Similarly, Lowell and Avato document how, despite earnings less than those of permanent immigrants or natives, foreign students and temporary workers enjoy higher earnings as their visa status becomes permanent.[29]

Mukhopadhyay and Oxborrow examine whether immigrants who are temporary workers actually earn less than those who received employment-based permanent residency. Using the 2003 NIS data and propensity-score matching, they find that receiving a work-based permanent residency visa results in an annual wage gain of approximately $11,000—a finding that "confirms popular belief . . . that H-1B workers are paid less than native workers."[30] In this volume, Lowell reports that temporary skilled workers earn significantly less than native- and foreign-born local workers such that young Indian-born H-1Bs concentrated in the IT sector earn less than native workers. Thomas, also in this volume, finds that African immigrants with STEM degrees earn more than those with non-STEM degrees, but the earnings premium disappears for college graduates who are overeducated for their jobs.

Although Mukhopadhyay and Oxborrow suggest that increasing the number of work-based permanent immigrant visas will help resolve this problem, others suggest reforming temporary worker visas.[31] In that vein, Orrenius et al. advocate for adjudicating high- and low-skilled visas (H-1Bs, H-2As, and H-2Bs) using an auction system that would subsequently raise government revenue, increase efficiency, and boost GDP.[32] Similarly, Casella and Cox suggest a system of auctioning pre-contract visas to firms, which would permit trading of these visas on a secondary market and transferring visa ownership to workers after employers sign contracts.[33]

Impacts of High-Skilled Immigration

A prolific literature has also examined the labor market outcomes of immigrants in STEM occupations, as well as with H-1B visas. For example, Hanson and Slaughter find strong positive impacts of high-skilled immigration for US native employment in STEM occupations.[34] They also report that wage differences between immigrants and natives in

STEM jobs were much smaller than in non-STEM jobs, and that immigrant workers in STEM jobs reached wage parity with natives more quickly than immigrants in non-STEM jobs. In a similar vein, Peri et al. find that STEM employment boosts total productivity growth in US cities.[35] Increases in the number of STEM workers are associated with significant wage gains for college-educated natives and smaller gains for non–college educated natives. In a second study, Peri and colleagues analyze how random H-1B visa variation across US cities affects labor market outcomes for computer-related workers.[36] Overall, negative H-1B supply shocks are associated with declines in foreign-born and native-born computer-related employment. Kerr and Lincoln consider the impact of high-skilled immigrants on technology formation.[37] Although higher H-1B admissions increase immigrant employment in science and engineering—as well as patenting by inventors with Indian and Chinese names by retaining foreign talent that contributes to innovation and growth—it has a limited impact on native employment or patenting.

Entering the United States as a foreign student often leads to work in high-skilled occupations, although a student visa, by itself, only offers temporary US residence. Using the 2003 National Survey of College Graduates, Hunt reports that immigrants who first enter the United States with a student or trainee visa enjoy higher wages and carry out more patenting, licensing, and publishing activities than natives, although part of this advantage is due to differences in human capital between the two groups.[38] In subsequent work, Hunt and Xie find that the mobility of skilled workers with temporary visas is comparable to that of natives, and that voluntary job changing increases when immigrants' immigration status becomes permanent.[39] Shih examines the effect that foreign students have on native enrollment in higher education.[40] Between 1995 and 2005, the relationship between foreign students and native enrollment was positive, suggesting foreign student tuition payments help offset the diminishing public funding of many universities.

A number of studies have documented the negative impacts of lowering the H-1B visa cap, including the presence of less foreign intellectual capital in the United States.[41] Others argue that lowering the H-1B visa cap discourages high-skilled foreign students from studying in the United States,[42] curtailing international student enrollments,[43] and reducing innovation in US science and engineering departments.[44] A recent study, however, reports mixed results. Mayda et al. find less international worker hiring in the private sector at the top and bottom of the wage distribution.[45] However, the lower H-1B visa caps were not associated with reductions in the hiring of H-1B skilled workers from India, workers in computer occupations, or among companies that intensively use the H-1B program.

Impacts of Low-Skilled Immigration

Although fewer in number, several studies have also examined the labor market impacts of low-skilled immigration. For instance, Cortés reports that a 10 percent increase in the share of low-skilled immigrants in the labor force lowers the price of immigrant-intensive services, such as gardening and housekeeping, by 2 percent.[46] In follow-up work, Cortés and Tessada estimate the effects of low-skilled immigration for high-skilled native women.[47] They find that the increased supply of low-skilled immigrants shifts the time use decisions of high-skilled women who reduce their time doing domestic work and increase their expenditures on domestic help. Amuedo-Dorantes and Sevilla underscore an additional channel, namely, a reduction in the time allocated to basic (as opposed to educational or recreational) childcare by college-educated mothers of non–school-aged children.[48]

Orrenius and Zavodny examine employer demand for temporary immigrant workers as unauthorized migration has declined.[49] When labor markets are strong and productivity is high, they report greater use by employers of H-2A and H-2B visa programs. The analysis also suggests that employers do not view these visa programs as alternatives to unauthorized migration, given that visas are not related to the numbers of less-educated US natives or Latin American immigrants in the labor force, or to the use of employment verification mandates (E-Verify), which should reduce the hiring of unauthorized immigrants.[50] However, Amuedo-Dorantes et al. find that, as enforcement intensifies, firms boost their demand for low-skilled foreign-born labor under the H-2B visa program.[51]

Immigration Multipliers, Backlogs, and Other Dynamics

Jasso and colleagues have published a variety of papers that offer important insights about dynamics of the authorized US visa system. For example, using longitudinal data on the 1971 cohort of legal immigrants and the 1970 census data, Jasso and Rosenzweig reveal that the immigration multiplier, e.g., the number of legal immigrants whose permanent residence derives from family reunification, varied by visa category but was lower than expected.[52] In a second study using 1977 longitudinal immigrant cohort data, Jasso and Rosenzweig compare initial and long-term occupational outcomes of immigrants who entered with work and family visas.[53] They report a narrowing of differences between the two groups due to occupational downgrading among work-based immigrants and occupational upgrading among family-based immigrants.

In one of the first published longitudinal studies of immigrant permanent residents, the New Immigrant Survey, Jasso et al. describe how visa categories of couples, such as those with one spouse who was the US citizen sponsor and those in which both spouses are immigrants, influence the dynamics of families.[54] Combining data from the NIS and administrative sources, they report that one-third of immigrant adults who received permanent residency visas in 1996 had previous unauthorized experience.[55] Jasso et al. examine the numbers of high-skilled immigrants waiting for legal permanent residence and find significant visa backlogs.[56] High-skilled immigrants far exceed the number of available employment-based permanent residency visas. Other findings using the NIS show that previous unauthorized entry has no effect on the wages of immigrant permanent residents after they are legalized.[57]

Other Related Findings

Other studies address a variety of important research questions. For instance, Bhatti (in this volume) examines highly skilled Pakistani women immigrants who experience devaluation of their foreign-earned degrees. Obinna uses data from the US Citizenship and Immigrant Services Performance Analysis System to describe approved, pending, and denied legal permanent residency applications between 1992 and 2006.[58]

Finding lengthy wait times for many immigrants, she suggests the visa queues lower immigrants' chances of upward mobility and successful integration. Logan and Thomas find evidence that suggests diversity visas are heavily skills-selective, resulting in the outmigration of highly skilled persons in well-paying jobs from Africa to the United States.[59] Using interview data from Indian-born IT workers with H-1B visas, Banerjee describes incidents of low wages and exploitative working conditions that involve frequent relocations without employment benefits.[60] Other work also suggests that the H-1B visa program governs more than immigrant entry, leading to subversive self-employment,[61] transcultural parenting,[62] and gendered experiences among dependent spouses.[63] Finally, Lee shows that, in 2004, children with fathers who arrived with student or tourist visas have greater odds of college attainment.[64]

Patterns and Trends in Visa Use

Next, we examine recent trends in US immigrant and nonimmigrant visas to understand how much change has occurred in the use of various visa types and in the national origin composition of visa recipients. For all the analyses, we rely on two data sources. For nonimmigrant visas, we use data on nonimmigrant visa issuances available from the US Department of State (DOS) for the 1997–2018 period. These data provide a better estimate of the number of beneficiaries of nonimmigrant visas than nonimmigrant admission data, which tend to be inflated and capture crossings as opposed to individual visa recipients.[65] For immigrant visas, we use data on the number of legal permanent residency visas issued (or the number of persons who obtained legal permanent residency) for the 2002–2017 period, which are available from the Department of Homeland Security.[66]

Together, data on nonimmigrant visa issuances from 1997 to 2018 and on types of immigrant entries from 2002 to 2017 contain information by detailed class of admission, permitting classification of visa issuances into broad categories. For example, for the number of low-skilled temporary worker visa issuances, we include H-2A and H-2B visas for agricultural and unskilled seasonal workers, H2R visas for returning unskilled seasonal workers, as well A-3 and G-5 visas. The latter two visa types are for attendants and employees of ambassadors, ministers, diplomats, consular officers, and other government officials and their families; and for employees or local workers of foreign nationals who are permanent members of a diplomatic mission, official government representatives, or those appointed to an international organization in the United States. Among high-skilled temporary worker visas, we include H-1B and related H-1BI, H-1C, H3 visas, as well as A1, A2, G1, I, L1, O1, O2, P1, P2, P3, R1, S5, S6, and TN visas. Generally speaking, all visas in this category are issued to high-skilled professionals, although there are some exceptions.[67]

Below we describe overall trends in nonimmigrant and immigrant visa use, and how it varies by national origin. We then discuss the estimates from fixed-effects panel data regressions modeling visa numbers as a function of specific country-of-origin attributes, US presidential administrations, and the 2008–2009 Great Recession.

Descriptive Findings

Figure 4.1 describes trends in nonimmigrant visas from 1997–2018 and in immigrant visas from 2002–2017. Early in the 2000s, trends in the two visa types move closely together but, after the Great Recession, the number of nonimmigrant visas increased considerably. Specifically, between 2009 and 2015, their numbers rose from 6 million to 11 million. Since then, the number of nonimmigrant visas declined to about 10 million. In contrast, immigrant visas fluctuated less, hovering around one million per year since 2004.

Figure 4.2 describes trends in different types of nonimmigrant employment visas. Between 1997 and 2018, the number of temporary nonimmigrant work-based visas grew from approximately 300,000 to 800,000. Moreover, high-skilled visas outnumbered low-skilled visas every year. However, during the Great Recession, the number of both high- and low-skilled visas declined. Although both types of work visas rose again after 2009, growth in low-skilled visas outpaced that for high-skilled visas. Between 2010 and 2015, low-skilled visas rose from 100,000 to almost 300,000, relative to the increase from 300,000 to 400,000 for high-skilled visas. In that regard, low-skilled employment visas appear especially responsive to the economic recovery that followed the Great Recession.

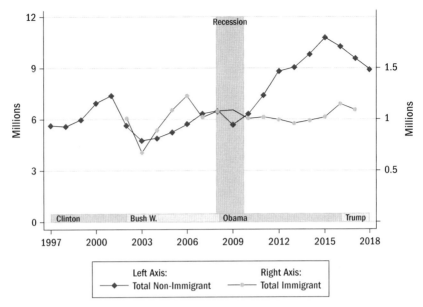

Figure 4.1: Nonimmigrant and Immigrant Visas, 1997–2018. Source: US Department of State, Bureau of Consular Affairs, Nonimmigrant Visa Statistics, FY1997–2018 NIV Detail; US Department of Homeland Security, Office of Immigration Statistics, Office of Strategy, Policy & Plans, Annual Flow Reports: Lawful Permanent Residents, August 2018.

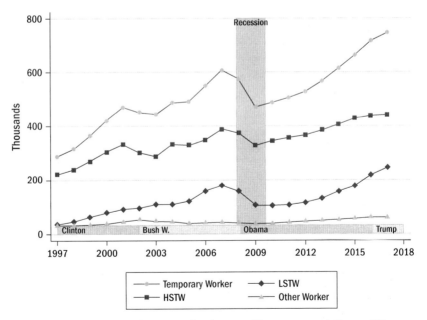

Figure 4.2: Nonimmigrant Temporary Employment Visas, 1997–2018. Source: US Department of State, Bureau of Consular Affairs, Nonimmigrant Visa Statistics, FY1997–2018 NIV Detail.

Figure 4.3 describes trends in low-skilled employment visas by the top ten immigrant national origins. Here, the story is quite clear. Since 1997, especially after 2009, low-skilled temporary visas—most of which are for unskilled seasonal agricultural workers—were increasingly issued to Mexicans. Between 2009 and 2018, visas issued to Mexicans increased from 130,000 to almost 250,000. In comparison, trends in this visa category for migrants from other national origins remained fairly unchanged.

Figure 4.4 describes shifts in high-skilled temporary nonimmigrant work visas by national origin. Migrants born in India are the main recipients of high-skilled nonimmigrant visas. This finding is consistent with the much larger numbers of H-1B petitions filed by Indian migrants since 2007, as reported by the US Citizenship and Immigration Statistics (USCIS). After the Great Recession, there were also some small increases in the number of high-skilled nonimmigrant visas issued to Mexican and Chinese migrants.

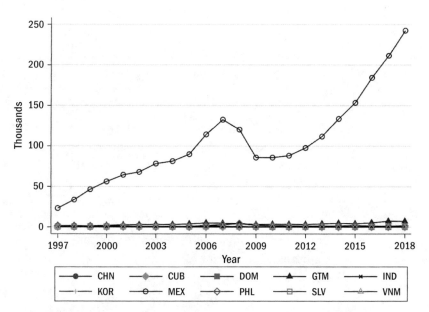

Figure 4.3: Low-Skilled Temporary Employment Visas by National Origin, 1997–2018. Source: US Department of State, Bureau of Consular Affairs, Nonimmigrant Visa Statistics, FY1997–2018 NIV Detail.

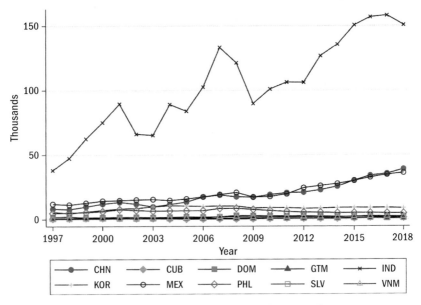

Figure 4.4: High-Skilled Temporary Employment Visas by National Origin, 1997–2018. Source: US Department of State, Bureau of Consular Affairs, Nonimmigrant Visa Statistics, FY1997–2018 NIV Detail.

Figures 4.5a and 4.5b describe similar trends in student and exchange visas by national origin. Prior to the Great Recession, no single nation stood out as the main recipient of either type of visa. However, student and exchange visas issued to Chinese migrants grew rapidly after the Great Recession. Between 2008 and 2015, the number of student visas issued to Chinese migrants rose from 50,000 to almost 275,000. Similarly, between 2006 and 2015, the number of exchange visas issued to Chinese migrants quadrupled from 10,000 to 40,000.

Figure 4.6 depicts trends in six types of immigrant visas. The volume of these visas is rather small when compared to nonimmigrant visas. However, although immigrant visas are rather stable for most of the period, a notable change occurred between 2002 and 2007. Permanent family-based, employment-based, and refugee/asylum visas dropped between 2002 and 2003, following the events of September 11. Nevertheless, the three types of immigrant visas rebounded during the 2003–2006 period of fast economic growth. In addition, during the

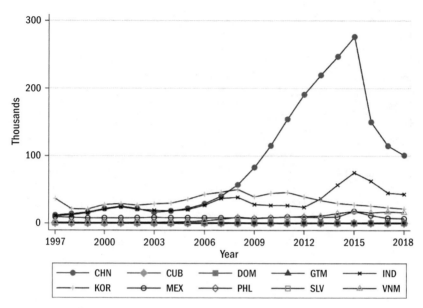

Figure 4.5a: Student Visas by National Origin, 1997–2018. Source: US Department of State, Bureau of Consular Affairs, Nonimmigrant Visa Statistics, FY1997–2018 NIV Detail.

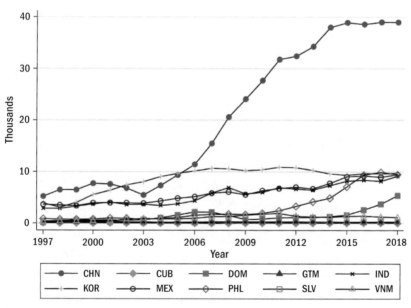

Figure 4.5b: Exchange Visas by National Origin, 1997–2018. Source: US Department of State, Bureau of Consular Affairs, Nonimmigrant Visa Statistics, FY1997–2018 NIV Detail.

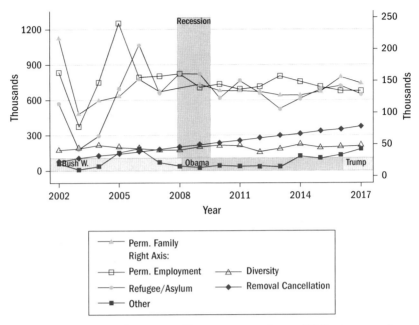

Figure 4.6: Main Types of Immigrant Visas, 2002–2017. Source: US Department of Homeland Security, Office of Immigration Statistics, Office of Strategy, Policy & Plans, "Annual Flow Reports: Lawful Permanent Residents," August 2018.

2002–2017 period, the number of removal cancellation visas steadily increased and diversity and other immigrant visas remained stable.

Figures 4.7 and 4.8 reveal differences by national origin for various types of permanent visas, including employment-based, family-based, diversity, and cancellations of removals visas. Starting with employment-based visas, the main recipients were migrants from India, China, South Korea, the Philippines, and Mexico. In contrast, most immigrant family–based visas went to Mexicans. Figure 4.8 also shows that diversity visas issued to Cubans ebbed and flowed. Recent growth is linked to Cuba's removal, in 2013, of travel restrictions that had been placed on its citizens. After eliminating these restrictions, Cubans became able to leave for the United States without an exit permit. Together with new diplomatic relations announced in 2014, diversity visas issued to Cubans grew. From January to March 2015, 9,900 Cubans entered the United States, more than double the 4,746 who arrived during the same

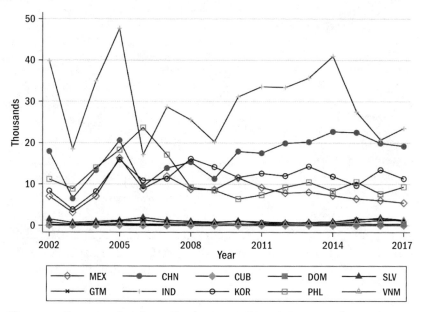

Figure 4.7a: Permanent Immigrant Employment and Family Visas: Employment Visas. Source: US Department of Homeland Security, Office of Immigration Statistics, Office of Strategy, Policy & Plans, "Annual Flow Reports: Lawful Permanent Residents," August 2018.

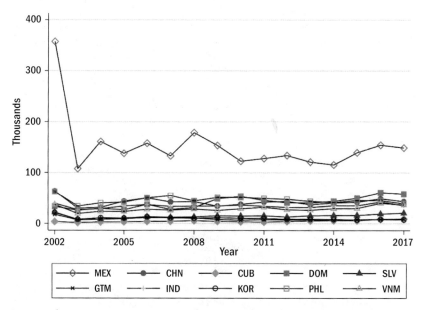

Figure 4.7b: Permanent Immigrant Employment and Family Visas: Family-Based Visas. Source: US Department of Homeland Security, Office of Immigration Statistics, Office of Strategy, Policy & Plans, "Annual Flow Reports: Lawful Permanent Residents," August 2018.

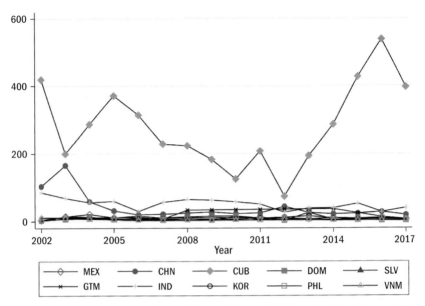

Figure 4.8a: Diversity Visas and Cancellation of Removals: Diversity Visas. Source: US Department of Homeland Security, Office of Immigration Statistics, Office of Strategy, Policy & Plans, "Annual Flow Reports: Lawful Permanent Residents," August 2018.

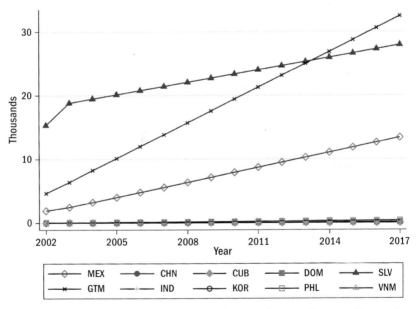

Figure 4.8b: Diversity Visas and Cancellation of Removals: Cancellations of Removals. Source: US Department of Homeland Security, Office of Immigration Statistics, Office of Strategy, Policy & Plans, "Annual Flow Reports: Lawful Permanent Residents," August 2018.

period in 2014. Finally, since 2002, three groups have received the greatest number of visas related to cancellations of removals: Salvadorians, Guatemalans, and Mexicans.

In sum, nonimmigrant visas have exhibited significant fluctuations. In what follows, we attempt to gain a deeper understanding about how unobserved and observed country-specific factors, as well as different US presidential administrations and the Great Recession, are related to visa trends.

Multivariate Results

In this section, we present findings from fixed-effects panel data models that account for country-specific traits associated with the volume of visas in each category, and the roles played by the Great Recession and recent US administrations. Specifically, we estimate the following benchmark model via Ordinary Least Squares (OLS) using data on approximately 200 countries in the 1997–2018 period when working with nonimmigrant visas, and in the 2002–2017 period when focusing on immigrant visas:

$$(1) \quad Y_{ct} = \alpha + X_{ct}\beta + Z_t^{U.S.}\gamma + d_c + d_t + u_{ct}$$

The vector Y_{ct} stands for the log volume of each type of visa granted to country c in year t. We first examine total, nonimmigrants, and immigrant visas. Subsequently, we distinguish among types of nonimmigrant visas, such as family, employment, low- and high-skilled work, student/exchange, tourism, visa waiver, and special visas. In the case of immigrant visas, we distinguish among family, employment, diversity, refugee/asylum, removal cancellation, and other visas.

We account for several country-specific and US-related factors potentially influencing the volume of any visa category. In particular, the vector X_{ct} contains information on country-specific and time-varying economic, developmental, and political traits that are often associated with migration flows. The latter include the origin country's Gross Domestic Product (GDP) per capita; its unemployment rate; its Human Development Index (HDI);[68] and an indicator of whether, politically, the country could be considered free (or somewhat free) versus not free.

GDP per capita, unemployment rates, and the HDI are all included in logs to facilitate the interpretation of the estimates as elasticities.

Next, the vector $Z_t^{U.S.}$ contains dummy variables indicating whether visas were granted during the Great Recession (i.e., 2008 and 2009), and/or during a specific US administration (i.e., Clinton, George W. Bush, Obama, or Trump administrations). These indicators tell us whether and how various US economic and political events are associated with the volume of visas issued.

Because we are working with panel data, equation (1) also includes a vector of year dummies (d_t) and a vector of country-specific fixed effects (dc) to account for unobserved country-level heterogeneity related to visa volumes. Finally, the vector u_{ct} is the idiosyncratic or time-varying error. Equation (1) is estimated using OLS, allowing for arbitrary correlations between country fixed-effect and other explanatory variables in equation (1) in any given period.

Table 4.2 shows the estimated coefficients from estimating our model using all visas, and separately for nonimmigrant and immigrant visas. Only total visa issuances prove sensitive to the state of the US economy, declining by 24 percent during the Great Recession. However, the issuance of nonimmigrant visas was higher during President Clinton's administration when compared to President George W. Bush's administration.

Table 4.2 also provides some information about the role played by the country of origin's socioeconomic and political traits. Richer countries receive a larger volume of nonimmigrant visas. A 10 percent increase in GDP per capita is associated with a 3 percent higher volume of nonimmigrant visas, but a 3 percent lower volume of immigrant visas. Aligned with the impact of higher GDP per capita on nonimmigrant visas, the estimates in table 4.2 reveal that a 10 percent increase in unemployment is associated with a 1.5 percent lower volume of nonimmigrant visas. Finally, table 4.2 also provides evidence of the importance of socioeconomic development as captured by the HDI. A 10 percent increase in the HDI (where a higher value indicates a higher human development level) is correlated to a 36 percent higher volume of immigrant visas and a 14 percent higher volume of nonimmigrant visas. In other words, migrants are more likely to originate from countries with higher human development indexes.

TABLE 4.2: Fixed-Effects Panel Data Model of Total, Immigrant, and Nonimmigrant Visas

	Total	Immigrant	Nonimmigrant
Recession	−0.243*	−0.114	0.0257
	(0.137)	(0.181)	(0.0189)
Clinton[a]	—	—	0.281***
			(0.0410)
Obama[a]	0.376	0.409	−0.172
	(0.275)	(0.323)	(0.112)
Trump[a]	0.414	0.442	0.0331
	(0.275)	(0.325)	(0.129)
Log GDP Per Capita	0.195	−0.349*	0.339***
	(0.139)	(0.202)	(0.121)
Log Unemployment Rate	−0.106	0.0404	−0.150**
	(0.0903)	(0.104)	(0.0740)
Log HDI	0.332	3.642***	1.355***
	(0.815)	(1.324)	(0.428)
Freedom index (not free)[b]	−0.115	−0.183	−0.0168
	(0.0918)	(0.186)	(0.0522)
Observations (c,t)	2,698	2,698	3,589
R-squared	0.079	0.052	0.123
Number of Countries	170	170	173

Source: Derived from a dataset that the authors compiled from various sources, including US Department of State, Bureau of Consular Affairs, Nonimmigrant Visa Statistics, FY1997–2018 NIV Detail, and US Department of Homeland Security, Office of Immigration Statistics, Office of Strategy, Policy & Plans, "Annual Flow Reports: Lawful Permanent Residents," August 2018.
Notes: [a]Reference group is Bush W.
[b]Reference group is somewhat free.
All models include country of origin and year fixed effects, and a constant term. Robust standard errors in parentheses ***$p < 0.01$, **$p < 0.05$, *$p < 0.1$.

In sum, several socioeconomic and political factors related to migrants' home countries, as well as in the United States, are associated with the volume of immigrant and nonimmigrant visas. Because relevant factors may differ by type of visa, tables 4.3 and 4.4 further differentiate by type of nonimmigrant and immigrant visa.

Based on estimates in table 4.3, the state of the US economy correlates with the number of nonimmigrant visas issued in some categories.

TABLE 4.3: Fixed-Effects Panel Data Model of Total Nonimmigrant Visas by Type

Dependent Variable	Total	Employment	LS Worker	HS Worker
Recession	0.0257	0.0140	0.900**	0.00331
	(0.0189)	(0.0313)	(0.396)	(0.0313)
Clinton[a]	0.281***	−0.0952***	0.122	−0.0341
	(0.0410)	(0.0275)	(0.261)	(0.0266)
Obama[a]	−0.172	−0.216	−1.982***	−0.179
	(0.112)	(0.143)	(0.459)	(0.143)
Trump[a]	0.0331	−0.262	−1.443***	−0.283*
	(0.129)	(0.167)	(0.497)	(0.167)
Log GDP Per Capita	0.339***	0.278	0.768*	0.259
	(0.121)	(0.237)	(0.460)	(0.238)
Log Unemployment Rate	−0.150**	−0.0806	0.426	−0.0689
	(0.0740)	(0.0555)	(0.316)	(0.0569)
Log HDI	1.355***	1.885***	−2.983	2.218***
	(0.428)	(0.465)	(2.087)	(0.468)
Freedom Index (not free)[b]	−0.0168	−0.154**	−0.222	−0.176***
	(0.0522)	(0.0614)	(0.468)	(0.0641)
Observations (c,t)	3,589	3,589	3,589	3,589
R-squared	0.123	0.093	0.049	0.092
Number of Countries	173	173	173	173

Source: Derived from a dataset that the authors compiled from various sources, including US Department of State, Bureau of Consular Affairs, Nonimmigrant Visa Statistics, FY1997–2018 NIV Detail, and US Department of Homeland Security, Office of Immigration Statistics, Office of Strategy, Policy & Plans, "Annual Flow Reports: Lawful Permanent Residents," August 2018.
Notes: [a]Reference group is Bush W.
[b]Reference group is somewhat free.
All models include country of origin and year fixed-effects, and a constant term. Robust standard errors in parentheses ***$p < 0.01$, **$p < 0.05$, *$p < 0.1$.

For instance, low-skilled worker visas increased by close to 90 percent during the Great Recession—supporting the notion that employers are seeking temporary labor that can easily be dismissed during uncertain economic times. In contrast, exchange student visas declined by almost 7 percent.

We also observe how visa categories fluctuated differently across the various US administrations. Nonimmigrant visas rose during the Clin-

Other Worker	Student	Exchange	Tourist	Spouses	Other
−0.0858	0.106	−0.0692**	0.0748***	−0.0872	−2.886***
(0.317)	(0.0784)	(0.0300)	(0.0272)	(0.218)	(0.400)
−3.095***	0.253**	0.0660	0.406***	−0.364***	-0.0363
(0.336)	(0.105)	(0.135)	(0.0585)	(0.124)	(0.134)
−3.669***	-0.177	0.561**	−0.242*	−0.503*	3.951***
(0.506)	(0.206)	(0.237)	(0.136)	(0.294)	(0.612)
−2.696***	−0.131	0.642**	0.0979	-0.540	3.721***
(0.596)	(0.213)	(0.267)	(0.163)	(0.330)	(0.734)
1.151**	0.424**	0.0176	0.321**	0.0573	0.202
(0.489)	(0.194)	(0.161)	(0.144)	(0.268)	(0.488)
−0.0962	0.102	−0.0177	−0.253**	0.110	−0.313
(0.320)	(0.0939)	(0.107)	(0.105)	(0.175)	(0.518)
2.195	1.780**	1.070	1.607***	-0.388	2.330
(2.075)	(0.755)	(0.827)	(0.537)	(0.879)	(3.054)
0.505	0.222*	−0.0963	−0.0136	0.0609	−0.665
(0.555)	(0.127)	(0.0844)	(0.0642)	(0.303)	(0.521)
3,589	3,589	3,589	3,589	3,589	3,589
0.08	0.058	0.072	0.100	0.011	0.246
173	173	173	173	173	173

ton administration, driven by increases in student visas (by 25 percent) and tourist visas (by 41 percent), despite some reductions in employment and spouse visas, for example. And, relative to the Bush administration, the Obama administration witnessed significant increases in exchange and other nonimmigrant visas but lower volumes of low-skilled worker visas, those for other workers, and tourist and spouse visas. Finally, the volume of exchange and other nonimmigrant visas rose during the

TABLE 4.4: Fixed-Effects Panel Data Model of Total Immigrant Visas by Type

Dependent Variable	Total	Family	Employment	Diversity	Refugee/ Asylum	Removal Cancella- tion	Other
Recession	−0.114	0.0544	0.175	−0.0737	0.346	−0.0376	0.248
	(0.181)	(0.176)	(0.145)	(0.199)	(0.247)	(0.163)	(0.214)
Obama[a]	0.409	0.146	0.504***	0.590	0.250	−1.335***	0.649
	(0.323)	(0.329)	(0.190)	(0.359)	(0.496)	(0.421)	(0.437)
Trump[a]	0.442	0.130	0.586***	0.129	0.0700	−1.563***	−0.153
	(0.325)	(0.345)	(0.205)	(0.425)	(0.507)	(0.448)	(0.479)
Log GDP Per Capita	−0.349*	−0.510**	−0.516**	−0.777**	−0.179	−1.208***	−0.330
	(0.202)	(0.241)	(0.242)	(0.391)	(0.389)	(0.405)	(0.474)
Log Unem- ployment Rate	0.0404	0.0467	−0.137	0.145	−0.149	−0.000539	0.369
	(0.104)	(0.168)	(0.0915)	(0.210)	(0.200)	(0.290)	(0.569)
Log HDI	3.642***	7.105**	2.432*	5.262**	4.037*	5.324*	9.570**
	(1.324)	(3.294)	(1.395)	(2.644)	(2.203)	(2.911)	(4.554)
Freedom Index (not free)[b]	−0.183	−0.282	0.0237	−0.0178	−0.113	−0.517	0.432
	(0.186)	(0.353)	(0.130)	(0.250)	(0.268)	(0.419)	(0.405)
Observa- tions (c,t)	2,698	2,698	2,698	2,698	2,698	2,698	2,698
R-squared	0.052	0.063	0.065	0.024	0.041	0.120	0.090
Number of Countries	170	170	170	170	170	170	170

Source: Derived from a dataset that the authors compiled from various sources, including US Department of State, Bureau of Consular Affairs, Nonimmigrant Visa Statistics, FY1997–2018 NIV Detail, and US Department of Homeland Security, Office of Immigration Statistics, Office of Strategy, Policy & Plans, "Annual Flow Reports: Lawful Permanent Residents," August 2018.

Notes: [a]Reference group is Bush W.

[b]Reference group is somewhat free.

All models include country of origin and year fixed-effects, and a constant term. Robust standard errors in parentheses ***$p < 0.01$, **$p < 0.05$, *$p < 0.1$.

Trump administration, when compared to the Bush administration; however, the opposite is true for low-skilled, high-skilled, and other worker visas.

Among the various country-specific traits playing a significant role in observed visa trends is the role of GDP per capita. Low-skilled and other worker visas, as well as student and tourist visas, rise by approximately 8 percent, 11 percent, 4 percent, and 3 percent, respectively, when GDP per capita increases by 10 percent. In addition, a larger volume of student visas is issued to countries that rank high on freedom, whereas the opposite is true for worker visas.

Consistent with the descriptive results, estimates in table 4.4 display no evidence of a statistically significant association between the Great Recession and the volume of immigrant visas. However, once again, immigrant visas fluctuate across US administrations. For instance, compared to the Bush administration, the Obama and Trump administrations granted anywhere between 50 percent and 59 percent more employment-based immigrant visas. Cancellations of removals, however, were lower.

Other traits predictive of the volume of immigrant visas include the home country's GDP and HDI. A 10 percent increase in the home country's GDP per capita lowers the volume of immigrant visas by 3.5 percent—a reduction driven by decreases in the number of family-based, employment, diversity, and cancellation of removal visas. Perhaps most interesting is the positive correlation between HDI and the volume of immigrant visas granted to a country. A 10 percent increase in the HDI is associated with a 36 percent higher volume of immigrant visas—an effect that stems from a 71 percent increase in family-based visas, a 24 percent rise in employment-based visas, a 53 percent growth in diversity visas, a 40 percent increase in refugee/asylum visas, and a 53 percent surge in cancellation of removals.

Discussion and Conclusion

In this chapter, we have examined recent shifts in the US visa system. We describe how the visa system increasingly reflects an interaction between policies derived from congressional legislation, and policies and practices embedded in executive orders and actions implemented by different presidential administrations. We use visa data to examine shifts across roughly two decades, and analyze whether and how the numbers and types of visas varied by national origin characteristics, US presidential administrations, and the Great Recession.

Descriptive findings point to dramatic growth in the number of temporary visas during the last fifteen years. The use of low-skilled temporary visas grew among Mexican-origin migrants, who, in any given year, relied more on these visas than any other national origin group. Similarly, the use of high-skilled temporary work visas rose among Indian-origin migrants, who relied on these visas much more than any other national origin group. Since 2011, Mexican and Chinese immigrants also increasingly entered with high-skilled temporary work visas. In addition, growing numbers of Chinese immigrants entered with temporary student and exchange visas, although their use of student visas peaked in 2015 and dropped by more than half afterward. However, for both visa types, the use by Chinese immigrants tripled or more after 2008.

We then examined US visa categories as a way to understand broad issues of concern for social scientists, such as inequality and labor demand for immigrants and presidential preferences. Our findings show how visa issuance has shifted in response to changes in migrants' country of origin characteristics, US administrations, and the Great Recession. Despite no major legislative change in the US visa system since 1990, visa issuance declined by 24 percent during the Great Recession. In the case of nonimmigrant visas, the decline was particularly noticeable among exchange visas, although visas for low-skilled workers and tourists rose. In addition, perhaps due to their long-term nature, immigrant visas did not significantly change as a result of the Great Recession.

We also uncover evidence of shifts in both nonimmigrant and immigrant visas across US administrations. For example, the Clinton administration issued more nonimmigrant visas, especially student and tourist visas, but fewer nonimmigrant visas for work-related purposes or for spouses. In addition, compared to the Bush administration, fewer high-skilled visas were issued during the Trump administration, and fewer low-skilled visas were issued in both the Obama and Trump administrations. Immigrant visas rose during both the Obama and Trump administrations compared to the Bush administration, led by increases in the number of employment visas. Finally, nonimmigrant visas rose with the per capita GDP of migrants' countries of origin, whereas the opposite is true for immigrant visas. In a similar vein, the volume of visas is positively correlated to migrants' country of origin development indexes—a finding that addresses concerns by some that visas are more likely to go to countries with lower levels of human capital development.

Thus, despite the lack of legislative policy reform during the last three decades, our findings reveal substantial shifts in the legal visa system. Some types of nonimmigrant visas seem especially sensitive to economic conditions and have shifted upward (low-skilled and tourists) or downward (exchange visas) during the Great Recession. Low-skilled and other work-related nonimmigrant visas declined during recent administrations, but permanent immigrant work-related visas rose during both the Obama and Trump administrations. The consistent and strong associations between the Human Development Index and visa issuance suggest that most legal migrants are not coming from the poorest countries. Overall, the substantial shifts in visa issuances—in the absence of legislative reforms—are symptomatic of differential levels of access to visa issuance.

Our analysis faces several limitations. First, nonimmigrant visa issuance data are, at best, an imperfect indicator of the number of persons who are the beneficiaries of certain types of nonimmigrant visas. Costa and Rosenbaum note that visa issuance data slightly overcount the number of high-skilled H-1B visas each year, and that the best data would derive from petitions that USCIS approve for H-1Bs.[69] Unfortunately, these data are difficult to obtain for years prior to 2010. This shortcoming is less serious for this analysis, given our focus on understanding overall visa trends rather than modeling visa issuance. A second limitation relates to the timing of the data. Because we are only able to capture three years of the Trump administration, which is when backlogs in some visa categories grew, our estimates should be interpreted cautiously. Indeed, one highly publicized shift that occurred during the Trump administration was prolonged processing times for most visas, which is likely to influence the data used in our analysis. Finally, we urge readers to remember that our analysis aims to display correlations, rather than to assess causality.

Despite these limitations, the analysis suggests that presidential actions and preferences underlie an upward shift in nonimmigrant visas.

During the last two decades, as the United States has become embroiled in highly polarized immigration politics, presidential executive actions and preferences are important correlates of shifts in visa use. Exactly what influences these observed shifts is not clear. For example, we cannot decipher whether Mexican immigrants who entered with low-skill work visas are part of the growing return (voluntarily or via deportation) trend. It is also unclear whether Chinese immigrants who entered with high-skill, student or exchange visas have become increasingly likely to return. If one or both hold true, then upward shifts in entering the United States with temporary visas for some national origin groups may represent a shift toward temporary-migration-and-return rather than temporary-migration-and-permanent US residence. Although the latter has been true in the past for both Mexican and Chinese immigrants, our findings may reflect a new shift toward temporary-migration-and-return. If true, it will have large impacts on the US economy. More research in the future must consider this question.

Since 1990, the United States has been unable to create and implement legislative policy reform, which helps to explain the rising use of presidential executive orders and actions, as well as other correlates of visa-use trends.[70] One consequence is the creation of an unequal visa system that is strongly differentiated by individual and country characteristics, as well as preferences of the administration in place. Some may posit that legislative reform is no longer needed, given that system change can occur through other means. Yet, US courts have ruled that the power for changing the immigration and naturalization system lies in the hands of Congress. We argue that the current US visa system—with its complex and contradictory forms of exclusion and inclusion—ultimately creates hardships for too many immigrants already in the United States and those hoping to enter in the future. For example, even if a migrant is highly successful after years of working with a skilled or unskilled employment visa, the current system does not offer them an opportunity to transition to a permanent visa. Only legislative reform can create a path to permanent residency for temporary workers, no matter how much they contribute to the United States. Only legislative reform can create new and dynamic mechanisms for legal US entry. Moreover, only legislative reform can resolve the underlying inequality in which the visa system exists.[71] Thus, until such reform occurs, the US visa system will remain one that is differentiated by political preferences and socioeconomic conditions that fail to account for the long-term benefits of immigration.

NOTES

1 We are very grateful to Vincent Ta for his expert assistance with the data management and statistical analysis that appear in this chapter. We are also grateful to the editors of this volume for their insightful comments, and to our universities for their generous support of this work.

2 Marc R. Rosenblum, "U.S. Immigration Reform: Can the System Be Repaired?" The Center for Comparative Immigration Studies, *CCIS Working Paper* 132 (January 2006), https://escholarship.org.

3 See Katharine M. Donato and Catalina Amuedo-Dorantes, eds., "The Legal Landscape of U.S. Immigration in the Twenty-First Century," *RSF: The Russell Sage Foundation Journal of the Social Sciences* 6, no. 3 (2020): 1–16.

4 Katharine M. Donato and Catalina Amuedo-Dorantes, "The Legal Landscape of U.S. Immigration: An Introduction," *RSF: The Russell Sage Foundation Journal of the Social Sciences* 6, no. 3 (2020): 2.

5 Mat Coleman and Austin Kocher, "Detention, Deportation, Devolution and Immigrant Incapacitation in the U.S., Post 9/11," *Geographical Journal* 177, no. 3 (2011): 228–237.

6 Katharine M. Donato and Leslie Rodriguez, "Police Arrests in a Time of Uncertainty: The Impact of 287(g) on Arrests in a New Immigrant Gateway," *American Behavioral Scientist* 58, no. 13 (2014): 1696–1722; Katharine M. Donato and Amada Armenta, "What We Know About Unauthorized Migration," *Annual Review of Sociology* 37 (2011): 529–543.

7 Sarah Pierce, "Immigration-Related Policy Changes in the First Two Years of the Trump Administration," Migration Policy Institute (May 2019); Sarah Pierce and Jessica Bolter, "Dismantling and Reconstructing the U.S. Immigration System: A Catalog of Changes under the Trump Presidency," Migration Policy Institute (July 2020); Donato and Amuedo-Dorantes, "The Legal Landscape of U.S. Immigration."

8 Senator Alan Simpson, "Statement on Senate Floor during debate about conference reform for the Immigration Act of 1990, S17109," *Congressional Record* 136 (October 26, 1990), S17109. See also Muzaffar Chishti and Stephen Yale-Loehr, "The Immigration Act of 1990: Unfinished Business a Quarter-Century Later," Migration Policy Institute, *MPI Issue Brief* (July 2016), www.migrationpolicy.org.

9 Stephen Yale-Loehr, *Understanding the Immigration Act: A Practical Analysis* (Washington, DC: Federal Publications, 1991).

10 In "The Immigration Act of 1990," Chishti and Yale-Loehr note that the United States tightened security and limited applicants to the VW program by excluding foreign nationals from Iraq, Syria, Iran, or Sudan entering after March 1, 2011;

dual nationals from one of these four countries and a country listed in the visa waiver list; and persons visiting Libya, Somalia, or Yemen after March 1, 2011. The Travel Ban proclamation issued by the Trump administration and upheld by the Supreme Court in 2017 bans foreign nationals from Iran, Libya, North Korea, Somalia, Syria, and Yemen from receiving most types of nonimmigrant and immigrant visas. In addition, the Travel Ban barred certain Venezuelan government officials from receiving B1/B2 visas.

11 See figure 1 in Chishti and Yale-Loehr, "The Immigration Act of 1990."

12 Since 2011, the US Labor Department's Wage and Hourly Division has had authority to authorize U visas, and, in 2015, it also started certifying T visas. However, immediately after the Trump administration appointed a new division head in 2019, all U and T visa certifications granting temporary status to persons who were trafficked or faced other forms of mental and physical abuse were suspended, creating new backlogs in processing and approvals. See Ben Penn, "Human Trafficking Victims Blocked from Visas by Trump Wage Boss," *Bloomberg Law*, June 24, 2019, https://news.bloomberglaw.com. This example reveals how executive and legislative actions interact to affect visa allocation.

13 William A. Kandel, "Permanent Legal Immigration to the United States: Policy Overview," Congressional Research Service, *CRS Report* (May 11, 2018), https://fas.org.

14 Chishti and Yale-Loehr, "The Immigration Act of 1990."

15 For more details about work-based immigrant and nonimmigrant visas, see Daniel Costa, "Temporary Migrant Workers or Immigrants? The Question for U.S. Labor Migration," *RSF: The Russell Sage Foundation Journal of the Social Sciences* 6, no. 3 (2020): 18–44.

16 Jill H. Wilson, "Diversity Immigrants' Regions and Countries of Origin: Fact Sheet," Congressional Research Service, *CRS Report* (February 13, 2018), https://fas.org.

17 Congressional Research Service, "Iraqi and Afghan Special Immigrant Visa Programs," *CRS Report* (April 2, 2020), https://fas.org.

18 Harriet Orcutt Duleep and Mark C. Regets, "Admission Criteria and Immigrant Earnings Profiles," *International Migration Review* 30, no. 2 (1996): 571–590.

19 Harriet Orcutt Duleep and Mark C. Regets, "Earnings Convergence: Does It Matter Where Immigrants Come From or Why?" *Canadian Journal of Economics* 29, no. S1 (1996): 130–134.

20 Harriet Orcutt Duleep and Mark C. Regets, "Social Security and Immigrant Earnings," *Social Security Bulletin* 59, no. 2 (1996): 20–30.

21 Harriet Orcutt Duleep and Mark C. Regets, "The Decline in Immigrant Entry Earnings: Less Transferable Skills or Lower Ability?" *Quarterly Review of Economics and Finance* 37, no. S1 (1997): 189–208.

22 Harriet Orcutt Duleep and Mark C. Regets, "Measuring Immigrant Wage Growth Using Matched CPS Files," *Demography* 34 (1997): 239–249.

23 Julia Gelatt, "Do Employer-Sponsored Immigrants Fare Better in Labor Markets than Family-Sponsored Immigrants?" *RSF: The Russell Sage Foundation Journal of the Social Sciences* 6, no. 3 (2020): 70–93.

24 In addition to social science research, journalists have reported wage and other labor abuses of migrants with temporary work visas. See Costa, "Temporary Migrant Workers or Immigrants?" For example, some described how migrant agricultural workers with H-2A visas and migrants with H-2B visas doing other low-wage jobs had salaries withheld and experienced horrific working conditions, including threats of deportation, if they complained. In addition, US government inspectors did not often penalize employers for these conditions. For migrant professionals with H-1B visas, and for those with J-1 visas, reports also revealed wage abuses as well as workers being forced into trafficking.

25 B. Lindsay Lowell, "A Long View of America's Immigration Policy and the Supply of Foreign-born STEM Workers in the United States," *American Behavioral Scientist* 53, no. 7 (2010): 1029–1044; Madeline Zavodny, "The H-1B Program and Its Effects on Information Technology Workers," *Federal Reserve Bank of Atlanta Economic Review*, Third Quarter (2003); National Research Council, *Building a Workforce for the Information Economy* (Washington, DC: National Academic Press, 2001); Jacob F. Kirkegaard, "Outsourcing and Skill Imports: Foreign High-Skilled Workers on H-1B and L-1 Visas in the United States," *Institute for International Economics Working Paper* no. 05-15 (2005).

26 Moira Herbst and Steve Hamm, "America's High-Tech Sweatshops," *Bloomberg Businessweek*, October 1, 2009, www.bloomberg.com.

27 Amy Melissa Gass-Kandilov, "The Value of a Green Card: Immigrant Wage Increases Following Adjustment to U.S. Permanent Residence" (PhD diss., Department of Economics, University of Michigan, Ann Arbor, Michigan, 2007).

28 Herbst and Hamm, "America's High-Tech Sweatshops."

29 B. Lindsay Lowell and Johanna Avato, "The Wages of Skilled Temporary Migrants: Effects of Visa Pathways and Job Portability," *International Migration* 52, no. 3 (2013): 85–98.

30 Sankar Mukhopadhyay and David Oxborrow, "The Value of an Employment-Based Green Card," *Demography* 49, no. 1 (2012): 234.

31 Mukhopadhyay and Oxborrow, "The Value of an Employment-Based Green Card."

32 Pia Orrenius, Giovanni Peri, and Madeline Zavodny, "Proposal 12: Overhauling the Temporary Work Visa System," Brookings Institute, The Hamilton Project, 15 Ways to Rethink the Federal Budget (February 2013), www.brookings.edu.

33 Alessandra Casella and Adam Cox, "A Property Rights Approach to Temporary Work Visas," *Journal of Legal Studies* 47 (2018): 195–227.

34 Gordon H. Hanson and Matthew J. Slaughter, "High-Skilled Immigration and the Rise of STEM Occupations in U.S. Employment," National Bureau of Economic Research, *NBER Working Paper* 22623 (October 2016), www.nber.org.

35 Giovanni Peri, Kevin Shih, and Chad Sparber, "Stem Workers, H-1B Visas, and Productivity in US Cities," *Journal of Labor Economics* 33, no. S1 (2015): 225–255.

36 Giovanni Peri, Kevin Shih, and Chad Sparber, "Foreign and Native Skilled Workers: What Can We Learn from H-1B Lotteries?" National Bureau of Economic Research, *NBER Working Paper* 21175 (May 2015), www.nber.org.

37 William R. Kerr and William F. Lincoln, "The Supply Side of Innovation: H-1B Visas Reforms and U.S. Ethnic Invention," *Journal of Labor Economics* 28, no. 3 (2010): 473–508.

38 Jennifer Hunt, "Which Immigrants Are Most Innovative and Entrepreneurial? Distinctions by Entry Visa," *Journal of Labor Economics* 29, no. 3 (2011): 417–457.

39 Jennifer Hunt and Bin Xie, "How Restricted Is the Job Mobility of Skilled Temporary Work Visa Holders?" *Journal of Policy Analysis and Management* 38, no. 1 (2018): 41–64.

40 Kevin Shih, "Do International Students Crowd-Out or Cross-Subsidize Americans in Higher Education?" *Journal of Public Economics* 156 (2017): 170–184.

41 Jeffrey Gower, "As Dumb as We Wanna Be: U.S. H1-B Visa Policy and the 'Brain Blocking' of Asian Technology Professionals," *Rutgers Race and the Law Review* 12, no. 2 (2011): 243–269.

42 Takao Kato and Chad Sparber, "Quotas and Quality: The Effect of H-1B Visa Restrictions on the Pool of Prospective Undergraduate Students from Abroad," *Review of Economics and Statistics* 95, no. 1 (2013): 109–126.

43 Kevin Shih, "Labor Market Openness, H-1B Visa Policy, and the Scale of International Student Enrollment in the United States," *Economic Inquiry* 54, no. 1 (2016): 121–138.

44 Eric T. Stuen, Ahmed Mushfiq Mobarak, and Keith E. Maskus, "Skilled Immigration and Innovation: Evidence from Enrolment Fluctuations in US Doctoral Programmes," *Economic Journal* 122, no. 565 (2012): 1143–1176.

45 Anna Maria Mayda, Francesca Ortega, Giovanni Peri, Kevin Shih, and Chad Sparber, "The Effect of H-1B Quota on the Employment and Selection of Foreign-Born Labor," *European Economic Review* 108 (2018): 105–128.

46 Patricia Cortés, "The Effect of Low-Skilled Immigration on U.S. Prices: Evidence from CPI Data," *Journal of Political Economy* 116, no. 3 (2008): 38–422.

47 Patricia Cortés and José Tessada, "Low-Skilled Immigration and the Labor Supply of Highly Skilled Women," *American Economic Journal: Applied Economics* 3, no. 3 (2011): 88–123.

48 Catalina Amuedo-Dorantes and Almudena Sevilla, "Low-Skilled Immigration and Parenting Investments of College-Educated Mothers in the United States," *Journal of Human Resources* 49, no. 3 (2014): 509–539.

49 Pia Orrenius and Madeline Zavodny, "Help Wanted: Employer Demand for Less-Skilled Temporary Foreign Worker Visas in an Era of Declining Unauthorized Immigration," *RSF: The Russell Sage Foundation Journal of the Social Sciences* 6, no. 3 (2020): 45–67.

50 E-Verify is an electronic program used by employers to confirm the employment eligibility of job applicants.

51 Catalina Amuedo-Dorantes, Esther Arenas-Arroyo, and Bernhard Schmidpeter, "Immigration Enforcement and the Hiring of Low Skilled Workers," American Economic Association, *AEA Papers and Proceedings*, vol. 111 (2021): 593–597.

52 Guillermina Jasso and Mark R. Rosenzweig, "Family Reunification and the Immigration Multiplier: U.S. Immigration Law, Origin-Country Conditions, and the Reproduction of Immigrants," *Demography* 23 (1986): 291–311.

53 Guillermina Jasso and Mark R. Rosenzweig, "Do Immigrants Screened for Skills Do Better than Family Reunification Immigrants?" *International Migration Review* 29, no. 1 (1995): 85–111.

54 Guillermina Jasso, Douglas S. Massey, Mark R. Rosenzweig, and James P. Smith, "Assortative Mating among Married New Legal Immigrants to the United States: Evidence from the New Immigrant Survey Pilot," *International Migration Review* 34, no. 2 (2000): 443–459.

55 Guillermina Jasso, Douglas S. Massey, Mark R. Rosenzweig, and James P. Smith, "From Illegal to Legal: Estimating Previous Illegal Experience among New Legal Immigrants to the United States," *International Migration Review* 42, no. 4 (2008): 803–843.

56 Guillermina Jasso, Vivek Wadhwa, Ben Rissing, Gary Gereffi, and Richard Freeman, "How Many Highly Skilled Foreign-Born Are Waiting in Line for U.S. Legal Permanent Residence?" *International Migration Review* 44, no. 2 (2010): 477–498.

57 Bilesha Weeraratne and Douglas S. Massey, "Does Past Unauthorized Immigrant Status Result in a Wage Penalty for Legalized Immigrants?" Paper presented at the annual meeting of the American Economic Association, January 2013.

58 Denise Obinna, "The Challenges of American Legal Permanent Residency for Family- and Employment-Based Petitioners," *Migration and Development* 3, no. 2 (2014): 272–284.

59 B. Ikubolajeh Logan and Kevin J. A. Thomas, "The U.S. Diversity Visa Programme and the Transfer of Skills from Africa," *International Migration* 50, no. 2 (2012): 1–19.

60 Payal Banerjee, "Indian Information Technology Workers in the United States: The H-1B Visa, Flexible Production, and the Racialization of Labor," *Critical Sociology* 31, nos. 2–3 (2006): 425–445.

61 Pallavi Banerjee, "Subversive Self-Employment: Intersectionality and Self-Employment Among Dependent Visa Holders in the United States," *American Behavioral Scientist* 63, no. 2 (2018): 186–207.

62 Pallavi Banerjee, "What Do Visas Have to Do with Parenting? Middle-Class Dependent Visa Holders and Transcultural Parenting," in *Contemporary Parenting and Parenthood: From News Headlines to New Research*, ed. Michelle Janning (New York: Praeger/ABC-CLIO, 2018), 237–257.

63 Pallavi Banerjee, "When Men Stay Home: Household Labor in Female-Led Families of Indian Migrant Families," in *Families As They Really Aare*, vol. 2., ed. Barbara J. Risman and Virginia E. Rutter (New York: Norton, 2015), 500–515.

64 Rennie Lee, "Immigrant Entry Visa Categories and Their Effects on the Children of Immigrants' Education," *Journal of Ethnic and Migration Studies* 44, no. 9 (2018): 1560–1583.

65 The file we used is FY1997–2018 NIV Detail, which contains annual issuance by national origin for each year: US Government, Department of State, Bureau of Consular Affairs, "Nonimmigrant Visa Statistics," https://travel.state.gov.

66 The file we used is available here: US Government, Homeland Security, Office of Immigration Statistics, Office of Strategy, Policy & Plans, "Annual Flow Report: Lawful Permanent Residents," August 2018, www.dhs.gov.

67 There is some debate whether all TN visas are issued to high-skilled workers. For example, some view Canadian nurses who have been issued TN visas as high-skilled workers, but others view them as lower-skilled employees. See Daniel Costa, "Temporary Migrant Workers or Immigrants? The Question for U.S. Labor Migration," *RSF: The Russell Sage Foundation Journal of the Social Sciences*, no. 3 (2020): 18–44.

68 The HDI is a composite measure reflecting GDP per capita, educational attainment, and life expectancy.

69 Daniel Costa and Jennifer Rosenbaum, "Temporary Foreign Workers by the Numbers: New Estimates by Visa Classification," Economic Policy Institute, March 7, 2017, www.epi.org.

70 Donato and Amuedo-Dorantes, "The Legal Landscape of U.S. Immigration."

71 See Banerjee's chapter in this volume.

5

Preferential Hiring

US Earnings of Skilled Temporary Foreign Workers

B. LINDSAY LOWELL

There are significant numbers of foreign workers employed on visas that permit only temporary stays in the United States, often in science, technology, engineering, and mathematical occupations (STEM).[1] Perhaps no other visa for highly skilled workers has received as much attention as the temporary H-1B visa. Originally, temporary programs were relatively small, and visa holders were provided temporary work as intended. The H-1B visa was refashioned in the Immigration Act of 1990 and it, as well as all other temporary working visas (as noted by Donato and Amuedo-Dorantes in their chapter in this volume), now exceed the number of visas awarded annually for permanent green cards. Today, the number of skilled visas awarded annually for temporary stays for work is roughly four times greater than those for permanent work.[2] Most observers would agree that these visas no longer supply employers with just-in-time foreign workers to deal with temporary labor short-ages. Many are unconcerned, arguing that temporary foreign workers are a boon to the US economy. Other observers argue that temporary visas like the H-1B tend to foster employer dependence and poor work-ing conditions.

The goal here is to investigate one temporary visa, with an eye toward unbundling how H-1B earnings vary by employment sector, age, and nation of origin. The theory of preferential hiring queues to meet flex-ible employment strategies, abetted by temporary visa regimes, drives our expectations of sector-specific effects. Wage differentials should emerge in sectors of preferential demand; in particular, the information technology (IT) sector or computer programming jobs in the profes-sional service industry. The long recognized concentration of young,

Indian-origin H-1Bs in computer programming can be attributed primarily to Indian-origin engineering education, employment in India-linked multinationals, a globally competitive job market driven by outsourced demand, and the reinforcing effects of the H-1B temporary visa system on hiring queues.

This chapter first elaborates on the analytic expectations and the temporary H-1B visa regulations that reinforce employers' preferences in the competitive market for highly skilled workers. We then review the manner in which the H-1B visa constrains foreign workers' bargaining power and examine the research literature on H-1B earnings. The statistical analysis is based on unique H-1B data and a straightforward multivariate analysis of H-1B earnings compared with all similar domestic workers overall, with those in STEM jobs and with those in narrowly defined IT sector jobs. After presenting the findings, we investigate how the results inform questions about H-1Bs' impact on the labor market, their status relative to permanent immigrants, and the incidence of employment abuse and discrimination. The conclusions summarize the topside findings and discuss possible policy reforms.

Theory and Review of H-1B Visa Regulations and Earnings

There are many reasons why employers tend to prefer foreign workers. Preferential hiring from well-defined hiring queues can concentrate the supply and demand of select foreign workers in select occupations and industries. Temporary visas can abet those preferences and the H-1B, for reasons of regulatory lacunae or simply the temporary status of the visa, may not ensure that visa holders will have the same pay or working conditions as other workers. While some research finds that H-1Bs earn less than natives, otherwise well-designed studies report that H-1Bs earn more than natives. Arguably, however, natives in all occupations are not the correct comparison.

Preferential Hiring and Temporary Work Programs

While the promise of higher wages may be the major allure beckoning international migrants, many factors affect where migrants come from and where they are employed. The classic theory is that targeted employer recruitment, not wage differentials, is the initial mover of international migration; and that employer strategies lead to foreign workers' concentration in segmented occupations and industries.[3] Highly competitive markets encourage employers to strategize ways to lower their labor costs, typically through some combination of defined control over the work process or lower pay. Subsequent research has not reliably found such dual labor market segmentation, but employer preferences associated with sector-specific concentrations of foreign workforces remains an oft-observed phenomenon.

One reason for employer preference can be a reliance on coethnic networks that source new workers at lower cost while vouching for a new worker's reliability. Migrant networks, especially among workers from the same country or city, tend to be strong. Another often reported reason is that migrants "work harder," which may be the case but it may also be an unspoken code for more work at the same pay as natives.[4] Foreign workers may also accept lower wages; their reservation wage is lower than that of natives, because they come from lower-wage origins so they still benefit. Foreign workers may also be highly motivated to stay with their employer, reducing employee turnover. Finding new employment can be difficult, especially if there are language, regulatory, or other barriers to changing jobs. Employers who selectively employ foreign workers can pursue a strategy that permits greater control over the workforce. For these reasons, foreign workers might be the first choice in hiring queues.[5]

Temporary work visas can abet such employer strategies. Worldwide, many temporary visa programs channel workers who are recruited or networked from specific national origins to well-defined industries, occupations, and employers.[6] Indeed, they are often expected to do so. The rules governing temporary work programs, even rules designed to protect working conditions, tend to limit the rights of the visa holder. They may constrain the ability of foreign workers to bargain for improved pay or working conditions if for no other reason than the nature of temporary residence, which limits future-looking bargaining power and yields an upper hand to employers.[7] Temporary visas in many countries are sometimes poorly regulated and abuse sometimes occurs. It does not follow, however, that all temporary work programs will generate substandard working conditions, and successful outcomes exist. Each program needs to be examined on its own.

Elements of the H-1B workforce can be described by preferential hiring, which can be characterized as employers choosing workers not only for their job qualifications, but for their network ties and demographic and working characteristics. There is extensive research on preferential hiring in terms of immigration, race, gender, age, and education, most of which falls outside the scope of this chapter.[8] The focus here is on why some employers might prefer foreign H-1B workers and how visa regulations relate to that demand. Observations of visas for highly skilled foreign workers elsewhere suggest they supply tractable workforces that optimize competitive employer strategies. For example, work permits issued to Indian computer programmers were found to undercut wages paid to the UK workforce, but the temporary permits facilitated the pursuit of a global IT business strategy. After about two years of training, the workers returned home to India and were better able to provide offshore contract-based services.[9] A similar process of global "body shopping," a strategy of flexible labor management geared to defined periods of contracted work, has been observed among Indians employed in Australia.[10]

During the 1990s, the IT sector, along with other industries, ramped up global supply chains and employment networks. A legacy of engineering education at Indian schools, along with widespread English language ability, put Indian computer programmers first in line to supply the historic boom in US and global demand.[11] The IT businesses based in South Asia extended their reach to the United States, and along with US multinationals, reinforced global supply chains for information services. While some of the immediate demand was for high-level programmers, software development and other IT services have become more routinized over time.[12] Many firms in the professional services industry, both abroad and onshore, use business models that rely on competitively priced computer programmers, as well as the ability to flexibly contract and yet retain workers in these high-churn occupations.[13] Somewhere between one-third and one-half of all new H-1Bs are employed by the visas' ten largest employers; all are in the professional services industries.[14] Most of these are multinational companies in a fast-moving, global marketplace for workers. At the same time, as Wotherspoon discusses in his chapter in this volume, college matriculation in source countries increased sharply, as did the number of international students globally. Large numbers of Indians attend US colleges and many hope to stay on, some of whom are hired as H-1B workers.[15] The United States surely benefits from Indian immigrants who are highly educated and are most often found in professional occupations.[16] The H-1B visa program merits careful evaluation.

Admission Policy and H-1B Visa Specialty Occupations

As conceived in the US Congress's major legislation on immigration in 1952, 1965, and 1990, permanent and temporary visas differ. As in other nations, this difference is rooted in more than a century of migrant behavior; the political sway of unions, along with the evolution of greater worker rights; the dominance of visas for family reunification; and the subsequent construction of targeted visa classes to supply domestic employment demand while protecting workers. Permanent visas favor family sponsorship, while targeted employment visas permit employers to address persistent labor shortages and, especially, to hire uniquely skilled individuals. Temporary visas were intended to supply employers in fast-growing industries facing worker shortages, say due to the lags required to educate workers in fields such as engineering.[17] Temporary visas can smooth labor bottlenecks; however, shortages should work themselves out as wages increase to attract domestic workers. The historic logic was both to protect domestic workers and facilitate the adjustment of domestic industries as they evolve and adapt to changing markets.

The Immigration Act of 1990, the framework of the current system, retained the structure of the legislation of 1965 with alterations to expand employment-based skilled immigration, as well as to facilitate the supply of skilled temporary foreign workers. The admission of permanent residents remains dominated by family-sponsored immigrants, and permanent admissions for employment are only about 15 percent of annual flows. Still, the 1990 Act increased the number of visas for the employment of permanent immigrants from 54,000 to 140,000.[18] The 1990 Act also expanded access to temporary work programs, creating the temporary H-1B with an initial cap of 65,000 visas. Soon thereafter, Congress made serial changes to the number of visas available, while successive administrations executed regulatory changes to employment conditions and admission processes—as remarked upon by Donato and Amuedo-Dorantes in their chapter in this volume. Legislation after the turn of the twenty-first century effectively increased the cap to 85,000, and unlimited visas are available for nonprofits and colleges. In recent years, the United States has awarded between 100,000 and 150,000 new H-1B visas annually, far in excess of the roughly 50,000–70,000 available slots originally set aside for principal employment-based permanent visas, accentuating a gap between expectations and the possibility of staying long term.[19]

The visa's terms of temporary employment and status adjustment confound expectations and weaken H-1Bs' market power. This had been a relatively small, diverse program, supplying mostly European and Japanese workers to healthcare and a variety of other industries.[20] The 1990 Act removed the requirement that temporary H-1Bs intend to return home after their permitted three- to six-year stay. Evidence of intent to return is a requirement for most temporary visas, and it makes a subsequent application for permanent residency more difficult. It was thought that the removal of that requirement would smooth the transition of foreign workers into available permanent slots. Many H-1Bs certainly want the option of staying permanently, an intent encouraged by today's visa, but the relative scarcity of permanent slots makes that difficult.[21] The pathway to permanency is further confounded because H-1B workers must either be continually employed or leave the country. Critics argue that it becomes a risky proposition for an H-1B to seek new employment. The H-1Bs who want to stay permanently are beholden to their current employers in the hope that they will sponsor them for further employment on a permanent visa. A change in employers or demands for better wages or working conditions puts the H-1B at risk if they want to stay.

Otherwise, the 1990s Act's H-1B does not take measures that would reinforce temporary demand. However flawed in execution, most other working visas require some evidence that the sponsoring employer faces a shortage of domestic workers in a given job and occupation. A test of any sort that provides some evidence of such shortages is no longer required for the H-1B, while the stipulation that the job is only for short-term assignments was jettisoned decades ago. The visa does set requirements for initial H-1B earnings, which can be seen as an indirect if weak test of demand.[22] Sponsoring employers must attest that they will pay H-1Bs the wage that prevails in their occupation for workers of similar qualifications and experience.[23] The prevailing wage requirement, however, may not ensure that the H-1B earns at least as much as an otherwise equally experienced worker.[24] One way this occurs is when an employer applies to pay a qualifying wage for a future worker with little experience,[25] but then hires a more experienced or qualified worker.[26] Other problems include the broad definition of occupations,[27] the (mis)classification of job requirements, exemptions for workers by graduate degree and earnings, and wage floors for employers who are dependent on H-1B workers. The way the dependent employer provision has been implemented varies over time, but suffice it to say that most employers will pay at least $60,000 for a new H-1B.

The upshot is that there is a misalignment between the intended temporary role of H-1Bs in the labor market, the visa's regulatory design, and the immigration system's framework, which, in turn, places downward pressures on the expected earnings of H-1B visa holders. This misalignment fuels long unresolved debates among observers with different concepts of the visas' purpose. Within the tedious legislative, regulatory, and administrative components of the visa system, always viewed within the context of employer demand, are the factors that condition H-1B outcomes. Past prevailing wage regulations have not been foolproof despite their goal of protecting earnings or serving as a screen for labor shortages. Then again, neither do the regulations dictate that foreign workers will be paid less, leaving the issue open to analysis.

Research Findings on H-1B Earnings

For the past three decades there has been heated debate over whether temporary H-1B workers earn more or less than other workers. The review here will be of analytic papers based on large samples, with adequate controls for age or skill, as well as on the major analyses discussed by those engaged in this debate.[28] While there are many valuable contributions to the literature, there are problems with the reliability of the available data and especially with the commonplace but narrow comparison of H-1B earnings to those of native-born workers.

Analyses of nationwide samples promise generalizable results, but almost none ask about detailed visa status. One analysis, which proxies for H-1B status, compares foreign workers in select industries to the native-born and concludes that the proxy H-1Bs earn more than US citizens.[29] The proxy classifies all foreign-born noncitizens in ten select STEM occupations as H-1Bs, which includes many non-H-1B immigrants, especially those who have substantially more US experience and workplace rights than temporary H-1Bs; and predictably higher earnings. The lack of an H-1B survey identifier is highly problematic, and other research demonstrates how an inappropriate proxy is biased by better paid foreign-born workers. The National Science Foundation (NSF) regularly samples all US college graduates (National Survey of College Graduates, NSCG) and identifies foreign workers by their current permanent or temporary visa class.[30] Analysis of the 2003 survey found that those identified as currently holding any temporary work visa in highly skilled jobs earn about 5 percent less than all other foreign- and native-born workers.[31] And skilled temporary foreign workers who either change employment or adjust to permanent status see a substantial increase in earnings in line with other research using these data.[32] These are useful findings, especially insofar as they find visa mobility improves earnings, but the sample captures "any" temporary work visa, thus conflating different skilled temporary visas. It is not an effective test of H-1B visa status alone.[33]

The use of independent or specially constructed samples is an alternative approach. A sample taken from a survey of readers of an IT magazine found that self-reported H-1Bs earned either the same or as much as 8 percent more than IT workers with US citizenship.[34] The authors also introduce other interesting analyses, including the finding that permanent residence status is associated with a 9–13 percent increase in earnings compared with US natives. This is a large sample with 50,000 cases, and the authors demonstrate a concern that the characteristics of the migrants sampled should be comparable to what might be expected from other data sources. Nevertheless, the sampled H-1Bs are nearly a decade older than the actual H-1B population, and the non-random nature of the sample does not inspire confidence. What these results, and those of the NSCG above, also demonstrate is that immigrants who adjust to permanent visas get a substantial increase in earnings. Either including non-H-1B immigrants in an H-1B proxy, or not including them with US natives, could substantially alter conclusions about relative H-1B earnings.

Two research papers use samples constructed from actual H-1B visa data along with a large nationwide sample which, as will be described below, are the same data to be used here. The first paper covers a lot of ground to support its basic finding that, on average, H-1Bs earn more than US native-born workers, even when comparing same-age workers within occupational groups.[35] The authors address technical criticisms of their data, but critics note their approach does not control for potential confounding factors. A similar data analysis finds that actual H-1Bs earn less than natives in IT occupations, while H-1Bs earn the same as natives in electrical engineering.[36] A more detailed regression analysis of the same datasets further unbundles workers by major occupational group comparing H-1Bs and US native-born workers.[37] It finds that OLS regression–adjusted H-1B earnings are greater than the earnings of natives in STEM and most other occupations.

However, comparisons of H-1Bs to native-born workers, commonplace in the literature, are arguably wrong. The correct comparison should be H-1Bs to all *domestic* workers, meaning natives *and* foreign-born workers who are not temporary work visa holders (say green card permanent residents, including youth arrivals and naturalized citizens). Of course, most analysts are entrenched in the voluminous literature on immigrant earnings assimilation, positing that, even if immigrants earn less than natives upon arrival, with US-specific experience, immigrant earnings catch up with natives over time. The logic on assimilation is to ask about long-run integration, and the comparison of foreign to native workers is specified. But H-1B visa regulations specify that employers pay the prevailing wage, which is measured as the average of *all* workers with the same work experience in a given occupation. No mention is made of earning more than native-born or naturalized US citizens. The underlying economic logic has little to do with assimilation; rather, the goal is to require an H-1B wage that does not undercut the labor market. Domestic workers, foreign and native, are the proper comparison because the appropriate test is whether or not H-1Bs earn at least as much as all other similar workers.

Data and Measurement

The analysis here uses two different datasets. One is a large H-1B dataset consisting of visa petitions released by the US Citizenship and Immigration Services (USCIS) under the Freedom of Information Act.[38] In order to compare the earnings of domestic workers, these data are combined with a large dataset from the US Census Bureau's annual American Community Survey (ACS). We describe these two data sources here and the sample restrictions made to ensure the two are comparative.

The H-1B microdata are for all approved employer petitions for H-1B workers from 2000 to 2010. While the US Department of Labor (USDOL) must first approve an employer's application for the right to seek an H-1B worker to fill a given job, that approval then triggers an employer's petition of the USCIS to have an H-1B visa awarded to a specific foreign worker. The available petitions data include information on age, education, country of origin, occupation, industry, and annual earnings of the hired worker.[39] These data, in turn, are combined with the Census's ACS microdata that are representative of the total US population. The ACS data are subsampled to be comparable, e.g., for all currently employed workers in the same occupations found in the H-1B petitions data.[40]

We place a few additional restrictions on the data to make them comparable. First, we top code the annual earnings of the H-1Bs using the same maxima used in the annual ACS files. Second, almost all H-1Bs are full-time workers, and their employers are expected to pay year-round annualized salaries.[41] We define full-time and year-round workers in the ACS, referred to as full-timing, as those ages 21–64 who worked 35 hours or more in the prior week and 50 weeks or more in the prior year. Self-employed ACS workers are excluded. Third, reviewers have questioned a comparison of H-1Bs with the ACS that includes the same workers. So we exclude from the ACS observations of an H-1B proxy defined as foreign-born non-citizen workers who arrived in the United States after age 21, have at least a bachelor's degree, and have been in the country no more than six years. While this exclusion may improve the reliability of the estimates, it hardly affects the results.

Next, we combine real 2010 earnings over three years, 2008–2010, to better compare annual H-1B events. The H-1B data capture annual petitions for new workers during a first three-year stay, as well as continuing workers during an additional three-year stay. The H-1B workers' earnings increase after receiving a continuation of their visa. This can occur within either three-year visa stay, although increases may not be as substantial as increases across the two three-year stay periods. Regardless, the H-1B petitions data do not identify individuals from an initial award of a visa to a continuation, so we cannot track change in earnings for workers granted a continuation—say, for a new job or a different employer, within or across either the first or subsequent three-year window of stay. Thus, a three-year time period captures the average change in initial-to-continuation earnings within those windows. Exploratory estimates are similar, nevertheless, using either single years or even longer periods.

Analysis of the Workforce by Age, Sector, and Origin

The H-1B workforce is very young and concentrated in STEM and IT occupations in the professional service industries; and those from South Asia are the lion's share of the 190 H-1B origin countries. Table 5.1 shows the concentration of Indian H-1Bs, who make up well over half of all H-1Bs, in STEM occupations. Figures 5.2 to 5.4 demonstrate the hyper-concentration of all H-1Bs under the age of 30 and the pattern of nominal earnings over the working ages. Table 5.2 examines H-1B earnings compared to domestic workers after controlling for several factors.

Sector Concentrations and Age-Earnings Profiles

First, we want to establish the well-known concentration of Indian H-1Bs—that is to say, the demand for H-1Bs from India has long been greatest in a subset of all occupations and industries. Table 5.1 shows that Indian H-1Bs are 57 percent, well over half, of all H-1Bs in all occupations. At the same time, Indian H-1Bs concentrate in core STEM jobs, where they make up 74 percent of all H-1Bs in STEM jobs (and 44 percent of all H-1Bs).[42] Indian H-1Bs further concentrate in the IT sector, where they constitute 91 percent of all H-1Bs in just the IT sector, defined as workers holding jobs in computer occupations in the professional computer services industry (and 29 percent of all H-1Bs). Indians

TABLE 5.1: Indian-born H-1Bs as Percentage of Only H-1B Workers by
Sector of Employment, 2008–2010

Sector	Total (%)	Workforce within sector that is:	
		Non-Indian (%)	Indian (%)
All H-1B occupations	100	43	57
Non-STEM occupations	100	69	31
STEM core occupations	100	26	74
Computer occupations in the professional computer services industry within STEM	100	9	91

Source: Authors' tabulations of USCIS H-1B petitions microdata.

are the largest number of H-1Bs overall and they are highly concentrated
in STEM and computer-programming jobs in the professional services
industry.[43]

Figure 5.1 shows the age distribution of the H-1B and domestic workforce in STEM jobs. The H-1Bs are younger than their domestic counterparts. For the H-1Bs, nearly half or 46 percent are under the age of
30; for the domestic workforce, 14 percent are under the age of 30. For
H-1Bs, 54 percent are older than 30 years of age; for domestic workers,
86 percent are older than 30 years of age.[44] While STEM workers tend to
be on the young side, the H-1Bs are not merely somewhat younger than
domestic workers, they are hyperconcentrated in the age group 21–29.
Thus, the commonplace observation that H-1B employers prefer to hire
very young H-1B young workers holds true.[45]

Figure 5.2 shows the average nominal earnings for all H-1B occupations, figure 5.3, the earnings for core-STEM occupations, and figure 5.4,
the earnings in the IT sector. Starting with figure 5.2, H-1Bs earn more
than all domestic workers until age 35, after which there is little difference in earnings. Next, in the core STEM occupations as shown in figure
5.3, H-1Bs earn more than domestic workers through age 29, after which
they earn less throughout most of the age distribution. Finally, for jobs
in the IT sector as shown in figure 5.4, H-1Bs earn more than domestic
workers through age 24, after which they earn less. The figure also shows
that for the youngest H-1B workers, the visa effectively sets a $60,000
floor on nominal earnings. Next, the individual earnings data are used
to compare average earnings after controlling for confounding factors.

Regression Results by Age, Sector, and Origins

This analysis explores different groupings of workers to evaluate overall effects, and then tests for simple sector and age-group differences in earnings. It should be expected that H-1Bs earn less than all domestic workers, e.g., both foreign-born residents and natives, although the difference may not be great. In sectors that analysts have identified with long ongoing concentrations of H-1Bs—STEM jobs in general and computer programming jobs or IT services in particular—it should be expected that H-1Bs earn less than all domestic workers in the same jobs. The focus on the youngest workers relates to H-1Bs' hyper age concentration and high nominal earnings. A weak expectation is that there

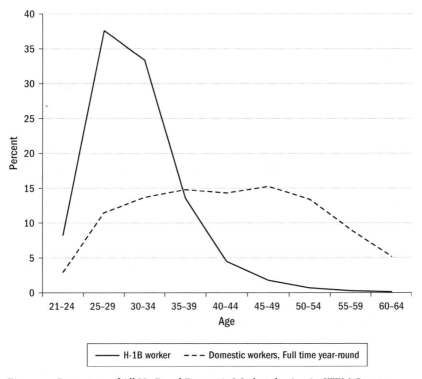

Figure 5.1: Percentage of All H-1B and Domestic Workers by Age in STEM Occupations, 2008–2010. Source: Author's tabulations of USCIS H-1B petitions and American Community Survey microdata.

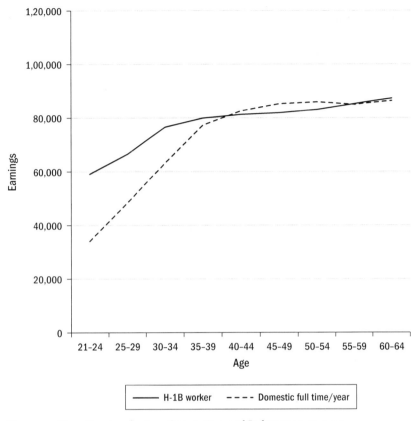

Figure 5.2: Mean Earnings by Age, Occupation, and Industry, 2008–2010.
Source: Author's tabulations of USCIS H-1B petitions and American Community
Survey microdata.

is no H-1B earnings advantage among young workers after controls, a
strong expectation is that average H-1B earnings among the youngest
differ by sector and national origins.

The first three columns in table 5.2 are for the three samples
described—all workers, STEM, and IT sector workers—and include the
years 2008–2010, while the fourth additional column shown includes
the years 2006–2007. Results for these years roughly contrast pre- and
post-recession periods, but only for the sample of computer programmers in the IT professional services industry. For all of the samples and
age-origin regressions, the top panel of table 5.2 shows the coefficients

for just H-1B earnings relative to domestic workers from separate regressions. The bottom panel shows the sample size and variance explained for each regression. Almost all of the coefficients and all of the model estimates are statistically significant.

The regression analyses are of annual earnings controlling for standard human capital and other factors associated with earnings. The regression results shown are Ordinary Least Squares estimates of the natural log of earnings controlling for years of work experience, experience squared, graduate degree dummy variables, and fixed-effects for industry and year. The domestic ACS workforce is restricted to full-

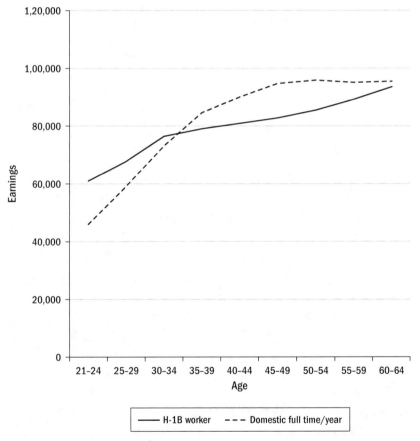

Figure 5.3: Mean Earnings by Age in Core STEM Occupations. Source: Author's tabulations of USCIS H-1B petitions and American Community Survey microdata.

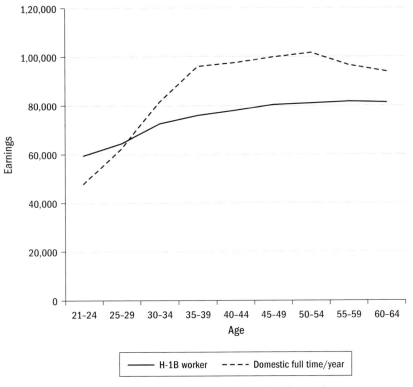

Figure 5.4: Mean Earnings by Age in IT Occupations and Professional Services Industry, 2008–2010. Source: Author's tabulations of USCIS H-1B petitions and American Community Survey microdata.

time, year-round workers with a bachelor's degree or better and proxy H-1Bs are excluded. The H-1B microdata have no variable for English ability, but research demonstrates that for highly educated workers, English language ability has no effect in earnings regressions.[46] We do not introduce a control for years in the United States, which is not called for because the issue here is not one of earnings assimilation.[47]

Consider first the results for the three samples shown across columns and for workers of all ages in the top row of table 5.2. For all workers of all ages, as well as workers just in STEM jobs, the coefficient comparing H-1Bs to domestic workers is statistically significant and negative. The H-1Bs earn about 1 percent less than either all domestic workers or just domestic workers in STEM jobs. On the other hand, for the sample of

TABLE 5.2: OLS Regression of the Natural Log of Annual Earnings Comparing US Domestic and H-1B Workers: Full-Time, Year-Round Employees

Age sample by row	All H-1B occupations, 2008–2010‡		STEM, 2008–2010‡		Computer occupations in Professional IT services†			
					2008–2010		2005–2007	
Cofficients of Earnings Relative to Domestic Workers								
(1) All ages								
H-1Bs, all countries	−0.010	***	−0.009	***	−0.125	***	−0.162	***
(2) Ages 21–29								
H-1Bs, all countries	0.190	***	0.150	***	0.043	***	−0.001	
(3) Ages 21–29, H-1B country/region of origin								
India	0.201	***	0.111	***	−0.045	***	−0.100	***
China	0.088	***	0.092	***	0.097	***	0.053	***
Philippines	0.104	***	−0.051	***	−0.121	***	−0.201	***
Asia, other	0.040	***	0.047	***	−0.015	**	−0.081	***
Western Hem.	0.078	***	0.036	***	0.078	***	0.001	**
English nations	0.278	***	0.246	***	0.264	***	0.198	***
Africa	0.161	***	0.095	***	0.051	***	−0.029	
Regression Sample Size and Fit Statistics								
(1) All ages								
N	1,124,216		468,853		212,944		259,877	
R^2	0.21	***	0.21	***	0.15	***	0.11	***
(2) Ages 21–29								
N	327,234		186,409		109,676		140,185	
R^2	0.26	***	0.17	***	0.06	***	0.04	***
(3) Ages 21–29, H-1B country of origin								
N	327,234		186,409		109,676		140,185	
R^2	0.27	***	0.18	***	0.08	***	0.06	***

Note: Domestic workers are natives and long-term foreign-born workers (see text).
‡Controls for experience, experience squared, education, industry and year.
†Controls for experience, experience squared, education and year.
*$p < 0.05$, **$p < 0.01$, ***$p < 0.001$.
Source: Author's tabulations of USCIS H-1B petitions and American Community Survey microdata.

all workers in computer programming jobs, H-1Bs earned 12 percent less than domestic workers in the years 2008–2010. Thus, H-1Bs of all ages earn a little less on average than domestic workers of all ages, while H-1Bs in IT computing/professional services earn substantially less than domestic workers of all ages. These results hold up for IT sector workers in the pre-recession years 2005–2007. These are reasonable results given our review above of nominal earnings across the age distribution; however, the nominal results also suggest a possible H-1B earnings advantage among the youngest workers.

Consider the second row of table 5.2, restricted to the youngest workers, ages 21–29. That shows, in columns one and two, that H-1Bs ages 21–29 have an earnings advantage of roughly 19 percent over young domestic workers in all occupations, and 15 percent more than core STEM domestic workers. Row two, column three, shows that even among computer programmers in the professional service industry, H-1Bs ages 21–29 earn roughly 4 percent more than domestic workers post-recession. In the pre-recession 2005–2007 period, however, no earnings difference is found. The results for the youngest computer programmers suggest an H-1B earnings advantage in recession years but no earnings advantage during the earlier, tighter labor market. It is possible that the visa regulations place an effective floor on H-1B earnings. As there would be lower demand and wages for domestic workers during a recession, the H-1B earnings floor yields an H-1B earnings advantage. These results mirror the nominal earnings differences seen in figures 5.2–5.4 but appear, at first, to counter expectations of lowered H-1B *ceteris paribus* earnings.

The third row, or bottom set of regression coefficients in the top panel of table 5.2, are also restricted to 21–29 year olds and show results for H-1B earnings by country/region of origin. In columns one and two, for young workers in all occupations and for those employed in STEM occupations, H-1Bs from all origins (except the Philippines) earn more than domestic workers—consistent with the findings of greater average H-1B earnings for all young workers combined (compared with row two results).

When we examine results by country/region of origin in the third and fourth columns for young workers in just the IT sector, however, young H-1B earnings show national-origin disadvantages. Young Indian

H-1Bs earn roughly 5–10 percent less than domestic computer programmers; and those from the Philippines, about 12–20 percent less. Young Chinese H-1B programmers are an exception, as they earn about 10 percent more than domestic workers. The relatively few Chinese H-1Bs and H-1Bs from non-Asian origins earn substantially more than domestic programmers. The few from highly developed English-speaking nations earn roughly 26 percent more than IT domestic workers.[48]

Discussion: What H-1B Earnings Can and Cannot Tell Us

These findings have several implications that we discuss below. Having already made the case for comparing H-1B earnings to the average of domestic workers, the results call for greater attention to the earnings of foreign workers who stay and leave H-1B status. We also respond to reviewers' questions about the impacts of H-1Bs on the labor market and economy, as well as about abuse of the visa program.

Group Averages and Implied Mobility

This analysis is relatively focused, and some readers may wonder about differences masked in group averages. For example, H-1Bs are compared to the average of native and foreign-born residents, but does one of the latter two groups earn more than the other? One could separately analyze these and other non-overlapping groups, or test interactions for the statistical significance of many occupation-industry or other group differences. But this parsimonious focus has advantages, and averages can suggest interesting findings.

For example, much of the literature reviewed above compares H-1Bs with the earnings of the native-born, while the analysis here is in line with research that compares H-1Bs with average occupational earnings (combined native and foreign-born). If H-1Bs earn more than natives, but less than combined native and (non-H-1B) foreign workers as found here, the foreign component must drive the difference. The foreign-born in certain ages and occupations must earn more than natives, bringing up the combined domestic worker average. The research literature, indeed, finds that H-1Bs who adjust to permanent status get a boost in earnings. This implies that the transition out of temporary status is empowering and/or selective—empowering in that adjustment to permanent status enhances workers' bargaining power, selective in that only a subset of skilled temporary foreign workers adjusts to permanent residency.[49] This reinforces the observation that temporary status restrains earnings and merits more research.

This analysis also breaks out the youngest H-1Bs from older workers. The graphs of nominal earnings show that H-1Bs younger than age 30 earn more than domestic workers, while H-1Bs aging into their thirties earn less. So the over-30 H-1Bs pull down the group average, resulting in lower H-1B earnings for workers of all ages. In turn, one could hypothesize that an analysis restricted to workers over the age of 30 would reveal substantially lower H-1B earnings. At the same time, the regression results still find a significant overall H-1B earnings advantage among the youngest 21–29-year-old workers. Seeing this, some observers argue that young workers are quite able to do routine work.[50] The employer strategy is to employ young H-1Bs who do much the same work for an amount that is still less than somewhat older workers. That reduces total labor costs, and the young H-1Bs are let go before they gain the tenure to command higher wages.[51] The findings here reinforce that line of thought because average H-1B earnings muddle national-origin effects. The youngest Indian-born H-1Bs, concentrated in the IT sector, earn substantially less than domestic workers, reinforcing the expectation of sector-specific preferential demand.

Questions of Labor Market Impacts

Can these research findings shed any light on questions about H-1B's impact on the US labor market? Unfortunately, this research offers little direct insight on the endless debates over H-1Bs or, generally speaking, the net impact of skilled migration on the labor market. It does, however, complicate arguments over domestic shortages, and implies that any positive impacts likely result from more complex processes than simple increases in "skill inputs."

As to whether H-1Bs offset domestic shortages of STEM or IT workers, it is very difficult to square nearly three decades of a sustained and large supply of H-1B workers, mostly to the same subset of occupations and employers, with the notion that those workforces face deep, chronic shortages of domestic labor. Theory and experience strongly militate against such a monumental failure of labor market response and, what is more, there is good evidence that putative shortages do not exist.[52] Also, the comparatively low H-1B earnings found here, particularly in IT jobs, are not consistent with a shortage of labor. Arguments as to whether shortages exist should be beside the point or, put another way, the nature of demand supplied by the H-1B seems to be more nuanced than to alleviate domestic labor shortages.

With regard to impacts, most economists argue that skilled foreign labor complements domestic labor and capital, boosting earnings, and that net effects may be complex.[53] Yet a team of economists from the National Academy of Sciences simulates a small, negative impact of all college-educated migrants on native earnings.[54] Then again, direct impacts on wages may not be readily measured; research finds that the increase in skilled immigration in the 1990s deterred natives from STEM education and jobs.[55] Simulation research also finds that foreign IT workers depress native earnings and employment; and that lower employment adversely reduces output.[56] In a somewhat different vein, it can be argued that lower H-1B earnings generate greater returns to employers or capital,[57] and skilled migration may also boost innovation and entrepreneurship, with the net effect of boosting economic growth.[58] Put another way, the lower earnings of H-1Bs benefits employers and can generate total economic returns that benefit the economy. At the same time, some research finds that H-1Bs boost innovation and employment.[59] With that in mind, the comparative earnings of H-1Bs alone cannot resolutely address the range of net impacts. However, if the findings had been that H-1Bs earned more than the market average, it would be fairly straightforward to argue that their high productivity generates positive spillovers on the economy. But it is difficult to reconcile lower H-1B earnings with that conclusion. The H-1B program does not appear to be a dynamic tide that lifts each and every boat.

Attrition from STEM employment is of concern and the potential number of domestic workers is large. For every two students graduating with a STEM degree, fewer than one is employed in STEM.[60] From the ACS data used here, separate tabulations were made of young workers who work both full- and part-time. Part-timing workers in H-1B occupations tend to be under the age of 35, although they are not as hyper age-concentrated as H-1Bs. Still, about 21 percent of all domestic STEM workers aged 21–29 are part-time workers. About 45 percent of those part-timers are enrolled in school and 10 percent are cross-state migrants. Fewer than 5 percent of same age full-time domestic workers, in contrast, are enrolled in school, and only 1 percent are cross-state migrants. The earnings of the part-time workers are about half that of full-time workers. In short, the hyper-concentration of full-time H-1Bs at the youngest ages coincides with a large part-time domestic workforce. This might imply that employers indeed find it difficult to recruit young full-time domestic workers. But might stronger demand attract some into full-time employment or help retain others who eventually take non-STEM jobs?[61]

Workplace Abuse and Discrimination

Many observers note workplace abuse of H-1Bs, while others report their precarious status and vulnerability. The statistical research here cannot directly evaluate those conditions, albeit the findings of lower wages are consistent with fieldwork that finds abuse and vulnerability. But the findings on migrant origins are not consistent with the contention that H-1Bs are uniquely vulnerable or racialized.

Fieldwork supports expectations that H-1B employers, particularly in the IT sector, pursue a flexible labor management strategy.[62] In the IT sectors of Houston and the Bay Area of California, H-1Bs were found employed in body shops, and either worked very long hours or were often benched without pay.[63] An intensive study of 40 H-1B workers also determined that subcontracting strategies created unstable working conditions.[64] Such field research, of course, cannot establish the prevalence of abusive practices. But their findings are consistent with a statistical analysis of the US labor force survey which found H-1Bs in IT were more likely to hold contingent jobs than natives, and those migrants in contingent jobs earned less.[65] The data used here do not have that type of detail on employment status, but the findings are consistent with the observation that the working conditions of H-1Bs can often be poor and may violate the terms of the visa.

Such findings and the expectations driving this analysis are consistent with those of Banerjee in her chapter in this volume, in terms of the reduced bargaining power of temporary programs and their concomitant global connectivity. She argues, however, that capitalism uniquely foments such policies, and advances additional arguments about adverse effects generated by capital and the US admission system in terms of surveillance and migrant racialization. The US Department of Homeland Security has been expanding the use of social media to screen immigrants and tourists, and is currently being sued for possible privacy violations of current visa holders.[66] At the same time, very real concerns about electronic surveillance are not restricted to immigrants, and it is implausible to attribute causal connections between evolving technologies and their ultimate use to "capital" when autocratic and socialist economies both abuse all forms of surveillance while also deterring immigration.

The findings reported here do not support a pattern of H-1B racialization, or the idea that lower H-1B earnings are caused by group-specific discrimination.[67] The findings show that Indian H-1Bs earn less than domestic workers in IT jobs, but outside of IT they tend to earn more. That pattern supports the expectation of preferential hiring driven by IT employer strategies, not of group racialization.[68] What is more, research indicates that the preponderance of H-1Bs in IT are hired by companies that have Indian management or are multinationals with global workforces that have strong linkages to India, which reinforces expectations about the role of business strategy.[69] At the same time, Chinese H-1Bs earn more than domestic workers across all employers, which is not consistent with racialization, unless all Chinese but only some Indians employed outside of IT are a "model minority." Consider too that H-1Bs from African origins earn more than domestic workers across the board. This is consistent with Thomas's findings in his chapter in this volume of African immigrant selectivity and earnings advantage in STEM jobs and not with visa racialization. The pattern of earnings across origin groups is not consistent with a visa policy that ineluctably racializes particular groups. There appears to be preferential hiring abetted by a regulatory regime that otherwise appears neutral, and the causal effect runs from business strategy to employment outcomes.[70]

Concluding Observations

Highly skilled foreign workers are admitted into the United States for temporary and permanent stays on a variety of visas. Over the past three decades, the number of skilled temporary foreign workers admitted annually into the United States has come to significantly exceed the number of permanent migrants. Temporary programs by their nature create challenges to worker rights and efficient labor markets. This chapter analyzes the earnings of H-1B specialty workers, the largest temporary program for skilled workers. A theory of preferential hiring to meet flexible employment strategies, abetted by the temporary regime, drives our expectations of sector and national-origin effects. The results are discussed for their implication for working conditions, worker mobility, and impacts on labor.

The findings support the expectation that H-1B earnings are lower than those of domestic workers, and there are substantial differences in earnings by sector, age, and national origins. On balance, the data and research designs used here are similar to that analyzed by Lofstrom and Hayes.[71] But whereas these authors find that H-1Bs earn more than *native-born* workers, the findings here are that H-1Bs earn less than *domestic* workers or the combination of native *and* foreign workers. Results will differ by comparison group: both the visa regime and its logic indicate that H-1B earnings should be compared with an occupational average, e.g., the average of native and foreign workers. On average, H-1Bs earn much less than domestic workers in the IT sector, while young Indian workers who comprise most of the IT sector's workforce earn less than similar domestic workers. The H-1B visa regulations fail in that regard, and policymakers should ask questions about the program's design and its role in the immigration system.

What do these results suggest for reforms to visa policy? A longstanding proposal is to enhance "visa portability," or the removal of barriers to job change, which might enhance H-1B's bargaining power and earnings. But the H-1B visa has been modified to enhance portability, and estimates suggest that 55–63 percent of H-1Bs obtain visa continuations in a given year,[72] while other research also suggests substantial mobility in the IT industry.[73] This indicates that the effectiveness of enhanced portability could be limited by the marketplace and other aspects of the visa.

The most commonly proposed alternatives, visa auctions or higher prevailing wage requirements, strive to price visas high enough to screen out employers who seek to hire foreign workers at low cost. Either approach to pricing visas promises desirable market-based incentives that should motivate employers to improve worker outcomes or pursue other business strategies. More restrictive screening of visa applications, along with higher prevailing wage requirements, were introduced toward the end of the Trump administration. Although this step lacks government tracking of visa outcomes, the effectiveness of such straightforward regulatory changes will likely remain mostly unknown. At the very least, a strong emphasis on effective visa statistics, tracking programs, and compliance audits backed by enforcement action, which are most often given short shrift, should be on the table for any meaningful reform.

More systemic solutions should involve redesigning the immigration system, expanding permanent migration, and carefully tailoring the supply of temporary labor. Perhaps an H-1B-like visa should be intended for two years' work with limited rights to stay, targeting supply to cyclical shortages rather than a standing supply that reinforces employer dependence and fosters migrant precarity.[74] Provisional temporary visas that optionally convert to permanent status sound promising; however, that would simply beg the question of how many visas the government should supply. In the absence of a way to determine an optimal number of migrants to admit on an ongoing basis, for which demand indexes or measures of job vacancies hold unproven promise, legislators preferably should confront the appropriate role of temporary visa programs. While temporary work programs hold the promise of benefiting both the US economy and foreign workers, they are problematic. They should be limited in scope, open to regulatory changes based on ongoing evaluation, and carefully monitored for employer compliance.

Finally, the H-1B visa program demonstrates features of contemporary migration that are often oversimplified. The H-1B visa holders certainly seek economic opportunity, as do their employers, but other factors shape their actions. It would be impossible to imagine the H-1B program without the reinforcing contexts of intensifying globalization, the ongoing IT revolution, and the ad hoc, conflicted nature of US immigration policy. These sociohistorical and contextual factors have enabled highly competitive global businesses, linked to India and other countries, and the highly skilled foreign workers to leverage a central role with first-mover advantages in a rapidly evolving segment of a global industry. The employment and incorporation of H-1B migrants, in the United States or upon return home, are conditioned by the way these factors play out. Those who have had their H1-B visas adjusted to *permanent* status appear to experience a substantial boost in earnings which, not to exonerate the low earnings of many temporary H-1B workers, can be explicated by how the H-1B visa interacts with business stratagems to control the employment of *temporary* foreign workers.

NOTES

1 I would like to express my appreciation to Magnus Lofstrom, who shared the microdata on H-1B petitions and generously answered questions on his analysis and the data. I also appreciate comments from Martin Ruhs, Hal Salzman, and participants at the presentation of an earlier version of this paper at the Society of Government Economists, as well as the participants at the Center for International and Regional Studies' Working Group on Economic Migration to the United States.

2 Megan Mathews, "The Impact of Counting Changes on Nonimmigrant Admissions: Preliminary Findings," US Department of Homeland Security, Office of Immigration Statistics, Fact Sheet (February 2012), www.dhs.gov.

3 Michael J. Piore, *Birds of Passage: Migrant Labor and Industrial Societies* (Cambridge, UK: Cambridge University Press, 1979).

4 Roger Waldinger and Mehdi Bozorgmehr, *Ethnic Los Angeles* (Chicago: University of Chicago Press, 1997).

5 Roger Waldinger and Michael I. Lichter, *How the Other Half Works: Immigration and the Social Organization of Labor* (Los Angeles: University of California Press, 2003).

6 Martin Ruhs and Bridget Anderson, *Who Needs Migrant Workers? Labour Shortages, Immigration, and Public Policy* (Oxford, UK: Oxford University Press, 2010).

7 Martin Ruhs, *The Price of Rights: Regulating International Labor Migration* (Princeton, NJ: Princeton University Press, 2013).

8 Preferential hiring is typically evoked when workers are paid less, often but not always because of discriminatory intent based on race or sex. The "preference" of employers for certain workers may provide advantages other than reduced wage costs, in language ability in customer-fronting occupations, for example, or when migrant networks reduce hiring costs.

9 Jane Millar and John Salt, "In Whose Interests? IT Migration in an Interconnected World Economy," *Population, Space and Place* 13, no. 1 (2007): 41–58.

10 Xiang Biao, *Global "Body Shopping": An Indian Labor System in the Information Technology Industry* (Princeton, NJ: Princeton University Press, 2006).

11 Binod Khadria, "Skilled Labour Migration from Developing Countries: Study on India," *International Migration Papers* no. 49 (2002): 1–71; Payal Banerjee, "Indian IT Workers in the U.S.: Race, Gender, and State in the Making of Immigrant Labor" (PhD diss., Syracuse University, 2009).

12 Peter Norlander, Christopher Erickson, Sarosh Kuruvilla, and Rangapriya Kannan-Narasimhan, "India's Outsourcing Industry and the Offshoring of Skilled Services Work: A Review Essay," *Labor Studies* 4, no. 1 (2015): 1–24.

13 Norman Matloff, "Are Foreign Students the 'Best and Brightest'? Data and Implications for Immigration Policy," Economic Policy Institute, *Briefing Paper* no. 356 (2013).

14 Ron Hira, "Immigration Reforms Needed to Protect Skilled American Workers," Testimony presented to a Hearing before the Judiciary Committee of the U.S. Senate (March 17, 2015), www.epi.org; Ron Hira and Anil Hira, *Outsourcing America: What's Behind Our National Crisis and How Can We Reclaim American Jobs* (New York: American Management Association, 2008).

15 John Bound, Breno Braga, Joseph M. Golden, and Gaurav Khanna, "Recruitment of Foreigners in the Market for Computer Scientists in the United States," *Journal of Labor Economics* 33, no. S1 (2015): 187–223.

16 Mary Hanna and Jeanne Batalova, "Indian Immigrants in the United States," Migration Information Source, October 16, 2020, www.migrationpolicy.org.

17 Richard B. Freeman, "A Cobweb Model of the Supply and Starting Salary of New Engineers," *International Labor Review* 29, no. 2 (1976): 236–248.

18 Michael J. Greenwood and Fred A. Ziel, "The Impact of the Immigration Act of 1990 on U.S. Immigration," U.S. Commission on Immigration Reform (1997), https://repositories.lib.utexas.edu.

19 US Citizenship and Immigration Services (USCIS), "Characteristics of H-1B Specialty Occupation Workers: Fiscal Year 2010 Report," Department of Homeland Security, 2011, www.uscis.gov. The permanent employment-based visa caps apply to both the principal worker and derivative family. Out of the 140,000 cap, perhaps no more than half go to the principal. Recall too that H-1Bs are only part of a larger supply of skilled temporary foreign workers, albeit their temporary intent requirement puts most second in line behind H-1Bs.

20 B. Lindsay Lowell, *Foreign Temporary Workers in America: Policies that Benefit the U.S. Economy* (New York: Quorum Press, 1999).

21 Given today's H-1B regime and the hurdles that remain, the standard temporary visa requirement of a clear intention to return would be more transparent and fair. Workers who obtain an H-1B earn more than if they had not migrated; nevertheless, those who return may have greater opportunities in marriage and job markets than workers who stayed home.

22 Ruhs, *The Price of Rights*.

23 The US Department of Labor states that the H-1B is intended to address labor shortages, while the employer attestation to pay the prevailing wage is designed to protect domestic workers. The attestation is a weak gauge of shortages.

24 Note that prevailing wages for hires on federal contracts under the Davis-Bacon Act may specify that those workers be paid more than, for example, union workers or a defined average of a segment of occupational earnings. The federal government's mandate is to protect all domestic workers, so the H-1B requires a wage higher than the occupational average.

25 Shari B. Hochberg, "United States-India Relations: Reconciling the H-1B Visa Hike and Framework for Cooperation on Trade and Investment," *Pace International Law Review* 24, no. 1 (2012): 233–257.

26 US Government Accountability Office (GAO), "*H-1B Visa Program.*" The GAO has reported that H-1B employers categorize more than half of their H-1B workers as entry level and only 6 percent as fully competent. They observe that the wage offered by the employer petitioning to fill a specific job will often be less than the experience and education of the H-1B who fills that job.

27 Some observers argue that the occupational classifications for wage determination are overly broad, effectively low-balling more specialized occupations embedded in the broader wage classification.

28 American Immigration Council, "The H-1B Visa Program: A Primer on the Program and Its Impact on Jobs, Wages, and the Economy," American Immigration Council, Fact Sheet (April 2020), www.americanimmigrationcouncil.org.

29 Nicole Kreisberg, "H1B Jobs: Filling the Skill Gap," American Institute for Economic Research, *Issue Brief* (2014). The analysis uses the American Community Survey, which is also used here in combination with unique H-1B data. The ACS, like almost all major surveys, only classifies immigrants by place of birth or as naturalized citizens. The results of Kreisberg's analysis reinforce the observation of our analysis that foreign-born citizens as well as long-term foreign residents tend to earn more than temporary H-1B workers.

30 National Science Foundation, National Survey of College Graduates (various dates), www.nsf.gov

31 National Science Foundation, National Survey of College Graduates (various dates), www.nsf.gov; B. Lindsay Lowell and Johanna Avato, "The Wages of Skilled Temporary Migrants: Effects of Visa Pathways and Job Portability," *International Migration* 52, no. 3 (2014): 85–98.

32 Jennifer Hunt and Bin Xie, "How Restricted Is the Job Mobility of Skilled Temporary Work Visa Holders?" *Journal of Policy Analysis and Management* 38, no. 1 (2019): 41–64; Xuening Wang, "US Permanent Residency, Job Mobility, and Earnings," *Journal of Labor Economics* 39, no. 3 (2021): 639–671.

33 Daniel Costa and Jennifer Rosenbaum, "Temporary Foreign Workers by the Numbers: New Estimates by Visa Classification," Economic Policy Institute (2017), https://files.epi.org. The H-1B workforce is roughly 37 percent of an estimated 1.2 million temporary highly skilled foreign workers in the United States. Visa programs in similar fields include L intracompany transferees (28 percent), F-OPT Optional Practical Training visa for students (11 percent), TNs for Canadians and

Mexicans (4 percent), and O extraordinary ability (3 percent). The remaining J exchange visitor visas (18 percent) include both summer jobbers and the highly skilled generally in nonprofit settings.

34 Sunil Mithas and Henry C. Lucas, Jr., "Are Foreign IT Workers Cheaper? U.S. Visa Policies and Compensation of Information Technology Professionals," *Management Science* 56 (2010): 745–765. The comparison group includes natives and foreign-born workers who have become naturalized citizens, biased toward a higher comparative average, and it excludes a large share of other foreign-born workers both temporary and permanent (see foregoing).

35 Jonathan T. Rothwell and Neil Ruiz, "H-1B Visas and the STEM Shortage: A Research Brief," SSRN (May 11, 2013), http://dx.doi.org.

36 US Government Accountability Office (GAO), "H-1B Visa Program: Reforms Are Needed to Minimize the Risks and Costs of Current Program," GAO-11-26 (2011), www.gao.gov. The GAO analysis is more limited but similar in nature to Rothwell and Ruiz's research in "H-1B Visas and the STEM Shortage." It also uses actual H-1B petitions data while capturing native-born earnings with the Current Population Survey. Yet, the GAO finds natives earn more in IT occupations.

37 Magnus Lofstrom and Joseph Hayes, "H-1Bs: How Do They Stack Up to US Born Workers?" *IZA Discussion Paper* no. 6259 (2011).

38 Lofstrom and Hayes, "H-1Bs." The FOIA data request to the USCIS was made by Dr. Lofstrom and he kindly shared the data upon request and helpfully responded to questions about the data.

39 These are not data on visas "issued" to H-1Bs but rather data on "petitions" for individual workers for whom visas are then either issued abroad or awarded within the United States (change of an existing visa).

40 The addition of the two datasets yields 5,175,000 observations, of which the petitions are a little more than half.

41 With few exceptions, particularly in STEM jobs, the H-1B visa is for full-time, year-round workers. Employers apply first to the Department of Labor (DOL) for approval to fill a job(s). The petition to Homeland Security for an individual worker follows DOL's approval. I tabulated data from the Office of Labor Certifications (OFLC), showing that 98 percent of IT employers' applications are for full-time and year-round workers paid an annual salary. See Department of Labor (DOL), "Performance Data: Employment and Training Administration," www.dol.gov.

42 Core STEM is defined as occupations in information technology, the natural sciences, and engineering. A broader definition of STEM includes social science jobs, of which there are relatively few among H-1B visaholders. Core STEM jobs also do not encompass, as sometimes thought, jobs in healthcare that employ few H-1Bs.

43 The "IT sector" as defined here excludes some occupations relevant to "IT" but is roughly limited to the strongest demand for Indian workers. The category is a subset of all STEM jobs.

44 In non-STEM jobs a still high but somewhat lesser 33 percent of H-1Bs and 15 percent of domestic workers are younger than 30 years of age.

45 Matloff, "Are Foreign Students the 'Best and Brightest'?"

46 Lowell and Avato, "The Wages of Skilled Temporary Migrants."

47 The H-1B data have no indicator of place of work so we cannot introduce a control for different metropolitan labor markets, which some observers argue markedly conditions earnings outcomes for STEM workers and might be expected to accentuate the findings.

48 The substantially greater earnings of the small share of young, non-Indian H-1Bs pulls up the group's average earnings, resulting in the findings for all young H-1Bs shown in row two of table 5.2.

49 This is double selectivity. International migrants are typically selected to be high performers. The immigration system, by limiting the number of temporary visaholders who can adjust to permanent status, generates additional selective forces on migrants already in the United States.

50 Matloff, "Are Foreign Students the 'Best and Brightest'?"

51 Hira and Hira, *Outsourcing America.*

52 Hal Salzman, Daniel Kuehn, and B. Lindsay Lowell, "Guestworkers in the High-Skill U.S. Labor Market: An Analysis of Supply, Employment and Wage Trends," Economic Policy Institute, *EPI Briefing Paper* no. 359 (2013).

53 Pia Orrenius, Madeline Zavodny, and Stephanie Gullo, "How Does Immigration Fit into the Future of the U.S. Labor Market?" Migration Policy Institute, *MPI Issue Brief* (August 2019).

54 National Academy of Sciences, *The Economic and Fiscal Consequences of Immigration* (Washington, DC: National Academies Press, 2017).

55 Tyler Ransom and John V. Winters, "Do Foreigners Crowd Natives out of STEM Degrees and Occupations? Evidence from the US Immigration Act of 1990," *Journal of Labor Economics* 74, no. 2 (2020): 321–351.

56 Bound et al., "Recruitment of Foreigners."

57 Kirk Doran, Alexander Gelber, and Adam Isen, "The Effects of High-Skilled Immigration Policy on Firms: Evidence from H-1B Visa Lotteries," National Bureau of Economic Research, *Working Paper* no. 20668 (2016).

58 Max Nathan, "The Wider Economic Impacts of High-Skilled Migrants: A Survey of the Literature for Receiving Countries," *IZA Journal of Migration* 3, no. 4 (2014): 1–20.

59 William R. Kerr and William F. Lincoln, "The Supply Side of Innovation: H-1B Visa Reforms and U.S. Ethnic Invention," *Journal of Labor Economics* 28, no. 3 (July 2010): 473–508.

60 Salzman et al., "Guestworkers in the High-Skill U.S. Labor Market." Jennifer Cheeseman Day and Anthony Martinez, "Does Majoring in STEM Lead to a STEM Job After Graduation?" US Census Bureau, *America Counts: Stories Behind the Numbers* (June 2021).

61 The evolving gig economy has already generated demand for young workers, and the future of this globalized industry will surely lead to further changes.

62 Briggs Depew, Peter Norlander, and Todd Sorensen, "Flight of the H-1B: Inter-Firm Mobility and Return Migration Patterns for Skilled Guest Workers," *IZA Discussion Paper* no. 7456 (2013); Banerjee, "Indian IT Workers in the U.S."

63 Jacqueline Hagan and Susana McCollom, "Skill Level and Employer Use of Foreign Specialty Workers," in *Foreign Temporary Workers in America: Policies that Benefit the U.S. Economy*, ed. B. Lindsay Lowell (New York: Quorum Press, 1999), 149–170; Michael P. Smith, "The New High-Tech Braceros: Who Is the Employer? What Is the Problem?" in *Foreign Temporary Workers in America: Policies that Benefit the U.S. Economy*, ed. B. Lindsay Lowell (New York: Quorum Press, 1999), 119–148.

64 Banerjee, "Indian IT Workers in the U.S."

65 Renee Reichl Luthra, "Temporary Immigrants in a High-Skilled Labour Market: A Study of H-1Bs," *Journal of Ethnic and Migration Studies* 35, no. 2 (2009): 227–250.

66 Faiza Patel, Rachel Levinson-Waldman, Sophia DenUyl, and Raya Koreh, "Social Media Monitoring: How the Department of Homeland Security Uses Digital Data in the Name of National Security," Brennan Center for Justice Report (May 22, 2019), www.brennancenter.org.

67 Payal Banerjee, "Indian Information Technology Workers in the United States: The H-1B Visa, Flexible Production, and the Racialization of Labor," *Critical Sociology* 32, nos. 2–3 (2006): 425–445.

68 Seiko Ishikawa, "The Racialization and Exploitation of Foreign Workers by the Law" (Master's thesis, City University of New York, 2017). Ishikawa argues that US visa law is, on its face, neutral, and that government agents favor Indians over other applicant groups. The research finds that institutional/business history also favors Indians in engineering jobs. Ishikawa concludes, nevertheless, that Indian H-1B workers are racialized.

69 Hira, "Immigration Reforms."

70 These data cannot distinguish between US-owned companies and foreign-owned multinationals. The former are sometimes argued to be better actors than the latter, others argue that there is no effective difference. That question cannot be addressed with these data.

71 Lofstrom and Hayes, "H-1Bs."

72 Xiaochu Hu and B. Lindsay Lowell, "Estimating the Temporary Workforce of H-1B Specialty Workers in the United States." Paper presented at the Society of Government Economists Annual Meeting, Washington, DC, May 13, 2016.

73 Depew et al., "Flight of the H-1B"; Hunt and Xie, "How Restricted Is the Job Mobility of Skilled Temporary Work Visa Holders?" These findings somewhat undercut the idea that H-1Bs are firmly tied to a specific job and/or employer,

which reduces their bargaining power. Regardless, H-1B workers may still temper their wage expectations in the hope of landing sponsorship for a permanent visa.

74 Gregory DeFreitas, "Nonimmigrant Visa Programs: Problems and Policy Reforms," in *Foreign Temporary Workers in America: Policies that Benefit the U.S. Economy*, ed. B. Lindsay Lowell (Westport, CT: Quorum Books, 1999), 171–178.

6

Elusive Permanent Residency

Democratic Deficit of Skilled Temporary Foreign Workers

SANGAY K. MISHRA

Recruitment of skilled foreign workers has been a significant part of economic migration to the United States. Greater migration of skilled professionals was triggered by the cold war rivalry between the Soviet Union and the United States, including the competition for superiority in the field of science and technology. The Immigration and Nationality Act of 1965 (the Hart-Celler Act), widely known for giving prominence to highly skilled workers, initiated a small stream of skilled workers in response to this competition. This stream of skilled workers kept growing over the years, and the shift to skilled immigration in 1965 also coincided with a change in the source of immigration—an overwhelming majority of skilled workers were now coming from different parts of Asia.[1] The wave of highly skilled immigration from Asia became stronger in subsequent years and changed dramatically with the information technology boom in the 1990s.[2]

One of the most significant developments in relation to highly skilled workers is the emergence of temporary work visas, such as the H-1B, L1, and J1, to manage the need for skilled temporary foreign workers.[3] The H-1B is a nonimmigrant visa that allows US employers to recruit foreign workers with needed skills and professional qualifications. The H-1B visa, however, also highlights the precarity of temporary work visas. The precarity does not simply pertain to restrictions regarding the time limit on the visa, terms of employment, and quality of job, but also relates to the possibility of the workers and their families settling down permanently in the United States after years of work. Even though H-1B is a dual-intent visa, unlike many other temporary employment visas, which allows a path for permanent residency and citizenship, many skilled workers with this visa have to wait for more than 10–15 years to acquire permanent residency.[4] This problem has become particularly vexing given the complicated nature of the immigrant visa (permanent residency, or green card) distribution system, with annual numerical limits combined with visa category limits and per-country caps. Since an overwhelming majority of H-1B workers are from India, the impact of wait time for a green card is disproportionately accentuated in their case.[5]

This chapter analyzes the precarity that the skilled temporary foreign worker visa produces, particularly in the context of acquiring permanent residency and long-term settlement in the United States. The chapter argues that the precarity experienced by H-1B workers goes against the democratic norm of equality and fairness. Precarity as a concept has been used in multiple contexts that deal with citizenship, immigration, minority identities, and mobility. The temporary status of migrants without the rights associated with permanent residency or citizenship produces particular forms of precarity that cut across skill levels of migrants. The literature on migration generally does not associate highly educated and well-paid skilled migrants with the notion of precarity, a concept deployed more commonly for low-wage migrants, undocumented populations, and refugees. However, the precarious nature of skilled migration has been highlighted by recent work on skilled migration that points to the neoliberal regime of flexible global labor combined with immigration policies of receiving countries that make permanent settlement difficult even for skilled migrants. A study by Shaohua Zhan and Min Zhou of Chinese and Indian skilled temporary migrants in Singapore points to the precarity these workers face due to the restrictive immigration policy of Singapore, which is further accentuated by a global flexible skilled labor regime that has weakened labor protections considerably.[6]

This chapter draws upon the discussion of precarity faced by skilled migrants in restrictive immigration regimes to understand the experiences of H-1B workers in the United States. It also engages with the literature in the field of political theory that highlights the value of time and how it is judged differently in the case of migrants. In the case of skilled workers, the longer wait for residency and citizenship could be temporally unjust given the arbitrary nature of wait time that these workers must withstand. The precarity and uncertainty the H-1B workers face are directly linked to the disproportional nature of wait time that they have to endure, but the scholarship on immigration has not focused on how delays due to wait time produce inequality and marginalization irrespective of skill levels. The centrality of wait time, the chapter argues, is an important element of the precarity that temporary foreign skilled workers sustain in the United States. The chapter also points to the racialized nature of skilled workforce recruitment and settlement policies that lead to disproportional wait time for particular national origin groups.

H-1B Visas and Emergence of Temporary Workers

The guest or temporary worker program was developed in the early- to mid-twentieth century to meet the growing demand for workers, with an implicit assumption that they would come to the United States for a relatively short period of time and return to their country of origin eventually.[7] It was created in the context of the restrictionist immigration regime that started with the 1924 quota act.[8] A new category of H1 visa was created through the Immigration and Nationality Act of 1952 to hire temporary workers without giving them a long-term right to stay in the country.[9] The restrictionist regime was more comfortable with temporary workers than immigrants who planned to settle in the United States.

The Bracero program (1942–1963) was one of the first such programs that brought millions of temporary low-skilled workers from Mexico, eventually creating a crisis moment that led to the large-scale deportation of Mexican workers as well as American citizens of Mexican descent. The Bracero program is now seen as a troubling period in American immigration history, where the use of the temporary worker category led to Operation Wetback, a draconian policy of deportation and racial profiling.[10] The Bracero program was rescinded eventually, but the temporary worker program became a feature of the American immigration system. In 1943, only a year after the creation of the Bracero program, Jamaican workers were recruited to work on Florida sugar plantations under a temporary visa program.[11] The H2 visa has been extensively used since its creation in 1952 to recruit low-skilled temporary workers for both agricultural and non-agricultural work. The H2 visa program—which was amended in 1986 as part of the Immigration Reform and Control Act, creating H-2A for agricultural programs and H-2B for non-agricultural programs—has been criticized for creating conditions for extreme exploitative labor practices. These workers remain completely dependent on their employers, who use workers' temporary status to deny them proper wages and place them in harmful working conditions. Exploitative practices of recruitment agencies and threat of deportation by employers are endemic features of the low-skilled temporary workers' program as implemented currently. Moreover, the protections available on paper are seldom enforced.[12]

A significant addition to the temporary workers' program came with the Immigration Act of 1990; the H-1B visa was created for highly skilled workers, with an annual cap of 65,000 visas. The H-1B visa allowed employers to hire foreign workers on a temporary basis for jobs that fell under the category of specialty occupations requiring theoretical and practical application of a body of highly specialized knowledge alongside a bachelor's degree or its equivalent. Classified under a nonimmigrant category, this particular visa could last up to six years. The legislation enacted in 1990 gave the H-1B an exalted status of dual-intent visa, which allowed these workers to apply for permanent residency provided an employer was willing to sponsor the application for permanent residency. The H-1B conversion to permanent residency, however, has been subject to multiple requirements and numerical caps, and the transition is often uncertain and extremely challenging, with no guarantees.[13]

When the H-1B visa was introduced in 1990, it was most widely used by the information technology (IT) sector. The IT industry lobbied the US Congress to raise the annual cap from 65,000 to make it possible to hire more workers on temporary visas. The Y2K moment—which anticipated major problems with computer programming systems in formatting the calendar year when year 2000 arrived—created a further rush to hire more tech workers on temporary visas to help manage the crisis in the late 1990s. The American Competitiveness and Workforce Improvement Act of 1998 increased the H-1B cap to 115,000 for the fiscal years 1999 and 2000. The demand for H-1B workers exceeded the cap and the US Congress was again approached to increase the cap. The American Competitiveness in the 21st Century Act of 2000 further raised the yearly cap to 195,000 for the years 2000 to 2003. Between 1991 and 2000, an estimated 900,000 skilled workers entered the United States on the H-1B visa. That figure has kept increasing over the years; between 2000 and 2016, the annual H-1B petition approval ranged between approximately 200,000 and 350,000.[14]

Overall, the demand for H-1B visas has been increasing sharply. In a given year, the number of petitions filed for H-1B visa far exceed the annual visa limit, forcing the government to introduce a lottery system to deal with the increasing number of applications. Currently, the law generally limits the annual H-1B admissions to 65,000, but a sizable section of H-1B workers are exempted from the annual limit because they are returning workers or work for universities or nonprofit research centers that are exempt from the limit. In 2014, the US Citizenship and Immigration Services (USCIS) approved 318,824 H-1B petitions, an increase from a twenty-first-century low point of 192,900 in 2010, possibly caused by the economic recession of 2007–2009.[15] The number of H-1B approvals have increased in subsequent years, with total annual petition approvals of 334,961 (2018), 389,378 (2019), and 426,710 (2020).[16] The increase in the number of H-1B visas over the years, however, was not accompanied by an increase in the annual number of green cards allotted under different employment categories, creating a crisis of exceptionally long wait time that accentuates the precarity produced by a flexible labor regime enhanced by temporary visas.

Scholarly and policy works have pointed to the problems of temporary visas, such as the H-1B for skilled workers, particularly underlining how it impacts the quality of jobs, protections against wage theft, and arbitrary harassment.[17] A big part of the problem is the way the H-1B visa is structured—it is not a type of work permit that allows one to work in the United States for any chosen employer. Rather, this visa is an employer-specific and employment-based visa. When employers want to hire a skilled foreign national, they petition the federal immigration agency, the USCIS, for visas so that potential employees may work for the petitioning employers specifically. An employer must agree to process an H-1B for the employee to be able to work legally for that employer. Individuals who work under the H-1B visa for their petitioning companies have no independent claim to this visa for working or residing in the country.

The complete dependence on the employer to maintain the visa is a major part of the H-1B visa regime that creates serious constraints for the employees. Payal Banerjee argues that the H-1B visas emerged as a part of the larger national pattern of creating a flexible labor force that does not encumber IT companies with a large number of employees that it cannot get rid of easily. The H-1B visa regime comes with a flexibility that creates complete dependence of the skilled workers on the employers as far as their ability to stay and work in the United States is concerned. Banerjee points to the regime of subcontracting and temporary employment, a model of employment that has become a part of the IT industry in cases of both migrant and native workers, that creates particular kinds of vulnerabilities for migrant workers. Banerjee explains:

> The organization of employment in IT occupations corresponds roughly to three segments: the clients, a set of consulting companies that place their employees on clients' projects, and subcontracting companies that supply contract workers to the consulting companies. The consulting company's project team for the client is created by mixing, on a temporary basis, a few of its own employees, usually placed at upper managerial levels on the projects, with several other IT professionals, variously referred to by the interviewees as "contract workers," "contractors," or "consultants," from a large number of companies serving as subcontractors. What is unique about the induction of Indian IT workers on the H-1B visa is that this group is overwhelmingly concentrated at the subcontracting level, where citizens are not to be found . . . workers on H-1B visas are virtually restricted from entering the upper tiers of relatively well-established consulting companies due to the dual impact of their immigration status and the logic of flexible production.[18]

The direct employment of H-1B workers by major firms has been less common, and the needs of these firms are met primarily through subcontracting firms. The dependence of migrant skilled workers on subcontracting firms "creates a set of contractual, dead-end, extremely transient positions without any benefits or job stability for people who are placed at these companies through subcontracting firms."[19] This feature of H-1B visas has become even more important since skilled immigration is now completely dominated by temporary workers who enter the United States through this visa.

Scholarly works suggest that the exploitative practices associated with the H-1B visas have worsened in recent years. Along the lines of analysis produced by Banerjee, Maria L. Ontiveros suggests that there are different kinds of skilled worker hiring practices through this visa category, and a sizable portion of these workers are employed in firms that operate like "body shops."[20] Ontiveros has constructed three typologies of H-1B workers: pure H-1B, outsourcing H-1B, and body shop workers. In this typology, pure H-1B are employees who arrive on visas sponsored by specific companies for which they will work. This kind of H-1B visa is generally considered to be the best and most desired because the worker is employed directly by the company and the possibilities of sponsorship for a green card are higher in such cases. These workers might feel that they have achieved their dream job in the United States and they think of a long-term future in the United States. However, even the pure H-1B employees often find themselves working excessive hours for substandard pay and are often afraid of protesting the work conditions for fear of being discharged and losing the visa. The biggest problem for them arises from being underpaid, overworked, and not being able to complain for fear of having their visas revoked. In some cases, these employees do protest their conditions. For example, a lawsuit brought by 800 workers, many with H-1B visas, at the Siebel Systems software company highlighted the conditions H-1B workers faced, particularity long working hours without overtime compensation. The media coverage of the lawsuit used the term "Siebel Slaves" to describe how the company deliberately chose temporary foreign skilled workers because these workers were grateful to come to the United States and were unlikely to protest. The lawsuit resulted in a $27.5 million settlement to compensate foreign workers who were misclassified as exempt employees ineligible for overtime.[21]

The outsourcing H-1B visa holders, the second kind in this typology, arrive on a visa sponsored by an outsourcing company that is contracted to perform work at a company in the United States. The outsourcing category of H-1B workers are often brought in to replace existing workers, and it becomes controversial because in many cases local workers are replaced by temporary foreign workers. There are multiple examples of legal disputes, for example, in cases such as Southern California Edison, Disney World, and Nor Cal Electric, among others. Ontiveros suggests that since H-1B workers are typically paid less and are subject to bad working conditions, they become the benchmark with which other workers must compete. She argues, "the conditions facing the outsourced labor, in effect, set the market price and terms and conditions for the entire labor force."[22]

However, it is the third type—the body shop workers—that captures the most exploitative aspect of temporary visas. It encompasses a significant segment of the H-1B workers. The companies characterized as body shops tend to be relatively small and they sponsor visas for a significant number of H-1B workers. Body shop employers bring H-1B workers to the United States without a specific job or plan. They often place these workers in a series of short-term positions, either at reputable companies or with outsourcing vendors, to meet their needs. Body shop employers often violate visa laws by charging the H-1B potential employee an exorbitant fee for the visa application process. To hide the illegal fee, the body shop companies require the employee to pay the fee to a subsidiary company in India or to a relative of the company's owner.[23] Body shop employees are often asked to sign a contract agreeing to pay a variety of fees to their employer—including liquidating damages, typically $10,000–$30,000—if the employee stops working before the end of the contract. This type of fee may seem reasonable to prevent an H-1B employee from leaving a subcontractor to work directly for a client or a competitor, but in reality these fees are more like a bondage fee, putting severe restrictions on an employee from challenging abusive work conditions. Scholars and journalists have pointed to instances where body shops have wielded this power and sued to enforce the provisions.[24]

Body shops produce one of the most distressing situations for H-1B workers since they often bring workers to the United States without a job waiting for them. They are technically employed by the body shop but do not necessarily have work. They are told to "sit on the bench" and wait. These workers do not get paid for the waiting period and are often forced to find temporary menial jobs to make ends meet.[25] The body shop might place them in short-term jobs and not pay for the time between jobs. The employer will often take money from the employee and run it through the payroll system of the body shop to make it appear as if the money came from a high-tech employer. The workers "on the bench" waiting for work sometimes live in cramped guesthouses provided by the body shops. These guesthouses might have eight to ten workers living in a small space and they are charged exorbitant amounts for rent. Guesthouses are also used as a form of control because the owners prevent the workers from leaving the premises. Because the body shop is the official employer for these workers, it controls workers' paychecks, and there are reports of wage theft and withholding of part of the salary to cover "expenses" and "taxes."[26] Another form of wage theft occurs when the body shop places an H-1B visa in a fictitious job in an area with a low prevailing wage rate (possibly the Midwestern or Southern states) and places the employee in an area (possibly the East Coast corridor) that requires higher wages, whereby the employee is paid a lower salary and the body shop keeps the difference.

These practices associated with H-1B visas are a product of a larger structural trend of labor flexibility that thrives on temporary labor, a lean workforce, minimal labor protections, and outsourcing of skilled work both inside the United States and outside. Temporariness and flexibility of the workforce are major features of the skilled labor regime that relies on H-1B visas for part of its labor recruitment. Moreover, the flexible skilled labor regime benefits from a significant trend within US immigration that has come to rely increasingly on the temporary work visa. The last thirty years have shown a consistent and significant change in the US immigration system, particularly employment-related immigration, that has come to rely on temporary employment visas to meet its labor needs for workers at all skill levels.

Proliferation of Temporary Work Visas

The H-1B visa is part of the larger trend of emergence and proliferation of the category of temporary workers—both skilled and unskilled. The proliferation of temporary work visa categories is a trend that has not been adequately highlighted in the immigration literature and policy debates. Traditionally, the United States allowed immigrants to settle down relatively quickly and acquire permanent residency with ease, but that ended with the decline of European immigration by the mid-twentieth century. A system of guest workers or the temporary worker program came to acquire a very important place in the current immigration system. As discussed earlier, the legacy of one of the first short-term work visa programs that brought Caribbean sugar workers in 1943 goes back to the Bracero program, lasting from 1942 to 1963, which brought 4.6 million contract workers from Mexico to work in agriculture and other unskilled industries. Even as the temporary worker programs through H-2A and H-1B visas have been highly beneficial for the American economy and contributed to the creation of a flexible labor market, they have resulted in producing a crisis by creating a segment of the labor force that retains temporary status for long periods of time; their wait for permanent status defies any sense of temporal justice.

Scholars of immigration have pointed to the trend of an increase in the volume of temporary or nonimmigrant visas over the last few decades, particularly to deal with the need for skilled workers. Katharine Donato and Catalina Amuedo-Dorantes compare the overall numbers of immigrant and nonimmigrant (temporary) visas over the years and show that both kinds of visas tracked closely in terms of numbers, but there was a dramatic increase in the gap between nonimmigrant visas and immigrant visas after 2008.[27] Between 2009 and 2015, temporary nonimmigrant visas increased from six million to eleven million, and declined thereafter to about ten million in 2018. In comparison, the number of permanent immigrant visas has remained significantly smaller and stable, around one million per year since 2004.

Moreover, Donato and Amuedo-Dorantes specifically look at the number of temporary nonimmigrant work visas to demonstrate how it has come to acquire a significant place in the US immigration system dealing with employment. Mapping trends of nonimmigrant temporary work visas between 1997 and 2018, they show that during this time period, temporary nonimmigrant work visas more than doubled, from approximately 300,000 to 800,000. In addition, every year, high-skilled temporary visas outnumbered low-skilled visas. However, both declined during the Obama administration due to the Great Recession. The authors further show that the number of immigrant employment visas that allow permanent residence has always been far smaller than temporary nonimmigrant employment visas. For instance, in 2017, approximately 150,000 immigrant employment visas were issued in comparison to 800,000 temporary work visas in the same year. Based on the trend over the years, the authors argue that the legal immigration system, particularly in the realm of employment, has become far more reliant on temporary nonimmigrant visas.

Daniel Costa also points to a similar trend and suggests that in the years following the 1990 Immigration Act, a clear pattern emerged where employment immigration became heavily tilted in favor of temporary nonimmigrant visas relative to immigrant visas that provided permanent residency. Costa elaborates how the creation of multiple categories of temporary work visas alongside expansion of existing ones in the 1990s led to a heavy reliance on temporary visas for recruitment of workers, both high- and low-skilled. Costa adds that wage theft, bad working conditions, and other exploitative practices have become a major feature of temporary visas. Furthermore, he suggests that temporary visas have become a serious impediment for long-term social and political incorporation of workers, since their path to permanent residency is prolonged and limited.[28] In the current immigration system, even those temporary workers who have a possible path to permanent residency (H-1B workers) are confronted with major delays and procedural hurdles due to numerical caps on different visa categories alongside country caps.

Being a modified continuation of the older guest worker program, the H-1B visa for skilled workers is seen by critics as the most recent program to bring in a racialized workforce—primarily Asian immigrant workers—and to keep them powerless through visa restrictions. This creates a flexible workforce that simultaneously benefits tech industries without burdening them too much with labor protections and wage restrictions. The temporary visa also does the work of not allowing the racialized workers to easily settle permanently in the United States and gives a nod to the lobbies that want to keep permanent immigration restricted. Analyzing the experience of Indian tech workers in the United States, Sharmila Rudrappa argues:

> Guest worker programs resolve the tensions the American state faces in nation-building. The needs of capital drive the demand for labor, pulling in non-white workers from various parts of the world, but the nation is built on the abstract citizen—a white (male) person. Although the needs of the nation and the needs of capital are diametrically opposed, these

contradictory needs are resolved through guest worker programs. These programs keep labor transaction costs low, but, by denying non-white workers citizenship, also expunge guest workers from the national body. As "guests," non-white workers are seen solely as value-adding, labor-bearing bodies to be deployed when needed for capital's benefit. Their human qualities and concrete social lives matter little; they are seen as inherently non-existent.[29]

The experience of the last thirty years, following the creation of high-skilled temporary visas in 1990, suggests that they have produced a large number of temporary workers. A restrictive immigration regime and a lack of consensus on immigration reform have resulted in a system of skilled immigration that is open to temporary work visas in high numbers but remains highly restrictive about providing a path to permanent settlement of these workers. A steady growth in the overall numbers of H-1B visas has been accompanied by a strict limit on green cards allocated for the category of employment. As a result, even as H-1B visa holders are eligible for green cards and potential permanent settlement, these temporary workers are confronted with a highly restrictive, racialized, and complex immigration system that devalues their time as well as their worth in US society.

Temporariness and Transition to Long-Term Settlement: The Indian Skilled Workers' Racialized Experience

Being a dual-intent visa, the attraction of transition to a permanent immigrant status—a green card—is a major incentive for H-1B skilled workers. A dual-intent visa allows foreign nationals to be temporarily present in the United States with the intention of possibly immigrating to the United States permanently. This is significant because most temporary visas require that the visitor intends to return home. However, notwithstanding the dual-intent nature of the H-1B visa, the path to permanent residency is not an easy one for H-1B visa holders in practice. Having an H-1B nonimmigrant visa adjusted to an immigrant visa depends on multiple contingencies, such as employer sponsorship, availability of green cards in relation to visa category, country limits, and efficiency of government bureaucracies. The structure of employment-based green cards is set up in a way that creates major bottlenecks and multiple uncertainties that render the process highly stressful for skilled workers. Moreover, the flow of high-skilled immigrants from India and China in large numbers has further aggravated vulnerabilities for workers from these countries, suggesting the racialized nature of immigration wait time.

High-skilled migration to the United States since the 1965 immigration reform has been dominated by migrants from Asia, and this trend has been further accentuated in recent years. The H-1B category, for instance, has been overwhelmingly dominated by workers from India. According to one estimate, more than 70 percent of H-1B workers currently are from India and in 2016, 74 percent of 345,000 H-1B visas went to migrants from India.[30] Given the fact that an overwhelming majority of H-1B visa holders are from India, the transition to permanent residency has become extremely difficult for this group of skilled workers, since the current system of country and category caps has resulted in extreme delays for highly skilled Indian workers, producing further precarity and uncertainty for them. The longer wait for green cards is thus part of the restrictive nature of temporary skilled visas that is based on the presumption that these workers are in the United States temporarily, producing an extremely restrictive regime of green cards for skilled workers.

The growing wait time for temporary skilled workers to obtain a green card reflects a certain level of anxiety about skilled economic migrants in American society. The ongoing debate about H-1B workers replacing native workers feeds into this anxiety of oversupply of high-skilled foreign workers, creating political support for a restrictive green card regime.[31] Scholars of immigration suggest that legal immigrants to the United States can face two different types of waits. Almost all immigrants experience the first kind—the time the government takes to process the petitions and applications for green cards. It is an administrative process that typically ranges from a few months to a couple of years at any given point. It is the second category of wait that is extremely daunting, and approximately a third of all immigrants experience it—the time it takes for a green card to become available under immigration quotas. Since the current immigration system has limited the number of green cards, not everyone who is eligible and applies for a green card is able to get one immediately. Some have to endure a long wait time before they are able to acquire a green card. The H-1B visa holders—particularly from India and, to a lesser extent, from China—belong to this category and they experience the wait time very differently in comparison to other H-1B skilled workers who apply for green cards.

The type of wait caused by a simple unavailability of green cards requires a longer explanation. The immigration categories with quotas and waiting lists are the "preference categories," which have been created for employment as well as family visa preferences. For example, under employment preference there are categories such as EB1 (Priority Workers), EB2 (Advance Degree or Exceptional), and EB3 (Other skilled Workers) with a pre-decided number of green card visas allotted for each preference category for each year. Moreover, the law also limits the number of green cards that any one nationality can receive. The rule is that one nationality cannot receive more than 7 percent of the total green cards in a category plus any unused green cards distributed to nationals on a first-come, first-served basis in a given category. For example, Indian nationals cannot receive more than 7 percent of green card slots allotted for the EB2 category and possibly more if there are unused visas. Nationality-based quotas, known as country limits, result in each nationality waiting in lines that move at different speeds within each category. For instance, the wait time for Mexican siblings of US citizens is different from that of Chinese siblings of US citizens. According to David Bier of the Cato Institute, for the most part, only four nationalities—Indian, Chinese, Filipinos, and Mexicans—reach the country limit of green cards, thereby leading to other nationalities passing them in the line.

Overall, the average wait time for a green card in all preference categories—family as well as employment—has doubled since 1991 when these preference categories were first introduced. The wait time in all employment categories has increased for all nationalities. The average wait time for all employment categories in 1991 was less than six months, which increased to approximately two years in 2018. However, the average wait time conceals the dramatic differences among nationalities and it is most pronounced for Indian-origin skilled workers, who comprise an overwhelming majority of H-1B visas. Many Indian professionals with a college degree (EB3) and Indian advanced degree holders (EB2) waited for a decade for their number to come up in a green card queue. A longer wait time lasting for more than a decade has become a highly common experience for skilled workers from India on the H-1B visa.

The future projections of green card wait times estimated by policy analysts paints a very bleak picture for skilled immigrants from India. According to an estimated projection made by the Cato Institute, H-1B skilled workers from India entering the United States in 2018 and applying under EB2 and EB3 preference categories may have to wait for an impossible half-century. Similar projections are made for multiple family preference categories for certain nationalities. To get a comparative sense, the backlog for Indian skilled workers under EB2 and EB3 preference categories is the second highest (548,641), second only to Mexico family unification preference category (F4) for siblings of adult US citizens (777,378). In fact, the waits are so long that many people waiting for green cards would die before their turn came.[32]

One of the major difficulties that employment-based green card applicants face is that an overwhelming majority of them are waiting for their green card while working in the United States on temporary visas, which is different from a large number of family-based green card applicants who wait in their country of origin. Both have their own challenges, but skilled workers employed in the United States while waiting for years for their green cards face some unique challenges: Their employment options are limited due to the fact that they are dependent on their employee for sponsorship of the green card applications. Their ability to settle down in the United States, acquire citizenship, and become part of the political process are indefinitely delayed. Their spouses and children in the United States, who are typically on dependent visas, are completely limited in terms of their mobility, jobs, and other needs. The H-1B visa has highly restrictive features not only in terms of dependence on one's employer but also in terms of rights that the family members are given while living as dependents on the primary visa holder's H-1B. The spouses of H-1B visa holders do not have the right to work in the United States while they live as dependents on H4 visas. Most spouses who are on H4 dependent visas leave promising careers to join their partners on H-1B in the United States and many of them are not able to return to their careers because of the long wait for green cards that could allow them to work.

A significant change enacted in 2015 by the Obama administration, giving employment authorization for those H4 dependents whose spouses on the H-1B were waiting to obtain green cards, eased the restrictions on dependent employment for a small segment of this group.[33] H4 dependents are eligible for work authorization only if their spouses have their I-140 (immigration petition for alien workers) approved and are waiting in line for their green card. This allowed some H4 dependents to gain employment, but a large number of them remain ineligible. An overwhelming majority of the H4 dependents are highly educated women from India who move to the United States with their husbands at a point in their lives that is critical for their professional careers. In her book *High-Tech Housewives: Indian IT Workers, Gendered Labor, and Transmigration*, Amy Bhatt takes a very close look at the phenomenon of dependent spouses of Indian H-1B male workers and points out how masculine mobility of the H-1B workers is dependent on women giving up their careers or putting them on hold in order to support labor migration. These women put their careers on hold while they wait for green cards or eligibility to work through employment authorization.

The restrictive immigration regime and the need for flexible labor by corporations creates this system of gendered marginality that has become an integral part of the temporary skilled workers program. The scholarship on the gendered dimension of immigration has pointed to multiple barriers that female skilled foreign workers encounter—one of the most important being credential or skill devaluation. Misba Bhatti, analyzing the experience of Pakistani women skilled workers in the United States, argues that women are more vulnerable to de-skilling and often end up taking jobs that are lower-level or unskilled in comparison to their education and skill levels.[34] The process of de-skilling is apparent among women on H4 dependent visas—they face a challenging labor market when they finally become eligible to work after a long gap, and often must accept jobs that are lower than their education and skill levels.

Scholars of immigration have analyzed how immigration and settlement policies of the receiving countries produce precarity for skilled migrants who are generally highly educated and well paid. Zhan and Zhou point to the restrictive permanent residency policy of Singapore that makes it highly precarious for skilled migrants from India and China to navigate the job market while their residency rights are restrictive.[35] The Indian skilled workers in the United States have similar experiences in which H-1B temporary visas not only limit their job choices and their ability to settle down on a permanent basis but also put restrictions on their spouses to pursue their careers.

The precarity created by bureaucratic restrictions on H-1B visa holders has been reflected starkly in the kinds of restrictions they have had to face during the COVID-19 pandemic. There have been multiple reports of COVID-19–related restrictions faced by H-1B visa holders who have lived in the United States for more than ten years while awaiting their green cards. Many of them had to travel to India during the pandemic to care for their parents or relatives but were not allowed to return to their families in the United States once travel restrictions were imposed after the second COVID-19 outbreak in India in March 2021. The US government allowed its citizens and green card holders to travel back, but anyone with temporary visas such as the H-1B faced restrictions.[36] Such crisis moments point to the precarity faced by H-1B skilled workers who have created a life for themselves in the United States but are subjected to multiple restrictions due to their prolonged wait time for green cards.

Wait Time as an Immigrant Democratic Deficit

One of the important points missing from the immigration debate, particularly those pertaining to high-skilled immigrants, is the way in which durational wait time is an important part of the experience of precarity faced by skilled migrants. In this section, I draw upon the concept of durational time and its relationship to the notions of justice and equality to suggest that a disproportionately prolonged wait time and its impact on temporal justice should be considered an important element of any policy discussion dealing with immigration. One might argue that as temporary migrants, H-1B visa holders cannot demand fairness and equality and that such claims are perhaps more appropriate for US citizens only. However, in many realms of the law, the temporary workers are eligible for equality and fairness under the law, and the framework discussed below explains why that is important.

Time is an equally critical asset for people across class, race, and gender divides. In social and political life, time measurements are almost ubiquitous. For instance, there is an age requirement for the right to vote, incarceration for crimes is measured in time, there is a time requirement for those who are eligible to naturalize, etc. Time is used to confer or deny rights, and such use of time is particularly stark in the case of immigrants. Skilled migrants from India are positioned such that their time in the immigration queue has no equivalence with those similarly positioned in terms of wait time. I draw upon Elizabeth Cohen's work on the political economy of durational time to analyze the experience of skilled workers with H-1B visas and the democratic implications of their wait time for permanent residency.[37]

Media reporting as well as scholarly and policy work on skilled migrants in the United States point to the centrality of wait time in their lives. The transition from temporary status (H-1B visa) to a permanent status (green card) is a highly significant change for these skilled migrants, and for a large number of these skilled workers the trend of increasingly long wait times has become one of their most frustrating realities. The bureaucratic immigration regime of green card numerical limits and country caps has led to a system that appears rational and impartial but in fact creates long wait times for a large number of workers. The need to think about the importance of time and injustice inherent in long wait times has never been greater. Recent scholarly works have pointed to the importance of durational time as a category while thinking about immigration policymaking.

Elizabeth Cohen describes how time plays an important role in structuring the ways in which states grant rights, mete out punishments, and distribute benefits. She draws upon examples from multiple facets of social and political arenas to illustrate the centrality of time as a category in granting rights or deciding punishments. To underline the significance of duration time in establishing the broader democratic principles of fairness and equality, she points to time-related issues such as gaining voting rights once a person turns eighteen, gaining retirement benefits upon turning sixty-two or sixty-six years old, and receiving prison sentences of varying durations, depending on the crime. Duration time, Cohen suggests, is a prerequisite for the acquisition and exercise of multiple rights in liberal democratic societies. It is virtually impossible, she argues, to find an arena of social and political life where durational time does not figure prominently. "Prison sentences, naturalization procedures, social welfare benefits eligibility, abortion restrictions, and probationary periods are only a few of the most prominent examples of laws and policies that confer or deny rights and political status based on formulae that include precise duration of time," argues Cohen.[38] In this analysis, durational time becomes a tool of power in the hands of the state and its institutions, determining whose time is valuable and who cannot make a claim to equality in the realm of valuation of time.

In every liberal democratic society, durational time has an assigned political value. The valuing of time in political processes transforms time into a political good that becomes a matter of negotiation when state and political subjects transact over power. Cohen's argument to treat durational time as a political good has important implications for how durational time is treated in political and policy debates. This conception of durational time demands a robust approach to wait time to understand the issue of justice in relation to durational time and temporal justice. The importance of temporal justice is underlined by the fact that in political and policy deliberations, a similarly situated person's time is not treated as having similar value. Wait time, which is at the center of this chapter, needs to be understood as a differential valuation of time, depending on the status of the person waiting. Cohen urges political thinkers and policy analysts to understand the relationship between duration time as used in political power distribution and social justice. She argues, "Racialized incarceration practices, delayed naturalization, and obstructionist abortion awaiting periods are all instances in which select people's time is appropriated as a means of denying them rights that others enjoy."[39]

Individuals on temporary employment visas with a possibility of acquiring permanent residency and eventual naturalization confront the issue of time while they wait for their turn. As discussed earlier, the wait for H-1B visa holders, particularly in the case of Indian skilled workers, who apply for green cards becomes endless. The emergence and proliferation of the category of temporary workers—both skilled and unskilled—is a trend that has become an important feature of the current immigration system and it brings the issue of temporal injustice to the fore of immigration conversations.

Cohen argues that time is supposed to apply to all individuals in an identical manner and time is preferable to measuring fitness for citizenship in comparison to property or more subjective judgments such as social and political incorporation. Time allows all persons an equal chance to demonstrate their capacity for citizenship and becoming a permanent member of society. To treat someone's time as valueless is tantamount to denying them equality at a fundamental level. When this argument is used to understand temporary workers who are in the process of becoming permanent residents, it is very clear that the state's willingness to take their wait time into account while deciding on green cards is almost non-existent. Cohen argues,

> Immigration is an ascribed status in much the same way as is racial classification. The state's refusal to grant credit to the time spent by temporary workers and other nonimmigrant foreign-born person in the U.S. is analogous to both racial and gender-based citizenship distinctions whose eradication is celebrated. The suggestion that equally situated persons are differentially capable of citizenship conjures the kind of arguments that were once used to claim that women and racial minorities were incapable of consent, patriotism, or other means of entering the demos.[40]

The larger political import of this argument is evident in the case of undocumented immigrants who might be living in the United States as long as 20–25 years but do not have a realistic path of acquiring legal status, and their time has no real value in pursuing legalization. It is a political crisis that connects to the idea of justice and fairness and the democratic problems of maintaining a permanent underclass without citizenship rights.

Cohen's argument points to the devaluing of immigrants as racial minorities, with immigrant women being particularly devalued in American society. The testimony by H-1B workers about the impact of wait times on their lives points to a lack of inclusion and suggests a differential treatment that does not take into account the amount of time they are required to wait just because they are from a particular nationality. There is no acknowledgment of the racialized nature of this wait, which gets produced through a bureaucratic labyrinth comprised of category limits and country caps. For a certain category of migrants, the dimension of duration time that lends itself to unequal treatment is not considered relevant. This non-egalitarian system of prolonged wait time has consequences that are similar to impacts caused by discriminatory treatment on the basis of race or gender and, in this case, it is made invisible by a bureaucratic process that often goes unnoticed.

Testimonies from those affected by prolonged wait times point to the real-life impact of discriminatory treatment. As reported in the *Washington Post*, Yogi Chhabra, an IT professional in his fifties based in Louisville, Kentucky, is on the verge of family separation due to the long wait for his green card.[41] His case epitomizes the disruptions and difficulties that skilled workers have to endure as they wait for their turn to come. Chhabra has lived in the United States for twenty-one years and has been in the green card backlog for nine years. His son is on a dependent visa connected to the father's H-1B visa, but twenty-one is the age limit for dependent children. Even though Chhabra's son has lived in Kentucky since he was three years old, has received a US education, and currently works as a mechanical engineer, he faces a possible deportation since he is now older than twenty-one and thus not eligible to stay on the dependent visa that he has been on through most of his life. The family considered leaving the United States multiple times, since the wait for their green cards has put them in a legal limbo of sorts with many restrictions. Anand Vemuri, an IT professional in his forties who is based in New Jersey, is in a similar position. His sons, now sixteen and thirteen, came to the United States as toddlers. The family has been in the green card backlog for seven years and Vemuri is fearful of his eldest son aging out of eligibility of being a dependent.[42]

The disruptions caused by prolonged wait times can be considered akin to the restrictive quotas imposed on certain nationalities by the 1924 quota act. The act was widely criticized for placing numerical limits on Southern and Eastern European immigration alongside immigrants from Asia. The scholarship on the quota act has demonstrated that the imposition of numerical limits was driven by racial animus against Southern and Eastern Europeans.[43] There is enough evidence in the public and policy discourse to suggest that imposing the quota act was the result of a racialized opposition to these groups. The prolonged wait time for Indian skilled workers due to numerical limits on green cards and country and category caps is similar to the quota act in its impact without explicitly articulating the racial animus. The disproportionately long wait for green cards introduces restrictions similar to the way the quota act imposed numerical limits on certain nationalities rationalized by complex calculations based on census data. In the case of skilled workers, the logic of limited green cards and country caps is used to rationalize the long wait. A more robust critique of durational time as a tool of restricting immigration is required to fully grasp the enormity and impact of the system of green card allocation for skilled workers.

The demands to devise an immigration system that puts a limit on wait times are being articulated by those who have closely observed this system of skilled immigration and green card acquisition.[44] There is an urgent need to foreground the importance of temporal justice in immigration policymaking and to consider wait time as a possible restrictive immigration tool.

Conclusion

The emergence of temporary employment visas as a major category in the US immigration system has produced new conditions of precarity for skilled workers who are generally not associated with the experiences of precariousness and marginality. In this chapter, I have shown that part of this precarity comes from the conditions of employment that are deeply connected to a flexible labor market reliant on a lean workforce as well as outsourcing to body shop companies. This precarity also stems from temporary visa–based employment for skilled immigrants who are dependent on employers and face multiple restrictions and bureaucratic hurdles. In the case of H-1B workers from India, and to a lesser extent workers from China, a large part of precarity is produced by an immigration regime that creates long green card wait times for select nationalities. The experiences of H-1B workers from India not only point to the challenges they face in terms of working conditions and wages—even as they are employed in relatively high-paying technology jobs—but also the huge barriers they encounter in acquiring permanent residency. The transition from temporary visa to a permanent status is one of the major challenges for skilled workers from India. The extremely disproportional nature of wait times demands an approach in immigration policy debates that should consider prolonged wait times as a substantive violation that denies justice and equality. This analysis suggests that immigrant labor—both high- and low-skilled—is constituted through a sociohistorical process where educational and class status intersect with immigration regimes and institutional mechanisms shaping immigrants' legal, social, and political inclusion.

This chapter has submitted that durational time is a political good and wait time should be approached through the lens of justice, equality, and distribution of power. The increased inequality for Indian skilled workers in terms of their wait time denies them the right to equality and justice and suggests a racialized devaluation of time that deprives certain populations of fairness and equal treatment integral to the experience of living in a liberal democracy. The immigration debate in the United States has not yet fully acknowledged how a restrictive temporary employment visa program, dominating both skilled and unskilled regimes of migration, has produced precarious conditions for migrant workers in the United States. The prolonged wait time for permanent residency for skilled migrants from India produces restrictions that parallel those introduced through historically restrictive immigration policies, such as the 1924 quota act, in terms of restricting immigration avenues for particular nationalities. The comparison to the 1924 quota act highlights the deliberate nature of the restrictive green card regime, which has produced a system that consistently excludes particular national groups by creating a wait time that could last longer than a decade. The prolonged wait time, however, is presented as a bureaucratic procedure produced through annual numerical limits and country caps and not a racialized restriction on particular nationalities. The chapter has noted that durational time has been used as a restrictive immigration tool to produce results that have delayed permanent residency for particular national groups, creating impacts that are akin to nation-of-origin–based restrictions. A focus on the restrictive role of durational time in future immigration research is needed for any sensible reform in the larger immigration system.

NOTES

1 Erika Lee, *The Making of Asian America: A History* (New York: Simon & Schuster, 2016).

2 Sangay Mishra, *Desis Divided: The Political Lives of South Asian Americans* (Minneapolis: University of Minnesota Press, 2016).

3 The J visa is a temporary nonimmigrant visa also known as the exchange visitors program. The program was created as part of the Mutual Educational and

Cultural Exchange Act of 1961 (the Fulbright-Hays Act) to allow foreign nationals to temporarily reside in the United States and participate in a variety of education or training programs and to promote cultural exchange between the United States and other countries. This visa typically requires returning to the home country. The L visa is divided between L-1A and L-1B and is also a temporary visa used for intracompany transferees, allowing qualified employees to work and live in the United States on a temporary basis. See Donato and Amuedo-Dorantes's chapter in this volume.

4 David Bier, "Immigration Wait Times for Quotas Have Doubled: Green Card Backlogs Are Long, Growing, and Inequitable," Cato Institute, *Policy Analysis* no. 873, June 18, 2019, www.cato.org.

5 The employment green card wait is also long for Chinese nationals. For certain categories of employment green card, Chinese nationals have similar wait times as Indians. However, the overall number suggests a bigger pool of Indian nationals waiting in the line. In 2018, 78 percent of the employment green card waiting line was comprised of Indian nationals in comparison to 17 percent that was comprised of Chinese nationals. See Bier, "Immigration Wait Times for Quotas Have Doubled."

6 Shaohua Zhan and Min Zhou, "Precarious Talent: Highly Skilled Chinese and Indian Immigrants in Singapore," *Ethnic and Racial Studies* 43, no. 9 (2020): 1654–1672.

7 Elizabeth F. Cohen, "The Political Economy of Immigrant Time: Rights, Citizenship, and Temporariness in the Post-1965 Era," *Polity* 47, no. 3 (2015): 337–351.

8 There is a longer history of exclusion of Asian immigrants that started with the 1882 Chinese Exclusion Act and continued with the 1917 Asiatic Barred Zone Act. This history of immigration exclusion was accompanied by exclusion from acquiring citizenship through naturalization that finally ended for all Asians only in 1952. This long exclusionary history shapes how Asian immigrants are treated in the United States. See Zhou's chapter in this volume; and Lee, *The Making of Asian America*.

9 Margaret L. Usdansky and Thomas J. Espenshade, "The H-1B Visa Debate in Historical Perspective: The Evolution of U.S. Policy Toward Foreign-Born Workers," The Center for Comparative Immigration Studies, University of California, San Diego, *CCIS Working Paper* no. 11 (May 2000), https://ccis.ucsd.edu.

10 Ronald L. Mize, *The Invisible Workers of the U.S.-Mexico Bracero Program: Obreros Olvidados* (Lanham, MD: Lexington Books, 2016).

11 Cohen, "The Political Economy of Immigrant Time."

12 Southern Poverty Law Center, "Close to Slavery: Guest Workers Programs in the United States," February 19, 2013, www.splcenter.org.

13 B. Lindsay Lowell, "A Long View of America's Immigration Policy and Supply of Foreign-Born STEM Workers in the United States," *American Behavioral Scientist* 53, no. 7 (2010): 1029–1044; B. Lindsay Lowell, "Temporary Workers and

Evolution of the Specialty H-1B Visa," *International Migration Review, In Defense of the Alien*, 23 (2000): 33–43; also see Lowell's chapter in this volume.

14 Sarah Pierce and Julia Gelatt, "Evolution of the H-1B: Latest Trends in a Program on the Brink of Reform," Migration Policy Institute, *MPI Issue Brief* (2018), www.migrationpolicy.org.

15 Ruth Ellen Wasem, "Temporary Professional, Managerial, and Skilled Foreign Workers: Policy and Trends," Congressional Research Service, CRS Report, January 13, 2016, https://fas.org.

16 US Department of Homeland Security, "Report on H-1B Petitions Fiscal Year 2020 Annual Report to Congress, October 1, 2019–September 30, 2020," February 16, 2021, www.uscis.gov.

17 For more on this, see in this volume chapter 1 by Banerjee, chapter 5 by Lowell, chapter 8 by Thomas, and chapter 9 by Bhatti.

18 Payal Banerjee, "Indian Information Technology Workers in the United States: The H-1B Visa, Flexible Production, and the Racialization of Labor," *Critical Sociology* 32, nos. 2–3 (2006): 433; see also Banerjee's chapter in this volume.

19 Banerjee, "Indian Information Technology Workers in the United States," 437.

20 Maria L. Ontiveros, "H-1B Visas, Outsourcing and Body Shops: A Continuum of Exploitation for High Tech Workers," *Berkeley Journal of Employment and Labor Law* 38 (2017): 21.

21 Ontiveros, "H-1B Visas, Outsourcing and Body Shops."

22 Ontiveros, "H-1B Visas, Outsourcing and Body Shops," 18.

23 Matt Smith, Jennifer Gollan, and Adithya Sambamurthy, "Job Brokers Steal Wages, Entrap Indian Worker in US," *Reveal*, October 27, 2014, https://revealnews.org.

24 Smith et al., "Job Brokers Steal Wages."

25 Moira Herbst and Steve Hamm, "America's High-Tech Sweatshops," *Bloomberg Business Week*, October 2, 2009, www.bloomberg.com.

26 Herbst and Hamm, "America's High-Tech Sweatshops."

27 Katharine M. Donato and Catalina Amuedo-Dorantes, "The Legal Landscape of U.S. Immigration: An Introduction," *RSF: The Russell Sage Foundation Journal of the Social Sciences* 6, no. 3 (2020): 1–16.

28 Daniel Costa, "Temporary Migrant Workers or Immigrants? The Question for U.S. Labor Migration," *RSF: The Russell Sage Foundation Journal of the Social Sciences* 6, no. 3 (2020): 18–44.

29 Sharmila Rudrappa, "Cyber-Coolies and Techno-Braceros: Race and Commodification of Indian Information Technology Guest Workers in the United States," *University of San Francisco Law Review* 44, no. 2 (2010): 372.

30 Pooja B. Vijayakumar and Christopher J. L. Cunningham, "An Indentured Servant: The Impact of Green Card Waiting Time on the Life of Highly Skilled Indian Immigrants in the United States of America," Industrial and Organizational Psychology Translational Research and Working Papers, 2019, https://scholar.utc.edu/iopsy/2.

31 Lowell, "Temporary Workers and Evolution of the Specialty H-1B Visa."

32 Bier, "Immigration Wait Times for Quotas Have Doubled."

33 One of the tragic cases of the H4 dependent visa was Sunayana Dumala, the wife of Srinivas Kuchibhotla, who was shot dead by a gunman in Olathe, Kansas, in 2017 in a hate-crime attack. Kuchibhotla was in line for his green card but due to the long wait had still not received it when he died. As a result, Sunayana Dumala lost her legal status and struggled to procure a visa to stay in the country. Her case shed light on the consequences of the long wait for green cards. See Chris Fuchs, "Widow of Kansas Shooting Victim Temporarily Lost Resident Status," *NBC News*, September 13, 2017, www.nbcnews.com.

34 See Bhatti's chapter in this volume.

35 Zhan and Zhou, "Precarious Talent."

36 Katie Meyer, "N.J. Man Stranded in India by COVID-19 Points to Immigration Problems, Menendez Says," May 24, 2021, *PBS*, WHYY, https://whyy.org.

37 Elizabeth Cohen, *The Political Value of Time: Citizenship, Duration, and Democratic Justice* (Cambridge: Cambridge University Press, 2018).

38 Cohen, *The Political Value of Time*, 2.

39 Cohen, *The Political Value of Time*, 4–5.

40 Cohen, "The Political Economy of Immigrant Time."

41 Abigail Hauslohner, "Employment Green Card Backlog Tops 800,000, Most of Them Indian. A Solution Is Elusive," *Washington Post*, December 17, 2019, www.washingtonpost.com.

42 Hauslohner, "Employment Green Card Backlog."

43 Kunal M. Parker, *Making Foreigners: Immigration and Citizenship Law in America, 1600–2000* (Cambridge: Cambridge University Press, 2015).

44 Marcela F. González, "Precarity for the Global Talent: The Impact of Visa Policies on High-Skilled Immigrants' Work in the United States," *International Migration* (May 2021), https://doi.org/10.1111/imig.12870.

7

International Students

Mobility and Resettlement

TERRY WOTHERSPOON

Rapid technological change combined with an aging workforce has increased the demand for highly skilled workers in the United States and other highly developed nations. Over the past two decades an increasing number of government agencies, scholars, and business organizations have signaled concerns that global competition to address shortages of appropriately qualified workers is intensifying. So explosive are calls to address the "global talent crunch" that many of these commentators are framing the issue as a "worldwide race for talent,"[1] or, in more militaristic terms, as a new "arms race" engaged in the "battle" or "war" for talent.[2] National and regional authorities, taking into account particular economic, labor market, and political circumstances, have adopted a variety of strategies and policy options to address these problems. Accelerated or streamlined investments in higher education, focusing especially on engineering, information, and communication technologies and other STEM (science, technology, engineering, and mathematics) fields in which demands for highly skilled workers, are expanding rapidly. These investments take time to yield results, though, and numbers of domestic students pursuing and completing programs in specialized areas often remain lower than anticipated.[3] Immigration policies and procedures are being streamlined to encourage recruitment of temporary workers and longer-term settlement for desired classes of workers from other nations. However, in many cases, nationalistic movements and political pressures have restricted or blocked options for significant immigration policy reform. Even without such restrictions, options to meet immediate demands through increased use of temporary foreign workers and work authorizations circumstances create vulnerability and risks for many employees while minimizing incentives for employers to invest in longer-term labor market development strategies.

These factors have generated increasing interest in many nations in a middle-ground or multistage strategy focused on initiatives to attract and retain international students in order to meet both short- and longer-term needs for highly qualified labor. International students, by virtue of their decisions to study abroad, present themselves as motivated, adaptable, and highly qualified. Studying in a foreign context provides them with additional opportunities to augment their credentials, training, social networks, and other capacities that enhance their employability as they navigate new social and institutional environments. For employers as well as immigration branches, these circumstances can act as informal screening mechanisms to complement wider immigrant selection processes, especially for those who have opportunities to work during their studies or immediately after graduation, contributing, in the process, to potential convergence of interests among potential employers, governments, and students who see international education as a gateway to longer-term careers and settlement.

This chapter explores recent trends and issues associated with potential pathways to longer-term settlement and immigration for international students. The discussion is focused on the United States, but is also informed by more general developments and experiences in other representative nations. It questions the extent to which policies to promote the retention and eventual settlement of international students are aligned with emerging labor market needs. The analysis begins with a summary of key dimensions and patterns related to the post-graduation plans of international students. It then explores the relationships between the flow of international students and global postsecondary growth, post-study visa options, and immigration prospects for highly skilled workers. It argues that discourses that employ the analogy of a race, while potentially useful for attracting attention to concerns about skills shortages in particular economic sectors, nonetheless fail to capture important nuances and interrelationships associated with the expansion of higher education and volatile labor market dynamics. These relationships, in turn, tend to produce considerable complexity and uncertainty for international students as they navigate diverse pathways from the start of their journey to study in a foreign setting.

Understanding Pathways to Settlement among
International Students

There has been long-standing interest to understand the relationships between status as an international student and prospects for permanent residency. As debates have shifted away from a narrow focus on issues of "brain drain," there has been more careful assessment of the potential contributions that foreign students may offer, relative to other immigrant streams and local workers, to meet demands for highly qualified labor in both host and home nations.[4] Relatively limited comprehensive data are available to enable systematic analyses of the phenomenon that could offer definitive understandings of trends in many national contexts and on a comparative basis.[5] This problem is further complicated by variations in visa categories, definitions and administrative records in diverse contexts, as well as the nature of transition processes across different phases of studies, employment, interim, and post-graduation experiences.[6] These processes have become more complex since the late twentieth century as technological, economic, political, and demographic changes have amplified transformations associated with growth and internationalization of higher education, transnational and cyclical flows of workers and migrants, the nature of employment, and the life course itself.[7] Nonetheless, a clearer picture about transitions is emerging as more nations begin to track initiatives to encourage international students to extend their stay after graduation, complementing literature that addresses economic, political, and social dimensions of highly qualified labor and migration.[8]

Numerous factors influence decisions to study and remain in or leave another country.[9] Substantial proportions of international students are motivated to study in the United States and other highly developed nations as a pathway to employment experience and permanent residence.[10] Data from several OECD nations suggest that about three-quarters (74 percent) of international students who changed their status from a study permit to visa categories enabling them to remain in the nation did so for work-related reasons.[11] However, relationships between studying and settling abroad are not at all straightforward and not always based on post-graduation work options in the nation in which students complete their studies. Many international students have no intention or desire to stay for long, if at all, after graduation. Some are attracted to programs in the United States and other nations in order to gain credentials at high-status institutions or pursue specialized programs, while others value opportunities to gain language skills, social interactions, and cultural experiences that are transferable across a number of settings. Many international students intend or are compelled to return home or settle elsewhere after completing their programs because of conditions associated with scholarships or sponsored funding, family commitments, financial constraints, individual preferences, or employment opportunities. Trajectories are not restricted to staying or returning home; some international graduates who have little desire or capacity to remain after they complete their programs eventually return, whereas others stay for short durations before returning home or to other nations.

Student surveys report that the majority of international students in most contexts—typically between 60 and 80 percent—indicate preferences to continue to stay after graduation for work or other opportunities in the nation in which they pursue their programs.[12] For a variety of reasons, the actual numbers of students who do stay after graduation, especially beyond the first year after completing their programs, are substantially lower than the anticipated levels. Although the data are now more than a decade old, the OECD estimates that across reporting nations, about 25 percent of international graduates, on average, remain for at least short periods after completing their programs.[13] While these figures do not include the United States, where requests for freedom of information are often required for access to relevant data, available records suggest that general trends have paralleled those in other OECD nations. The numbers of those who wish to remain are well below those authorized to stay, though policy changes beginning in 2008 have made it possible for increasing proportions of international students, especially among those with advanced STEM credentials, to stay and to remain for longer periods following graduation.[14] Foreign students who achieve PhD credentials in science, engineering, and other technical fields are most likely to be granted short-term visas to stay in the United States after graduation as well as extensions for longer-term or permanent residence.[15] In specialized areas such as Artificial Intelligence, where there is extensive competition for highly specialized personnel, as many as 90 percent of international students who completed PhDs in relevant fields in the five-year period up to 2019 remained in the United States.[16] While increasing numbers of highly qualified international students have been able to fulfill their aspirations to extend their stay in the United States—in part through advocacy of high-profile figures from high-tech and innovation sectors along with proponents of more fundamental immigration reform—pathways from status as international student to temporary or longer-term worker and potential citizenship continue to be daunting and, for most who set out on the journey, highly restrictive and uncertain.

Despite administrative and policy changes to facilitate greater capacity to retain qualified students after graduation, existing regulatory systems are not equipped to accommodate the significant growth in the numbers of students who have responded to signals that their degrees will enhance prospects for immigration and settlement. These circumstances have heightened concerns by some commentators that without substantial immigration reform the United States risks losing its status as the favored destination for international students and highly qualified workers.[17] Before examining the extent to which evidence supports these concerns and parallel notions of a global competition for talent, the next section presents a framework for understanding relationships between higher education, employment, and immigration.

Conceptual Framework

The relationship between international studies and permanent residency has been explored from alternative theoretical orientations, focusing especially on factors related to human capital, labor market structures, and policy.[18] These phenomena do not operate independently of one another. Pierre Bourdieu's relational theory of social practice suggests a framework that takes into account how the social locations occupied by autonomous actors and organizations within broader structural contexts influence their life chances, decisions, and social interactions. Bourdieu conceptualizes social organization as a series of independent but overlapping fields, each of which is coordinated around the mobilization of particular types of resources, knowledge, and organizational principles.[19] Social actors' options and actions are strongly influenced (though not determined) by their position in the field in relation to the resources (forms of capital) that they may be able to draw upon in conjunction with their habitus (predispositions and perceptions of the world cultivated through significant life experiences, and the extent to which these are aligned with what counts or is important for success within a given field).[20] Any given field is relatively autonomous, with a distinct logic in which particular kinds of resources or capitals and forms of habitus are more significant than others, but it is also likely to intersect with and be partly configured in relation to other fields.[21]

This framework provides a useful analytical lens through which to understand issues associated with pathways from student to immigrant status. Higher education and labor markets are distinct but overlapping fields for which the fields of policy and economy, in particular, maintain an active role in relation to the definition and regulation of immigration and visas as well as in related matters such as trade, international relations, and economic development. Higher education has become increasingly more crucial for providing access to valued jobs and social opportunities. The economic advantages associated with a degree are complemented by the cultural capital derived from access to formal knowledge acquired in the education process as well as status associated with particular credentials. Education also enhances social capital by facilitating access to personal connections and networks that may increase options for employment and other types of opportunities.[22] These resources, Bourdieu emphasizes, help to confer social advantage based on access to specific forms or volumes of capital as well as options to convert one kind of capital to another type.[23] For foreign students and migrant workers, variances in migration status serve as forms of capital in which designation as migrant workers, citizens, or other legal categories facilitate or restrict access to particular kinds of positions and entitlement.[24] While decisions to study overseas may be unsettling for students who find they are not adequately equipped with the social and cultural resources essential for functioning in a new environment, over time they can expect to cultivate important cultural skills, forms of habitus, social connections, and other experiences and credentials that improve their employability and socioeconomic options at home or abroad.[25] These opportunities, at the same time, are only meaningful to the extent that appropriate institutional and structural conditions are in place to enable access to visas, funding support, jobs, and other crucial factors.

Transitions between education and work facilitate some convergence across, but also potential tensions between, higher education and labor markets. Postsecondary institutions, like labor markets, are strongly influenced by economic conditions and technological developments, and much of their activity is oriented toward professional training, preparation for work, and development of competencies and credentials recognized or valued by employers. Nonetheless, important differences exist in the logics and structural arrangements within each field. Often to the dismay of business lobbies, the missions and mandates of most institutions of higher learning extend well beyond matters of economic utility. Intersections of these fields with the state, or field of policy, are also complex. Each field has distinct time orientations (immediate skills shortages versus the length of time to complete degree programs, for instance), as well as unique fiscal and governance structures. In some instances, a given policy or practice may have mutual advantages. As postsecondary institutions seek to increase revenue streams in part by targeting growth in the numbers of international students paying high tuitions in specialized fields, for instance, employers may benefit through the dampening wage impact generated by an oversupply of highly qualified workers. Nonetheless, the fields are not necessarily aligned, and in some cases are likely to be in competition, with one another. These dynamics are reflected in the growing complexity associated with international students' study-to-post-graduation trajectories and initiatives by employers and governments to support recruitment and retention of highly qualified workers.

Changing Labor Markets and Work-Related Visa Options for International Students

As many universities and employers signal that international markets are valuable sources of highly qualified students and employees, expectations have risen among students that their investments in studying abroad will be rewarded.[26] These aspirations are reflected in dramatic increases in the past two decades in the numbers of international students applying for visas to extend their stays in the United States after graduation. Existing options, shaped in part but not solely by immigration policies and regulations, have not kept pace with demand.

The current immigration framework is based on the *Immigrant Act of 1990*, which enacted major reforms oriented in large part to recognition of the growing importance of changing education and skill requirements in the global economy. As observed in some detail in chapters in this volume by Donato and Amuedo-Dorantes and Lowell, the legislation addressed many of its initial aims, but subsequent economic, technological, and demographic changes combined with a patchwork of more specific measures have revealed that further adjustments are necessary to ensure that the immigration policy is more closely aligned with emerging labor markets and social contexts.

Several visa categories differentiate status as student, worker, and family member. For international students, the predominant routes toward post-graduation work authorization are based on the classification of those who have completed full-time academic programs as F-1 visa holders who subsequently become eligible for either Optional Practical Training (OPT) or H-1B visas. An H-1B visa, which can be held for up to six years (three years plus possible renewal for an additional three-year period), offers greater prospects for those who are seeking permanent residency over time, but yearly caps limit the number that are issued each year, applicants must be sponsored by eligible employers, and applications are highly time-sensitive. Except for a brief period beginning in 1998 when numbers were increased to meet a surge in demand for high-tech workers, annual quotas remained at 65,000 from the time they were introduced in 1991 until 2004, when 20,000 additional dedicated spaces were opened each year for international students who arrived to complete graduate-level degrees in the United States. Because particular categories of applicants and employers are exempt from the annual caps, the actual number of H-1B visas issued each year is well above (typically about 2.5 times higher than) the annual ceilings, but the number of applicants to the H-1B pool, substantial proportions of whom are not international students, far exceeds the number of visas issued.[27]

The OPT option, by contrast, has greater flexibility with regard to eligibility and employment options, but status to remain in the United States is only valid for a twelve-month period, with the exception of graduates in STEM fields who are eligible to renew for up to two additional years.[28]

The US focus on employer sponsorship or support in attracting highly qualified workers is attractive in minimizing the chances of creating a pool of underemployed credentialed graduates. This is a common problem in nations like Canada, which have moved to implement more open immigration policies but few guarantees of appropriate work options.[29] Employers in the United States often welcome opportunities to sponsor or hire international students to meet their workforce requirements, but there are several concerns about the current system. Some employers are not aware of options to recruit international students, while others avoid doing so because of negative stereotypes or misconceptions about international students.[30] These perceptions are reinforced by critics who claim that lower-paid foreign workers and graduates are being used to replace qualified Americans. Aside from a few high-profile cases there is little systemic evidence to support contentions that the system as a whole is being abused.[31] The application process for H-1B and other work authorization visas can discourage prospective employers from sponsoring strong applicants. Intensified scrutiny of applications imposed by the implementation of the "Buy American and Hire American" executive order in April 2017, followed by the temporary suspension of new H-1B visa authorizations in mid-2020 and other measures, placed additional roadblocks to make it more difficult to negotiate the administrative demands associated with work authorization processes. Many university and business organizations are strongly opposed to these initiatives, which have simultaneously intensified anxieties and insecurities among international students questioning whether their heavy investments in academic work and their search for post-graduation employment in the United States are worthwhile.[32]

Efforts to keep pace with rapidly changing labor market conditions since the 1990 legislation was enacted have contributed to the emergence of a complicated patchwork of programs, regulations, and obstacles. Post-study work options and opportunities for international students to stay in the United States after graduation have increased, but remain constrained and difficult to navigate. The National Association of Colleges and Employers, which surveys member organizations about their employment plans, reports that between 2014 and 2019, one-quarter to one-third of respondents indicated that they planned to hire international student graduates in the coming year.[33] Alongside the

H-1B stream, the OPT has become an increasingly more attractive option for international students, especially after provisions for extensions were introduced for STEM graduates in 2008 and again in 2016.[34] These arrangements are especially appealing to foreign students who value the opportunity to gain US-based work experiences while broadening their repertoires of cultural and social resources after graduation to enhance employment and career prospects in their home countries or other nations.[35] For those seeking to position themselves for longer-term stays or eventual permanent residency, the OPT option makes it possible to open new connections and doorways, though its designation as a training program means that applicants must declare an intent to return home.

Although periodic regulatory and administrative initiatives have been introduced to streamline the system—such as the "Cap and Gown" provision, which enables foreign students to remain in the United States during the period between the completion of their program and the issuing of work authorizations—more fundamental problems remain. Extensive backlogs in visa processing and immigration recruitment have compounded uncertainty for many applicants confronted with a somewhat complex and unpredictable immigration system. Shifting policy frameworks have left many international students vulnerable to risks such as exploitation by employers, recruitment to low-quality educational programs, and threats of potential termination of status in instances where immigration officers reject or question their claims.[36] The resurgence in recent years of nationalism, populism, and overt racism has heightened a sense of insecurity and perceptions of being unwelcome and unsafe among some international student populations.[37] While these factors may over time be tempered by economic opportunities and a more welcoming environment, they have reinforced the growing tendency for potential international students and workers to consider destinations other than the United States.

The juxtaposition of these divergent policy, administrative, and political factors has had mixed consequences. Interest among foreign nationals seeking to study and work in the United States remains high. However, the inability to secure adequate employment has resulted in high proportions of international graduates leaving despite aspirations to remain in the United States after completing their programs and, while international students are issued post-graduation visas contingent on having work, unemployment rates among this temporary workforce are rising.[38] The next section explores labor market options in relation to trends in higher education contributing to accelerated supplies of highly qualified graduates in the United States and globally.

The Changing Field of Higher Education: Dynamics of Student Mobility and Settlement

Postsecondary enrollment and international student mobility have risen dramatically on a global basis during the twenty-first century. The United States continues to maintain its status as the leading destination for international students, though its share of the global international student market decreased from 28 percent in 2001 to 21 percent in 2019.[39] During this period, the number of highly qualified graduates in STEM and other fields has increased substantially both in the United States, heightening demand for post-study visa and work authorizations, and globally.[40]

Figure 7.1 reveals that both levels and rates of growth of international student enrollment have remained very high in the United States relative to most of the other principal destination countries since 2007. These patterns are somewhat misleading insofar as total international student numbers in the United States include those with OPT authorization due to their classification as trainees. Figure 7.2, which includes separate data for OPT holders, indicates that while international student enrollments continued to grow steadily until 2016, OPT expansion has had a marked impact in driving growth in the total numbers, especially with respect to graduates in STEM fields. By 2011, three years after the OPT was extended for STEM graduates, the annual number of OPT authorizations surpassed H-1B capped allocation levels, with the proportion of total OPT authorizations allocated to STEM graduates rising from 10.2 percent in 2010 to 27.5 percent by 2017.[41]

Along with policy and institutional practices related to higher education and immigration, student migration trends reflect two additional interrelated sets of dynamics. These include longer-term patterns of economic and social development in specific national or regional contexts, and disruptions produced by significant new political or economic

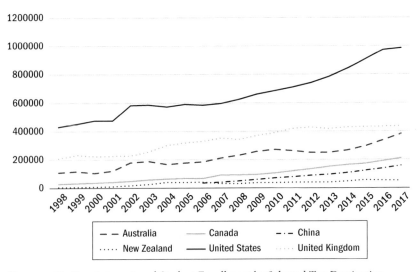

Figure 7.1: Tertiary International Student Enrollment by Selected Top Destination Countries. Source: Data compiled from UNESCO UIS, "Net flow of internationally mobile students," http://data.uis.unesco.org/#, and OECD OECD.Stat, "Enrollment of international students over time," https://stats.oecd.org/#

developments or unanticipated "shocks"—such as terrorist attacks, racialized violence, or health pandemics—that destabilize existing relationships.[42] The pool of highly skilled labor may be considered a global pool insofar as mobility patterns among students and prospective workers is influenced, either positively or negatively, by particular policy interventions and social and political conditions across different nations or regions as well as those within their preferred national destination. In practice, individuals, like governments, employers, and universities, typically streamline their strategies and adjust their actions through reference to a selective range of indices and comparators. Patterns of international student recruitment, migration, and hiring, like those associated with foreign workers and immigrants more generally, are more segmented than unified in nature. They are influenced by a rich confluence of historical relations of colonization and trade, linguistic and cultural connections, and economic, geographic, and geopolitical factors.[43] As migration flows change in relation to globalization and other significant developments, there is some convergence among migration policy models, but multiple orientations and hybrid models have emerged to accommodate conditions, needs, and challenges specific to particular contexts.[44]

In order to facilitate employment experience and longer-term immigration, OECD member nations have introduced an extensive range of policies to extend student visas, to issue post-graduation work authorizations or, where such measures are already in place, to adjust eligibility criteria and extend the period in which international students are able to remain after graduation—evident in a leapfrog effect as nations progressively extend work authorization periods.[45] The most comprehensive measures are being introduced in countries that have made it a priority to recruit international students as a source of permanent residents, especially oriented to those pursuing advanced degrees in STEM fields and other specializations in which demand for highly qualified workers is great. High proportions of science and engineering students from India, for instance, suggest that their decisions to study in the United States are significantly influenced by prospects to achieve permanent

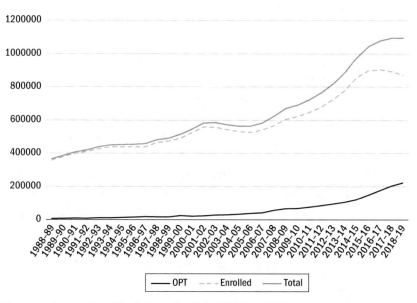

Figure 7.2: International Students in the United States, 1988/89 to 2018–2019.
Source: Data compiled from Institute of International Education, "International Students Enrollment Trends, 1948/49–2018/19," *Open Doors Report on International Educational Exchange*, Institute of International Education, https://opendoorsdata.org.

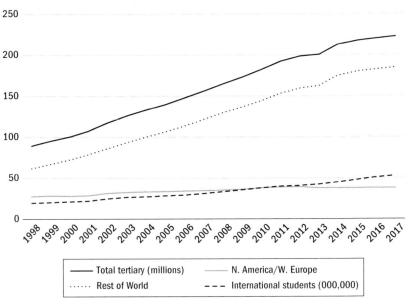

Figure 7.3: Global Tertiary Education Enrollment. Source: Data compiled from UNESCO, UIS.Stat, "Education," http://data.uis.unesco.org.

residency status.[46] In other nations, including Canada, Australia, and New Zealand, extended time frames in which international students are authorized to seek employment and work after graduation are being accompanied by the introduction of specialized immigration streams that make it possible to prioritize or fast-track those who gain relevant job experience in designated fields. Many other nations in Europe and elsewhere are taking a longer-term approach, complementing incentives—such as visa flexibility, with a broad range of services related to housing, healthcare, and other domains—to attract and retain international students considered as important resources for future economic and social development.[47]

OECD nations are not unique in their attention to the transformation of higher education and migration landscapes.[48] Initiatives to attract international students and skilled workers to Western nations are compounded by complex shifts occurring in other parts of the world. Figure 7.3 reveals that the accelerated development of mass higher education systems on a worldwide basis since the late 1990s has been most pronounced outside of North America and Western Europe, in regions that traditionally have been the main sources of international students. There is some complementarity as the production of greater numbers of students receiving initial degrees in their home nations increases the pool of students eligible to pursue graduate degrees and credentials validated from established institutions in other nations.

Transitions in student mobility patterns also reflect the interaction of demographic and economic trends with transformations in postsecondary policy and delivery in an increasing number of contexts. The OECD projects that by 2030, universities in China and India could produce as many as half of all graduates and more than 60 percent of those with STEM qualifications among those aged 25–34 years with tertiary degrees in OECD and G20 nations.[49] Figure 7.3 illustrates that overall rates of growth in the numbers of international students, until recently, have not matched those for total enrollments, but, since 2011, the numbers of international students worldwide has exceeded total postsecondary enrollments in North American and Western European nations. There is no shortage in the supply of international students, though prospective students have an increasing range of options from which to select. Returning to the data presented in figure 7.1, the United States and the United Kingdom remain the top destinations for international students, while there has been substantial growth in international student numbers in response to initiatives in Australia, Canada and, to some extent, New Zealand to attract foreign students. Especially striking is the emergence in the new millennium of China as one of the top five destination countries for international students.

The next sections explore these relationships more fully, focusing on how intersections of broader policy and regulatory reforms with more fundamental transformations unfolding within global political economies of student mobility and migration have shaped the trends illustrated in figures 7.1 and 7.2.

Intersections between the Field of Higher Education and High-Skilled Labor Markets

Several nations—most notably China and India—that have typically been the top sources of international students in the United States and other OECD nations overall (and especially in STEM fields) are undertaking dual strategies to increase numbers of highly qualified graduates domestically while mitigating the impact of brain drain. These initiatives typically include targeted funding initiatives along with broader protocols to enhance program quality and expand research productivity and innovation.[50] China and other nations have introduced various initiatives designed to encourage highly qualified graduates with PhDs and other specialized credentials to return (referred to as "sea turtles" in China) after completing programs in other nations. These include a combination of fiscal incentives and tax breaks supported by measures such as enhanced research infrastructure and start-up subsidies for scientific research.[51] Return migration has been hastened by the absence of a secure immigration pathway for foreign-born US-trained workers with short-term post-study visas in high-tech industries, but it has also contributed to an accelerator effect through technology transfer from one context to other settings, which then benefit from increased innovation and demands for skilled labor.[52]

These trends and projections have further alarmed some employers, governments, and analysts in the United States and other nations concerned about global competitiveness for talent, but it is essential to exercise caution in three major respects. First, the data demonstrate that the supply of graduates in STEM fields and other desired areas is growing rapidly, both in specific contexts and on a global basis. Second, rapid changes in technology and work organization have made the connection between specific credentials and forms of training more tenuous; there is no necessary connection between highly specialized credentials and work in many fields, and skills and capabilities may be transferable across various occupations and sectors.[53] Third, the development and deployment of high-skilled workers is not configured as a uniform global market. Demographic, technological, economic, and social conditions vary substantially across national and regional contexts, contributing to diverse labor market and training regimes. Migration trends associated with study and work often parallel one another, but there is not always a direct correspondence and, in some cases, different conditions may have offsetting impacts. National variations in economic conditions and unemployment rates can have a profound effect on international students' decisions about staying or returning after graduation.[54] While highly developed nations are attractive destinations for foreign students, as long as economic opportunities remain viable, rates of return tend to increase for nations where employment options are supported by wage and tax structures favorable to highly qualified graduates.[55]

Emphasis on labor market factors alone, especially those related to STEM and innovation areas, obscures other factors that may be important in determining what and where postsecondary students study. Some of these may reflect relatively short-term responses to major disruptions or shocks within or beyond particular local or national systems. Specific events typically reverberate in different ways across other systems or within the global system as a whole without necessarily affecting longer-term patterns. The trend lines in figures 7.1 and 7.2 indicate overall trajectories of continuing growth in international student recruitment despite brief periods of slowed growth or decline. The disruptions to the trends reflect the impact of particular events or developments that have not had longer-term impact in part because of quick attention to subsequent policy reforms and new measures to attract foreign students. In the United States, for instance, international student enrollments declined after the tightening of immigration regulations and intensified screening of applicants in response to terrorist activities—the 1993 World Trade Center bombing in New York and the 9/11 events in 2001—in which individuals on student visas were involved.[56] In New Zealand, an observed decline in the number of international students after 2003 occurred after Chinese embassy officials raised concerns about racial profiling and recruitment fraud. In Australia, media reports of attacks on students from India and the politicization of immigration policy in 2009 similarly resulted in sharp declines in the total number of international students over the next four years.[57] In each of these cases, previous patterns of growth were renewed within five years.

Several more recent developments have had an impact on international student movements, though it remains too early to determine what the longer-term consequences might be in a global context that has changed in important ways since those earlier events. In the UK, the negotiation of the terms of Britain's departure from the European Union has elevated concerns over the flattening of growth trends in a nation that has figured prominently as a top destination country for international students.[58]

Similarly, figure 7.2 reveals declining numbers of international students enrolled in the United States after the 2016 election, parallel with measures to constrain immigration and prioritize local workers and product chains accompanied by increasing incidences of racism and xenophobia. Evidence reveals that at least some prospective international students turned to programs in Canada and other nations as a result of these developments. The National Foundation for American Policy, examining the impact of recent changes to US visa requirements, observed that enrollment of students from India in graduate programs in computer science and engineering in the United States declined by more than 25 percent between 2016–17 and 2018–19, whereas parallel enrollments in Canadian universities increased by more than 127 percent.[59] Similarly, immediately after the June 2020 announcement of a presidential proclamation to suspend entry of foreign workers on H-1B and other visas until the end of the year, firms and immigration consultants in Canada positioned themselves to recruit many of those likely to be affected by the measures.[60] These dynamics are compounded by additional developments, illustrated in the case of enrollment trends for international students from China studying in the United States. Previously high growth rates began to slow down after 2013 due in part to measures introduced in China to encourage both domestic enrollment and the return of highly skilled graduates after studies abroad. The numbers began to level off more sharply in response to subsequent developments, including restraints on immigration to the United States, strained trade relations between the two nations, and student concerns about safety and the relative costs of higher education.[61]

International border closures and disruptions in postsecondary operations and student intakes after the emergence of the COVID-19 pandemic in early 2020 have had an especially pronounced impact, sharply restricting or diverting flows of international students and migrants on a near-global basis. Though it is too early to determine the longer-term consequences of these developments, some of the adjustments are likely to have lasting impact. Most prospective international students who were surveyed in early spring 2020 were confident that they would be able to pursue their plans to study abroad, but these expectations eroded over time. By May, slightly more than one-third of those who intended to study in the United States, United Kingdom, Canada, and Australia had already changed their plans. At the start of the 2020–21 academic year, two-thirds of prospective international students surveyed indicated that the coronavirus had affected their plans to study abroad; slightly more than one in five indicated that they had either abandoned their plans to study abroad or changed their desired destination in which to pursue their studies.[62] The pandemic has had significant fiscal and program consequences for universities in general, but especially jeopardized the sustainability of some universities and programs dependent on state funding and tuition revenue from international students.[63] Severe inequalities in the health impact and social and economic consequences of the crisis for different populations—with low-income and minority populations especially hard hit—have shifted global flows of students. One of the most significant changes is an increase in regional mobility relative to the conventional flows of international students from East to West.[64]

The pandemic has complicated a planning landscape that has become increasingly more uncertain amidst developments within and across various contexts, but it has not suppressed the growing supply of prospective international students in STEM and other fields in Western nations. Figure 7.4 reveals the strong representation of international students in graduate-level programs in five comparison nations, especially at the doctoral level where international students constitute between one-quarter (in the United States) to nearly one-half (in New Zealand) of total enrollments. The proportions of international students in information and communications technologies (ICT) and engineering and related fields is well above these totals in every case. However, the figure also reveals important variations across nations and degree levels in both overall concentrations of international students and fields in which they study. In the United States, proportions of international students at the doctoral level are about double corresponding rates for master's-level programs overall. In business, administration, and law programs, however, rates are similar for both levels, while in ICT-related fields they are lower at the doctoral level than at the master's level. International students are also highly represented in non-STEM fields such as health and welfare, in which international students constitute at least one in five doctoral-level students in all five nations.

Policies that prioritize recruitment and retention of international students in STEM fields may be warranted in areas where there is high

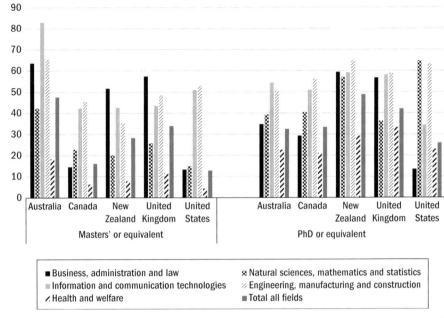

Figure 7.4: International Students as Proportion of All Students Enrolled by Selected Fields of Graduate Education, 2017. Source: Data compiled from OECD.Stat, "Distribution of Graduates and Entrants by Field," 2021, https://stats.oecd.org.

Note: Fields included in the total but not shown as separate categories include arts and humanities; education, social sciences; journalism and information; agriculture, forestry, fisheries, and veterinary; and services.

demand to sustain innovation and high-tech growth, but the data in figure 7.4 indicate the strong presence of highly qualified international students in other important disciplinary areas. Some jurisdictions have turned to international student graduates in order to address shortages in healthcare, teaching, business administration, entrepreneurial development, and other key areas in which college or university credentials in non-STEM fields are required.[65] Many businesses, governments, and community organizations recognize the close affinity between forms of skills and knowledge that are important for operating in globally connected environments and characteristics that motivate students to study abroad. Foreign graduates typically have much to offer by way of proficiency in more than one language, connections with broader and more diverse social networks, understandings derived from alternative knowledge systems and pedagogical approaches, and various soft skills and workplace competencies that are crucial for organizations operating in a cosmopolitan environment.[66] Despite these potential advantages, however, opportunities for international students graduating from non-STEM fields to pursue immediate pathways to work and settlement remain much more limited than for their STEM counterparts.

International Students: Beyond Human Capital

Discourses associated with the recruitment and retention of highly skilled workers are commonly framed in relation to a global talent pool made up of human capital, skilled workers, STEM students, and other abstract referents. By shifting the focus beyond technical aspects of skills and credentials to take into consideration important socioeconomic characteristics, it becomes clear that patterns of mobility and settlement among international students and highly qualified workers—like those associated with higher education more generally—are highly segmented, revealing systemic inequalities associated with class, race, gender, and other factors.

In the United States, young people from lower socioeconomic families and African Americans frequently encounter financial and other barriers that restrict access to quality STEM training, which, over time, reduce options to pursue further studies and careers in relevant fields.[67] International students and graduates contribute to greater racial and cultural diversity in the United States and other major destinations. Although they do not compensate for inequalities in the domestic high-skill labor force, they facilitate the broadening of perspectives, experiences, and interactions in ways that can enliven communities, foster social and economic innovation, and open doors for other minorities. Foreign student graduates represent a highly educated and relatively young cohort with attributes that many nations are looking for to support social and economic development. Nonetheless, access to work and potential settlement for international students is not equitably distributed, due in part to national quotas and other measures built into current visa and immigration program structures as well as selective foreign recruitment strategies employed by many universities. India and China are the predominant sources of graduate-level students in STEM fields. More than half of all initial H-1B visas are issued to applicants from India (an average of about 56 percent in 2018 and 2019) and close to 20 percent (18.8 percent in 2018 and 2019) to those from China.[68] While some representation by students from other nations contributes to greater workforce and population diversity, post-study prospects in the United States are especially limited for students from the global South, which is home to steadily increasing numbers of qualified prospective international students and immigrants. Thomas's chapter in this volume demonstrates that while there are economic opportunities for many immigrants from these regions, substantial inequalities remain to be addressed, as illustrated by the mismatches between education and work and reduced wage premiums experienced by African immigrants with STEM degrees. The barriers that racialized minorities must navigate have been heightened by the increasing prevalence of racial discrimination fueled by racially charged pronouncements and actions by prominent political leaders and public figures in the United States, UK, and other nations. International students, especially those from China and southeast Asia, have reported increased concerns over their safety and well-being in the United States, with many encountering xenophobia and harassment amidst the COVID-19 pandemic.[69]

Gender-related barriers and inequalities also influence pathways for international students. Elsewhere in this volume, Bhatti demonstrates the particular challenges that highly skilled female immigrants from Pakistan encounter through devaluation of credentials and other experiences. Figure 7.5, employing the most recent comparative data, reveals that, in 2016, males constituted more than two-thirds of international students graduating from master's and doctoral programs in the STEM fields represented (ICT and engineering and related) in the United States and four other primary destination nations for international students. Similar patterns of gender inequality are evident in data concerning programs that encourage international students to work after graduation. The United States does not report OPT, H-1B, and other special visa categories by gender, but there are high degrees of gender selectivity associated with fields and occupational practices related to these authorizations. Among those who submit H-1B petitions, males regularly outnumber females by a ratio of three to one (gender is not reported in annual summaries of those petitions that are successful).[70] Increasing numbers of international women are studying in STEM fields

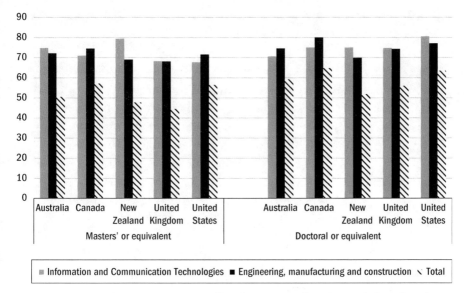

Figure 7.5: Male Graduates as Proportion of Total International Students Who Graduated from Master's and Doctoral Programs, by Selected Program Types, 2016. Source: Calculated from data compiled from OECD.Stat, Graduates by field, "International graduates by origin," https://stats.oecd.org.

in the United States, but the same three-to-one male/female ratio is observed in the overall distribution of graduate-level degrees awarded to international students in engineering and computer sciences fields.[71] However, evidence suggests that, among foreign students who remained in the United States after completing their doctorates between 1980 and the early twenty-first century across all fields of studies, women were more likely than men to stay.[72] Despite strong concerns about shortages of talent in these areas, relatively little policy attention has been paid to how gender-related factors influence international student pathways and to how visa and immigration processes may reinforce gender inequalities.

The combined impact of sociodemographic factors and program structures contributes to the development of a high-skill labor force in which young men, particularly those from India and China, are overrepresented relative to most other groups. While recruitment and immigration practices contribute to some diversity that may help offset inequalities observed in the domestic production of highly skilled labor, these arrangements give rise to concerns about logistical as well as deeper moral and equity considerations. The characteristics that employers are likely to value in a high-skill labor force constituted in large part by younger men—especially those with no immediate family responsibilities, who are well-positioned to take on roles as highly productive, flexible workers—are the same attributes that position these workers favorably as part of a mobile transnational labor force with employment options in other nations and corporate settings. Reliance on temporary visas, requirements for employer sponsorship, and other factors that create insecurity for those seeking longer-term career and settlement prospects increase the likelihood that many of these highly skilled prospects will pursue opportunities elsewhere, at the same time that other qualified potential employees may be overlooked.

Consideration of intersections among gender, race, and other social factors brings into focus the need to pay attention to a wide range of non-economic dimensions that shape students' experiences and pathways, such as community interactions and marriage/partnership and family relationships. In several policy contexts, attention is being paid to approaches that transcend a market-oriented focus on global talent driven by competition among independent nations or firms pursuing their own interests, seeking to achieve more effective outcomes without magnifying inefficiencies and mismatches characteristic of many previous labor force development strategies.[73]

The analysis throughout this chapter has emphasized that, far from targeting or competing for a single pool of international talent, most nations have developed distinct approaches for attracting international students and highly qualified labor based on a diverse range of economic, social, and regional interests. Although skills shortages may be particularly acute in some types of workplace settings, overall issues of mismatch between jobs and skills are highly complex in nature. Alongside variances in how skills are defined, developed, and utilized in particular settings, training in most cases is oriented more to skills sets and competencies that are relatively broad, which is especially important in a context where the capacities to perform a specific job are changing rapidly or more likely to be developed on the job than in prior training.[74] Moreover, attention to the human and social dimensions embodied in skilled workers highlights the importance of acknowledging that decisions to migrate or remain after graduation are influenced by important factors beyond the mechanics associated with immigrant policy and visa processing. These factors are evident in several emerging comprehensive policy frameworks that take into account family considerations, social conditions and living standards, and other factors to increase the likelihood that newcomers will be fully integrated and well-positioned to support broader social and economic development objectives.[75]

International Students as Prospective Workers and Citizens

Parallel with efforts by national governments to reshape policies and practices related to student visas and immigration has been increased engagement by governments and organizations at regional and local levels. Much of this subnational activity has focused on initiatives that supplement economic considerations with infrastructural and organizational support to promote successful integration into particular communities or regional structures.[76] In several nations, including Australia, New Zealand, and numerous EU members, international graduate students factor prominently within programs and initiatives dedicated to provide greater flexibility and local autonomy to recruit immigrants for employment and social development in locales outside of the major metropolitan centers.[77] In Canada, provincial Immigrant Nominee Programs have complemented federal strategies to increase immigration levels. These programs, which are sensitive to regional and local contexts in conjunction with broader immigration initiatives, typically feature provisions to recruit international students and streamline procedures to retain qualified graduates after completing their programs.[78] Similar programs are being developed in many parts of the United States. The co-presence of high-quality universities and high-tech and innovative industries has accelerated the growth of a highly skilled international labor force in New York and surrounding metropolitan areas, southern California/Silicon Valley, Boston and vicinity, and a few other concentrated clusters. Centers in some other regions, including many hard hit by population loss, deindustrialization, and economic stagnation, have begun to implement more aggressive strategies to ensure that they are not left out of the equation. Strategic partnerships such as the Partnership for a New American Economy and Welcoming America have brought together business leaders, prominent national and civic figures, and other community representatives to promote immigration as a core element for economic development through shared ideas, resources, and expertise to foster urban renewal and growth in mid-size and smaller urban centers as well as the largest metropolitan areas.[79] In the Detroit region, for instance, the Michigan Global Talent Retention Initiative, recognizing the many international students completing programs in STEM fields and other key areas as a valuable regional resource, has introduced measures to link students with local employers and assist in securing employment complemented by support from settlement agencies and other services organizations to ensure successful integration into local communities.[80]

International students feature prominently in these programs. They are recognized as valuable resources who may be motivated to remain upon completion of their programs. These regional initiatives do not take settlement for granted, focusing on the need to adopt several interrelated measures in which support to navigate visa and immigration policy and procedures is part of a more holistic approach to facilitate successful social and community, as well as economic, integration.

Conclusion: The Complex Dynamics of International Student Mobility and Settlement

Increasing numbers of students are attracted to options to study, and potentially settle, abroad. These patterns, combined with worldwide expansion in university enrollment in STEM and other highly skilled programs, suggest that, except in a few highly specialized or rapidly changing occupational fields, fears that a global talent shortage is looming are not likely to be realized. Nonetheless, ongoing monitoring of education and labor market trends, supported by reliable empirical evidence, are essential as social and economic changes play out in diverse ways within and across national contexts. The United States and other Western nations continue to be favored destinations for students seeking opportunities for study and work abroad, but student migration flows are shifting amidst a complex array of changing, often uncertain, circumstances. It is essential that policies and practices related to international student recruitment and retention are sensitive to the varied motivations and interests of students in pursuing studies in other countries. Desires to work and settle abroad after graduation factor prominently in decisions about where to study, but other considerations are also important, especially for those who intend to return home after graduation. Growing numbers of nations are recognizing the value of international students as part of broader strategies to meet labor market and immigration targets, but in most cases, to date, the proportion of international students who remain for more than short periods of time continues to be relatively low.

Several factors influence international student pathways, especially for those who initially intend to remain. Individual circumstances such as financial strain, academic struggles, family obligations, or opportunities for employment compel many students to return home or depart for other settings. For others, decisions to return are influenced by lack of social connections, racism, safety concerns, difficulties in finding a job, or unanticipated obstacles encountered in a foreign environment. Many international students are discouraged from remaining after graduation because of problems in securing visas, whether through restrictive immigration policies, technical regulations, administrative delays, or other difficulties. Several organizations and postsecondary institutions have responded by implementing programs to support retention, academic advancement, and post-work guidance for international students, but these are limited by the extent to which broader policy frameworks are developed in order to address rapidly changing economic and political environments.

While various nations have developed diverse strategies to encourage international student settlement in conjunction with distinct labor market, social, demographic, and political circumstances, several key messages can be derived from an overview of comparative experiences. First, streamlining visa processes increases the likelihood of conveying clear signals and guidelines to applicants and potential employers, making it possible to integrate opportunities for work experience with pathways to immigration in a more timely and direct manner. Second, monitoring and adjusting desired targets or quotas for particular visa categories, on a more regular and systematic basis, along with broader immigration objectives, can ensure greater coordination between supply and demand, including but not limited to STEM and other specialized fields of study. Third, consistent with themes highlighted throughout this book, it is crucial to recognize that the understanding of international students and prospective immigrants is misleading and incomplete if it is reduced to economic terms. The most effective settlement policies and practices take into consideration their rights and status as human beings and active social participants whose broader social circumstances are characterized by diverse capabilities, needs, interests, family and social connections, and more.

NOTES

1 Ben Wildavsky, *The Great Brain Race: How Global Universities Are Reshaping the World* (Princeton, NJ: Princeton University Press, 2012).

2 Ed Michaels, Helen Handfield-Jones, and Beth Axelrod, *The War for Talent* (Boston: Harvard Business School Press, 2001), 6; Korn Ferry, "The Global Talent Crunch," 2018, www.kornferry.com; Remco Zwetsloot, James Dunham, Zachary Arnold, and Tina Huang, "Keeping Top AI Talent in the United States: Findings and Policy Options for International Graduate Student Retention," Center for Security and Emerging Technology, Georgetown University, 2019, https://cset.georgetown.edu.

3 OECD, *Education at a Glance 2019: OECD Indicators* (Paris: OECD Publishing, 2019), 9–10.

4 Much of the earlier analysis and debates about brain drain often posed as justification to restrict immigration. See, e.g., John C. Shearer, "In Defense of Traditional Views of the 'Brain Drain' Problem," *International Educational and Cultural Exchange* 2 (Fall, 1966): 12–25. Rubén Rumbaut, "Origins and Destinies: Immigration to the United States since World War II," *Sociological Forum* 9, no. 4 (1994): 583–621.

5 Paulina Trevena, "Post Study Work Visa Options: An International Comparative Review," Scottish Government 2019, www.gov.scot; Zwetsloot et al., "Keeping Top AI Talent in the United States."

6 Reinhard Weisser, "Internationally Mobile Students and Their Post-Graduation Migratory Behaviour: An Analysis of Determinants of Student Mobility and Retention Rates in the EU," *OECD Social, Employment and Migration Working Papers* no. 186, www.oecd-ilibrary.org.

7 Phillip G. Altbach, "Impact and Adjustment: Foreign Students in Comparative Perspective," *Higher Education* 21 (1991): 305–323; Phillip G. Altbach, "The Realities of Mass Higher Education in a Globalized World," in *Higher Education in a Globalized Society*, ed. Donald Bruce Johnstone et al. (Cheltenham, UK: Edward Elgar, 2010), 25–41.

8 Lesleyanne Hawthorne and Anna To, "Australian Employer Response to the Study-Migration Pathway: The Quantitative Evidence 2007–2011," *International Migration* 52, no. 3 (2014): 99–115; Trevena, "Post Study Work Visa Options."

9 Weisser, "Internationally Mobile Students and Their Post-Graduation Migratory Behaviour"; Xueying Han, Galen Stocking, Matthew A. Gebbie, and Richard P. Appelbaum, "Will They Stay or Will They Go? International Graduate Students and Their Decisions to Stay or Leave the U.S. upon Graduation," *PLoS ONE* 10, no. 3 (2015).

10 Bryce Loo, Ning Luo, and Ziyi Ye, "Career Prospects and Outcomes for U.S.-Educated International Students: Improving Services, Bolstering Success," World Education Services, 2017, https://files.eric.ed.gov.

11 OECD, *Education at a Glance 2011: OECD Indicators* (Paris: OECD Publishing, 2011), 329–330.

12 Brett Berquist et al., "Global Perspectives on International Student Employability," International Education Association of Australia, 2019, www.ieaa.org.au.

13 OECD, *Education at a Glance 2011*, 329–330.

14 Neil G. Ruiz and Abby Budiman, "Number of Foreign College Students Staying and Working in U.S. After Graduation Surges," Pew Research Center, May 10, 2018, www.pewresearch.org.

15 Neil G. Ruiz, "The Geography of Foreign Students in U.S. Higher Education: Origins and Destinations," Global Cities Initiative, a Joint Project of Brookings and JPMorgan Chase, 2014, www.brookings.edu; Loo et al., "Career Prospects and Outcomes for U.S.-Educated International Students."

16 Zwetsloot et al., "Keeping Top AI Talent," 8–9.

17 Han et al., "Will They Stay or Will They Go?"; Giovanni Peri and Gaetano Basso, "Opportunity Lost: The Economic Benefit of Retaining Foreign-Born Students in Local Economies," The Chicago Council on Global Affairs, 2016, http://giovanni peri.ucdavis.edu; Zwetsloot et al., "Keeping Top AI Talent."

18 Dongbin Kim, Charles A. Bankart, and Laura Isdell, "International Doctorates: Trends Analysis on Their Decision to Stay in US," *Higher Education* 62, no. 2 (2011): 141–161; Rey Koslowski, "Selective Migration Policy Models and Changing Realities of Implementation," *International Migration* 52, no. 3 (2014): 26–39.

19 Pierre Bourdieu, *The Logic of Practice*, trans. Richard Nice (Stanford, CA: Stanford University Press, 1990); Pierre Bourdieu and Jean-Claude Passeron, *Reproduction in Education, Society, and Culture*, trans. Richard Nice (London: Sage, 1990).

20 Bourdieu, *The Logic of Practice*.

21 Elliot B. Weininger, "Class and Causation in Bourdieu," in *Bringing Capitalism Back for Critique by Social Theory*, ed. Jennifer M. Lehmann (Bingley, UK: Emerald Group Publishing, 2002), 49–114.

22 Bourdieu, *The Logic of Practice*; Bourdieu and Passeron, *Reproduction*.

23 Bourdieu and Passeron, *Reproduction*.

24 Herald Bauder, "Citizenship as Capital: The Distinction of Migrant Labor," *Alternatives* 33, no. 3 (2008): 315–33.

25 Sara Landolt and Susan Thieme, "Highly Skilled Migrants Entering the Labour Market: Experiences and Strategies in the Contested Field of Overqualification and Skills Mismatch," *Geoforum* 90 (2018): 36–44.

26 Rahul Choudaha, "Three Waves of International Student Mobility," *Studies in Higher Education* 42, no. 5 (2017): 825–832.

27 Sarah Pierce and Julia Gelatt, "Evolution of the H-1B: Latest Trends in a Program on the Brink of Reform," Migration Policy Institute, *MPI Issue Brief* (2018), www.migrationpolicy.org.

28 Emma Israel and Jeanne Batalova, "International Students in the United States," Migration Policy Institute, January 14, 2021, www.migrationpolicy.org.

29 Yao Lu and Feng Hu, "Over-Education Among University-Educated Immigrants in Canada and the United States," Statistics Canada, Analytical Studies Branch Research Paper Series, 2019, www.150.statcan.gc.ca.

30 Ruiz, "The Geography of Foreign Students in U.S. Higher Education"; Berquist et al., "Global Perspectives on International Student Employability."

31 Stuart Anderson, "Top 10 Myths About Hiring Foreign Nations," *International Educator* 17, no. 2 (2008): 6 and 8–10; Pierce and Gellatt, "Evolution of the H-1B," 9–10; see also Lowell's chapter in this volume.

32 Ian M. Lértora and Jerry M. Sullivan, "The Lived Experiences of Chinese International Students Preparing for the University-to-Work Transition: A Phenomenological Qualitative Study," *The Qualitative Report* 24, no. 8 (2019): 1877–1996; Abrar Al-Heeti, "As Trump Suspends New H-1B Visas, Many Tech Workers Face an Uncertain Future," *cnet*, July 24, 2020, www.cnet.com.

33 National Association of Colleges and Employers, "International Student Hiring Climbs for Class of 2020," February 24, 2020, www.naceweb.org.

34 Chris Mackie, "OPT's Critical Importance to Enrollment and Other Takeaways from the 2019 Open Doors Report," World Education News and Reviews, December 10, 2019, https://wenr.wes.org; Zwetsloot et al., "Keeping Top AI Talent."

35 Chiang-nan Chao, Niall Hegarty, John Angelidis, and Victor F. Lu, "Chinese Students' Motivations for Studying in the United States," *Journal of International Students* 7, no. 2 (2017): 257–269; Loo et al., "Career Prospects and Outcomes for U.S.-Educated International Students."

36 Ruiz, "The Geography of Foreign Students in U.S. Higher Education"; Adam Grimm, "Studying to Stay: Understanding Graduate Visa Policy Content and Context in the United States and Australia," *International Migration* 57, no. 5 (2019): 235–251; Matthew La Corte and Sam Peak, "Recruiting, Retaining, and Capitalizing on International Students at U.S. Universities," *Niskanen Center Policy Brief* (May 2019), www.niskanencenter.org; see also the chapter by Donato and Amuedo-Dorantes in this volume.

37 Julie Baer, "Fall 2017 International Student Enrollment Hot Topics Survey," IIE Centre for Academic Mobility Research and Impact, November 2017, www.iie.org; NAFSA: Association of International Educators, "Losing Talent 2020: An Economic and Foreign Policy Risk American *Can't* Ignore," March 2020, www.nafsa.org.

38 David Zweig, "Learning to Compete: China's Efforts to Encourage a 'Reverse Brain Drain,'" in *Competing for Global Talent*, ed. Christian Kuptsch and Eng Fong

Pang (Geneva: International Institute for Labour Studies, International Labour Organization, 2006), 187–213; Loo et al., "Career Prospects and Outcomes for U.S.-Educated International Students."

39 Baer, "Fall 2017 International Student Enrollment Hot Topics Survey"; NAFSA, "Losing Talent 2020."

40 National Academies of Sciences, Engineering, and Medicine, *Graduate STEM Education for the 21st Century* (Washington, DC: The National Academies Press, 2018).

41 Calculated from data in US Citizenship and Immigration Services (USCIS), "Characteristics of H-1B Specialty Occupation Workers: Fiscal Year 2019 Annual Report to Congress," Homeland Security, March 5, 2020, www.uscis.gov.

42 Choudaha, "Three Waves of International Student Mobility."

43 Hein de Haas et al., "International Migration: Trends, Determinants, and Policy Effects," *Population and Development Review* 45, no. 4 (2019): 885–922.

44 Koslowski, "Selective Migration Policy Models"; de Haas et al., "International Migration."

45 OECD, "Recruiting Immigrant Workers: Canada," 2019, www.oecd-ilibrary.org.

46 NFAP, "Analysis of International Student Data," 2.

47 Trevena, "Post Study Work Visa Options."

48 Agnieszka Weinar and Amanda Klekowski von Koppenfeis, *Highly-Skilled Migration: Between Settlement and Mobility* (Cham, Switzerland: Springer, 2020).

49 OECD, "How Is the Global Talent Pool Changing (2013, 2030)?" *Education Indicators in Focus* no. 31 (April 2015), www.oecd-ilibrary.org.

50 Angela Yung Chi Hou, "The Quality of Mass Higher Education in East Asia: Development and Challenges for Asian Quality Assurance Agencies in the Glonacal Higher Education," in *Mass Higher Education Development in East Asia: Strategy, Quality, and Challenges*, ed. Jung Cheol Shin, Gerard A. Postiglione, and Futao Huang (Cham, Switzerland: Springer, 2015), 307–323.

51 Wei Sun, "The Productivity of Return Migrants: The Case of China's 'Sea Turtles,'" *IZA Journal of Migration* 2, no. 1 (2013): 1–19; Zwetsloot et al., "Keeping Top AI Talent," 23–24.

52 AnnaLee Saxenian, "From Brain Drain to Brain Circulation: Transnational Communities and Regional Upgrading in India and China," *Studies in Comparative International Development* 40, no. 2 (2005): 35–61.

53 B. Lindsay Lowell, "A Long View of America's Immigration Policy and the Supply of Foreign-Born STEM Workers in the United States," *American Behavioral Scientist* 53, no. 7 (2010): 1029–1044; B. Lindsay Lowell and Philip Martin, "Managing the Dynamic Science and Engineering Labor Market in the United States," *International Migration Review* 46, no. 4 (2012): 1005–1012.

54 Zweig, "Learning to Compete"; Loo et al., "Career Prospects and Outcomes for U.S.-Educated International Students"; Zwetsloot et al., "Keeping Top AI Talent."

55 Kim et al., "International Doctorates."

56 These are summarized in Ruiz, "The Geography of Foreign Students in U.S. Higher Education," 4.

57 Gaby Ramia, Simon Marginson, and Erlenawati Sawir, *Regulating International Students' Wellbeing* (Bristol: Policy Press, 2013), 73–74; Peter Gale, "Beyond Fear and Towards Hope: Transnationalism and the Recognition of Rights Across Borders," in *Migration, Diaspora and Identity: Cross-National Experiences*, ed. Georgina Tsolidis (Dordrecht: Springer, 2014), 123–137.

58 Gavan Conlon, Rohit Lader, Maike Halterbeck, and Sophie Hedges, "EU Exit: Estimating the Impact on UK Higher Education, Department of Education," UK Government Research report (February 2021), https://assets.publishing.service .gov.uk.

59 National Foundation for American Policy, "Analysis of International Student Data for the 2018–19 Academic Year," *NFAP Policy Brief* (June 2000), https://nfap.com.

60 See, e.g., Josh O'Kane and Sean Silcoff, "Canadian Tech Executives Urge Skilled Immigrants to Come Here as Trump Expands U.S. Visa Halt," *The Globe and Mail*, June 23, 2020, www.theglobeandmail.com.

61 Makala Skinner, "The Financial Risk of Overreliance on Chinese Student Enrollment," World Educational Services World Education News and Reviews, December 17, 2018, https://wenr.wes.org.

62 QS Quacquarelli Symonds, "The Impact of the Coronavirus on Prospective International Students," QS Quacquarelli Symonds (May 2020), https://info.qs.com; QS Quacquarelli Symonds, "Higher Education in 2020: How COVID-19 Shaped This Year," QS Quacquarelli Symonds (December 2020): 11–12.

63 Dick Startz, "University Finances and COVID-19: Different Schools, Different Risks," Brookings Institute Brown City Chalkboard, June 18, 2020, www.brook ings.edu.

64 Simon Marginson, "Global HE as We Know It Has Forever Changed," *Times Higher Education*, March 26 2020, www.timeshighereducation.com.

65 La Corte and Peak, "Recruiting, Retaining, and Capitalizing on International Students at U.S. Universities," 3.

66 World Economic Forum, "The Future of Jobs Report 2018," 2018, www.weforum .org.

67 Laura Betancur, Elizabeth Votruba-Drzal, and Christian Schunn, "Socioeconomic Gaps in Science Achievement," *International Journal of STEM Education* 5, no. 38 (2018), www.ncbi.nlm.nih.gov; Maya Corneille, Anna Lee North, Kimberly N. Harris, K. T. Jackson, and Megan Covington, "Developing Culturally and Structurally Responsive Approaches to STEM Education to Advance Education Equity," *The Journal of Negro Education* 89, no. 1 (2020): 48–57.

68 Data from USCIS, "Characteristics of H-1B Specialty Occupation Workers," 7.

69 Igor Chirikov and Krista M. Soria, *International Students' Experiences and Concerns During the Pandemic* (University of California–Berkeley and University of Minnesota: SERU Consortium, July 1, 2020), www.cshe.berkeley.edu.

70 US Citizenship and Immigration Services, *H-1B Petitions by Gender and Country of Birth Fiscal Year 2018* (Washington, DC: US Citizenship and Immigration Services, October 5, 2018).

71 Paul Schulmann, "International Women: The Key to Gender Parity in U.S. Science & Engineering Departments?" *World Education News and Reviews* (June 7, 2016), https://wenr.wes.org.

72 Kim et al., "International Doctorates."

73 Ayelet Shachar, "The Race for Talent: Highly Skilled Migrants and Competitive Immigration Regimes," *New York University Law Review* 81, no. 1 (2006): 148–206.

74 D. W. Livingstone, "Skill Under-Utilization," in *The Oxford Handbook of Skills and Training*, ed. Chris Warhurst, Ken Mayhew, David Finegold, and John Buchanan (Oxford: Oxford University Press, 2017), 281–301; Peter H. Cappelli, "Skill Gaps, Skill Shortages and Skill Mismatches: Evidence and Arguments for the United States," *ILR Review* 68, no. 2 (2015): 251–290.

75 Demetrios G. Papademetriou and Madeleine Sumption, "Attracting and Selecting from the Global Talent Pool–Policy Challenges," Migration Policy Institute (September 2013), www.migrationpolicy.org; Weisser, "Internationally Mobile Students and Their Post-Graduation Migratory Behaviour," 61.

76 Irene Bloemraad, "Becoming a Citizen in the United States and Canada: Structured Mobilization and Immigrant Political Incorporation," *Social Forces* 85, no. 2 (2006): 667–695.

77 Madeleine Sumption, "Giving Cities and Regions a Voice in Immigration Policy: Can National Policies Meet Local Demand?" Migration Policy Institute (July 2014), www.migrationpolicy.org.

78 Creso M. Sá and Emma Sabzalieva, "The Politics of the Great Brain Drain: Public Policy and International Student Recruitment in Australia, Canada, England, and the USA," *Higher Education* 75, no. 2 (2018): 231–253.

79 Marie Price, "World Migration Report 2015. Cities Welcoming Immigrants: Local Strategies to Attract and Retain Immigrants in U.S. Metropolitan Areas," International Organization for Migration (December 2014), www.iom.int.

80 Steve Tobocman, "Revitalizing Detroit: Is There a Role for Immigration?" Migration Policy Institute (August 2014), www.migrationpolicy.org.

8

Highly Skilled African Immigrants

Fields of Study, Education-Occupation Matching, and Earnings in the US Labor Market

KEVIN J. A. THOMAS

African immigration to the United States has increased considerably in recent decades. While only about 46,000 Africans immigrated to the country during the one-hundred-year period between 1861 and 1961, the number of African immigrants in the United States now stands at more than two million.[1] In response to these trends, a growing number of studies have examined how well African immigrants are integrated into US society.[2] As a result, we now have a clear portrait of their social and demographic characteristics.

This portrait indicates that the African immigrant population contains one of the highest concentrations of highly educated individuals in the country.[3] However, as noted in previous studies,[4] the antecedents of their human capital profile are found in determinants of recent African migration trends. To be sure, these determinants are diverse.[5] Nevertheless, the central role of economic factors in driving these trends is indisputable.[6] There is no question that declining incomes at home are among the most important influences of African migration to the United States.[7] Correspondingly, recent changes in US immigration policy, including those reviewed in Donato and Amuedo-Dorantes's chapter in this volume, have helped to accelerate the process by providing new mechanisms of immigration for highly skilled African professionals.[8] What we know about the economic outcomes of these immigrants is limited, however, by the tendency to focus on the outcomes of selected groups of professionals.[9] With few exceptions,[10] studies that provide a comprehensive portrait of the economic outcomes of highly skilled African immigrants are generally lacking. Consequently, very little is known about how the outcomes of African professionals compare with those of similarly skilled US natives or immigrants from other countries. Moreover, it is not clear whether there are disparities in the economic outcomes of these groups that are shaped by qualitative differences in their human capital endowments.

This study uses data from the 2014–2018 sample of the American Community Survey (ACS) to provide clarity on these issues by examining the labor force outcomes of highly skilled African immigrants. The analysis focuses on three objectives. First, it investigates education-occupation mismatch status among these immigrants, examining whether their matching patterns vary depending on their field of study. Second, the study examines the implications of both education-occupation mismatch status and field of study for earnings inequalities among highly skilled Africans. Third, using two outcomes of interest, i.e., education-occupation matching and earnings, the analysis investigates how highly skilled Africans fare in the labor market in comparison to other similarly skilled immigrants and US natives.

Background

Contemporary African immigration to the United States has its origins in the 1965 immigration reform, which eliminated origin-country quotas that had restricted immigration from countries outside of Western Europe. However, it took about a decade for the first notable increases in African immigration to be observed. The human capital characteristics of these first immigrant cohorts were largely shaped by their response to economic motivations as predicted by early theories of migration. Lee, for example, argued that when incomes are substantially higher in destination than in origin countries, the first migrants responding to these differences will be positively selected on their human capital endowments.[11] Consistent with this perspective, the first African migrants to arrive in the contemporary period included students and skilled professionals.[12] By the 1980s, however, African economic conditions had declined so precipitously that many of these immigrants chose to permanently resettle in the United States.

Notwithstanding the significance of these trends, a more important shift in African immigration occurred a decade later. With the passing of the Immigration Act of 1990, the Diversity Visa (DV) program was established, and subsequently provided the central mechanism for increasing economically motivated migration from Africa to the United States. In part, this was due to the fact that the program was established during a period of considerable economic hardship in Africa and Latin America—usually referred to as the lost decade.[13] More important, eligibility for participation in the program was based on skills. Applicants were required to either have a minimum of a completed high school education or be employed in an occupation that required at least two years of training or experience. In the context of declining economic conditions at home, the DV program became the primary channel through which highly educated Africans in professional, managerial, and technical occupations chose to migrate to the United States.[14]

Subsequent increases in the number of highly skilled Africans in the United States were quickly followed by the expansion of research on their incorporation into society.[15] Yet, this expansion has provided mixed evidence on their levels of socioeconomic attainment. On the one hand is the work of scholars who use evidence of African migrants' high levels of educational attainment, to describe them as a new model minority.[16] This perspective is reinforced in studies showing that African immigrants have higher incomes than US-born Blacks and other Black immigrants.[17] On the other hand, several studies provide a more critical perspective on the socioeconomic attainment of African immigrants. They show, for example, that highly educated African immigrants are largely limited in their ability to translate their human capital into income gains in the US labor market.[18] Studies on whether this constraint is dependent on the composition of their skill endowments are generally absent from the literature. As a result, it is difficult to systematically identify the institutional barriers that prevent the optimal utilization of African immigrants' human capital in the US labor market.

A major factor typically linked to such barriers is the mismatch between educational attainment and occupation of employment. Such education-occupation mismatches occur when individuals have either more or less than the level of education considered normative for their occupation.[19] Education-occupation mismatches have been found to have a number of negative implications. Accordingly, research indicates that they have adverse effects on psychological well-being, wages, job motivation, and the economic outcomes of children.[20]

It is now clear from previous studies that immigrants are generally more likely to experience education-occupation mismatches than the native-born.[21] For highly skilled immigrants, this may result in not only the suboptimal utilization of their human capital endowments but limitations to their prospects of occupational mobility as well. Existing studies nevertheless give very limited attention to the investigation of how education-occupation mismatch status can shape the labor market experiences of highly skilled African immigrants. Beyond the question of the prevalence of such mismatches is the need for systematic assessments of whether African immigrants are more likely than other immigrants to experience these constraints. If they are, it will be important to understand what this implies for wage inequalities among immigrant groups.

Conceptually, however, there are at least two explanations for why we should expect to find a higher risk of education-occupation mismatch among highly skilled African immigrants. The first is the limited transferability of foreign schooling. Education earned abroad receives lower rewards in the labor market compared to education earned in destination countries.[22] As prior studies suggest, this constraint is more frequently encountered by immigrants from less developed countries than by immigrants from more developed countries.[23] More discussion on this is found in Bhatti's analysis of the experiences of highly skilled Pakistani female immigrants in the United States.[24] In the same vein, some scholars have argued that education earned in Africa is usually perceived to be of a lower quality than education earned in more industrialized countries.[25]

Despite the significance of the problem associated with foreign schooling, few studies have examined whether exposure to the problem varies by field of study. In some cases, the problem is assumed to be more of a constraint to the outcomes of foreign STEM graduates. For example, foreign medical graduates are required to go through complex processes of recertification and complete a three- to eight-year residency period.[26] This residency requirement is expected to be fulfilled regardless of whether foreign medical graduates have completed a similar residency period in their home countries.[27] Among immigrants with degrees in engineering, the problem of foreign schooling is slightly different. While they are not required to complete similar processes of recertification, it is typically difficult for them to find employers who recognize their foreign credentials. As a result, they are often advised by recruiters to take lower-level jobs to help them accumulate more US certified skills.[28]

A second explanation for expecting a higher risk of education-occupation mismatch among highly skilled African immigrants is associated with their race. Racial minorities are more likely to have lower levels of occupational attainment and returns to their human capital compared to Whites.[29] Moreover, the available evidence suggests that the labor market disadvantage associated with racial minority status is more pernicious among African immigrants. As maintained by Batalova and colleagues,[30] highly educated Black African immigrants are more likely to work as security guards, dishwashers, and in other low-level occupations compared to immigrants from other regions. Regardless of their field of study, therefore, highly skilled African immigrants are expected to experience a higher level of exposure to the risk of job mismatches given the fact that the majority of them are Black.

The Current Study

All told, there are at least two principal gaps in the existing literature that this study aims to address. First, the study addresses the lack of systematic research on the occupational attainment patterns of highly skilled African immigrants by investigating how their education-occupation matching patterns compare with those of other highly skilled persons. In the process, the study also examines whether education-occupation mismatches have a more adverse influence on earnings among the former compared to the latter. Second, given the lack of research examining whether the education-occupation matching outcomes of immigrants vary by their field of study, this chapter incorporates these variations into the analysis of the economic attainment patterns of highly skilled African immigrants. Specifically, it investigates whether Africans trained in STEM have more suboptimal job match patterns and earnings patterns than their counterparts trained in other fields of study. In doing so, the analysis provides new insights into how variations in fields of study shape immigrant integration into the US labor market.

Data and Methods

These objectives are examined using data from the 2014–2018, 5-year sample of the ACS available at the Integrated Public Use Microdata Series (IPUMS) database.[31] The sample contains information on indicators of educational attainment, labor force participation, and occupation of employment, which are useful for measuring the main outcomes of the study. Given the fact that the occupational constraints to the use of human capital are more defined among individuals who are highly skilled,[32] the analysis focuses on respondents with at least a bachelor's degree. The analysis is further restricted to individuals between ages 25 and 65.

Two dependent variables are used in the analysis. The first is *education-occupation matching status* and it is estimated using information on educational attainment and occupation of employment. Most previous studies use worker job assessments, worker self-assessments, or realized matching procedures to identify job matching status.[33] However, this analysis uses realized matching methods,[34] because they are best suited for the type of data available in the ACS. Using these methods, the following three education-occupation matching categories are defined. *Correct matches* are defined as having the occupation-specific modal level of schooling. *Over-education* and *under-education* are respectively defined as having more and less than the modal level of education for each occupation. The second outcome is weekly earnings, estimated as the sum of wage and salary income plus any positive business or farm income. This total is then divided by the number of weeks worked in the previous year to estimate weekly earnings. To account for the fact that weekly earnings have a nonlinear distribution, these estimates are further log-transformed before using them in the analysis.

The primary independent variables are *immigrant status* and *field of study*. Immigrant status is determined using data on place of birth. On this basis, the study identifies immigrants from five major regions— Africa, Asia, Europe, Latin America and the Caribbean (LAC), and other regions. US natives are identified as individuals born in the United States. Field of study is used as a proxy measure of skills, and is determined using data on the fields of study of college graduates.[35] Accordingly, all college graduates are classified into five broad areas of study: Arts/Humanities, Business, STEM, Social Sciences, and other fields (e.g., Cosmetology Services and Culinary Arts; Physical Fitness, Parks, and Recreation). As in research conducted by Mattoo and colleagues,[36] foreign *schooling* is measured using data on age at arrival and educational attainment to identify persons who arrived in the United States at ages before which specific levels of education are typically completed. For example, immigrants who arrived in the United States before age fifteen, whose highest level of educational attainment is a bachelor's degree, are assumed to have earned their degrees in the United States. On the contrary, similarly educated immigrants who arrived at age thirty-five are assumed to have foreign schooling credentials.

The control variables in the analysis include *English proficiency, decade of arrival, work experience,* and other demographic measures. English proficiency is measured as a dummy variable indicating whether individuals speak English very well or only English. Work experience is estimated as age minus six (i.e., the earliest schooling age), minus years of schooling; and decade of arrival is used to account, among other things, for the changing human capital profile of immigrant arrival cohorts. Additionally, the analysis controls for *marital status, race, region of residence, age, sex,* and highest level of educational attainment.

Analytical Strategy

The analysis starts by using multinomial regression models to examine the determinants of education-occupation matching. The dependent variable is education-occupation matching status. The regression models are used to examine how factors, such as differences in fields of study, mediate inequalities in matching outcomes. For ease of interpretation, coefficients estimated by the models are transformed into Relative Risk Ratios (RRR).[37] Next, OLS regression models are used to examine disparities in weekly earnings and the extent to which they are determined, among other things, by education-occupation matching status as well as fields of study.

The empirical analyses are conducted in two stages. The first stage examines the education-occupation matching and wage outcomes of highly skilled African immigrants. The second stage compares these immigrants with other immigrants and US natives to identify group-level inequalities in the two outcomes of interest.

Results

Table 8.1 presents the descriptive statistics of the five major immigrant groups and the US-born. Although African immigrants are the second smallest group in the sample, their educational profile is distinguished in several important ways. The majority of them have degrees in either STEM (45.6%) or business (22.3%). About 7 percent of African immigrants also have doctoral degrees. However, approximately half of them (49.1%) earned their college credentials abroad, which is the highest in the sample. This finding suggests that African immigrants are disproportionately more likely to be exposed to the labor market disadvantages associated with foreign schooling than other immigrants.

A closer look at the educational profiles of the other subgroups further reveals several interesting patterns. For example, more than half of all immigrants from Asia (56.3%) had STEM degrees, which reflects increasing trends in the recruitment of STEM graduates from the region.[38] Regardless of region of origin, however, all immigrant graduates had higher percentages of individuals with STEM degrees and doctoral degrees compared to their US-born counterparts.

Our first impression of the distribution of matching status across groups is also shown in table 8.1. Consistent with previous studies,[39] immigrants are generally less likely to be correctly matched for their jobs than US natives. The exception to this disparity is found among immigrants from other regions, the majority of whom are from Canada and Australia. Immigrants in this group are about as likely to be correctly matched for their jobs as US natives. Significantly, however, table 8.1 shows that African immigrants have the least favorable matching outcomes in the sample; they had the lowest percentage of correct matches (39.3%) and the highest percentage of individuals who were over-educated (54%).

Additional group-level differences are observed in other labor market indicators. Average weekly earnings are highest among immigrants from other regions, as well as their European counterparts, and lowest among immigrants from LAC and Africa. Interestingly, these differences do not

TABLE 8.1: The Descriptive Statistics of College Graduates Between Ages 25 and 65, by Place of Birth

	Africa	Asia	Europe	LAC	Other	US
Field of study						
Arts and Humanities	6.6	6.4	9.8	6.6	10.8	10.4
Business	22.3	18.5	18.5	25	18	21
STEM	45.6	56.3	42	35.8	39.1	29.3
Social Science	18.2	13.6	20.3	20.1	22.2	22.8
Other fields	7.3	5.2	9.3	12.5	9.9	16.4
Education-Occupation match						
Correct match	39.3	43	43.4	41	53.7	52.9
Under-education	6.1	5.2	6.2	7.4	7.1	8.8
Over-education	54.5	51.7	50.4	52	39.1	38.4
Weekly earnings (Mean)	1,515	1,760	1,905	1,305	2,231	1,622
Weeks worked (Mean)	43.8	43.9	44.2	44.1	44	44.8
Age (Mean)	44.1	43.2	44.6	44.2	44.9	44.5
Female	40.7	48.6	49.8	54.3	47.9	53.2
Married	70	77	71	65	71	66.8
English proficient	39.7	35.8	53.3	38.4	83.8	94.1
Has a PhD	6.7	8.6	9.7	3.8	9	3.6
Foreign immigrant graduate	49.1	39.7	36	40.9	39.9	—
Work experience (Mean)	21	19.3	21.2	21.3	21.6	21.6
Hispanic	0	0	3.3	73.6	1.0	5.3
Black	62.5	0	1.9	13.6	1.4	6.3
White	30.4	10.5	91.2	8.7	84.4	83.9
Asian	4.4	85.9	1.6	1.6	9.5	2.4
Other race	2.7	3.6	2	2.5	3.7	2.1
Decade of arrival						
2009 to 2018	21.7	21.8	17.8	17.1	19.8	—
1999 to 2008	32.2	26.8	22.9	26.2	22.2	—
1989 to 1998	23.7	23.3	26.9	23.3	23.5	—
1979 to 1988	14.7	17.9	13.1	18.7	14	—
Before 1979	7.7	10.2	19.3	14.7	20.5	—
Metro-area resident	96	96.8	93.3	95.8	90.9	82.7
N	25,236	221,694	84,280	93,962	18,956	2,186,773

Data source: ACS 2014–2018 five-year sample.

appear to be driven by variations in work effort or work experience. As table 8.1 indicates, all groups in the analysis worked for an average of about forty-four hours per week and had an average of about twenty years of work experience.

There are no major group-level differences in demographic characteristics. Mean ages range from 43.2 among Asians to 44.9 among immigrants from other regions. With the exception of African immigrants, who are about 60 percent male, the sex distribution for all groups in the sample is approximately even. Compared to these similarities, there are notable differences in immigrant-specific attributes across groups. For example, African immigrants (53.9%) have the highest percentage of individuals who arrived in the last two decades, while immigrants from other regions have the highest levels of English proficiency (84%) followed by immigrants from Europe (53.3%).

Field of Study and the Labor Market Outcomes of African Immigrants

Results from multinomial regression models examining the relationship between field of study and education-occupation mismatch status among African immigrants are presented in table 8.2. Baseline estimates of the risks of experiencing various matching statuses, conditional on fields of study, are presented in Model 1. These estimates show two critical findings. First, the lowest risks of under-education among African immigrants are found among graduates with business degrees followed by their counterparts with STEM degrees. Compared to their peers with degrees in other fields (i.e., the reference group), the risks of under-education among immigrants with degrees in business and STEM are lower by about 65 percent and 60 percent, respectively. Second, there are smaller disparities in the risks of over-education compared to those associated with under-education. In terms of over-education, the lowest risks are observed among STEM graduates, whose risks are approximately 20 percent lower than those of graduates with degrees in other fields. Taken together, these baseline differences have one major implication. They suggest that, among highly skilled African immigrants, graduates with STEM degrees have the lowest risk of experiencing any kind of job mismatch in the US labor market.

TABLE 8.2: Relative Risk Ratios Estimated from Multinomial Regression Models Examining the Predictors of Education-Occupation Matching Status Among Highly Skilled African Immigrants

	Under-education		Over-education	
	Model 1	Model 2	Model 1	Model 2
Field of study				
Arts and Humanities	0.79	0.82	1.05	0.91
Business	0.35***	0.36***	1.06	1.28***
STEM	0.40***	0.43***	0.77***	0.76***
Social Science	0.60***	0.61***	1.05	1.06
Other fields (Reference)	(1.00)	(1.00)	(1.00)	(1.00)
Age	0.99***	1.18***	1.00	1.81***
Female	1.33***	1.35***	0.73***	0.79***
Married		0.91		0.90**
English proficient		1.00		1.059*
Has a PhD		0.00		0.15***
Foreign immigrant graduate		0.89		0.96
Work experience		0.81***		0.55***
Work experience squared		1.00***		1.00*
Decade of arrival				
2009 to 2018		2.48***		3.22***
1999 to 2008		1.41*		2.17***
1989 to 1998		1.23		1.53***
1979 to 1988		0.97		1.26***
Before 1979 (Reference)		(1.00)		(1.00)
Metro-area resident		0.70**		1.032
Constant	0.50***	0.10***	1.72***	0.00***
Log likelihood	−21652.525	−20302	−21652.525	−20302.6
N	25236	25236	25236	25236

Note: Base outcome is Correct match. *$p < 0.05$, **$p < 0.01$, ***$p < 0.001$.

Controlling for the full range of demographic and social character-istics in Model 2 leads to few changes in the relative risks of either type of job mismatch across the various fields of study. The lowest risks of under-education continue to be found among Africans with business degrees, followed by their peers with STEM degrees. Likewise, dispari-ties in the risks of over-education largely remain the same, except for what is observed among Africans immigrants with business degrees. As Model 2 indicates, these graduates have the highest risks of over-education after other factors are controlled, implying that their base-line risks of over-education shown in Model 1 were partly suppressed by their comparatively more favorable demographic attributes. At the same time, Model 2 shows that, at least within the population of Afri-can graduates, having foreign degrees is not significantly associated with job mismatches after other factors are controlled. Moreover, the highest risks of experiencing any kind of job mismatch are observed among Af-rican graduates who arrived in the last two decades.

Table 8.3 turns our attention to earnings differences and examines whether fields of study and education-occupation mismatch status are associated with earnings inequalities among African graduates. Base-line estimates shown in Model 1 indicate that the most notable predictor of earnings inequalities is whether African immigrants have STEM de-grees. Compared to graduates with other degrees, STEM graduates have weekly earnings that are 64 percent higher (i.e., exp (0.49) −1), which is consistent with research showing that, on average, STEM graduates have higher salaries compared to non-STEM graduates.[40] Business graduates appear to have the second highest earnings among highly skilled Af-ricans; however, their suggested earnings advantage is not statistically significant. In terms of mismatch status, Model 1 provides clear evidence that there are wage penalties associated with education-occupation mis-matches. Under-educated and over-educated Africans have earnings that were lower by 57% (i.e., exp (−0.85) −1) and 37% (i.e., exp (−0.46) −1), respectively, compared to the earnings of their counterparts who have jobs that correctly match their schooling.

Most of these disparities remain unchanged after including controls for the full set of demographic and social characteristics in Model 2. After controlling for these factors, for example, STEM graduates still earned the highest wages, which were 46% (i.e., exp (0.38) −1) higher

TABLE 8.3: Coefficients from OLS Regression Models Showing the Predictors of Earnings Differences Among Highly Skilled African Immigrants

	Model 1	Model 2	Model 3
Field of study			
Arts and Humanities	−0.152	−0.19	−0.199
Business	0.032	0.07	0.36*
STEM	0.493***	0.38***	0.77***
Social Science	−0.054	−0.110	0.06
Other fields (Reference)	(0.00)	(0.00)	(0.00)
Education-Occupation match			
Correct match (Reference)	(0.00)	(0.00)	(0.00)
Undereducation	−0.85***	−0.69***	−0.84***
Overeducation	−0.46***	-0.55***	0.02
Age	0.010***	0.23***	0.24***
Female	−0.88***	−0.92***	−0.92***
Arts and Humanities * Overeducation			−0.21
Arts and Humanities * Undereducation			1.23**
Business * Overeducation			−0.58*
Business * Undereducation			0.19
STEM * Overeducation			−0.77***
STEM * Undereducation			0.07
Social Science * Overeducation			−0.36
Social Science * Undereducation			0.05
Married			−0.20***
English proficient		−0.20***	−0.03
Has a PhD		−0.612***	−0.62***
Foreign immigrant graduate		−0.31***	−0.32***
Work experience		−0.55	−0.06*
Work experience squared		−0.00***	−0.00***
Decade of arrival			
2009 to 2018		−0.93***	−0.94**
1999 to 2008		−0.08	−0.09
1989 to 1998		0.12	1.09
1979 to 1988		0.04	0.04
Before 1979 (Reference)			
Metro-area resident		0.33***	0.34**
Constant	5.95***	0.04	−0.41
R-squared	0.02	0.05	0.06
N	25,236	25,236	25,236

Note: *$p < 0.05$, **$p < 0.01$, ***$p < 0.001$.

than the wages of graduates in other fields. Similarly, the wage disadvantages associated with both under-education and over-education continue to persist, although the penalty associated with under-education declines slightly after accounting for the full set of controls. Among other things, Model 2 also confirms that graduates with foreign degrees have lower incomes than graduates with degrees earned in the United States. However, group-level differences in the distribution of foreign degrees do not necessarily explain the earnings inequalities associated with field of study and job mismatches among highly skilled African immigrants.

Model 3 specifically investigates whether the adverse effects of education-occupation mismatches on wages vary by field of study, and the results show several important findings. First, they show that the wage penalty associated with over-education is most severe among African immigrants with STEM degrees. In other words, despite the fact that African STEM graduates have the highest earnings, this wage premium effectively disappears if they work in occupations that require less education than they possess. A similar wage penalty is also found among business graduates who are over-educated. In relative terms, however, the size of their wage disadvantage is smaller than that observed among over-educated STEM graduates.

Additionally, the results show that under-education is generally associated with lower wages, except among Africans with degrees in the arts and humanities. While the reasons for this are unclear, it may reflect the fact that arts and humanities graduates are mostly individuals with degrees in foreign languages. As such, they may have access to niche markets that provide greater rewards for their skills than for their actual level of schooling.

In summary, the analysis of the outcomes of highly skilled African shows at least four important findings. First, STEM graduates are less likely to experience any kind of job mismatch compared to graduates with degrees in other fields. Second, STEM graduates also have the highest incomes. Third, education-occupation mismatches are associated with lower wages compared to correct matches. Finally, the adverse effect of over-education on wages is most severe among African immigrants with STEM degrees, followed by their peers with business degrees.

Field of Study and the Labor Market Outcomes of Africans,
Other Immigrants, and the US-Born

The next stage of the analysis compares the outcomes of African immigrants with those of immigrants from other regions and US natives. To begin this process, table 8.4 examines the predictors of education-occupation mismatch status in the full sample. Baseline differences shown in Model 1 indicate that the highest risks of under-education are observed among African immigrants, followed by immigrants from LAC. Both groups have estimated risks of under-education that are approximately 20 percent higher than those of the US-born, controlling for field of study and demographic differences. A similar pattern of disparity is observed in the risks of over-education. These risks are highest among African immigrants, who are about twice as likely to be over-educated as their US-born peers.

For the most part, the elevated risks of experiencing any kind of mismatch observed among immigrants from Africa persist after controlling for other factors (Model 2). For African immigrants, this finding is particularly instructive. It underscores the fact that their more adverse matching outcomes are not entirely explained by variations in factors, such as fields of study, possession of foreign credentials, or their racial characteristics. Indeed, after accounting for these factors, African immigrants continued to have one of the highest risks of education-occupation mismatches in the sample.

For all immigrants, however, having degrees in the arts and humanities, business, STEM, and social sciences is associated with a lower risk of over-education than having degrees in other fields (Models 1 and 2). Unlike what is observed in the African sample in table 8.2, STEM graduates do not have the lowest risks of being either under-educated or over-educated. In terms of under-education, the lowest risks are found among business graduates, while the lowest risks of over-education are found among immigrants with other degrees. Model 2, however, underscores the importance of several factors associated with an elevated risk of over-education. These factors include foreign schooling, racial minority status (i.e., being Black or Hispanic), and recent immigration status.

The final set of results are presented in table 8.5, which examines earnings differences between African immigrants and other highly

TABLE 8.4: Relative Risk Ratios Estimated from Multinomial Regression Models Examining the Predictors of Education-Occupation Matching Status Among Immigrants and the US-Born

	Undereducation		Overeducation	
	Model 1	Model 2	Model 1	Model 2
African immigrants	1.24***	3.21***	1.91***	1.73***
Asian immigrants	0.97***	3.41***	1.67***	1.86***
European immigrants	0.99	2.95***	1.59***	1.06***
LAC immigrants	1.21**	2.72***	1.74***	1.89***
Other immigrants	0.91**	2.87***	1.00	1.06***
U.S. Born (Reference)	(1.00)	(1.00)	(1.00)	(1.00)
Field of study				
Arts and Humanities	0.46***	0.46***	1.14***	1.25***
Business	0.17***	0.16***	1.03***	1.42***
STEM	0.26***	0.26***	1.04***	1.09***
Social Science	0.36***	0.37***	1.14***	1.21***
Other fields (Reference)	(1.00)	(1.00)	(1.00)	(1.00)
Age	0.99***	0.74***	1.00***	1.76***
Female	1.70***	1.74***	0.94***	0.90***
Married		1.06***		0.79***
English proficient		0.94***		1.02***
Asian		0.72***		0.89***
Black		1.10***		1.23***
Hispanic		1.20***		1.06***
White		0.91***		0.86***
Other (Reference)		(1.00)		(1.00)
Has a PhD		0.00***		0.26***
Foreign immigrant graduate		0.51***		1.11***
Work experience		1.31***		0.56***
Work experience squared		1.00***		1.00***
Decade of arrival				
2009 to 2018		3.08***		1.69***
1999 to 2008		1.56***		1.72***
1989 to 1998		1.23***		1.44***
1979 to 1988		1.07*		1.20***
Before 1979/US natives (Reference)		(1.00)		(1.00)
Metro-area resident		0.70***		0.81***
Constant	0.41***	185.9***	0.60***	0.00***
Log likelihood	−2342903	−2192285	−2342903	−2192285
N	2630394	2630394	2630394	2630394

Note. Base outcome is Correct match. $^*p < 0.05$, $^{**}p < 0.01$, $^{***}p < 0.001$.

TABLE 8.5: Coefficients from OLS Regression Models Showing the Predictors of Earnings Differences Among Highly Skilled Immigrants and the US-Born

	Model 1	Model 2	Model 3	Model 4
African immigrants	−0.26***	−1.33***	−1.39***	−1.09***
Asian immigrants	−0.21***	−1.37***	−1.43***	−1.39***
European immigrants	−0.00	−1.29***	−1.34***	−1.31***
LAC immigrants	−0.26***	−1.33**	−1.37***	−1.13***
Other immigrants	0.08**	−1.17***	−1.12***	−1.46***
US Born (Reference)	(0.00)	(0.00)	(0.00)	(0.00)
Field of study				
Arts and Humanities	0.10***	0.06***	0.07***	0.10***
Business	0.47***	0.52***	0.53***	0.57***
STEM	0.60***	0.57***	0.57***	0.54***
Social Science	0.23***	0.18***	0.18***	0.19
Other fields (Reference)	(0.00)	(0.00)	(0.00)	(0.00)
Education-Occupation match				
Correct match (Reference)	(0.00)	(0.00)	(0.00)	(0.00)
Undereducation	−0.56***	−0.36***	−0.33***	−0.36***
Overeducation	−0.49***	−0.67***	−0.69***	−0.67***
African immigrants * Overeducation			0.13*	
African immigrants * Undereducation			−0.31**	
Asian immigrants * Overeducation			0.15***	
Asian immigrants * Undereducation			−0.35**	
European immigrants * Overeducation			0.13***	
European immigrants * Undereducation			−0.19***	
LAC immigrants * Overeducation			0.05	
LAC immigrants * Undereducation			0.10*	
Other immigrants * Overeducation			−0.08	
Other immigrants * Undereducation			−0.25*	
Age	−0.03***	0.28***	0.28***	0.28***
Female	−0.89***	−0.90***	−0.90***	−0.90***
African * Arts & Humanities				−0.33*
African immigrant * Business				−0.48**
African immigrant * STEM				−0.20*
African immigrant * Social Sciences				−0.33**
Asian immigrant * Arts & Humanities				−0.38**
Asian immigrant * Business				−0.29***
Asian immigrant * STEM				0.20***
Asian immigrant * Social Sciences				−0.16**

TABLE 8.5: (cont.)

	Model 1	Model 2	Model 3	Model 4
European immigrant * Arts & Humanities				−0.08
European immigrant * Business				−0.16***
European immigrant * STEM				0.14
European immigrant * Social Sciences				−0.08
LAC immigrant * Arts & Humanities				−0.17**
LAC immigrant * Business				−0.47***
LAC immigrant * STEM				−0.12**
LAC immigrant * Social Sciences				−0.23***
Other immigrant * Arts & Humanities				0.16
Other immigrant * Business				0.33**
Other immigrant * STEM				0.35***
Other immigrant * Social Sciences				0.28*
Constant	7.92***	0.07	0.08	0.11
R-squared	0.03	0.07	0.07	0.07
N	2,630,394	2,630,394	2630394	2,630,394

Note: *$p < 0.05$, **$p < 0.01$, ***$p < 0.001$. Models 2 through 4 also control for marital status, race, English proficiency, foreign schooling, educational attainment, decade of arrival, work experience, work experience squared, and residence in metropolitan areas.

skilled individuals. Overall, Model 1 indicates that African and LAC immigrants have the lowest earnings among college graduates, after accounting for their mismatch statuses, fields of study, and demographic differences (i.e., age and sex). On average, the earnings of both groups are about 23% (i.e., exp (−0.26) −1) lower than those of US natives. Additionally, European immigrants earn as much as US natives, while Asian immigrants earn wages that are comparatively lower by about 19% (i.e., exp (−0.21) −1).

To put things in perspective, it is important to juxtapose these findings with the inequalities in weekly wages observed in table 8.1. For example, gross weekly earnings for US natives are 7 percent higher than those of African immigrants (table 8.1). Therefore, the results in Model 1 (table 8.5) imply that this wage difference would have been greater had there been no demographic differences or variations in the distribution of fields of study among graduates in both groups. Similarly, Model 1 implies that Asian immigrants would not have earned the higher gross weekly incomes they had compared to the US-born shown in table 8.1 if there were no differences in the respective distributions of both groups.

Controlling for the effects of field of study, the results also show lower earnings among graduates of other fields of study compared to their counterparts with degrees in each of the four other major fields (Model 1). Once again, STEM graduates are shown to have the highest earnings. As observed among African immigrants (table 8.3), the results further show that over-education and under-education are both associated with lower earnings than correct matches (Model 1). For the most part, however, neither earnings inequalities based on immigrant status nor those related to field of study are substantially transformed after including the full set of controls (Model 2).

Interaction terms are used in Model 3 to test whether there are differences in the additional effects of mismatch status on wages across immigrant groups. Subsequently, over-education is shown to be positively associated with earnings among immigrants from Europe, Asia, and Africa. This finding implies that immigrants in these groups are more likely to be buffered from the negative effects of over-education on earnings than other graduates in the sample. On the contrary, Model 3 indicates that under-education is negatively associated with earnings and that this association is strongest among immigrants from Asia and Africa.

The second set of interaction terms examined (Model 4) are used to investigate variations in the additional effects of field of study on earnings. Subsequently, the results show that there is an additional negative influence on wages associated with having a degree in the Arts and Humanities. This implied wage penalty is strongest among Asian and African immigrants. Model 4 also shows a negative association between wages and having business degrees, but this relationship is strongest among immigrants from LAC and Africa. Additionally, having STEM degrees has a negative association with relative earnings among immigrants from Africa and LAC. Interestingly, these are also the only two groups of immigrants who do not experience a wage premium associated with STEM degrees when compared to the US-born. For Social Science degrees, the results reveal a negative association with wages that is notably more adverse among African immigrants.

Taken together, these results show at least one consistent pattern. Among graduates in every field of study, African immigrants are among the least likely to earn an additional wage premium for their human capital. This disadvantage persists, even after controlling for factors such as foreign schooling and race.

Conclusion

Changes in US immigration policy along with declining economic conditions in Africa have combined to produce one of the largest increases in African immigration to the United States in recent years.[41] Scholars maintain that these migrations have accelerated the African brain drain because, in most cases, they include highly educated migrant professionals.[42] More concerning, however, are emerging questions about the disconnection between African immigrants' poor economic outcomes on one hand and their high levels of human capital on the other.[43] In its attempt to clarify these issues, this study has investigated how structural constraints associated with education-occupation matching influence the use of African immigrants' human capital. Moreover, it has examined whether this influence varies across fields of study. Based on its empirical analysis, the study provides three critical insights into the economic incorporation of highly skilled Africans into US society.

First, it demonstrates that highly skilled Africans have suboptimal outcomes in the labor market because of their disproportionately high risk of being employed in jobs that do not match their levels of educational attainment. Of critical importance is their high exposure to the risks of over-education, given the fact that most African immigrant graduates are employed in jobs with educational expectations that are below their level of schooling. These findings are important for several reasons. For one, they show that prior concerns about the tendency of highly educated African immigrants to work as security guards or in other low-level occupations are not without merit.[44] Beyond these job-related implications, over-education could have negative consequences for other outcomes such as children's economic welfare.[45] As such, the study's findings provide reasons for concern that the negative consequences of over-education for highly skilled African immigrants may carry over into other social domains.

Second, the results demonstrate that the risks of experiencing any kind of job mismatch are strongly conditional on variations in fields of study. Within the African immigrant population, the most important variation that matters is that between STEM versus non-STEM degrees. African immigrants who graduated with STEM degrees generally had lower risks of experiencing any kind of education-occupation mismatch than their peers with non-STEM degrees. This finding is inconsistent with prior claims that immigrants with STEM degrees are particularly more vulnerable to being employed in jobs below their levels of schooling.[46] Instead, it underscores the importance of STEM education for buffering skilled African immigrants against the under-utilization of their skills in the US labor market.

Third, the results show that variations in both fields of study and education-occupation matching status among immigrants are important because of their direct implications for earnings. Among African immigrants, STEM graduates had higher earnings compared to non-STEM graduates. Similarly, graduates who were correctly matched for their jobs had higher earnings than their under-educated or over-educated counterparts. The analysis further provides more nuanced perspectives on the earnings implications of job mismatch status and fields of study. It suggests that African immigrants received lower earnings for their STEM degrees compared to other similarly educated immigrants. Unlike STEM graduates from Asia and Europe, who received higher additional earnings associated with possession of STEM credentials, African STEM graduates received lower earnings. Similar inequalities were observed in comparisons between African immigrants and other immigrants with degrees in business and the social sciences. In fact, across all fields of study, African immigrants were among those least able to translate their field-specific skills into higher earnings in the US labor market.

On the basis of these findings, we can conclude that the labor market incorporation of African immigrant graduates does not appear to result in the same degree of success as that observed among other immigrant groups. While it is difficult to identify the major explanations for these findings, they may be the consequences of several related factors. One of these is the fact that African immigrants may find it more difficult to move from lower-status to higher-status jobs. Although traditional constraints to labor market mobility such as racial minority status and foreign credentials may not necessarily explain their cross-sectional, labor market outcomes, these constraints may be more important in restricting their longer-term occupational success.

Other possibilities include the absence of occupational niches among highly skilled Africans, and cultural stereotypes that could limit their access to better job opportunities. Unlike STEM graduates from Asia, for example, African STEM graduates have not been able to develop specific occupational niches in the labor market. Asian immigrants have established a large presence in Silicon Valley, expanding their access to employment networks within the tech industry.[47] In terms of cultural stereotypes, some scholars suggest that US employers may be affected by lingering biases resulting from negative media representations of Africa.[48] Whether such biases have more negative consequences on the outcomes of African immigrants than the effects of similar biases against other immigrant groups remains to be determined. What is still clear is that the labor market integration of African immigrants remains a work in progress because it lags behind those of many similarly educated workers in the US labor market.

For these reasons, it is problematic to simply refer to highly skilled African immigrants as "economic" migrants. There is no doubt that declining economic performance in their countries of origin and the attraction to higher wages in the United States are among the principal factors driving their migration. After their arrival, however, their labor market experiences are mostly disconnected from what we would expect to observe among individuals with high levels of education. Instead, their experiences are shaped by a combination of factors including institutional forces that limit their ability to find employment in jobs appropriate for their education and individual-level factors such as their fields of study.

NOTES

1 Monica Anderson, "African Immigrant Population in U.S. Steadily Climbs," Pew Research Center (February 14, 2017), www.pewresearch.org; Kwadwo Konadu-Agyemang and Baffour K. Takyi, "An Overview of African Immigration to U.S. and Canada," in *The New African Diaspora in North America: Trends, Community Building, and Adaptation*, ed. Kwadwo Konadu-Agyemang, Baffour K. Takyi, and John Arthur (Lanham, MD: Lexington Books, 2006), 4.

2 Kristen McCabe, "African Immigrants in the United States in 2009," Migration
   Policy Institute (July 21, 2011), www.migrationpolicy.org; Joseph Takougang,
   "Contemporary African Immigrants to the United States," *Ìrìnkèrindò: A Journal
   of African Migration* 2, no. 1 (2003): 187.

3 Randy Capps, Kristen McCabe, and Michael Fix, "Diverse Streams: African
   Migration to the United States," Migration Policy Institute (April 2012), www.
   migrationpolicy.org; McCabe, "African Immigrants in the United States in 2009."

4 Arun Peter Lobo, "U.S. Diversity Visas Are Attracting Africa's Best and Brightest," Population Reference Bureau, July 1, 2001, www.prb.org; Ikubolajeh B. Logan
   and Kevin J. A. Thomas, "The U.S. Diversity Visa Programme and the Transfer of
   Skills from Africa," *International Migration* 50, no. 2 (2012): 1–19.

5 Baffour K. Takyi and Kwadwo Konadu-Agyemang, "Theoretical Perspectives on
   African Migration," in *The New African Diaspora in North America*, ed. Kwadwo
   Konadu-Agyemang, Baffour K. Takyi, and John Arthur (Lanham, MD: Lexington
   Books, 2006), 13–16; Kevin J. A. Thomas, "What Explains the Increasing Trend in
   African Emigration to the US?" *International Migration Review* 45, no. 1 (2011):
   3–28.

6 Lobo, "U.S. Diversity Visas Are Attracting Africa's Best and Brightest"; Thomas,
   "What Explains the Increasing Trend in African Emigration to the US?"

7 Takyi and Konadu-Agyemang, "Theoretical Perspectives on African Migration";
   Thomas, "What Explains the Increasing Trend in African Emigration to the US?"

8 Capps et al., "Diverse Streams"; Logan and Thomas, "The U.S. Diversity Visa
   Programme and the Transfer of Skills from Africa."

9 Amy Hagopian, Matthew J. Thompson, Meredith Fordyce, Karin E. Johnson,
   and L. Gary Hart, "The Migration of Physicians from Sub-Saharan Africa to the
   United States of America: Measures of the African Brain Drain," *Human Resources
   for Health* 2, no. 17 (2004): 1–10.

10 Francis Nii-Amoo Dodoo, "Assimilation Differences among Africans in America,"
    Social Forces 76, no. 2 (1997): 527–546.

11 Everett S. Lee, "A Theory of Migration," *Demography* 3, no. 1 (1966): 47–57.

12 Konadu-Agyemang and Takyi, "An Overview of African Immigration to U.S. and
    Canada."

13 Shuffield Seyram Asafo, Adelajda Matuka, and Nyendu Dominic, "External Debt
    and Economic Growth: Two-Step System GMM Evidence for Sub-Saharan Africa
    Countries," *International Journal of Business, Economics and Management* 6, no. 1
    (2019): 39–48.

14 Lobo, "U.S. Diversity Visas Are Attracting Africa's Best and Brightest"; Logan
    and Thomas, "The U.S. Diversity Visa Programme and the Transfer of Skills from
    Africa."

15 John A. Arthur, *Invisible Sojourners: African Immigrant Diaspora in the United
    States* (Santa Barbara, CA: Greenwood Publishing, 2000); Mary M. Kent, *Im-
    migration and America's Black Population* (Washington, DC: Population Reference
    Bureau, 2007); Omiunota N. Ukpokodu, "African Immigrants, the 'New Model

Minority': Examining the Reality in U.S. K-12 Schools," *The Urban Review* 50 (2018): 69–96.

16 Ukpokodu, "African Immigrants, the 'New Model Minority': Examining the Reality in U.S. K-12 Schools."

17 Tod G. Hamilton, "Selection, Language Heritage, and the Earnings Trajectories of Black Immigrants in the United States," *Demography* 51, no. 3 (2014): 975–1002.

18 Capps et al., "Diverse Streams"; Augustine J. Kposowa, "Human Capital and the Performance of African Immigrants in the U.S. Labor Market," *Western Journal of Black Studies* 26, no. 3 (2002): 175–183.

19 Martin Nordin, Inga Persson, and Dan-Olof Rooth, "Education-Occupation Mismatch: Is There an Income Penalty?" *Economics of Education Review* 29, no. 6 (2010): 1047–1059.

20 Harminder Battu, Clive R. Belfield, and Peter J. Sloane, "Overeducation among Graduates: A Cohort View," *Education Economics* 7, no. 1 (1999): 21–38; Val Burris, "The Social and Political Consequences of Overeducation," *American Sociological Review* 48, no. 4 (1983): 454–467; Chantal Pohl Nielsen, "Immigrant Overeducation: Evidence from Denmark," World Bank Policy Research Working Paper no. 4234 (2007); Rebbeca Tesfai, "Racialized Labour Market Incorporation? African Immigrants and the Role of Education-Occupation Mismatch in Earnings," *International Migration* 55, no. 4 (2017): 203–220; Kevin J. A. Thomas, "Occupational Stratification, Job-Mismatches, and Child Poverty: Understanding the Disadvantage of Black Immigrants in the US," *Social Science Research* 50 (2015): 203–216.

21 Jeanne Batalova, Michael Fix, and Peter A. Creticos, "Uneven Progress: The Employment Pathways of Skilled Immigrants in the United States," National Center on Immigrant Integration Policy, Migration Policy Institute (2008); Barry R. Chiswick and Paul W. Miller, "Educational Mismatch: Are High-Skilled Immigrants Really Working at High-Skilled Jobs, and What Price Do They Pay If They Are Not?" In *High-Skilled Immigration in a Globalized Labor Market*, ed. Barry R. Chiswick (Washington, DC: American Enterprise Institute, 2011), 109–154.

22 Chiswick and Miller, "Educational Mismatch"; Rachel M. Friedberg, "You Can't Take It with You? Immigrant Assimilation and the Portability of Human Capital," *Journal of Labor Economics* 18, no. 2 (2000): 221–251; Aaditya Mattoo, Ileana Cristina Neagu, and Çağlar Özden, "Brain Waste? Educated Immigrants in the US Labor Market," *Journal of Development Economics* 87, no. 2 (2008): 255–269.

23 Friedberg, "You Can't Take It with You?"

24 See Misba Bhatti's chapter in this volume.

25 Dodoo, "Assimilation Differences among Africans in America."

26 Linda Rabben, "Credential Recognition in the United States for Foreign Professionals," Migration Policy Institute (May 2013).

27 Rabben, "Credential Recognition in the United States for Foreign Professionals."

28 Rabben, "Credential Recognition in the United States for Foreign Professionals."

29 Kevin J. A. Thomas, "Racial and Ethnic Disparities in Education–Occupation Mismatch Status among Immigrants in South Africa and the United States,"

Journal of International Migration and Integration/Revue de l'integration et de la migration internationale 11 (2010): 383–401.

30 Batalova et al., "Uneven Progress."

31 Steven Ruggles et al., "IPUMS USA: Version 10.0 [dataset]. Minneapolis, MN: IPUMS; 2020," (2020).

32 Thomas, "Occupational Stratification, Job-Mismatches, and Child Poverty."

33 Greg J. Duncan and Saul D. Hoffman, "The Incidence and Wage Effects of Overeducation," *Economics of Education Review* 1, no. 1 (1981): 75–86; Stephen Rubb, "Overeducation in the Labor Market: A Comment and Re-Analysis of a Meta-Analysis," *Economics of Education Review* 22, no. 6 (2003): 621–629; Stephen Vaisey, "Education and Its Discontents: Overqualification in America, 1972–2002," *Social Forces* 85, no. 2 (2006): 835–864.

34 Rubb, "Overeducation in the Labor Market."

35 Information on field of study in the ACS applies to those reported by individuals with bachelor's degrees. However, research suggests that only 10–25 percent of STEM undergraduate students change their majors when they graduate. See Jerilee Grandy, "Graduate Enrollment Decisions of Undergraduate Science and Engineering Majors: A Survey of GRE Test Takers," *ETS Research Report* 92–51 (1992): i–45; María Pennock-Román, "Precollegiate Curricula, University Characteristics, and Field Persistence Among Science Majors," *ETS Research Report* 99–10 (1999). No information on graduate field of study is available. However, the analysis includes controls for whether individuals have PhD degrees to account for the independent effects of educational attainment that are observed over and beyond the influence of the study's measure of fields of study.

36 Mattoo et al., "Brain Waste?"

37 A RRR = 1 indicates no difference in the relative risks, < 1 indicates a decreased risk, and > 1 indicates an increased risk.

38 Neil G. Ruiz and Abby Budiman, "Number of Foreign College Students Staying and Working in U.S. after Graduation Surges," Pew Research Center (2018), www.pewresearch.org.

39 Chiswick and Miller, "Educational Mismatch."

40 Douglas A. Webber, "The Lifetime Earnings Premia of Different Majors: Correcting for Selection Based on Cognitive, Noncognitive, and Unobserved Factors," *Labour Economics* 28 (2014): 14–23.

41 Anderson, "African Immigrant Population in U.S. Steadily Climbs"; McCabe, "African Immigrants in the United States in 2009."

42 Lobo, "U.S. Diversity Visas Are Attracting Africa's Best and Brightest"; Ikubolajeh and Thomas, "The U.S. Diversity Visa Programme and the Transfer of Skills from Africa."

43 Capps et al., "Diverse Streams"; Kposowa, "Human Capital and the Performance of African Immigrants in the U.S. Labor Market."

44 Batalova et al., "Uneven Progress."

45 Thomas, "Occupational Stratification, Job-Mismatches, and Child Poverty."

46 Rabben, "Credential Recognition in the United States for Foreign Professionals."

47 Willow Lung-Amam, "Malls of Meaning: Building Asian America in Silicon Valley Suburbia," *Journal of American Ethnic History* 34, no. 2 (2015): 18–53.

48 Dodoo, "Assimilation Differences among Africans in America."

9

Highly Skilled Female Pakistani Immigrants

Devalued Credentials

MISBA BHATTI

The United States annually attracts the highest number of college-educated immigrants compared to other economically advanced countries. However, previous studies conducted on the subject indicate that many foreign-trained highly skilled immigrants in the United States face numerous labor market obstacles.[1] Immigrants who arrive in the United States with foreign degrees and professional experiences have to overcome systematic and structural barriers of not having their credentials recognized in the US labor market.[2] Further, the effects of migration on accessibility to the labor market in the host country are gendered. Highly skilled female migrants often face different challenges from their male counterparts in their socioeconomic incorporation in the host country.[3]

With almost half of all international migrants being women, there is a need to study the effects of migration and the process of integration in the host country for this cohort. In addition to being dependents of male migrants, or what is unfortunately termed "trailing spouses,"[4] women migrate independently, seeking better employment opportunities and career development.[5] In fact, according to the Organization for Economic Co-operation and Development (OECD) data, female migrants with tertiary education now account for an increased proportion of highly skilled migrants.[6] According to the Migration Policy Institute, female migration to the United States has been on the rise since the 2000s, as compared to the rest of the world. The majority of this migration flow is dominated by family reunification, where female migrants enter the United States as spouses of either highly skilled male migrants or US citizens.[7]

However, despite their high social and human capital, migrant women, and especially highly skilled migrant women in the United States, not only remain underrepresented in the field of migration studies, compared to skilled male migrants, they face systematic disadvantages when it comes to their social and economic integration.[8] Immigration visa categories and occupational entry policies play a vital and often deterring role toward economic integration of female skilled migrants and are important for understanding the gendered experiences of migration for skilled migrants.[9] Female migrants who immigrate to the United States in their capacity as spouses, regardless of their qualifications, find their pathways to employment compromised by the constraints of their visa status.[10]

Credential de-evaluation also has a gendered skew. Female migrants are often placed at a greater academic or occupational disadvantage than their male counterparts.[11] Moreover, skilled female migrants with foreign credentials from developing countries, while facing systematic discrimination like their male counterparts, are treated differently in the US labor market compared not only to their male counterparts but also to other skilled female migrants from developed countries.[12] However, the scholarly literature has largely been focused on the experiences of skilled migrant men, overlooking the unique experiences of skilled migrant women.

This chapter aims to fill the gap by focusing on a group of Pakistani women who attained their qualifications from foreign institutions, in mainly science, technology, engineering, and mathematics (STEM) fields. I argue that highly skilled migrant women, especially those from developing countries, face a dual disadvantage when it comes to their credential evaluation and their underrepresentation in the US labor force. This dual disadvantage is based on their gender, immigration statuses, and country of origin of their foreign degrees.[13] Using primary data, collected via semistructured interviews with twenty highly skilled Pakistani female migrants to the United States, I examine the experiences of highly skilled Pakistani women and provide details about the ways in which their foreign-earned degrees are devalued in the US labor market. The study aims to shed light on understanding the gender-specific barriers that highly skilled South Asian migrant women face.

Migrant Women from Pakistan to the United States:
An Overview

The United States is the fifth most common destination country for Pakistan-born international migrants.[14] At the time of writing, it is estimated that around 554,000 Pakistani immigrants and their children reside in the United States, with the majority of highly skilled Pakistani immigrants arriving in the United States after the 1960s.[15] Before this, the national origins quota system was introduced under the Emergency Quota Act of 1921 to restrict migration of "undesirables," which allowed a very limited number of immigrants from South Asia into the United States. The Luce-Celler Act of 1946 removed the ban on South Asians but allowed only one hundred immigrants per year.[16] As will be discussed later in the chapter, such policies discriminated against migrants based on their country of origin, and were drafted to regulate, control, and limit immigration from what was considered less desirable countries in East and South Asia.

The Immigration and Nationality Act amendments of 1965 (the Hart-Celler Act) ended the quota system and increased the number of immigrants from 150,000 to 290,000 per year. The introduction of this Act enabled many Pakistanis, particularly skilled professionals, such as doctors and engineers, to migrate to the United States in the coming years.[17] However, the flow of people migrating to the United States was seriously reduced post–9/11, and in the subsequent years during the "war on terror," which led US authorities to adopt a rigid stance on migrants from Pakistan. This change in policy is reflected in a decline in the number of Pakistanis admitted to the United States, from 16,448 in 2001 to 9,444 in 2003.[18] This trend was reversed in 2019, which indicated an increase in skilled migration flows from Pakistan.[19] The data from 2020 were not available at the time of writing.

The vast majority of Pakistanis who migrate are male, including those who live in the United States. According to the International Labor Organization (ILO), overall global female migration from Pakistan remains low at 0.21 percent.[20] According to the Bureau of Emigration and Overseas Employment (BE and OE), a Pakistani government body that oversees migration, between 1971 and July 2019, only 40,807 Pakistani registered female migrants traveled overseas for work.[21] This low figure is attributed to many factors, among which is that women in Pakistan face a series of economic and social challenges to access the labor market, including opportunities to migrate for work.[22] This is also perhaps related to the preconceived notions of the public and private labor sectors in Pakistan: that Pakistani women are neither substantial nor equal contributors to the country's overall economic and social growth.[23]

There is also cultural resistance in Pakistani society against women working. These cultural and gender norms, which attribute to women the role of "house maker," contribute to impeding women's economic productivity both at home and abroad. Other sociocultural factors that make migration for work difficult for women in Pakistan include reluctance to leave the familiar surroundings and way of life in Pakistan, marriage, and uncertainty about whether family members could accompany them. In addition, the negative emphasis from Pakistani media on migration, incidences of exploitation, and lack of proper agencies that specialize in finding work for women overseas, all hinder women from migrating for work.[24]

The majority of female migration from Pakistan to the United States is dominated by family reunification, and the number of women migrating on their own to work is still very low. According to the recent data released by the Statistical Yearbook, in 2019, the United States admitted around 5,400 immigrants from Pakistan under the family renunciation visa systems, the majority of which was made up of females.[25] The Yearbook did not provide data on levels of education and work experiences of these immigrants. Exact figures of Pakistani highly skilled migrant women to the United States are not known due to the unavailability of gender-disaggregated data by official agencies in Pakistan.

According to the American Community Survey, approximately 37,000 women of Pakistani origin aged twenty-five and older are employed in the civilian labor force in the United States.[26] The data issued by the US Census Bureau show that among the ethnic groups, Pakistani females have the lowest rates (41.8 percent) of workforce participation in the United States.[27] Pakistani female immigrants in the United States face numerous hurdles to getting their foreign credentials recognized and are underrepresented in the job market. For the majority of female skilled immigrants from Pakistan, a major hurdle to integration in the job market is the immigration policy, which prevents migrants on certain visa categories, such as HB4, from entering the labor market.[28] This, coupled with lengthy and complex credential evaluation systems in the United States, often lead to Pakistani female skilled migrants being discouraged, by their family and spouses, from entering the labor market.

Migration Policies and Gender Roles

While the migration of independent female skilled and highly skilled migrants is on the rise internationally, family reunification still dominates female migration flows to the United States, particularly from South Asian countries.[29] The majority of skilled female migrants from Pakistan currently residing in the United States entered the country as dependents of either skilled male immigrants on H-1B visas or as spouses of US citizens. Many of these women arrive in the United States on spouse visa programs, such as HB4, which creates several barriers for them, as their legal and financial statuses are contingent upon their partners' legal status in the United States.[30] These migrant women are denied legal work permits and are unable to join the workforce upon arrival in the United States.[31] For the majority of highly educated and professional female migrants from Pakistan, US immigration policy restrictions impose a formidable hurdle as their dependent status keeps them out of the labor force. These US immigration policy restrictions shape and largely impact Pakistani female workforce participation in the United States.

Importantly, US visa regimes and migration policies replicate Pakistani gender cultural norms and roles for females residing in the United States.[32] By denying these educated and skilled female migrants the legal status to work, US visa regimes perpetuate gender hierarchies that designate men as wage earners and women as homemakers.[33] Furthermore, foreign credential recognition in the United States is a lengthy and expensive process, which often becomes a barrier, compelling Pakistani women to compromise and give up on work.[34] These Pakistani female immigrants, already burdened with gender and discriminatory immigration policies, find credential devaluation further hindering their ability to join the workforce in a manner that corresponds with their education and skills.

Credential Recognition in the United States

Immigration has always played an important role in the development of the US economy. However, the increasing demand for highly skilled migrants has not changed the receptivity of the immigrants in the host country, especially those from developing economies.[35] Highly skilled migrants are labeled "knowledge workers," and are often defined based on their educational attainment, qualifications, earning levels, and occupations.[36] When foreign-educated and foreign-trained professionals come to the United States, despite having attained quality higher education, they have to overcome numerous hurdles, such as complex credentialing systems, in order to become integrated into the US labor market. This issue has deep roots in the systematic structure of the United States and in both past and present policies.

Foreign credentials are defined as any formal education, certification, and qualification, including diplomas and certificates, received outside of the United States. Although regulations in the United States are not as exclusionary as other OECD countries, an estimated 20–30 percent of jobs in the United States require licensure and certification.[37] Due to the lack of a centralized federal system in the United States, there is no single governing body that regulates and standardizes the process of professional certification recognition. There exists a profusion of overlapping and contradictory local, state, and national rules, policies, procedures, and examinations that make the process of recertification complicated, confusing, time-consuming, and expensive for immigrants in the United States. The vast network of organizations that exist, from professional associations at state or federal levels to credential assessment services, is difficult to navigate and requires considerable effort on the part of the immigrant.[38]

Many professions, and especially those related to the fields of medicine, engineering, and information technology, are licensed by the state, and each state has its own complex system of rules, regulations, procedures, and costs. A professional license issued and recognized in one state, for example, is not always acknowledged or approved in another. Further, each profession also has its own classification of recognizing credentials, and in addition to stating the required academic qualifications, some jobs require internship training and additional diploma courses. Many immigrants have limited resources available to them in order to navigate these complex procedures, which often results in years of struggle in navigating this cumbersome system.[39]

Many highly skilled immigrants in the United States, and especially those from developing countries, face difficulty in getting their credentials recognized and are less able to pursue the same professions they occupied in their home countries.[40] They are often relegated to unemployment or underemployment due to the reluctance of professional organizations to accredit foreign degrees. This reluctance of the accreditation institutions in the United States arises because either they are not familiar with the foreign awarding institute or the credentials are difficult to assess.[41] Many Pakistani and other South Asian institutions are neither well known nor recognized by agencies in the United States, and this leads to graduates from these institutions not getting their degrees recognized in the United States. In a survey conducted between 2009 and 2013 examining "skill wastage" in the United States, it was estimated that 32 percent of foreign-educated highly skilled women were underemployed or unemployed as compared to 27 percent of foreign-educated highly skilled men.[42] Furthermore, systematic discriminating practices affect immigrants differently. In terms of credential recognition, studies have shown that women from advanced or developed countries, such as Britain, Canada, and Australia, are treated differently than those from the third world or developing countries, such as India, Pakistan, and Bangladesh.[43]

Though both male and female migrants must deal with many of the credential recognition hurdles, family dynamics further complicate matters for migrant women from developing countries. Norms borne out of a mix of religious and patriarchal cultural heritage dictate most of the women's lives, including the decision to work and pursue a career.[44] Within these communities, marriage and family are considered integral to a woman's identity and often take precedence over a woman's career. This is a hurdle that male migrants, both skilled and unskilled, rarely have to overcome. The interviewees included in this study are women from developing countries, many of whom reiterated the dual disadvantage—based on their gender, immigration statuses, and country of origin—of their foreign degrees that marginalizes them, whereas their counterparts from developed countries do not face the same obstacles.

Theoretical Framework

For women who come from conservative cultures, migration can be a means of liberation from restrictive family control and rigid gender roles.[45] However, this opportunity can also be a major challenge. With a rise in the number of high-skilled women migrating for employment, the term "feminization of migration" has rapidly become a core dimension of the international migration discussion.[46] High-skilled migrant women are more likely to end up with jobs for which they are over-qualified, resulting in their "de-skilling," or they may engage in "career laddering" by starting with lower-level jobs.[47] Both of these occur because of credential devaluation in the host country. The literature on the credential devaluation of immigrants' foreign degrees suggests that the magnitude of devaluation depends on many factors, including gender, race, country of origin, and age at migration, among other features.[48] Gender roles and immigration policies combined with credential devaluation of foreign-earned degrees impact and shape female immigrants' workforce participation, as these factors add an additional layer of complexity and hurdles to entering the labor force.

This chapter maintains that the United States does not fully recognize immigrants' foreign credentials because of an epistemological misconception of differences in knowledge. Epistemology is a field of study that deals with the nature and origin of knowledge. However, an individual's epistemic style determines how they define and constitute true and valuable knowledge.[49] Due to their epistemological understanding, the host societies of advanced economies allege any foreign knowledge attained, particularly from countries with developing economies, as deficient, lacking, inferior, and incompatible to the labor market in the host country.[50]

According to critical theorists, advanced economies such as the United States and Canada use knowledge as power. Though this holds true globally, the host societies of the developed economies in particular constitute and use knowledge as "socially constructed, culturally mediated, and historically situated," however, "knowledge is never neutral nor objective."[51] Previous work on this area has given rise to the debate that the way the understanding of knowledge has been constructed in these societies is a reflection of social relations, according to which knowledge gained from developed economies is deemed to be valuable and legitimate, compared to knowledge acquired from developing countries.[52] Thus, credentials from developing economies are greatly devalued in the United States. Immigrants from these countries encounter difficulties proving their foreign credentials and work experience, while those from developed countries, such as the United Kingdom (UK), Australia, Canada, or New Zealand, often face minimum hurdles and have relatively successful experiences.[53] Knowledge brought to the United States by immigrants from the "least desirable" countries is deemed by the host country as less valuable, incompatible with the social and cultural fabric, and unable to meet the demands of the labor market. This universal epistemological misconception, used to differentiate and categorize knowledge, gives rise to processes and practices that attribute differential values to credentials and certificates produced and issued in foreign countries, though this is a global trend and not just specific to the United States.

This demeaning attitude toward foreign credentials also occurs due to US employers' reluctance to recognize degrees from institutions unknown to them or from countries perceived to have a weaker regulatory environment. This suspicion of foreign degrees arises partially as a result of educational fraud and corruption that takes place, which devalues foreign higher education and undermines the academic integrity of certain institutions.[54] Fraudulent accreditation can include diploma mills and counterfeit academic documents, as well as bribery to ensure the licensing of academic institutions, the passing of examinations, admission into education programs, and the awarding of degrees. While academic corruption is a worldwide phenomenon, and might occur in the United States as well, the United States employs stricter measures as employers often are more likely to question the merits of the educational systems and awarding of credentials in universities from developing countries. Thus, immigrants from these countries—and, particularly, skilled migrant women—have to undergo retraining and re-education in order to improve their employment prospects.[55]

The classification of "desirable versus undesirable" immigrants is a form of "gatekeeping" constructed to manage the labor market as well as the flow of immigrants into the United States and is a by-product of patriarchal and supremacist philosophy. This hierarchy has been regulated by various US administrations and is rooted in the immigration policies of the country, in which the "undesirable" immigrant is often from the third world versus the "desirable" immigrants from Canada, Europe, and Australia.[56]

Methodology

While the previous discussion about the existing structures of foreign credential recognition in the United States and female migration from Pakistan was based on a review of academic literature, there are very few secondary sources available on the experiences of highly skilled South Asia migrant women in the United States. In order to fill this gap in the literature, twenty highly skilled migrant women to the United States from Pakistan were interviewed for this study, using in-depth, semistructured questionnaires administered by the author during April–May 2020, in order to collect primary data and information. The format of the interview was open-ended questions, followed by a second set of questions and discussions between the author and the respondents to gain an understanding of their experiences in the United States.

The participants were identified through the author's social and professional networks. The author had planned to conduct in-person interviews, but due to the travel restrictions imposed as a result of the ongoing COVID-19 pandemic, eighteen interviews were conducted through various telecommunications applications, such as Zoom, Skype, and Google Meet.[57] Due to time differences and interviewee work schedules, face-to-face online interviews could not be arranged with two respondents, who provided written responses to the questions. Verbal consent to collect and use the information was given prior to the interview, and pseudonyms have been used to anonymize the information and quotes used in the chapter.

The women interviewed for this chapter are highly skilled Pakistani immigrants, with considerable professional experience in their country of origin. The main purpose of the interviews was to gather information on the interviewees' knowledge, views, and personal experience on foreign degree devaluation in the United States and the various ways they overcame the hurdles faced. The women had migrated to the United States under various visa categories: Five interviewees had come to the Unites States as spouses of US citizens; three entered the United States under family reunification schemes; four came as international students; and eight had entered the United States under independent visa categories, such as H-1B. All had attained their tertiary degrees from institutions in Pakistan. Out of the twenty interviewees, five had medical degrees, four held engineering degrees, two were IT professionals, three had degrees in economics, and the remaining six had various degrees in the field of science and technology.

Findings

The following sections detail the findings of this interview-based study, organized under two methods, i.e., de-skilling and career laddering, through which the respondents argued their foreign-earned credentials were devalued in the United States.

The women interviewed for this study expressed that the most significant barrier to employment they faced after migrating to the United States was the devaluation of their foreign credentials. These female skilled migrants, who are already burdened with gender and discriminatory immigration policy, find credential devaluation adding to their inability to join the workforce in the host country. Despite having relevant educational backgrounds and years of professional experience in Pakistan, they did not have a positive experience in getting their credentials recognized after migrating to the United States. Instead, having a foreign degree became a liability. They were faced with systematic barriers when attempting to enter into the US workforce. The inaccessibility to professional occupation for which the interviewees had prior training and work experience led them to either pursue careers in a different professional field or retrain and attain entry-level experience in the United States. Faced with expensive licensing tests, or having to repeat an entire course of study, these high-skilled migrant women with advanced skills took lower-paying "survival jobs" and had to face de-skilling and career laddering. The following sections expand on the ways through which highly skilled migrant women, particularly from South Asia, face devaluation of their foreign credentials in the United States.

Career Laddering

"Career laddering" is defined as the progression of an individual from entry-level jobs to higher levels of pay, position, and authority.[58] However, with regard to credential devaluation, foreign-trained highly skilled migrants are often advised to progress toward professional certification by retraining and starting from entry-level jobs when they move to the United States.[59] Regardless of years of professional training and experience in a certain field, South Asian migrant women are often encouraged by US employers to attain attestation and recognition of their credentials through working in lower-level jobs. Highly skilled migrant women from developing countries often encounter a labyrinth of obstacles when applying for jobs in the United States, frustrating not only their ambitions but also their earning potential as they settle for lower-skill positions. Many express that the accomplishments, training, education, and expertise they bring to the United States often go to waste. Lengthy recertification processes and employers' unfamiliarity with foreign credentials limit immigrants' efforts to find the same level of work in their professional fields.[60]

One of these industries is the healthcare sector, where formal and informal barriers are the highest. As a result of various shifts and modifications that started around the 1980s, the medical sector in the United States underwent a transformation that resulted in a surplus of International Medical Graduates (IMGs) migrating to the United States.[61] As a result, many foreign graduates and trained medical professionals migrated to the United States and currently, out of the 16 million workers employed in the healthcare sector, more than 25 percent of the physicians practicing in the United States attended medical school abroad.[62] Official figures indicate that there are around 13,000 Pakistani doctors, or 6 percent of all foreign-born physicians and surgeons, practicing in the United States.[63] The majority of these are male doctors; the proportion of female doctors is very low.[64] Many of the female doctors of Pakistani origin working in the United States are wives of male physicians and moved to the United States after their husbands were admitted to residency programs.[65] Four out of the five female doctors interviewed for this study expressed that many medical programs prefer US clinical experience and applicants who have graduated within the past five years. Thus, despite years of experience working as a licensed medical doctor in Pakistan, these women were disqualified when they applied for jobs in the United States at the same professional levels they occupied back home. They had to start from the very bottom of the professional ladder and retake entry-level training in order to work their way up in their occupations.

Prior to her move to the United States, Saba, a physician from Pakistan, worked in one of the largest and most prestigious hospitals in the country. She had two years of experience and was a licensed medical practitioner back home. Saba's husband, who has a Master's degree in economics from the UK, was able to find a job in the United States. Saba moved to the United States in 2018 on a spouse visa. Since then, she has received her green card but is still trying to get a job and practice medicine. Saba notes:

[I face] more problems in the United States as I am not a licensed physician here like I was in my country. I need to complete the United States Medical Licensing Examination, USMLE, to be a licensed physician in the United States and they required additional time to prepare for. The state I live in does not have a lot of opportunities in the medical and related fields. I am as qualified as any US medical graduate and went through rigorous medical training back in Pakistan. But apparently, it all counts for nothing here and I have to retake postgraduate medical training in order to practice in the States.[66]

When asked how her experience with the entrance examination differed from those educated in US institutions, Saba replied:

Medical College graduates from the United States already take their USMLEs during their medical school years. It is easier for them as they are taught in their medical school years in the same format. For international medical graduates it is different because although the course is the same, the way it is applied and tested is entirely different and requires a lot of hard work over a period of months to a few years to complete. Another factor is that not all hospitals/institutions offer jobs to international medical graduates, citizens are preferred.[67]

Another highly skilled female migrant from Pakistan, Maha, narrated similar issues about the hurdles she faced to get her credentials recognized and to find work. She attained a Doctor of Pharmacy degree from Pakistan and worked for about a year and a half before she moved to the United States to join her husband, who is a US citizen. Maha received her green card ninety days after arrival to the United States, and although she had legal rights to work in the country, she faced various obstacles to getting licensed. She explained:

> I am working as a pharmacy technician instead of as a pharmacist, which I had studied for and worked as in Pakistan. Initially, being on a spouse visa meant I wasn't allowed to work. To work as a pharmacist, I had to become licensed and to become licensed, I was required to pass multiple exams: first a foreign equivalency exam, the TOEFEL and TSE, a year of internship and then finally a two-part licensing exam. I passed the initial tests while waiting and as soon as I received a Green Card /Permanent Residency, and was allowed to work, I started looking for the internship which was a requirement to apply for the licensing exam and I got an internship after a few months of trying. After the internship, I sat for the final licensing exam. The whole process felt like retaking the same exams and training that I had already cleared back home.[68]

She added:

> Graduates from the United States are placed into internships while they're still enrolled in pharmacy school and their school helps with the placement. They can apply for the licensing exam right after graduating and most of the time the college helps them prepare for the exam too. I haven't run into graduates from countries such as Canada, Australia, etc., but graduates from other countries like China, India and others, have to prepare for the multiple exams on their own and work independently to obtain an internship. So yes, in my field it is harder to get a license and job for a foreign graduate. None of the foreign pharmacy graduates I know were able to immigrate on an H-1B visa.[69]

Another medical graduate from Pakistan, Ayesha, was able to migrate to the United States on an H-1B visa, an independent visa category, after she was accepted into a residency program. She conveyed her frustration with the system: After having completed her house-job training,[70] gaining a year's experience working as a General Practitioner (GP) in Pakistan, and after having passed the USMLE examination, she still had to work under the supervision of a senior medical physician in the United States. She expressed that the residency program feels like repeating the intern-level medical training she had undergone in Pakistan:

> I am treated as a fresh graduate, even though I have the experience, but it counts for nothing at the hospital I work at. It is like repeating my house-job training.[71]

When questioned about their decision to move to the United States, all five participants with medical degrees highlighted that the United States represents a tremendous professional opportunity. With a rigorous system of graduate medical education, a merit-based structure of professional rewards, a culture of academic nurturing, and the worldwide recognition of residency training attained in the United States, migrating presented better opportunities than practicing in Pakistan. Material rewards were also emphasized as a major factor: In Pakistan, an intern earns approximately $150 per month (the same salary as an unskilled, illiterate worker in the United States).[72] Whereas, according to the Association of American Medical Colleges in the United States, an average intern can earn $4,000–$5,000 per month in the first year of residency.[73] The interviewees also reiterated that one can expect a better quality of life after residency in the United States.

Similarly, another interviewee, Maheen, who has an engineering degree in telecommunications from Pakistan, came to the United States on a spouse visa. As a spouse of a US citizen, she received her green card within a few months and has been living in the United States for the past four years. She stated that in her experience, despite having a tertiary degree, all the jobs that she had applied for required her to complete further education and diploma courses in the United States. She noted that graduates from Europe, Canada, and Australia with degrees in telecommunications and other engineering fields are treated differently.

People with foreign degrees from developed countries get priority over people from third-world countries because of the method of teaching. And training in almost all developed countries is the same. Their students get more hands-on experience during studies as compare to the students from underdeveloped countries.[74]

Maheen added that over the course of four years in the United States, she understands that there is an established assumption that the standards of teaching in developing countries, such as Pakistan, are not on par with US standards. It is one of the main reasons why employers in the United States have a preference for workers with experience and degrees attained from developed countries.

Other interviewees also expressed that the systematic challenges in the evaluation of their professional degrees led them to start all over again in their field of specialization. When asked how they felt about starting from the bottom of the professional ladder, they articulated that the whole process was very disheartening and undermined their confidence in their intellectual capacities. This phenomenon often results in many women giving up on their pursuit of a professional career in the United States, leading them to either take jobs unrelated to their professional education and training or give up on professional lives altogether. Many also expressed that they are advised by their family members to stay at home and concentrate on child-rearing and taking care of the house instead of going through the whole retraining process. The interviewees also conveyed that the case is different for highly skilled migrant men from Pakistan with the same qualifications. Men from South Asian countries, either single or married, are never encouraged to stay at home.

Perceptions of women's roles in a marriage and family and social norms that exist in a society like Pakistan can have a strong influence on a woman's decision to work. Though a change in mindset of Pakistani society at large can be observed in some sectors of Pakistan, many still firmly assert that a woman should stay at home. This ingrained belief in Pakistani society is a key variable that influences women's employment. Further, some of the visa categories, such as F-2, F-1, and H-4 dependent visas, do not allow a visa holder to legally work in the United States, and so can emphasize traditional patriarchal norms around marriage and gender roles within the family.[75] Donato and Amuedo-Dorantes's chapter in this volume addresses the developments of some of the visa categories and how they impact the wages of different immigrants granted entry into the United States on these visa categories. By reinforcing the roles of males as the breadwinner and financial provider of the family and curtailing employment opportunities for the women for a majority of the Pakistani families, these visas indirectly shape similar family structures and social norms of patriarchal societies and impact women's success in the US labor market.[76] The majority of these dependent visa recipients are women, around 80 percent of all H-4 visa holders, with relatively few men migrating to the United States as "trailing husbands."[77] In cases where a Pakistani man is excluded from the workforce, gender power struggles within the families assume difficult and complex forms. Ghazal, an interviewee with a Master's in the field of microbiology, reported:

> I didn't work for many years because of being unable to get licensed to work here in the field that I preferred and also because of being unable to handle my household and work outside the house at the same time. My family [parents and in-laws] asked me to stay at home while my husband worked to support the family.[78]

All the interviewees who were employed in their field of education were employed at levels lower than their occupational designations prior to immigration to the United States. Even for these lower-level jobs, they had to undergo retraining and sit for examinations before they could get licensed or obtain work permits. They noted that this was because their education and professional training attained in Pakistan were rated at lower standards than those gained in the United States.

De-Skilling

Underutilization of skills is a common issue faced by many high-skilled migrants to the United States, especially migrant women. The creation of jobs and skilling and de-skilling of the labor force depends on the labor market dynamics in any given context.[79] Though a well-functioning labor market operates with a balance between labor market needs and available skills, migrant women, and especially highly skilled professionals, encounter more hurdles and difficulties in continuing with their former careers as their education and credentials are valued differently than those of men. After migrating to the United States, many women professionals work part-time or in jobs for which they are overqualified. The change in the employment situation is often related to either the demands of the employers who request work experience in the United States or the unwillingness of professional organizations to accredit developing country credentials. This is also often related to gender-biased filtering and marginalization of women from professional jobs that limit their employment options.[80]

Many sectors that draw high-skilled migration to the United States and other developed economies are still very gender-specific, i.e., these sectors hire and draw upon specific sets of skilled male migrants.[81] Thus, the foreign degrees and training obtained by migrant women, particularly those who fall under the category of highly skilled, are subjected to dismissal or scrutiny.[82] One such sector is Information Technology (IT), where male migrants with critical skills, especially from the Indian Subcontinent, are readily recruited.

One of the women interviewed, Neha, is a Pakistani female IT professional with a computer engineering degree and three years of work experience at an IT firm in Pakistan. She has been facing numerous obstacles in attaining employment in the United States. Neha's parents moved to the United States after her father was transferred to his company's US branch. At the time, she was pursuing an engineering degree in Pakistan and decided to stay back to complete her education. After graduation, she immediately got a job offer from a reputable IT firm in Pakistan and delayed moving to the United States to join her family. Over the course of the three years that Neha worked in Pakistan, two of her male colleagues from the IT firm had found employment and moved to the United States and encouraged her to do so. After three years of work experience, Neha was confident that, like her male counterparts, she would also be successful in gaining employment in the IT sector in the United States. However, being a female with foreign credentials proved to be a liability and she was unable to get a job offer. Neha finally moved to the United States under family-based immigration and continued to look for a job.[83] She explains:

> I came to the United States and was still unable to get a job in the IT sector. It is quite sad how despite all my education and years of experience I still can't find a full-time job [in the IT sector]. In order to fill my time, I started to work odd jobs, like babysitting and tutoring. In short, it was difficult to obtain an offer due to my credentials and also maybe because the IT sector is very male-dominated.[84]

Neha continues to work part-time jobs and joined Pakistani Women in Computing (PWiC), a global organization established by Pakistani women working in the tech industry, aimed at supporting, mentoring, and providing learning and growth opportunities for women and to help them navigate the labor market in the IT sector. Neha is hopeful that she will get a job in the tech industry eventually, and that she will be able to make use of her education and professional training.

Heba, another Pakistani interviewee and IT professional, also failed to find employment in the tech industry in the United States. She decided to travel to the United States to pursue a second Master's degree in accounting and finance, in order to expand her career options. Heba conveyed that many foreign females who are educated and trained in traditionally male-dominated fields, such as IT, come to the United States and complete a second degree in a field with greater demand for a female labor force, such as finance or education. She is currently in her final year and plans to use her university's placement program to get an internship, noting:

> When I applied for jobs in the United States [in the IT sector] I was unsuccessful. Since my goal was to migrate to the United States, I decided to come here on a student visa. I applied to a Master's program and got accepted. After I graduate, my university will help me apply for Optional Practical Training and get temporary employment.[85]

The experiences of women who are not considered to be highly skilled but have a high level of education, including PhDs, are also quite similar. Alize, another Pakistani female interviewee, came to the United

States to join her husband, a US citizen, almost forty years ago. She held a doctoral degree in chemistry after having worked as a lecturer at a university in Pakistan. In the initial years after her move, Alize had to work odd jobs, such as a cashier, as her attempts to find a job as a professor were unsuccessful. She narrates,

> I was made aware of colleges offering positions. I personally went to the colleges to understand more about them. I filled in the application form and provided my portfolio, but was never short-listed. I was once called for an interview for an adjunct professor position. They assessed my knowledge in the subject and my teaching skills but then never offered me the job.[86]

Alize finally received a full-time job offer from a university, but for an administrator position. Though she felt overqualified for the position, she accepted the offer in order to get back in professional circles. Thirty years later, she retired from a senior-level position and a successful career in administration but feels disheartened that she could never go back to teaching, which was her passion.

Other interviewees also recounted similar cases of having to give up previous professions to work in positions that do not make full use of their skills, education, and training. Many reasons to take up these jobs were enumerated, among which access to the job market and professional circles was predominant, followed by the need for socialization and making financial contributions to the family. The de-skilling of migrant women is also associated with a lack of finances required for the costly re-skilling programs and examinations.[87] One of the interviewees, Rida, who recently moved to the United States on a family reunification visa and is a Physical Medicine and Rehabilitation (PM and R) physician, said that she took a job as a part-time receptionist at a women's center in order to earn and save money for her Foreign Medical Graduate Exam:

> This [the receptionist position] helps me financially so that I don't have to depend on anyone to pay the fee for my exams and other expenses. I don't mind working below my professional training as the income will help me pay the expenses and finally get licensed to practice. I also enjoy working at the center, so it is not so bad.[88]

Other interviewees emphasized that upon migration they had expected to find skilled jobs and employment in their field of specialization. However, due to their foreign credentials or because of their
gender, they are pushed into periods of unemployment or jobs that do
not match their skills—both of which often lead to a complete change of
profession for many South Asian migrant women in the United States.

Credentialing Future in the United States: The Need for a New and Revised System

Prior to the outbreak of the COVID-19 pandemic in 2020 and the
resulting loss of economic activity and border closures, 450,000 new
immigrant workers were being admitted annually into the US labor market.[89] These included professionals required to fill jobs in some of the
essential industries, such as health, medicine, innovation, and research.
The worsening overall health conditions in the United States due to
coronavirus and the loss of lives have brought to the front the need and
importance of trained professionals in these fields. Due to insufficient
US-educated and trained professionals, the labor market will need to
rely on foreign-trained professionals to fill the gap.[90]

Unfortunately, the need for immigrant professionals to fill the jobs
does not translate into an easy transition in the United States. Social and
political policies prevent smooth assimilation of South Asian migrants
into the workforce, with credential devaluation cited as one of the main
reasons for underemployment and unemployment. The case for highly
skilled migrant women from South Asia is severe as they face a dual disadvantage when it comes to recognition of their foreign-earned degrees.
Hence, there is a crucial need for a system that would make the process
simple, centralized, non-denigrating toward knowledge gained from developing countries, as well as less gender-skewed.

During the Obama administration, the White House Taskforce on
New Americans explored a system to streamline professional certification and licensure at the federal level.[91] However, no such system was
drafted or implemented. Under the Trump administration, there were
no plans to design or introduce a federal credentialing system. Conversely, there had been reports about introducing an immigration system that would be merit-based and where an applicant's eligibility to get

a US green card would be based on certain factors, such as high-valued skills, age, education, job prospects, English language proficiency, and so on.[92] The proposed Reforming American Immigration for Strong Employment Act (the RAISE Act) aimed to create "a fair, modern, and lawful system of immigration."[93] The mechanics of the system adopted the points-based schemes used by other high-income countries, such as Canada, Australia, and New Zealand, for selecting economic migrants, and incorporates some elements of prior US legislative proposals. However, if the proposal had been passed it would unlikely have changed the profile of those entering the job market, as graduates with western or US education would have been able to score more points. There is a growing need to provide agencies, national experts, and local leaders at the federal level to develop and provide tools and resources to address credentialing and licensing issues that skilled immigrant professionals confront when seeking to enter the workforce and ease degree devaluation practices, particularly those associated with gender.

Conclusion

This chapter seeks to identify the gap in the literature that exists on credential devaluation and underrepresentation in the US job market for skilled migrant women, with a focus on those from Pakistan. Very few studies have explored the challenges highly skilled South Asian women face when attempting to have their foreign earned degrees accredited in the United States. This study has tried to incorporate and shed light on experiences of skilled women who migrated to the United States for various reasons—i.e., employment, education, family reunification, and as dependents—and were residing in the United States either under a visa category or as a citizen or resident.[94]

Using examples and experiences of skilled and highly skilled migrant women from Pakistan, the study argued that while migrant professionals from developing countries in general face devaluation and denigration of their prior education and work experience, there is an additional gender skew, with women often being placed at a greater academic or occupational disadvantage than their male counterparts. This is more visible in sectors, such as IT, that hire certain sets of skilled migrants and that are usually biased in favor of male skilled migrants.

Family dynamics and gender norms add another layer of complexity for female skilled migrants from developing countries. When family members of these women require them to give priority to family and children, their careers and integration into the job market often get neglected. Furthermore, the foreign credentials of migrants from South Asia are treated differently—as not having the same standards as those attained from developed economies. As a combined result of these factors, these women are more vulnerable to de-skilling and career laddering practices and often end up taking lower-level or unskilled jobs. These practices arise from a misconception in the epistemological understanding of knowledge in host societies, which assumes that knowledge brought by immigrants from developing countries and economies is incompatible with the US social and cultural fabric and unable to meet the demands of jobs in developed economies. Thus, immigrants from developing economies are often deemed unsuitable based on the ethnic and national origins of the knowledge they bring.

In the process of prior education assessment and recognition of immigrants' professional training in the United States, there is a lack of a centralized body that can facilitate the processes and procedures. The current system consists of overlapping and contradicting local, state, and national policies and rules that make the whole process of degree and certificate recognition confusing, complicated, and time-consuming. The United States has the added barrier of varying state policies regarding professional degree and license recognition, which may differ from one state to another. In addition, different professions have their own classifications and procedures, with some being relatively easier to navigate than others. Moreover, many sectors require US work experience or internship training as a prerequisite to getting hired. This complex network of degree recognition processes in the United States is identified by the participants of this study as a predominant hurdle in their path to getting jobs in their preferred field of professional training.

While this study focuses on the experience of highly skilled migrant women from Pakistan, it provides important insight into understanding underrepresentation among foreign-trained migrant women, as well as migrant men, in professional jobs in the United States. Although the cultural norms of the home country may have a persistent effect on the labor market disadvantage of migrant women in the receiving country, this study shows that home-country cultural norms and patterns interact with host-country structural conditions and immigration policies to exacerbate gender disadvantages. In order to facilitate and assimilate these highly skilled migrant women, there is a need for government organizations, professional associations, educational institutions, and prior learning assessment agencies to dismantle barriers based on gender and ethnic and national backgrounds and adopt an inclusive framework that fully embraces all human knowledge and experiences. It is also imperative for government agencies to work with employers to map out a system to acknowledge previous work and training experiences so that immigrants do not have to start at the bottom of the professional ladder and can advance their careers rather than restart them.

NOTES

1 See in this volume chapter 5 by Lowell and chapter 8 by Thomas.

2 Linda Rabben, "Credential Recognition in the United States for Foreign Professionals," Migration Policy Institute (May 2013), www.migrationpolicy.org.

3 Grit Grigoleit-Richter, "Highly Skilled and Highly Mobile? Examining Gendered and Ethnicised Labour Market Conditions for Migrant Women in STEM-Professions in Germany," *Journal of Ethnic and Migration Studies* 43, no. 16 (2017): 2738–2755.

4 Jacqueline Andall, "Gendered Mobilities and Work in Europe: An Introduction," *Journal of Ethnic and Migration Studies* 39, no. 4 (2013): 525–534.

5 Kyoko Shinozaki, "Career Strategies and Spatial Mobility among Skilled Migrants in Germany: The Role of Gender in the Work-Family Interaction," *Tijdschrift voor economische en sociale geografie* 105, no. 5 (2014): 526–541.

6 International Organization for Migration, *Harnessing Knowledge on the Migration of Highly Skilled Women* (Geneva, Switzerland: IOM, 2014), 2.

7 Jeanne Batalova, "Immigrant Women and Girls in the United States," *Migration Policy*, March 4, 2020, www.migrationpolicy.org.

8 Anna Boucher, "Female High-Skill Migration," in *High-Skilled Migration: Drivers and Policies*, ed. Mathias Czaika (Oxford: Oxford University Press, 2018), 65–86.

9 Deborah J. Moon, "Dependents and Deviants: The Social Construction of Asian Migrant Women in the United States," *Affilia* 36, no. 3 (September 2020): 391–405.

10 Sabrina Balgamwalla, "Bride and Prejudice: How US Immigration Law Discriminates against Spousal Visa Holders," *Berkeley Journal of Gender, Law & Justice* 29, no. 1 (2014): 25.

11 Bandana Purkayastha, "Skilled Migration and Cumulative Disadvantage: The Case of Highly Qualified Asian Indian Immigrant Women in the US," *Geoforum* 36, no. 2 (2005): 181–196.

12 Shibao Guo, "Difference, Deficiency, and Devaluation: Tracing the Roots of Non-Recognition of Foreign Credentials for Immigrant Professionals in Canada," *Canadian Journal for the Study of Adult Education* 22, no. 1 (2009): 37–52; see also Thomas's chapter in this volume.

13 International Organization for Migration, and OECD Development Centre, *Harnessing Knowledge on the Migration of Highly Skilled Women*. International Organization for Migration, 2014.

14 Migration Policy Institute, "The Pakistani Diaspora in the United States," 2015, www.migrationpolicy.org.

15 Abby Budiman, "Pakistanis in the U.S. Fact Sheet," Pew Research Center's Social and Demographic Trends Project, April 29, 2021, www.pewsocialtrends.org.

16 Yunas Samad, "The Pakistani Diaspora: USA and UK," in *Routledge Handbook of the South Asian Diaspora*, ed. by Joya Chatterji and David Washbrook (London: Routledge, 2013), 295–305.

17 Samad, "The Pakistani Diaspora," 299.

18 Oda Hisaya, "Pakistani Migration to the United States: An Economic Perspective," Institute of Developing Economies, Japan External Trade Organization (JETRO), Discussion Paper no. 196 (March 2019), www.ide.go.jp.

19 Themrise Khan, "Female Labour Migration from Pakistan: A Situation Analysis," International Labour Organization (2020), www.ilo.org.

20 Khan "Female Labour Migration from Pakistan," 1.

21 Between 2008 and 2013, a high percentage (22.3 percent) of female economic immigrants from Pakistan fell under the category of domestic workers/housemaids, with the majority of them heading to the Gulf Cooperation Council (GCC) countries; Government of Pakistan, Bureau of Emigration & Overseas Employment, "Reports & Statistics," 2019, beoe.gov.pk/reports-and-statistics.

22 Khan, "Female Labour Migration from Pakistan," 18.

23 Khan, "Female Labour Migration from Pakistan," 13.

24 Khan, "Female Labour Migration from Pakistan," 19.

25 The Statistical Yearbook, "Table 32. Nonimmigrant Temporary Worker Admissions (I-94 Only) by Region and Country of Citizenship: Fiscal Year 2019," March 12, 2021, www.dhs.gov.

26 Jeanne Batalova and Uriah Ferruccio, "Spotlight on the Foreign Born of Pakistani Origin in the United States in 2006," *Migration Policy*, March 4, 2020, www.migrationpolicy.org.

27 The Status of Women in the States, "Table B2.3. Data and Ranking on Women's Employment and Earnings by Detailed Racial and Ethnic Groups, United States, 2011–2013," March 30, 2021, https://statusofwomendata.org.

28 Divya Ravindranath, "Visa Regulations and Labour Market Restrictions: Implications for Indian Immigrant Women in the United States," *Indian Journal of Labour Economics* 60, no. 2 (2017): 217–232.

29 Batalova, "Immigrant Women and Girls in the United States."

30 Balgamwalla, "Bride and Prejudice," 28–29.

31 Maneesha Kelkar, "South Asian Immigration in the United States: A Gendered Perspective," *Asian American Policy Review* 22, no. 1 (2012): 55–61.

32 Ravindranath, "Visa Regulations and Labour Market Restrictions," 223.

33 Monica Boyd, "Migration Regulations and Sex Selective Outcomes in Developed Countries," in *International Migration Policies and the Status of Female Migrants: Proceedings of the United Nations Expert Group Meeting on International Migra-tion Policies and the Status of Female Migrants, San Miniato, Italy, 28–31 March 1990* (New York: United Nations Population Division, 1995), 83–98.

34 Ravindranath, "Visa Regulations and Labour Market Restrictions," 223.

35 Shahid Javed Burki and Swamy Subramanian, "South Asian Migration to United States: Demand and Supply Factors," *Economic and Political Weekly* 22, no. 12 (1987): 513–517.

36 Mathias Czaika, "High-Skilled Migration," in *High-Skilled Migration: Drivers and Policies*, ed. Mathias Czaika (Oxford: Oxford University Press, 2018), 6.

37 Rabben, "Credential Recognition in the United States for Foreign Professionals," 2.

38 Rabben, "Credential Recognition in the United States for Foreign Professionals," 3.

39 Rabben, "Credential Recognition in the United States for Foreign Professionals," 4.

40 Ramya M. Vijaya and Bidisha Biswas, *Indian Immigrant Women and Work: The American Experience* (London: Routledge, 2016), 37.

41 Purkayastha, "Skilled Migration and Cumulative Disadvantage," 181–196.

42 Jeanne Batalova, Michael Fix, and James D. Bachmeier, "Untapped Talent: The Costs of Brain Waste among Highly Skilled Immigrants in the United States," Migration Policy Institute (December 2016), www.migrationpolicy.org.

43 Guo, "Difference, Deficiency, and Devaluation."

44 Khan, "Female Labour Migration from Pakistan," 27.

45 Yen Le Espiritu, "Gender, Migration, and Work: Filipina Health Care Profession-als to the United States," *Revue européenne des migrations internationales* 21, no. 1 (2005): 55–75.

46 Gloria Moreno Fontes Chammartin, "The Feminization of International Migra-tion," *Migrant Workers: Labour Education 2002/4*, no. 129 (Geneva: ILO, 2002): 37–40.

47 Rabben, "Credential Recognition in the United States for Foreign Professionals," 3.

48 Guo, "Difference, Deficiency, and Devaluation."

49 Deanna Draze, "A Study of the Relationship Between Epistemic Style and a Study of the Relationship Between Epistemic Style and Evaluation Practice" (PhD diss., Western Michigan University, 2000), 1–3.

50 Guo, "Difference, Deficiency, and Devaluation."

51 Phyllis M. Cunningham, "A Sociology of Adult Education," in *Handbook of Adult and Continuing Education*, ed. Arthur L. Wilson and Elisabeth Hayes (San Fran-cisco, CA: Jossey-Bass, 2000), 573–591.

52 Education and training are associated with objective values in the labor market. Collins argues that credentials have become a social stratifier, and "the rise of a

competitive system for producing abstract cultural currency in the form of educational credentials has been the major new force shaping stratification in twentieth-century America." See Randall Collins, *The Credential Society: An Historical Sociology of Education and Stratification* (New York: Columbia University Press, 2019), 125.

53 Guo, "Difference, Deficiency, and Devaluation."
54 Jacques Hallak and Muriel Poisson, "Academic Fraud and Quality Assurance: Facing the Challenge of Internationalization of Higher Education," in *Accreditation and the Global Higher Education Market*, ed. Gudmund Hernes and Michaela Martin (Paris: UNESCO, 2008), 190–206.
55 Guo, "Difference, Deficiency, and Devaluation."
56 Hongxia Shan, "Shaping the Re-Training and Re-Education Experiences of Immigrant Women: The Credential and Certificate Regime in Canada," *International Journal of Lifelong Education* 28, no. 3 (2009): 353–369.
57 The author is based in Doha, Qatar, whereas all the interviewees were living in various states in the United States at the time of the interview.
58 Merriam Webster Dictionary, "career ladder," www.merriam-webster.com.
59 Rabben, "Credential Recognition in the United States for Foreign Professionals," 3.
60 Emmanuel Dean Osaze, "The Non-Recognition or Devaluation of Foreign Professional Immigrants Credentials in Canada: The Impact on the Receiving Country (Canada) and the Immigrants" (Master's thesis, York University, United Kingdom, 2017), 5–6.
61 Rabben, "Credential Recognition in the United States for Foreign Professionals," 5.
62 American Immigration Council, "Foreign-Trained Doctors Are Critical to Serving Many U.S. Communities," Special Report, January 2018, www.americanimmigrationcouncil.org.
63 Aaron Young et al., "FSMB Census of Licensed Physicians in the United States, 2018," *Journal of Medical Regulation* 105, no. 2 (2019): 7–23.
64 According to the Association of Physicians of Pakistani Descent of North America (APPNA), an American nonprofit organization headquartered in Westmont, Illinois, United States, there are around 15,000 physicians of Pakistani descent in the United States. The data on the number of male and female physicians are not available.
65 Khan, "Female Labour Migration From Pakistan," 20.
66 Author interview with Saba, April 22, 2020, United States. The American Medical Association notes that "residency or postgraduate training is specifically a stage of graduate medical education. It refers to a qualified physician, podiatrist, dentist, or veterinarian (one who holds the degree of MD, DPM, DDS, DMD, DVM, DO, BDS, or BDent; or MB; BS, MBChB, or BMed) who practices medicine, usually in a hospital or clinic, under the direct or indirect supervision of a senior medical clinician registered in that specialty such as an attending physician or consultant. In many jurisdictions, successful completion of such training is a requirement in order to obtain an unrestricted license to practice medicine, and in particular a license to practice a chosen specialty." See American Medical Association, 2021, www.ama-assn.org.

67 Author interview with Saba, April 22, 2020, United States.

68 Author interview with Maha, April 30, 2020, United States.

69 Author interview with Maha, April 30, 2020, United States.

70 A house job in Pakistan is a year of medical internship and clinical training under the supervision of a senior physician at a hospital. During the internship, medical graduates gain clinical experience and skills via applied training. It is mandatory to complete a year of supervised training before commencing independent medical practice.

71 Author interview with Ayesha, April 25, 2020, United States.

72 Saad Shafqat and Anita KM Zaidi, "Pakistani Physicians and the Repatriation Equation," *New England Journal of Medicine* 356, no. 1 (2007): 442–443.

73 Amy Paturel, "Closing the Gender Pay Gap in Medicine," American Association for Medical Colleges (AAMC), April 16, 2019, www.aamc.org.

74 Author interview with Maheen, May 3, 2020, United States.

75 Pallavi Banerjee, "Constructing Dependence: Visa Regimes and Gendered Migration in Families of Indian Professional Workers" (PhD diss., University of Illinois at Chicago, 2013), 123–125.

76 Banerjee, "Constructing Dependence," 125.

77 Pallavi Banerjee, "Housewife Visas and Highly Skilled Immigrant Families in the U.S." Paper presented at the Council on Contemporary Families Symposium, August 8, 2018.

78 Author interview with Ghazal, May 5, 2020, United States.

79 Guo, "Difference, Deficiency, and Devaluation."

80 Shahrzad Mojab, "De-Skilling Immigrant Women," *Canadian Women Studies* 19, no. 3 (1999): 123–128.

81 Ruby Gropas and Laura Bartolini, "Southern European Highly Skilled Female Migrants in Male-Dominated Sectors in Times of Crisis: A Look into the IT and Engineering Sectors," in *High-Skill Migration and Recession*, ed. Anna Triandafyllidou and Irina Isaakyan (London: Palgrave Macmillan, 2016), 160–192.

82 Mojab, "De-Skilling Immigrant Women," 124.

83 Neha's family had settled in the United States and her parents were green card holders able to sponsor her under the Immediate Relative visa category, which allows for a US Lawful Permanent Resident to sponsor an immediate relative; i.e., a spouse or unmarried offspring.

84 Author interview with Neha, May 4, 2020, United States.

85 Author interview with Heba, May 10, 2020, United States.

86 Author interview with Alize, April 30, 2020, United States.

87 Mojab, "De-Skilling Immigrant Women," 125.

88 Author interview with Rida, May 2, 2020, United States.

89 The figure includes low-skilled workers employed in industries such as farming, construction, food processing, manual labor, etc., as well as skilled and highly skilled immigrants; Budiman, "Key Findings About U.S. Immigrants."

90 Michael S. Teitelbaum, "High-Skilled Migration Policy Challenge from a US Perspective," in *High-Skilled Migration Drivers and Policies*, ed. Mathias Czaika (Oxford: Oxford University Press, 2018), 130.

91 In 2014, President Barack Obama established the White House Task Force on New Americans to facilitate better integration of immigrants and refugees into American communities. The task force was officially launched in 2015; "White House Task Force on New Americans," The White House, 2015, https://obam awhitehouse.archives.gov.

92 Muzaffar Chishti and Jessica Bolter, "'Merit-Based' Immigration: Trump Proposal Would Dramatically Revamp Immigrant Selection Criteria, but with Modest Effects on Numbers," Migration Policy Institute, May 30, 2019, www.migration policy.org.

93 Chishti and Bolter, "'Merit-Based' Immigration."

94 According to the Fourteenth Amendment to the Constitution of the United States of America, "All persons born or naturalized in the United States, and subject to the jurisdiction thereof, are citizens of the United States and of the State wherein they reside." See Cornell Law School, Legal Information Institute, "14th Amendment," 2021, www.law.cornell.edu. According to US Citizen and Immigration Services, "a resident is identified as any person holding a green card, officially known as the Permanent Resident Card and is allowed to live and work permanently in the United States." See US Citizen and Immigration Services, "Green Card," 2020, www.uscis.gov.

10

Transnationalism and Gender among Immigrants

Economic, Political, and Social Challenges

SILVIA PEDRAZA

More than anyone else, immigrants live their lives in a transnational social field. They typically develop subjectivities, engage in communication, take actions, and live many aspects of their social lives across two or more nations. Focusing on immigrants to the United States, in this chapter I first review the major approaches to understanding why people migrate and how they assimilate. I also evaluate the major concepts that arose over time—from assimilation to incorporation to transnationalism.[1] I argue that while immigrants have always been transnational, the advent of modern communications qualitatively changed the immigrant experience in the last half century. Today's immigrants routinely live their lives across two or more nations; they also, at once, live life in the past and the present.

I strive to show that transnationalism has a threefold impact: on the societies of origin, the societies of destination, and the immigrants themselves. Through myriad examples from the history of many immigrant groups to the United States, I provide evidence of the three major types of transnationalism: economic, political, and social, while highlighting the role that gender plays in all three. Long ago, I made a call to incorporate gender into the study of migration, as doing so would not only fill the void regarding our knowledge of women as immigrants but would also "elucidate those aspects of the process of migration that were neglected by the exclusive focus on men."[2] As Talcott Parsons underscored, a conceptual scheme is like a searchlight that brightly illuminates a "spot," leaving what lies outside it in darkness: "the point is, what lies outside the spot is not really 'seen' until the searchlight moves."[3] Any theory illuminates certain aspects of reality while simultaneously obscuring others. As research on gender and migration has matured, now we can appreciate its many contributions.

Migration and Gender

The traditional, individual macro approach to the study of migration was best developed by Everett Lee's theory that focused on the individual migrant's decision to migrate—the "push" and "pull" factors at the origin and the destination (e.g., the perceived lack of a future in the homeland vs. the availability of jobs in the United States).[4] The journey was mediated by "intervening obstacles" (e.g., distance, immigration laws, cost), the influence of personal traits (e.g., stage in the life cycle), and the effect of personal transitions (e.g., marriage or divorce).

Focusing on the disruption that migration caused in the lives of the immigrants, Oscar Handlin in *The Uprooted* (1951) told the history of European immigration to America in the nineteenth century.[5] He focused on the pain of alienation and nostalgia the immigrants experienced as the transition from feudalism to capitalism propelled them. The movement, he emphasized, began "in the peasant heart of Europe"[6] from countries such as Ireland, Great Britain, Scotland, Germany, Scandinavia, Italy, Poland, Hungary, Greece, Croatia, Syria, and Armenia. The exception were the Jews from the Russian and Austrian empires who had not been allowed to own land and were already urban, often literate, able to handle money and credit, already modern.[7] Handlin described them as dissenters. All told, the movement involved 35 million people. For all, the central institution was the family—an emotional and an economic unit. All of this was lost when they entered an industrializing society and became the labor force for the new factory system. Handlin underscored the pain the immigrants felt when they lost their roots: their language, homes, village, family, and friends. In the New World, oftentimes only the religion survived the transfer. When they were uprooted, alienation and nostalgia pervaded their lives.

A generation later, John Bodnar in *The Transplanted* (1985) offered another plant image to describe the immigrant experience.[8] He focused on immigrants being transplanted when they put out new roots through the new institutions they developed to defend themselves and their culture. Through the development of their own institutions, the immigrants were able to find a new home and a new—most often hybrid—identity. Yesterday, as well as today, the immigrants founded churches and synagogues, newspapers, radio and (eventually) television stations, dance and music halls, theaters, sports, credit unions, and mutual aid societies. In so doing, they wove a new identity from the threads of their old culture and language together with the new threads of their American present.

The structural, macro approach superseded the micro, traditional approach. For a generation, American sociology was heavily influenced by the structural Marxism that came across the Atlantic Ocean with Louis Althusser and Etiénne Balibar's political economy.[9] Beginning in the mid-1970s, various authors developed a structural theory of migration, focusing on world patterns of development as the developed countries of North America and Western Europe remained the magnet that attracted the world's poor.

Arguing independently but in a similar vein, Manuel Castells, Michael Burawoy, and Alejandro Portes stressed that immigrant labor performed an important economic function for the developed, capitalist nation that received it.[10] Burawoy emphasized that the migration took place within a system of economic migration that institutionally separated the renewal of the labor force (that took place in the underdeveloped country) from the maintenance of the labor force (that took place in the developed country). The migration of low-skilled, cheap labor provided countries such as the United States or Germany with a dependable source of cheap labor; it also provided countries such as Mexico or Turkey with a "safety valve" as allowing the exodus served to satisfy the needs of their poor and lower-middle classes. Pedraza-Bailey extended this structural approach, arguing that refugee flows could similarly be part of a system of political migration.[11] The exodus of the opposition to communism served to externalize dissent from countries such as East Germany and Cuba, while also providing West Germany and the United States proof of the rightness of their cause.

A typology of immigrants was developed by Alejandro Portes and Rubén G. Rumbaut: labor migrants, refugees, entrepreneurial immigrants, and professional "brain drain" migration.[12] Given the frequency of devastating natural disasters in recent years, to this typology we may need to add immigrants who are forced to migrate as a result of earthquakes, hurricanes, floods, mudslides, and tornadoes.

When women joined the academy in substantial numbers, roughly from the 1980s on, their research highlighted that all human lives are gendered (woman—wife, daughter, mother, grandmother, sister; man—husband, son, father, grandfather, brother). Soon, the relationship between migration and gender was established. As Monica Boyd pointed out, the division of labor in society is gendered.[13] Thus, the study of migration and gender became one of the major ways of linking micro and macro levels of analysis. It also linked the immigrants' past in their homelands with their present in the United States—what we now call transnationalism.[14] Douglas S. Massey underscored that migration is a social process driven by social networks.[15] Massey et al. analyzed the contemporary Mexican migration to the United States from the perspective of social networks, comparing towns in Mexico with a history of migration to those that had no history of migration, over the course of several trips (documented and undocumented).[16] They emphasized that while the historical causes of a migration flow may well be structural (e.g., poverty in the sending society or lack of cheap labor in the advanced nation), once migrants' social networks grow and mature, the networks support and channel migration on a continuously widening scale, and the migration comes to fuel itself. That, indeed, has now happened among contemporary immigrants from Latin America and Asia to the United States.

Migration is a process that can be sex-selective. Migration flows can be overwhelmingly composed of men (as is typical of labor migrations, such as the Italian migration in the nineteenth century and the one from Mexico in the nineteenth and twentieth). They can also be overwhelmingly composed of women (such as the Irish migration in the nineteenth century, the Dominican one in the twentieth century). Or they can be overwhelmingly composed of families (as is typical of refugees, such as the Jews, Cubans, Cambodians, and Vietnamese throughout the twentieth century).

Katharine Donato and her colleagues examined the shifts in the sex composition of adult immigrants to the United States, age-standardized, from 1860 to 2006.[17] They showed that in the nineteenth century, the immigrant population went from being gender-balanced to being male-dominated, as women hovered around 45 percent. From 1930 on, as the number of immigrants increased, so did the number of women; by 1970, it reached a high of 54 percent. After 1970, the period that marks a dramatic growth in undocumented migration from Mexico, the proportions changed. However, when the authors excluded those from Mexico, women represented 51 percent of the immigrant population. Comparing the United States with twenty-five other nations, they showed that there were global shifts toward more women joining the migrations but there was "no consistent trend toward feminization."[18] Interesting contrasts were obtained among various nations. For example, Spain's foreign-born population was female-dominated with 53 percent in 1981, but the proportion dropped to 49 percent in 2001; while in France, the proportion of females rose from 43 percent in 1962 to 48 percent by 1999. In my view, to explain these contrasts we must take into account each country's own economic history of labor supply and demand; different cultural and religious patterns among its ethnic groups; and varying public policies that shape the migration flows.

Hasia Diner's study of Irish immigrant women in the nineteenth century best illustrates the causes and consequences of sex selectivity.[19] In *Erin's Daughters in America*, Diner showed that Irish migration responded to the "push" that prevailed in Europe at the time: poverty, landlessness, and the social dislocations that accompanied the transition from agrarian feudalism to industrial capitalism. The famine of 1848 as well as British oppression of its Irish subjects exacerbated these conditions. Diner demonstrated that, coupled with the Irish cultural pattern of single inheritance and single dowry, Ireland increasingly became the home of the unmarried and the late married. Unable to come up with a dowry for marriage, one escape from family and spinsterhood was for women to join a religious order; another was emigration. Thus, as the century wore on, the migration became a female mass movement.

Domestic service was a major occupational niche for immigrant women, then, as it still is today. Irish women found ready employment by the rising middle class, particularly for single women who could "live in." Moreover, Diner showed that domestic service was a good job for young women whose alternative was the unhealthy spaces of the textile factories with their meager wages. As live-in maids, with paid room and board, the young women were able to save, and used their savings to bring over other relatives, pay off the family mortgage back home, support the Catholic Church, finance the upward mobility of their young family in America, or secure an American marriage. Thus, work was central in the lives of these women.

Religion was inextricably bound with migration. Robert Orsi underscored the importance of Catholic traditions of worship that, as with the Italians, often had a Madonna at the center.[20] While the Madonna of 115th Street in New York City was a patron saint and symbol to all Italians of nation, history, and tradition, above all, she was a woman's devotion. Italian immigrant women turned to Our Lady of Mount Carmel with petitions for help with the hardship and powerlessness of their lives—as women bound by a strong, patriarchal tradition, and as immigrants mired in poverty, toil, and trouble. Today, we can see a similar welding of religion and national identity when Mexican women turn to the patron saint Our Lady of Guadalupe,[21] or Cuban women turn to Our Lady of Charity.[22] Most recently, both the Catholic and Protestant churches aided the undocumented in their dangerous journey from Mexico and Central America to the United States, journeys that often consisted of resting in the churches along the way for physical and spiritual assistance.[23] Religion also played a supportive role when the churches, particularly the Protestant churches, gave women the opportunity to play a leadership role. In her analysis of Afro-Caribbean women who left their small island of birth to work in the more prosperous Caribbean islands, Paula Aymer showed that with their work as domestics these women often took on the role of providers (traditionally male), working single-handedly to send remittances back to their families.[24] At the same time, they found their own identity as leaders in their new churches.

Race or color has always made a difference in America. Evelyn Nakano Glenn's study of three generations of Japanese women in domestic service depicted domestic service as one of the few occupations open to women of color from the nineteenth century through World War II.[25] The first generation *issei* of Japanese immigrants migrated to fill the labor in California agriculture and were able to become domestic servants. The second generation *nisei* benefited from a more open society but suffered the humiliation of the massive internment during World War II, out of fear that these Americans would side with the enemy. Japanese Americans were relegated to living in internment camps all along the West Coast, isolation that destroyed their tightknit business community.[26] The war brides generations suffered less than the other cohorts.[27]

The garment industry was another important niche for women, particularly in New York City, for Jewish, Italian, and Puerto Rican women. It allowed them to work not only outside their home in factories but, particularly, inside their home where they could look after their children while doing "piece work." This advantage led women to accept low wages and exploitative conditions when a market for ready-made mass-produced clothing developed and New York became the center of the garment industry,[28] eventually expanding to other cities, particularly Los Angeles and Miami.[29] The garment industry remained equally important in the lives of more recent immigrants, particularly for women from Puerto Rico and the Dominican Republic,[30] ceasing in importance only when the American garment industry collapsed under the weight of cheap imports of clothing from China, India, and Korea, from the 1970s onward.

Many immigrant women came from traditional societies where women did not work outside of the home. Yesterday as well as today, the immigration gave them a chance to break with the traditional gender norms and join the labor force, providing them with autonomy and earnings. More often than not, they saw work as an opportunity to help the family, rather than as a form of self-actualization.[31] Self-actualization was the goal for the mostly White, middle-class American women influenced by the women's movement. For most immigrant women, helping the family to succeed in America was the goal that gave meaning to their lives.[32]

Studies that focused on gender and migration also made writing the history of the private realm possible. Sydney Weinberg's *The World of Our Mothers* (1988) was a deliberate corrective to Irving Howe's *The World of Our Fathers* (1976),[33] both focusing on the Jewish immigrant experience in New York City at the turn of the nineteenth to twentieth century. Interviewing elderly, Jewish women who lived in nursing homes, Weinberg enabled us to see how women who lived their lives through those of their husbands and children contributed to their success as an immigrant family. As she emphasized, today we may not easily understand the satisfactions of those who lived for and through others, but the services and sacrifices these mothers made left a deep impression on their daughters.

Studies of gender and migration have served to link structure (the macro reasons why people left their countries—economic, political, religious, and natural disasters) and agency (the micro behavior of women who try to partly shed and partly retain the old cultures, reinventing themselves). Sherri Grasmuck and Patricia Pessar analyzed the movement of women who migrated from the island of Dominican Republic to the island of Manhattan.[34] They focused on the household political economy to show that gender lay at the center of decision-making. The family made various decisions guided by a family strategy: the major decision to migrate; who in the family would migrate first or next; what resources would be allocated to the journey; what remittances the family could expect; whether the migration would be temporary or permanent; and who would return.

Legal status is particularly important among contemporary immigrants. There have always been two immigrant Americas—one working-class, another professional. In their study of immigration and women, Susan Pearce, Elizabeth Clifford, and Reena Tandon interviewed women who represented both: domestics, factory workers, small-business employees, doctors, lawyers, and artists.[35] They also interviewed women who were legal and undocumented; those who followed their husbands; those who were "gender pioneers"; those who left for economic reasons; and those who were refugees. In Los Angeles, they interviewed Mexicans and Iranians; in Houston, Vietnamese; in Miami, Cubans and Haitians. They demonstrated that the difference between the legal and the undocumented is not as stark as many imagine it to be, as the women had often made a transition from one to the other. Women who arrived as legal immigrants (e.g., who came on a student visa) often lost that status and became undocumented. Women who were undocumented (e.g., who crossed the border without papers) often became legal (e.g., through marriage to a US citizen). They showed their agency not only as resistance (as usually understood) but also as creativity, reinvention of the self, and leadership.[36]

Grasmuck and Pessar also found gender involved in the decision to return.[37] Men who immigrated often lost the respect that was due to them in the traditional, patriarchal family they came from; thus, they

longed to return to their homeland, living an austere, frugal life to accumulate savings for the return. By contrast, women who immigrated
often found their capacity to participate as equals in the household enhanced, and their self-esteem heightened as they could see the fruits of
their labor outside the home; thus, they defended their newfound, if
meager, freedoms and staked themselves in their new place by spending
large sums of money on furnishings. As a result, often a struggle developed over finances and return, which was really about the traditional
gender roles in their culture.

The relationship of gender and migration also depends on the level
of education and stage of the life cycle. Using the Mexican Migration
Project data, together with her own fieldwork,[38] Shawn Malia Kanaiaupuni examined the gendered pattern of migration among 14,000
persons in forty-three Mexican villages in Jalisco,[39] Michoacán, and
Guanajuato—Mexico's traditional migrant-sending states—over several
trips across the life cycle. Kanaiaupuni found several gendered patterns.
For example, single women migrated more often than married women
did. Contrary to the prevailing notion that women migrate for family
reunification, she found that most wives of migrants did not migrate
(74 percent), often despite their husband's rather long migrant careers.
Also, greater education lowered the chances of migration among men,
while it raised them among women. In all, Kanaiaupuni argued, rather
forcibly, that "a theory of migration that does not consider the macro-
and micro-level effects of gender falls far short of an accurate portrayal
of human behavior."[40] I concur. However, in my view, before we can
develop a theory of gender and migration, we must do research considering these relationships in very different nations with respect to culture
and development, so we can understand which gendered patterns are
nearly universal and which are culturally bound or historically contingent. Still, gender is inextricably bound with migration.

Assimilation

Studies of assimilation, however, have mostly ignored gender differences.
The study of immigrants was closely wedded to the beginnings of social
science in America from the late nineteenth to the early twentieth century.[41] Immigrants and their plight were the focus of vivid studies from

the early days of "the Chicago school."[42] They shared the expectation that the outcome would be a process of assimilation. Yet from the outset, there was an ambiguity in the idea that Robert E. Park himself underscored.[43] "Assimilation" meant to become alike. But, like whom? And in what way? That ambiguity remained until Milton Gordon distinguished among types of assimilation: cultural versus structural.[44] However, the fundamental characteristic of assimilation theory was already evident: As time passed, new immigrant groups would inevitably adapt to the mainstream culture. In other multi-racial societies, a different concept took hold. In Cuba, Fernando Ortiz called it transculturation—how one culture expresses itself inside another.[45] But the leading influence was that of the assimilation school.

Research on immigrants and their eventual outcomes, however, began to wane until, in the 1960s, it all but disappeared. Under the pressures of Anglo-conformity, the children of those European immigrants went on to assimilate in American society at a time when the price of success was often one's ethnicity and identity. Like Paul Cowan, writer for *The Village Voice*,[46] whose real name was Saul Cohen, many successful Americans became orphans in history, having lost their ethnic legacies. In the process, what is really distinctive about immigrants was lost.

What is distinctive about immigrants? At the micro level, that they experienced a whole other life in another country and culture, which they bring with them and decisively continues to influence them; at the macro level, that the state in two societies is the gatekeeper that regulates migration through a body of law. Immigrants are also distinct in that they bring with them a whole host of social resources (their language, traditions, mores, social class, education, occupations, and values). I underscore that their outcomes, their success, in American society will be partly a function of those initial resources, partly a function of the nature of their migration (whether they are political or economic immigrants, victims of genocide, settlers, or sojourners), and partly a function of the social context that greeted them. Immigrants enter a particular social context (welcoming, neutral, or rejecting) at a particular moment in history (e.g., 1810, 1910, 2010) that presents them with varying possibilities in particular regions or cities, in particular industries or occupations, in the forms of discrimination or exclusion faced.

Beginning in the mid-1970s, the concept of assimilation was super-seded by the more neutral concept of incorporation. Joe Feagin argued that we needed to focus on the varying ways in which different ethnic groups were incorporated—became a part of the society—by paying at-tention to the initial and continuing placement and access of various groups within the economic, political, and educational institutions of the society.[47] Still, the concept of incorporation, like its predecessor, as-similation, assumed a one-way process, failing to take into account that yesterday as well as today, immigrants did not just become incorporated into American society, they also transformed it. They transformed its culture (high and popular both)—in sports, film, music, and dance. They transformed its institutions—educational, health, commercial, and neighborhoods. Immigrants made and remade America and are fash-ioning it still.

Other concepts came to challenge those of assimilation and accul-turation, such as internal colonialism, incorporation and, more recently, transnationalism. Nonetheless, Richard Alba and Victor Nee argued in *Remaking the American Mainstream* that it is still a necessary concept.[48] In their view, assimilation is a grand narrative that served to aptly de-scribe the experience of the Southern and Eastern European immi-grants, as well as the Asian immigrants who arrived at the turn of the nineteenth to twentieth century. They went on to join the mainstream of American life in terms of their levels of educational attainment, patterns of suburbanization, and intermarriage. Alba and Nee emphasized that their assimilation was partly historically contingent—dependent on the economic growth and new industries created by two World Wars and the greater openness of higher education resulting from the GI Bill. The GI Bill made it possible for working-class Americans to achieve the two markers of the middle class: home ownership and a college education.

Their success, however, was also racialized—that is, exclusive to those who had become "white" in the process. Thus, Pedraza and Rumbaut distinguished discrimination from exclusion.[49] Without doubt, many of the old European immigrants faced discrimination resulting from the deep nativism that treated them as strangers in the land.[50] The Irish, despised for their Catholicism and their low levels of education, were confronted with signs that told them "No Irish Need Apply" when jobs were advertised. Neither were well-educated Jews able to join the best social clubs for gentlemen nor live in the best Anglo neighborhoods. Nor could the Italians and Poles gain admission to the best Ivy League colleges that valued gentlemen and ladies' manners. But the people of color—African Americans, Native Americans, Mexicans, Puerto Ricans, the old Asian immigrants—faced exclusion as the strong color line in American society prevented even those who managed to become well-educated from attaining good jobs or living in decent neighborhoods. While the color line that obliterated social class differences could not be crossed in the Deep South,[51] most institutions in the North also engaged in forms of racial exclusion. Everywhere, those who faced exclusion found that schools, banks, credit lenders, and real estate developers kept them from joining the mainstream of life through practices such as "red lining" to prevent them from attaining loans, and "restrictive covenants" to prevent them from moving into better neighborhoods. Over several generations, such practices prevented them from accumulating wealth.[52]

Structurally, assimilation meant that even those formerly excluded groups made progress. Reynolds Farley and Richard Alba showed that even for those immigrant groups dominated by low-wage labor in the first generation (such as Mexicans, Central Americans, and Afro-Caribbeans), there was considerable improvement in the average occu-pational position in their second generation, though not to the point of parity with native-born Whites.[53] Progress was uneven, however, as Mexicans, in particular, and Central Americans showed less progress than other immigrant groups. Vilma Ortiz and Edward Telles in *Genera-tions of Exclusion* (2008) traced the progress of Mexican Americans in California across several generations, focusing on the cumulative costs of exclusion over several generations.[54] By contrast, immigrants who arrived recently, bringing with them high levels of human capital (such as many Asians and South Americans), did soon achieve parity with native-born Whites in those social indicators that pertain to education, income, and occupations.

The Civil Rights movement was a major watershed in American his-tory, as it brought about the development of anti-discrimination laws (the Voting Rights Act, the Civil Rights Act, and the Fair Housing Act, in particular). It also brought about a profound change in values that made racism as a belief lose its public legitimacy, doing away with the hold of the old White supremacy groups, such as the Ku Klux Klan.

While racism—the belief in the innate superiority of some races over others—has not fully left the American scene, and today we witness the rise of new White supremacy groups, surveys consistently provide evidence of an enormous decline over time. Young Americans hardly share it. They grew up in a vastly more open and tolerant society in which classmates and neighbors were often of other ethnicities and races, influencing their ability to understand and cope with difference.

Culturally, assimilation entails indicators that are essential for identity, such as dress, marital behavior, language, and social expectations. Margaret Gibson studied Sikh immigrants, whose manner of dress (long hair, turban) is essential to their identity.[55] She underscored that the price of assimilation need not always be the erasure of one's culture, and proposed the concept of accommodation, rather than assimilation. Focusing on immigrant youth and their identity development, Min Zhou highlighted that "dissonant acculturation" between the first and second generations can lead to substantial family conflict and estrangement between parents and children.[56] Such acculturation pressures may also vary by gender, as boys may have a more difficult time accommodating themselves to the new expectations than girls, and may seek to secure their masculine reputation within peer networks.

Gibson also underlined that cultural differences that may have been neutral to begin with can become politically charged. For example, in Europe, Muslim children resist school and its authorities when symbols of their ethnic and religious identity—such as the *hijab* (headscarf) worn by Muslim girls—become a marker of ethnic and religious identity "not to be compromised or sacrificed."[57] If teachers pressure the students to remove the headscarves to conform to the mainstream culture, it becomes a source of conflict in schools. "Thus, Muslim children may come to experience transitions between home and school not as neutral acts of switching between two cultural systems but as politically charged border crossings."[58] Student defiance and resistance may result.

The mainstream does not remain fixed over time. It changes and is transformed as immigrants progressively join it. Alba and Nee underscored that historically, "the American mainstream which originated with the colonial northern European settlers evolved through the incremental inclusion of ethnic and racial groups that were formerly excluded and as parts of their culture became part of the composite culture that was America."[59] Thus, with the vast migration from Germany, American culture became less puritanical as it incorporated many features of German culture: their love of music and drama, as well as card playing and drinking. With the enormous migration of Catholic and Jewish immigrants, the mainstream boundary that originally was Protestant eventually became Judeo-Christian.

However, for most of the twentieth century, the price of success in America was often one's ethnicity. I find the Hollywood film industry in the mid-twentieth century gives us evidence of the change. We can see that famous movie stars who were the children of immigrants and who cast a spell on all Americans did so by changing their names and Anglicizing them. For example, Doris Day was really Doris Kappelhoff and Kirk Douglas was really Issur Danielovitch, both of Jewish origin; Dean Martin was really Dino Crocetti, of Italian origin; Rita Hayworth was really Margarita Carmen Cansino, of Spanish origin. Such handing over of one's culture seems unnecessary today, in the first quarter of the twenty-first century. Now people of Latin American, Asian, and African origins who achieve Hollywood fame do keep their names, such as the Mexican director Alejandro González-Iñárritu, the Korean director Bong Joon-ho, and the Kenyan actress Lupita Nyong'o—all recent Oscar winners. Still, a substantial amount of name changing continues to take place, mostly among Hispanic movie actors. As Alba and Nee stressed, assimilation is still driven by the decisions of immigrants and their descendants, given the enticing rewards the mainstream offers. Today, those "enticing rewards" do not seem to have "as corrosive an impact" on the cultures of the new immigrants as they did yesteryear.[60]

This process of incorporation is likely to continue, as Alba and Nee forecasted. It has cultural as well as structural dimensions. Culturally, today we see that Latin music has outstripped country music in popularity; Americans now play not only football but also soccer; yoga and meditation are now ubiquitous; and sales of salsa top sales of ketchup. Structurally, today, Asian Americans match White Americans in levels of education and income, arenas in which Black Americans and Hispanics lag far behind. However, Asian American political incorporation remains very low, where African American representation is now high, and Latinas/os have made real progress. Since 1968, when Shirley Chisholm was elected the first Black American woman to Congress, the

117th Congress at present has record numbers of Blacks, Hispanics, and women. Of the 435 members of the House of Representatives, 118 are women—27 percent. Of the 100 senators, 25 are women—as Kamala Harris (the daughter of Jamaican and Indian immigrants) left to become vice president of the country. Counting all 535 lawmakers in both the House and Senate, now 61 are Black-Americans (12%) and 44 are Hispanic (8%), while only 18 are of Asian origin (3%) and one is Native American. While the Black-White divide remains the deepest of all in America today, one should not deny the extent to which Black Americans were able to draw on their talents and skills to achieve substantial political incorporation.

Although, overall, the American story has been one of upward mobility from the immigrant generation to their children and grandchildren, Alejandro Portes and Min Zhou raised the possibility that, at present, there may be segmented assimilation—upward mobility for some groups, downward for others.[61] In evaluating patterns of assimilation, however, gender is remarkably absent, unlike in studies of migration. Future studies of assimilation should consider gender differences.

Transnationalism and Gender

Beginning in the middle of the twentieth century until today, modern communications—jet air travel, faxes, email, the internet, videos, social media, and videoconferencing—flourished and developed to such an extent that they allowed immigrants to live vicariously in their former homelands while also living currently in the United States. The concept of transnationalism arose when social scientists noticed that, under the impact of these changes, many immigrants failed to shed their old identities and totally assimilate. Instead, they developed new bicultural identities and lived their lives and were quite involved in more than one nation, more than one world—in effect, making the home and adopted countries both one lived social world. In his study of Mexican working-class immigrants living in Redwood City, California, Roger Rouse found that "while they lived in Redwood City, they were also living deep in western Mexico," which resulted in "cultural bifocality."[62]

Linda Basch et al. formalized the definition of transnationalism now in use: the process by which immigrants "forge and sustain multi-stranded social relations that link together their societies of origin and settlement."[63] Thus, they underscored, immigrants "take actions, make decisions, and develop subjectivities and identities embedded in networks of relationships that connect them simultaneously to two or more nations."[64] It has economic, political, and social dimensions and challenges, in both its causes and consequences.

Barry Goldberg suggested that the concept of transnationalism be considered an important heuristic device for historians since, in "crucial respects, it argues, the present is not a replay of the past."[65] He argued that the European immigrant experience should not be the "model" experience for framing other histories, particularly not for understanding the re-Hispanicization of the Southwest or Puerto Rican and Filipino arrivals from the US global empire. Goldberg was critical of David Reimers's *Still the Golden Door* (1985), viewing it as a historian's inclination to see the past in the present, or "to remain more or less Whiggish (Reimers)."[66] In my view, one should take into account the difference between voluntary immigrants (the old Europeans), involuntary immigrants (due to slavery, conquest, and annexation), and refugees (in-between, as they flee because circumstances coerce them). Many of the post-1965 immigrants from Latin America and Asia are also voluntary immigrants who hope the golden door will still be open to them.

Soon after the concept of transnationalism exploded, the cry arose that transnationalism was not new, though much of the literature sounded as if it were.[67] Comparing immigrants at the turn of the twentieth century with contemporary immigrants to New York, Nancy Foner showed that many transnational patterns actually have a long history.[68] For example, at the turn of the twentieth century, Italian and Russian immigrants also kept ties of sentiment and family alive with those back home by living in transnational households and sending remittances back home; and by making political contributions for particular causes, such as the Irish support for the nationalist cause of the Irish Republican Army (IRA) back home. Moreover, except for Russian Jews who fled from political and religious persecution, the return rates for many immigrant groups, like the Italians, were extremely high, around one-third, even higher than today's.

While these critiques were valid, I argued that, nonetheless, much is distinctive about our current transnationalism. In today's global economy, changes in the technologies of transportation and communication (jet air travel, faxes, electronic mail, the internet, videos, social media, and videoconferencing) changed the qualitative experience of immigration. Modern communications enabled immigrants to maintain more frequent and closer contact with their home country and to participate regularly, even immediately, in the life they left behind.[69]

In all of my research, including this chapter, my methodology consists of substantial participant observation in various immigrant communities; formal and informal interviews with representatives of many immigrant groups; and observing the changes over time in my own transnational relationship to my homeland. To these I add demographic, survey research, and economic data. Based on these multiple forms of data, I argue that a profound qualitative difference exists in the transnational experiences immigrants live today. Because new technologies allow immediate communication, immigrants can experience the world they left behind as if they were still there—vicariously. For example, today, Costa Ricans can rapidly travel between "home" (in Central America) and "host" society (in the United States), rather than spending many weeks at sea, as Italians did in the nineteenth century on the return voyage from New York City to Italy. Likewise, cable television has brought Greece, with its colorful festivals and Olympics, right into the living room of Greek immigrants in Detroit. Moreover, while in the past, communication was unreliable and painfully slow, today it is nearly certain, and fast. For example, in the early twentieth century, the "overseas Chinese" that lived scattered throughout South East Asia often paid a letter writer to write the letter they could not, to send their affection, and implore their family's help in China. However, the letter often did not reach those in the rural areas, or it took months to arrive, by which time the news had grown old. By contrast, in recent years, a fax sent to a temple or a benevolent association penetrated deep in rural China immediately. Even Cuban Americans, whose travel is so restricted by the perennial conflicts between the US and Cuban governments, now communicate regularly with relatives and friends back on the island through electronic mail, Facebook, and WhatsApp. In the nineteenth century, Irish immigrants heard that a new baby was baptized in Ireland long after the event, while today Mexican immigrants can quickly see the baptism that took place back in their village on video, and even participate in the ceremony. Rather than being substantially cut off from the past, today's immigrants live—existentially speaking—both in the past and the present at once. A strong emotional thread now ties the two realities, as never before.

Immigrants today are there not just in their memories and imaginations, but vicariously, in that very moment; they are able to participate—economically, politically, socially, and emotionally—in a regular, constant way. Thus, a new form of intimacy has developed that cuts across national borders. As a result, they often create two "homes" that rest on the pillar of an identity (or identities) that incorporates two or more nations, cultural worlds, at once. This is true even when, as Roger Waldinger pointed out, dual loyalties can be conflicting.[70] My point is not to emphasize a past/present divergence, as Waldinger put it, but to emphasize that we do now live in a brave new world that is both vastly more impersonal and personal at once. It is more impersonal in that telephone menus now answer most of our questions automatically, without the sound of a human voice; clothing is bought and sold online, without our ever touching the cloth for its feel. Yet, it is far more personal across great distances than ever before, as new technology allows us immediate intellectual and emotional communication with those we love who remained behind.

Those sustained affective, emotional bridges also constitute a form of transnationalism, along with return travel, as Elizabeth Aranda showed for Puerto Rican migrants.[71] In creating and sustaining these bridges, women are centrally involved. For many immigrants in their new American "home," such as in Orlando or Detroit, this communication with their families and friends back in their old "home," such as Puerto Rico or Somalia, is the foundation of their emotional and economic well-being. Thus, we do want to know how and why "now" differs from "then."[72] However, as both David Hollinger and José Moya stressed, the major differences are often between groups who show remarkable variation in the development of diasporic identities and political and social involvement.[73] In my view, both perspectives are necessary.

Economic Transnationalism

Luis Eduardo Guarnizo and Michael Peter Smith considered the locations of transnationalism by distinguishing transnationalism from above (of multinational corporations and international organizations) from transnationalism from below (of immigrants, at times in resistance to the former).[74] They argued that we should see transnationalism neither from a dystopian nor from a celebratory point of view. They highlighted the tension in the literature on transnationalism between post-modern cultural studies' conception of identity as a "free-floating" process of individual self-formation and the empirical studies of binational migrants and transnational social movements that envisage personal identity as "socially determined."[75] Thus, they counterpoised the prevailing post-modernist metaphors of "deterritorialization" and "unboundedness" that abound in cultural studies against their being seen as a new structural feature of society. My own taste inclines me to the latter. Immigrant transnationalism is shaped by varying social contexts, cultural and legal, as Ernesto Castañeda showed when his fieldwork contrasted the life experiences of immigrants in New York, Barcelona, and Paris—cities with contrasting possibilities and constraints.[76]

Like all social forms, transnationalism can have both positive and negative impacts—economically, politically, and socially. Transnationalism is quite salutary for the economic health of the countries of origin. Data from the World Bank, based on the International Monetary Fund (IMF) statistics on formal transfers, in 2019, in US dollars, showed that the top remittance recipient countries were: India (82.2 billion), China (70.3 billion), Mexico (38.7 billion), the Philippines (35.1 billion), Egypt (26.4 billion), Nigeria (25.4 billion), and Pakistan (21.9 billion). The impact of remittances on the poorest countries is enormous. As a percentage of Gross Domestic Product (GDP), they constitute 34.3 percent of Haiti's GDP, 29.9 percent of Nepal's, 29.7 percent of Tajikistan's, 21.4 percent of Honduras's, and 20.8 percent of El Salvador's. The link between economic remittances and development is indisputable; they are critical to the survival of the poorest nations.

In 2019, Latin America and the Caribbean saw the fastest growth in remittances, given the healthy economy then (prior to the COVID-19 pandemic) and the large size of its immigrant populations.[77] Women often play an important role in these transactions. In the case of Cuba, part of the very vocal exile community insists on the political task that no dollars be sent back to Cuba because that props up Fidel Castro's regime. Yet another sizable part of the Cuban exile community insists on the moral task of putting families on the island first—and quietly sends dollars back to the family left behind. Susan Eckstein showed that the "New Cubans" from recent migrations transformed Cuban society with their remittances.[78] They still have family there they want to help, and they remembered their own hardship, while most of the "Old Cubans" from the early waves of the exodus neither have family there nor do they know what it means to experience hunger. Moreover, the "New Cubans" often do not see themselves as "exiles" but as "immigrants." Given the demographic weight of the Cuban American community, Miami and Hialeah are filled with small businesses that specialize in delivering food and money to the island. One can even send a typical Christmas Eve meal with all the trappings (roast pork, rice, black beans, and plantains) to the family back home. While women in exile are on both sides of this political divide, their traditional gender role of nurturer inclines them to help the family left behind.[79]

Given recent reforms in Cuban society, the émigrés are now also investing in the island—in small businesses and in real estate. They give the family loans so that, together, they can open up a small business. The small businesses allowed by the Cuban government are very small— e.g., restaurants with a small number of tables and chairs, beauty shops, music shops, taxis, party shops, and souvenir shops. For the sixty-plus years of the revolution, the market as such was absent, and few small businesses were allowed. This is all the more remarkable because in Miami and Hialeah it is evident that Cubans have a tradition of buying and selling, the foundation of the ethnic enclave on which, Alejandro Portes and Robert Bach argued, the success of Cuban Americans depended.[80] Clearly, some groups and cultures have a tradition of buying and selling—such as the Chinese, the Jews, and the Middle Easterners. Wherever they went, these immigrants lifted themselves up by their success in small business enterprises. Cubans also had a tradition of buying and selling but could not express it during the revolution. Only now family property and the small business sector have begun to return and Cubans overseas began to provide the capital for their family's small business.

Remittances have various impacts. Not only does migration result in remittances, but remittances also result in migration. In her study of the cumulative causation of migration to the United States from Costa Rica, the Dominican Republic, Nicaragua, Mexico, and Puerto Rico, Elizabeth Fussell found that in all of them, except Puerto Rico, larger amounts of remittances sent to households in a given year were associated with higher migration prevalence ratios the following year.[81] This was especially true in places with older migration streams, such as Mexico and the Dominican Republic. As Fussell underlined, immigrants who send back remittances demonstrate the rewards to migration, thus enticing more members of the sending community to go to the United States. Puerto Rico was an exception because, as US citizens, Puerto Ricans migrate freely back and forth; so much so that Jorge Duany investigated how a "nation on the move" constructs its identity.[82] Data from the US Census, American Community Survey, tell us that in 2017, 5.6 million people of Puerto Rican origin lived in the continental United States, while only 3.4 million people lived on the island.[83] While language (Spanish) and culture (Latin American) used to be the cultural markers of the Puerto Rican identity, such a large diaspora—many of whom hardly speak Spanish and are rather American—challenges the very markers of that identity. Yet Duany found that, nonetheless, the Puerto Rican identity was rather tenacious.

While overall the impact of immigrant remittances is positive for buoying the sinking economies back home, it can also create imbalances. Sarah Blue's survey of Cuban families in Havana who received remittances from their relatives abroad showed that the remittances were relinking the family that both the Cuban government and the exile community had torn asunder.[84] They certainly provided some measure of material comfort for those left behind, improving their lives; however, they also served to exacerbate racial inequality. Since the first two waves of the Cuban exodus (from 1959 to 1974) were predominantly White,[85] Black and Mulatto Cubans on the island have fewer immigrant networks abroad they can rely on.

Economic transnationalism also has social class and cultural dimensions. Most studies of the Mexican migration have focused on the lives of the poor immigrants. Upper-class Mexicans also migrate, however. Harriett Romo's study of the transnational lives of the Mexican elite in San Antonio, Texas, described the major influence they had on the cultural and artistic life in the city of San Antonio itself.[86] She also highlighted the role they played of "broker" between the Mexican communities, on the one hand, and the Anglo elite, on the other, on behalf of the Mexican community.

Several questions around the economic aspects of transnationalism remain for future research: To what extent is it possible in different social and political contexts? What are the impacts of remittances? What is the role of gender?

Political Transnationalism

Yesterday as well as today, immigrants aimed to influence the political outcomes in their homelands. Over the course of American history, some remarkably influential ethnic lobbies (such as the Irish, Jewish, Armenian, and Cuban) sought to influence US foreign policy.

The Irish American lobby sought to gather funds to achieve Irish independence from British rule in Northern Ireland, as well as for the unification of Ireland. The IRA's guerilla tactics and bombings against the British army and the Royal Constabulary resulted in a couple of thousand deaths and many thousands imprisoned during the thirty-year period of "the troubles" in Northern Ireland and England. To fund its campaign, the IRA was involved in armed robberies, kidnappings, and other criminal activities, but they also raised funds from Irish Americans who loved Ireland.

The Armenian lobby in the United States had quite a different aim: They wanted the United States to recognize the Armenian genocide. For years, they sought recognition that the systematic massacres and forced deportations of Armenians committed by the Ottoman Empire during and after World War I were not just the result of war but constituted genocide—state-sponsored mass murder—of the Christian minority by the Muslim Turkish government. While Armenia received the second highest US aid per capita, just behind Israel, and while forty-six US states recognized the genocide, the US government did not—up until recently. For decades, the strength of the Turkish lobby and the Turkish government itself achieved this impasse.

As Ronald Suny pointed out, President Barack Obama acknowledged the genocide before his election, and continued to insist that his opinion had not changed. Nevertheless, Suny highlighted, Obama "refused to use the inflammatory 'G' word as a matter of policy." Instead, he used "'*meds yeghern*,' the Armenian word for 'great crime' or 'catastrophe.'" Thus, "Realpolitik usually trumps historical truth and morality."[87] At last, under President Joe Biden, the Armenian lobby achieved its aim.

Congressional representation can also behave like an ethnic lobby. Cuban Americans serving in the House of Representatives and the Senate over the years also influenced American policy toward Cuba, especially via the Cuban Democracy Act sponsored by the Cuban American National Foundation. Cuban Americans serving in the House of Representatives and the Senate over the years also influenced US policy toward Cuba. Almost all were Republicans and opposed the lifting of the US embargo. Donatella della Porta and Sidney Tarrow called this internalization—playing out on domestic territory conflicts that have their origin externally.[88] They identified this as one of three transnational political processes, along with diffusion and externalization. Immigrants do also engage in externalization when they target a supra-national organization (e.g., the European Parliament or the United Nations) as an arena through which to present their social movement claims regarding human rights abuses in their homeland. In this external organization, their transnational collective action can be recognized as legitimate.

Political transnationalism increasingly takes the form of party politics. Immigrants living abroad are becoming a part of the political life in their home country, not only through absentee voting but also as representatives overseas. Enormous variation exists. At one end of the spectrum is the participation of Mexican immigrants in Mexico's elections; at the other end is the participation of Dominican immigrants in the Dominican Republic's elections. Since 2006, Mexican immigrants living in the United States can participate in the elections in Mexico, but the process involved is arduous, as they must return home to fill out the paperwork, risking the return to American soil if undocumented. In the 2012 presidential election in Mexico, only 30,000 Mexicans living in the United States voted. In the most recent 2018 election for President Andrés Manuel López-Obrador, founder of the National Regeneration Movement Party (*Morena*), more than twice the number in the previous election were registered to vote.[89] However, their participation remained quite small.

By contrast, in the Dominican Republic, participation has become representation, to such an extent that Dominicans living overseas (approximately 5 percent of the electorate) can decide the results of the presidential elections in the Caribbean island.[90] The 2012 presidential election was hotly contested, as the popular incumbent president, Leonel Fernández, could not serve another term. It was also the first to involve participation by Dominican citizens abroad who no longer had to fly to the island to vote. From afar, they not only voted for the president and the vice president, they also voted for the Chamber of Deputies. In this election, 6.5 million Dominican voters were eligible to vote. Fully 38 percent of the expatriate electorate resided in the United States, and 19 percent resided in Spain, with more than 100,000 of the eligible voters residing in New York. As José Itzigsohn pointed out, the Dominican Republic has become a transnational nation—one where the boundaries of belonging are no longer circumscribed by the territorial boundaries of the nation.[91]

The immigrants' legal status and type of migration matter. Groups that encompass a large number of undocumented workers, such as Mexicans or Salvadorans, have less voting power than their sheer numbers would imply, even when they are very concentrated, as in California and Texas. By contrast, Cubans encompass few undocumented workers because from the early 1960s on, they were easily granted refugee status. They were seen as victims of communism, as President Lyndon B. Johnson put it, when he passed the Cuban Adjustment Act that allowed Cubans to become legal residents one year (and a day) after a legal entry. Similarly, a large concentration in certain states matters, but is not sufficient. In California, for example, the Mexican and Salvadoran populations are very large, but since the state itself always votes with the Democrats, in national elections politicians do not court the state of California. By contrast, Florida has become critical because in national elections it is a swing state that carries a great deal of weight. Thus, Donald Trump did everything he could to court the Cuban American vote. Concentration in a swing state, such as Florida, gives immigrant groups there—whether Cubans, Puerto Ricans, Colombians, Nicaraguans, or Venezuelans—more political say than if they resided elsewhere.

Immigrants seek to influence the political life of their home country as well as their host country. More often than not, the political life rests on the work of women volunteers who organize the gatherings, do the legwork, bring the food, recruit new members, and mail the announcements. However, in the traditional societies that immigrants often come from, women are seldom at the forefront of politics. Immigrant politics is still very much a man's game, though resting on the volunteer work of women.

The immigrants' return migration and their involvement with life in their homelands was due not only to their bonds of love and loyalty for the family and nation left behind, but was also due to their lack of acceptance in America. Michel Laguerre used the broader concept of diasporic citizenship to underline that Haitian immigrants became politically involved with life in Haiti to "escape complete minoritization since the link with the homeland allows one to enjoy the majority status one cannot exercise in the adopted country."[92] Thus, Laguerre underscored the difference that race—being Black and immigrant—made. With Haiti's long history of political repression, the diaspora was playing the role of the missing political center—between the army and the government, siding with the people, thus helping the development of civil society and democracy in Haiti. As David Hollinger underscored, the new immigration, like the old, "displays a variety of degrees of engagement with the United States and with prior homelands, and it yields some strong assimilationist impulses along with vivid expressions of diasporic consciousness."[93]

Immigrants whose community is composed of large numbers of labor migrants, many of whom lack legal status, as with Mexicans and Central Americans, are marginalized and experience hostility where they live. Thus, they are more likely to seek political identification with their homeland and seek to effect change there. Immigrants whose community is composed of large numbers of refugees who do have legal status and high rates of naturalization, such as Cubans, Vietnamese, Cambodians, Laotians, Hmong, and Somalians, are better able to express their political views through the ballot box and through lobbying Congress.

The immigrants' engagement with life in their old country may express a very different political agenda than that of those who remained behind. That has always been the case for Cuban immigrants, many of whom sought to undermine the Cuban revolution since they saw it as illegitimate and anti-democratic, given its lack of elections, as well as anti-American. By contrast, Cubans who remained on the island saw their revolution as a legitimate expression of the people and its socialism-*cum*-communism as a democratic form; the intrusion of the United States, such as the trade embargo as well as the exile invasion at Bay of Pigs, rendered their extreme nationalism legitimate.

The governments of the nations the immigrants left behind at times also actively court the support of their émigrés, if it is to their benefit, particularly if it serves to counter their lack of popularity at home. For example, in Turkey, the autocratic, Islamist government of Recep Tayyip Erdoğan has actively courted the Turkish diaspora in Germany since they are seen as being in favor of his conservative, populist policies and his Justice and Development Party (*AK Parti* in Turkish). The government went as far as changing voting policies to allow Turks in Germany to participate in the last presidential election in Turkey in 2018. Yet another example is the way in which the Israeli government, through its Ministry of Aliyah and Integration, courts the identification of American Jews with Israel through a scholarship that pays for their *Aliyah*, which in Hebrew means "ascent." Jewish tradition views traveling to the land of Israel as an ascent, both geographically and metaphysically. However, given Israel's militarism and discriminatory treatment of Palestinians, for many young American Jews, their identification with Israel as their own Jewish state has now become increasingly problematic. Just as often, the governments of the nations the immigrants left behind also try to keep the participation of their émigrés at bay, afraid of the political impact they may have.

A diaspora that has developed over a long time can also become a political actor, particularly among refugees. As I have argued, this may give rise to an "impossible triangle" developing among three poles: the homeland government, the host government, and the exile community.[94] When the host government sides with one, it betrays the other. When the exile community is divided between intransigents and moderates, as among Cuban exiles, every move the host government makes betrays part of that community. Thus, when President Obama re-established relations with Cuba, after fifty-four years of their severance, the moderates felt encouraged, while the intransigents felt betrayed; when President Trump undid most of Obama's new policies toward Cuba and issued new sanctions that resembled those during the Cold War, the intransigents felt vindicated and the moderates felt betrayed.

To date, while the issue of gender has made a lot of headway in studies of economic transnationalism, it is mostly absent from studies of political transnationalism—perhaps because politics is still, largely, a man's game. Occasionally, there are women who stand out (e.g., Kamala Harris, the vice president of the United States) as playing an important political role—but they do so as an exception.

Governments do try to restrict the flows of communication involved in transnationalism, as was the case in the United States in 2004, under President George W. Bush, and in 2019, under President Donald J. Trump. But these restrictions only temporarily reduce the flow of people, goods, and money. Governments may try to stop the immigrants' transnationalism, but they will not be able to do so because transnationalism is a fact of the modern (or post-modern) world in which we live, a result of the spread of new forms of communication. Immigrants develop a bicultural identity that is loyal to their new country as well as to their original homeland. Such an identity is not only fragmented but also sharper in its sensibility—not unlike Park's concept of the "marginal man" at the beginning of the twentieth century.[95] A bicultural identity is not only the result of transnationalism but is that on which transnationalism rests. Precisely because transnationalism depends on such a bicultural identity, one can expect that the second generation, the children of immigrants, will participate in such a transnational social field to a much lesser extent.[96] However, even a small group of the second and third generations can play an influential role transferring ideas and resources.

Several questions around the political aspects of transnationalism remain for future research: To what extent is transnationalism possible in different social and political contexts? What is the role of immigrants' political identification in party formation, in voting, and in the development of political lobbies? What is the role of gender?

Social Transnationalism

Remittances can also be of a social nature—the ideas, behavior, identities, social capital, and knowledge that migrants acquire during their residence abroad that can be transferred to their homelands.[97] In *Migrating Faith* (2017), Daniel Ramírez's study of the spread of

Pentecostalism in Mexico and the United States, he added the notion of religious remittances—those symbolic goods sent or brought by migrants to prompt or maintain their families' and friends' conversion and new religious identity.[98] These involved repairing Catholic temples, financing the feast of the patron saint, creating ex-voto *retablos* (images of what they prayed for) on tin sheets, and writing songs and singing in choruses that expressed the migrants' faith. This research naturally considered gender.

Transnationalism depends on the network of family and friends left behind; it also strengthens those networks. People involved in a transnational social field often develop a more cosmopolitan outlook.[99] Yet traditional gender norms may constrain the movement of women between their two homes—for example, between Italy and Morocco. Women who shared the experience of migration from their country (e.g., Spain) to lend their labor to another (e.g., Germany) can develop very strong bonds with other such women.

Since migration often separates family members, numerous articles have focused on the issue of transnational motherhood. Pierrette Hondagneu-Sotelo and Ernestina Avila addressed the motherhood of Latinas who worked as nannies or housekeepers in Los Angeles while their children remained in their homeland.[100] Based on a survey, ethnography, and interviews, they examined how such women transform the meanings of motherhood to accommodate these separations.

José Itzigsohn and Silvia Giorguli-Saucedo stressed that social transnationalism refers to those social practices that are more affective-oriented and less instrumental than political or economic transnationalism.[101] They are those involving a sense of solidarity based on ethnicity or nationality, religion, or place of origin, such as township committees, ethnic and cultural clubs, charity organizations, churches, and disaster-relief organizations. These may assist the process of incorporation. In 1997–98, they conducted a survey of 1,202 immigrant households: Dominicans in Providence and New York City; Colombians in New York City; and Salvadorans in Washington DC and Los Angeles. They distinguished three types of transnationalism: reactive transnationalism, linear transnationalism, and resource-dependent transnationalism. They focused on three different immigrant groups to consider different histories of migration. Salvadorans largely left for political reasons, escaping a civil war. Dominicans largely left for economic reasons. Colombians left for political reasons, to escape the drug-related violence and the civil war. Contrary to expectations, through their index of sociocultural transnationalism, they found that the more education, the more involvement in transnational activities; and that incorporation and transnationalism seemed to go hand in hand. In addition, the authors found clear gender differences. Men's transnational involvement was more likely to be of the reactive transnationalism type—i.e., that discrimination, in general, did lead to men's increased transnational participation. For women, their transnational involvement was more likely to be resource-dependent. In general, they found that the greater the exposure to life in America, the higher the socioeconomic status, and the more satisfaction with the opportunities they encountered, the more transnational involvement by the immigrants. In fact, they found the two processes of transnationalism and incorporation were intertwined and concurrent.

Overall, the available research paid little attention to the psychological well-being or mental health outcomes of transnationalism. An exception was the work of Eleanor Murphy and Ramaswami Mahalingam.[102] They developed a "Transnationalism Scale" with twenty-one items that pertained to five major factors. Their sample came from English-speaking West Indian immigrants. While they often assimilated into the Black American population, they came from countries where they were the majority, so they could leave the experience of slavery and colonization far behind. Like most immigrants, they came believing that their hard work would be fairly rewarded. Murphy and Mahalingam found that transnationalism had important implications for the immigrants' social adaptation as well as their psychological well-being. Of the five factors, Social and Family-related Communication yielded the highest score, as it was significantly correlated with social support, ethnic identity, and perceived stress. Clearly it served as an emotional buffer.

Several questions around the social aspects of transnationalism remain for future research: To what extent is social transnationalism possible in different social and political contexts? What are the impacts of social and religious remittances? What is the role of gender? Moreover, what is the role of sexuality?

As we have seen, transnationalism has both positive and negative consequences. The positive consequence is that transnationalism gives immigrants and their family emotional health—a present that is tied to their past, a family that remains united, albeit at a distance. It also gives immigrants and their families left behind substantial economic health. It also matters in fostering the development of their homeland overall and their village or town, in particular. But the negative consequence is that this may well come at the price of the immigrants becoming incorporated, assimilated—both culturally and structurally—in America.

It is quite likely that the shift in concepts—from assimilation to transnationalism—will only be useful to describe the lived experience of the immigrant generation. That, however, is a necessity at a time like now when America is not only "a nation of immigrants"—whose history was written by immigrants—but is also an immigrant nation—whose present relies on immigration. Despite the current efforts to stem the rising tide of immigration into America, the nation's future will be shaped by the new waves of immigrants—as was its past. America's future depends on everyone: its old, established groups of immigrants (such as Irish Americans, German Americans, Italian Americans, Polish Americans, Jewish Americans); its old and new racial minorities (such as Black Americans, Mexican Americans, Native Americans, Korean Americans, Japanese Americans); as well as its new, not yet settled groups of immigrants (such as Colombian Americans, Peruvian Americans, Cuban Americans, Salvadoran Americans, Arab Americans, Chinese Americans, Vietnamese Americans). To my mind, America's capacity to weave a cloth from all these cultural threads has always been its strength. It remains so as we continue to expand America's diversity buttressed by greater equality.

NOTES

1 Silvia Pedraza, "Assimilation or Transnationalism? Conceptual Models of the Immigrant Experience," in *Cultural Psychology of Immigrants*, ed. Ramaswami Mahalingam (Mahwah, NJ: Lawrence Erlbaum, 2006), 33–54.

2 Silvia Pedraza, "Women and Migration: The Social Consequences of Gender," *Annual Review of Sociology* 17 (1991): 304.

3 Talcott Parsons, *The Structure of Social Action* (New York: Free Press, 1968), 16.

4 Everett S. Lee, "A Theory of Migration," *Demography* 3 (1966): 47–57.

5 Oscar Handlin, *The Uprooted: The Epic Story of the Great Migrations that Made the American People* (Boston, MA: Little, Brown, 1951).

6 Handlin, *The Uprooted*, 7.

7 Steven J. Gold and Bruce Phillips, "Mobility and Continuity among Eastern European Jews," in *Origins and Destinies: Immigration, Race, and Ethnicity in America*, ed. Silvia Pedraza and Rubén G. Rumbaut (Belmont, CA: Wadsworth, 1996), 182–194.

8 John Bodnar, *The Transplanted: A History of Immigrants in Urban America* (Bloomington: Indiana University Press, 1985).

9 Louis Althusser and Etiénne Balibar, *Reading Capital* (London: NLB, 1970); Silvia Pedraza, "Talcott Parsons and Structural Marxism: Functionalist Theories of Society," *Current Perspectives in Social Theory* 3 (1982): 207–224.

10 Manuel Castells, "Immigrant Workers and Class Struggles in Advanced Capitalism: The Western European Experience," *Politics & Society* 5, no. 1 (1975): 33–66; Michael Burawoy, "The Functions and Reproduction of Migrant Labor: Comparative Material from Southern Africa and the United States," *American Journal of Sociology* 81, no. 5 (1976): 1050–1087; Alejandro Portes, "Migration and Underdevelopment," *Politics & Society* 8, no. 2 (1978): 1–48.

11 Silvia Pedraza-Bailey, *Political and Economic Migrants in America: Cubans and Mexicans* (Austin: University of Texas Press, 1985).

12 Alejandro Portes and Rubén G. Rumbaut, *Immigrant America: A Portrait* (Berkeley: University of California Press, 2006).

13 Monica Boyd, "Family and Personal Networks in International Migration: Recent Developments and New Agendas," *International Migration Review* 23, no. 3 (1989): 638–670.

14 Pedraza, "Women and Migration."

15 Douglas S. Massey, "Why Does Immigration Occur? A Theoretical Synthesis," in *The Handbook of International Migration: The American Experience*, ed. Charles Hirschman, Philip Kasinitz, and Josh DeWind (New York: Russell Sage Foundation, 1999), 34–52.

16 Douglas S. Massey, Rafael Alarcón, Jorge Durand, and Humberto González, *Return to Aztlan: The Social Process of International Migration from Western Mexico* (Berkeley: University of California Press, 1987).

17 Katharine M. Donato, Joseph T. Alexander, Donna R. Gabaccia, and Johanna Leinonen, "Variations in the Gender Composition of Immigrant Populations: How They Matter," *International Migration Review* 45, no. 3 (2011): 495–526.

18 Donato et al., "Variations in the Gender Composition of Immigrant Populations," 512.

19 Hasia R. Diner, *Erin's Daughters in America: Irish Immigrant Women in the Nineteenth Century* (Baltimore, MD: Johns Hopkins University Press, 1983).

20 Robert A. Orsi, *The Madonna of 115th Street: Faith and Community in Italian Harlem, 1880–1950* (New Haven, CT: Yale University Press, 1985).

21 Daniel Ramírez, *Migrating Faith: Pentecostalism in the United States and Mexico in the Twentieth Century* (Chapel Hill: University of North Carolina Press, 2017).

22 Thomas A. Tweed, *Our Lady of the Exile: Diasporic Religion at a Cuban Catholic Shrine in Miami* (New York: Oxford University Press, 1997).

23 Jacqueline Maria Hagan, *Migration Miracle: Faith, Hope, and Meaning on the Undocumented Journey* (Cambridge, MA: Harvard University Press, 2008).

24 Paula L. Aymer, *Uprooted Women: Migrant Domestics in the Caribbean* (Westport, CT: Praeger, 1997).

25 *Issei, nisei,* and *sansei* are Japanese words for first-generation, second-generation, and third-generation immigrants. Evelyn Nakano Glenn, *Issei, Nisei, War Bride: Three Generations of Japanese American Women in Domestic Service* (Philadelphia, PA: Temple University Press, 1986).

26 See Zhou's chapter in this volume.

27 Glenn, *Issei, Nisei, War Bride.*

28 Irving Howe, *World of Our Fathers: The Journey of the East European Jews to America and the Life They Found and Made* (New York: Simon & Schuster, 1976); Roger Waldinger, "Immigrant Transnationalism," *Current Sociology* 61, nos. 5–6 (2013): 756–777.

29 María Patricia Fernández-Kelly and Anna García, "Power Surrendered, Power Restored: The Politics of Home and Work among Hispanic Women in Southern California and Southern Florida," in *Women, Change, and Politics,* ed. Louise A. Tilly and Patricia Gurin (New York: Russell Sage Foundation, 1991), 130–149.

30 Patricia R. Pessar, "The Linkage between the Household and Workplace in the Experience of Dominican Immigrant Women in the United States," *International Migration Review* 18, no. 4 (1984): 1188–1211; Helen I. Safa, "Female Employment and the Social Reproduction of the Puerto Rican Working Class," *International Migration Review* 18, no. 4 (1984): 1168–1187.

31 Yolanda Prieto, "Cuban Women in the U.S. Labor Force: Perspectives on the Nature of the Change," *Cuban Studies* 17 (1987): 73–91.

32 Pessar, "The Linkage between the Household and Workplace in the Experience of Dominican Immigrant Women in the United States"; Min Zhou, *Chinatown: The Socioeconomic Potential of an Urban Enclave* (Philadelphia, PA: Temple University Press, 1992).

33 Sydney S. Weinberg, *The World of Our Mothers: The Lives of Jewish Immigrant Women* (Chapel Hill: University of North Carolina Press, 1988); Howe, *World of Our Fathers.*

34 Sherri Grasmuck and Patricia R. Pessar, *Between Two Islands: Dominican International Migration* (Berkeley: University of California Press, 1991).

35 Susan C. Pearce, Elizabeth J. Clifford, and Reena Tandon, *Immigration and Women: Understanding the American Experience* (New York: New York University Press, 2011).

36 Pearce et al., *Immigration and Women.*

37 Grasmuck and Pessar, *Between Two Islands.*

38 Massey et al., *Return to Aztlan.*

39 Shawn Malia Kanaiaupuni, "Reframing the Migration Question: An Analysis of Men, Women, and Gender in Mexico," *Social Forces* 78, no. 4 (2000): 1311–1348.

40 Kanaiaupuni, "Reframing the Migration Question," 1312.

41 Alejandro Portes, Samuel A. McLeod, Jr., and Robert N. Parker, "Immigrant Aspirations," *Sociology of Education* 51, no. 4 (1978): 241–260.

42 Robert E. Park, "Human Migration and the Marginal Man," *American Journal of Sociology* 33, no. 6 (1928): 881–893; Robert Ezra Park, *Race and Culture* (New York: Free Press, 1950); William I. Thomas and Florian Znaniecki, *The Polish Peasant in Europe and America*, 2 vols. (New York: Alfred A. Knopf, 1927).

43 Park, *Race and Culture*.

44 Milton M. Gordon, *Assimilation in American Life: The Role of Race, Religion and National Origins* (New York: Oxford University Press, 1964).

45 Fernando Ortiz, *Contrapunteo Cubano del Tabaco y el Azúcar* [Cuban counterpoint: tobacco and sugar] (La Habana, Cuba: Editorial de Ciencias Sociales, 1983 [1963]).

46 Paul Cowan, *An Orphan in History: Retrieving a Jewish Legacy* (New York: Doubleday, 1982).

47 Joe R. Feagin, *Racial and Ethnic Relations* (Englewood Cliffs, NJ: Prentice-Hall, 1978).

48 Richard Alba and Victor Nee, *Remaking the American Mainstream: Assimilation and Contemporary Immigration* (Cambridge, MA: Harvard University Press, 2003).

49 Silvia Pedraza and Rubén G. Rumbaut, eds., *Origins and Destinies: Immigration, Race, and Ethnicity in America* (Belmont, CA: Wadsworth, 1996).

50 John Higham, *Strangers in the Land: Patterns of American Nativism, 1860–1925* (New Brunswick, NJ: Rutgers University Press, 1955).

51 Allison Davis, Burleigh B. Gardner, and Mary R. Gardner, *Deep South: A Social Anthropological Study of Caste and Class* (Los Angeles: Center for Afro-American Studies, University of California, 1988).

52 Melvin L. Oliver and Thomas M. Shapiro, *Black Wealth/White Wealth: A New Perspective on Racial Inequality* (New York: Routledge, 2006).

53 Reynolds Farley and Richard Alba, "The New Second Generation in the U.S.," *International Migration Review* 36, no. 3 (2002): 669–701.

54 Edward E. Telles and Vilma Ortiz, *Generations of Exclusion: Mexican Americans, Assimilation, and Race* (New York: Russell Sage Foundation, 2018).

55 Margaret A. Gibson, *Accommodation without Assimilation: Sikh Immigrants in an American High School* (Ithaca, NY: Cornell University Press, 1998).

56 Min Zhou, "Growing Up American: The Challenge Confronting Immigrant Children and Children of Immigrants," *Annual Review of Sociology* 23 (1997): 63–95.

57 Margaret A. Gibson, "Complicating the Immigrant/Involuntary Minority Typology," *Anthropology and Education Quarterly* 28, no. 3 (1997): 442.

58 Gibson, "Complicating the Immigrant/Involuntary Minority Typology," 442.

59 Alba and Nee, *Remaking the American Mainstream*, 12.

60 Alba and Nee, *Remaking the American Mainstream*, 270.

61 Alejandro Portes and Min Zhou, "The New Second Generation: Segmented Assimilation and Its Variants," *The Annals of the American Academy of Political and Social Science* 530, no. 1 (1993): 74–96.

62 Roger Rouse, "Making Sense of Settlement: Class Transformations, Cultural Struggle, and Transnationalism among Mexican Immigrants in the United States," Special issue titled "Towards a Transnational Perspective on Migration," ed. Nina Glick Schiller, Linda Basch, and Cristina Blanc-Szanton, *Annals of the New York Academy of Sciences* 645 (1992): 45.

63 Linda Basch, Nina Glick Schiller, and Cristina Szanton Blanc, *Nations Unbound: Transnational Projects, Postcolonial Predicaments, and Deterritorialized Nation States* (Langhorne, PA: Gordon and Breach, 1994).

64 Basch, Schiller, and Blanc, *Nations Unbound*, 7.

65 Barry Goldberg, "Historical Reflections on Transnationalism, Race, and the American Immigrant Saga," Special issue titled "Towards a Transnational Perspective on Migration," ed. Nina Glick Schiller, Linda Basch, and Cristina Blanc-Szanton, *Annals of the New York Academy of Sciences* 645 (1992): 205.

66 Goldberg, "Historical Reflections on Transnationalism," 205.

67 Nancy Foner, "What's New about Transnationalism? New York Immigrants Today and at the Turn of the Century," *Diaspora: A Journal of Transnational Studies* 6, no. 3 (1997): 355–375; José Moya, "Diaspora Studies: New Concepts, Approaches, and Realities?" Paper presented at the meeting of the Social Science History Association, Chicago, IL, November 18–21, 2004); Waldinger, "Immigrant Transnationalism."

68 Foner, "What's New about Transnationalism?"

69 Pedraza, "Women and Migration."

70 Waldinger, "Immigrant Transnationalism."

71 Elizabeth M. Aranda, *Emotional Bridges to Puerto Rico: Migration, Return Migration, and the Struggles of Incorporation* (Lanham, MD: Rowman & Littlefield, 2006).

72 Waldinger, "Immigrant Transnationalism."

73 David A. Hollinger, *Postethnic America: Beyond Multiculturalism* (New York: Basic Books, 1995); Moya, "Diaspora Studies."

74 Luis Eduardo Guarnizo and Michael Peter Smith, "The Locations of Transnationalism," *Transnationalism from Below: Comparative Urban & Community Research*, vol. 6, ed. Michael Peter Smith and Luis Eduardo Guarnizo (New York: Routledge, 1998): 3–34.

75 Guarnizo and Smith, "The Locations of Transnationalism," 20.

76 Ernesto Castañeda, *A Place to Call Home: Immigrant Exclusion and Urban Belonging in New York, Paris, and Barcelona* (Stanford, CA: Stanford University Press, 2018).

77 Dilip Ratha et al., "Data Release: Remittances to Low and Middle-Income Countries on Track to Reach $551 Billion in 2019 and $597 Billion by 2021," World Bank, October 16, 2019.

78 Susan Eva Eckstein, *The Immigrant Divide: How Cuban Americans Changed the U.S. and Their Homeland* (New York: Routledge, 2009).

79 Pedraza, "Women and Migration."

80   Alejandro Portes and Robert L. Bach, *Latin Journey: Cuban and Mexican Immigrants in the United States* (Berkeley: University of California Press, 1985).

81   Elizabeth Fussell, "The Cumulative Causation of International Migration in Latin America," *The Annals of the American Academy of Political and Social Science* 630, no. 1 (2010): 162–177.

82   Jorge Duany, "Nation on the Move: The Construction of Cultural Identities in Puerto Rico and the Diaspora," *American Ethnologist* 27, no. 1 (2000): 5–30.

83   Luis Noe-Bustamante, Antonio Flores, and Sono Shah, "Facts on Hispanics of Puerto Rican Origin in the United States 2017," PEW Research Center, Hispanic Trends, September 16, 2019.

84   Sarah A. Blue, "The Erosion of Racial Equality in the Context of Cuba's Dual Economy," *Latin American Politics and Society* 49, no. 3 (2007): 35–68.

85   Silvia Pedraza, *Political Disaffection in Cuba's Revolution and Exodus* (New York: Cambridge University Press, 2007).

86   Harriett D. Romo, "First Class: Transnational Lives of the Upper Middle Class in San Antonio, Texas." Paper presented at the meetings of the Latin American Studies Association, Las Vegas, Nevada, October 9–11, 2004.

87   Ronald Grigor Suny, "The Cost of Turkey's Genocide Denial," *New York Times,* April 24, 2015, www.nytimes.com.

88   Donatella della Porta and Sidney Tarrow, eds., *Transnational Political Protest and Global Activism* (Lanham, MD: Rowman & Littlefield, 2005).

89   Jonathan Blitzer, "Inside the Campaign to Register Mexicans in the U.S. to Vote—in Mexico," *The New Yorker,* April 12, 2018, www.newyorker.com.

90   Robert Courtney Smith, "Contradictions of Diasporic Institutionalization in Mexican Politics: The 2006 Migrant Vote and Other Forms of Inclusion and Control," *Ethnic and Racial Studies* 31, no. 4 (2008): 708–741.

91   José Itzigsohn, "A 'Transnational Nation'? Migration and the Boundaries of Belonging," in *Politics from Afar: Transnational Diasporas and Networks,* ed. Peter Mandaville and Terrence Lyons (London, UK: Hurst, 2012), 181–196.

92   Michel S. Laguerre, *Diasporic Citizenship: Haitian Americans in Transnational America* (New York: St. Martin's Press, 1998), 192.

93   Hollinger, *Postethnic America,* 153.

94   Pedraza, *Political Disaffection in Cuba's Revolution and Exodus;* Silvia Pedraza and Carlos A. Romero, *Revolutions in Cuba and Venezuela: One Hope, Two Realities* (Gainesville: University of Florida Press, forthcoming).

95   Park, "Human Migration and the Marginal Man."

96   Peggy Levitt and Mary C. Waters, *The Changing Face of Home: The Transnational Lives of the Second Generation* (New York: Russell Sage Foundation, 2002).

97   Peggy Levitt, *The Transnational Villagers* (Berkeley: University of California Press, 2001).

98   Daniel Ramírez, *Migrating Faith: Pentecostalism in the United States and Mexico in the Twentieth Century* (Chapel Hill: University of North Carolina Press, 2017).

99 Steven Vertovec, "Transnationalism and Identity," *Journal of Ethnic and Migration Studies* 27, no. 4 (2001): 573–582.

100 Pierrette Hondagneu-Sotelo and Ernestina Avila, "'I'm Here, but I'm There': The Meanings of Latina Transnational Motherhood," *Gender & Society* 11, no. 5 (1997): 548–571.

101 José Itzigsohn and Silvia Giorguli-Saucedo, "Incorporation, Transnationalism, and Gender: Immigrant Incorporation and Transnational Participation as Gendered Processes," *International Migration Review* 39, no. 4 (2005.): 895–920.

102 Eleanor J. Murphy and Ramaswami Mahalingam, "Transnational Ties and Mental Health of Caribbean Immigrants," *Journal of Immigrant Health* 6, no. 4 (2004): 167–178.

11

Remittances as Transnationalism

The Case of Bangladeshi Immigrants in Los Angeles

HASAN MAHMUD

It is not about the money being sent home, it is about the
impact on people's lives. The small amounts of $200 or
$300 that each migrant sends home make up about 60 per
cent of the family's household income, and this makes an
enormous difference in their lives and the communities in
which they live.
—Gilbert F. Houngbo[1]

One of the most obvious outcomes of international migration is migrant
remittances. Migration theories started investigating remittances as a
scholarly topic in the 1980s with the introduction of the New Economics
of Labor Migration (NELM) perspective, which conceptualizes remittances as the primary goal of economic/labor migrants.[2] In reality, it is
not just economic migrants, but all kinds of migrants who send remittances to their families at some points in their migratory life.[3] In 2015,
the United Nations (UN) began celebrating June 16 as the International
Day of Family Remittance (IDFR), to recognize the contribution of
migrant remittances "to the wellbeing of their families back home and
to the sustainable development of their countries of origin."[4] This for-
malization of the idea that remittances constitute a development fund
was supported by twenty-two UN organizations, joined by money transfer operators (MTOs), mobile phone companies, savings banks, and
several individual private sector entities. But the migrants themselves
were absent from this recognition and celebration of the developmental
consequences of remittances. This alludes, on one hand, to a general
tendency in the discourses on *migration-development nexus*, whereby

academics and policymakers talk about the developmental potentials of remittances without including the migrants. On the other hand, scholars focus on various other forms of transnationalism with marginal attention to migrant remittances. In this chapter, I shed light on the migrants' perspective about their remittances as a transnational practice.

Remittances—or, the money migrants send back home—has emerged as one of the most visible forms of immigrant transnational practices.[5] According to a World Bank estimate, immigrants sent home a total of $508 billion in 2020, out of which $409 billion went to developing countries.[6] In addition, migrants held more than $500 billion in annual savings, which, together with remittances, created a substantial source of financing for projects that could improve lives and livelihoods in developing countries. Little wonder that scholars have been enthusiastic about migrant remittance as a new "development mantra."[7] Development-related optimism regarding migrant remittance emerged in a period when scholars were recognizing that traditional Official Development Assistance (ODA) was unable to deliver on its promise to help poor countries achieve their millennium development goals.[8] Scholars recognize that the UN's recommended increase in development spending by 0.7 percent of the GDP of the donor countries is unlikely to happen, an acknowledgment that further strengthens development-related optimism about migrant remittance.[9]

Why do migrants send remittances? An adequate understanding of remittances involves examining not only the motivations but also the kind of migrants sending remittances. In the discourse of migrant remittances, the dominant notion is that migrants go abroad to work and earn money to send home. This implies that most international migrants are economic migrants, a category distinct from refugees and asylees.[10] But conceptualizing economic migrants in terms of an absence of the defining characteristic (i.e., not being refugees or asylees) makes the category "economic migrant" an open-ended one, which becomes difficult to examine empirically. For instance, while refugees and asylees are precisely defined by the United Nations High Commissioner for Refugees (UNHCR) as those fleeing to avoid persecution in their home country,[11] all other migrants *without* such threats are conceived as going abroad in search of better opportunities. That is, those migrating without a recognized threat to life are all economic migrants, assumed to have been motivated by their economic interests—a rational subject to be studied as an autonomous individual voluntarily deciding to maximize self-interest in the labor market. But people do migrate for reasons other than the purely political or economic ones, and may end up migrating to join their families abroad through marriage or to be unified with their parents, for instance.

Take Bangladeshi immigrants as an example. Nearly all Bangladeshi immigrants are categorized as economic migrants. They often migrate to other countries with clear economic motivations, including sending home remittances as one of their most prominent motives. Most Bangladeshi immigrants stay abroad for a certain period, while some settle in their destination countries for their entire professional career (e.g., those in the Middle East), or permanently (those in the UK, the United States, Australia, and so forth). They build coethnic communities and frequently engage with their families and relatives back in Bangladesh.

Transnationalism among these migrants has been explored by several scholars looking at the formation of ethnic community, transnational identity, religious and political engagement, marriage practices, and developmental consequences seen in the transformation of gender roles, property relations, and infrastructural development in the origin communities in Bangladesh.[12] With the oldest connections through colonial relations, it is not surprising that most of these studies looked at Bangladeshi migrants living in the UK. Recently, scholars began to study Bangladeshi migrants in other countries and to explore their transnationalism, including in the United States,[13] Italy,[14] Malaysia,[15] and Portugal.[16]

Bangladesh has been recognized as one of the top remittances-receiving countries, with $20 billion received in 2020, constituting more than 6 percent of the country's total GDP.[17] Remittances have become the second largest source of foreign currency earnings for Bangladesh after the ready-made garments industry. The largest portion of remittances to Bangladesh comes from the earnings of Bangladeshi temporary migrant workers in Gulf countries in the Middle East, followed by those in Southeast Asia. According to Bangladesh central bank data for the fiscal year 2018–2019, the highest amount of remittances were $3,110.39 million from the Kingdom of Saudi Arabia, followed by $2,540.41 million from the United Arab Emirates, and $1,197.63 million from Malaysia.[18] Another source of remittances is the Bangladeshi diaspora in developed countries, including the UK, the United States, Australia, and Italy. In the 2018–2019 fiscal year, Bangladesh received $1,842.66 million from the United States, $1,175.63 million from the United Kingdom, and $757.88 million from Italy.[19]

Despite scholarly recognition of remittances as one of the most common forms of migrants' transnationalism, studies of Bangladeshi remittances have attracted hardly any attention from the transnationalism perspective. In fact, most studies of Bangladeshi remittances have approached the phenomenon from an economistic perspective, focusing on the developmental consequences of remittances. This alludes to a conundrum in migration research: whereas the transnationalism perspective is adopted to explore how apparently powerless migrants effectively navigate through structural barriers in the pursuit of economic as well as sociocultural well-being of themselves and their families,[20] less attention has been paid on understanding their agency or looking at how migrants perceive their remittances. Studies adopting the NELM approach tend to highlight individual migrants' motivations, but due to limitations in the theoretical framework fall short of adequately explaining why migrants send remittances.[21] In contrast, studies adopting the transnationalism approach highlight the social and cultural factors shaping migrant remittances in both the origin and destination countries.[22]

The transnationalism perspective recognizes the importance of migrants' ties across borders and how transnational social and cultural fields embed migrants' practices, including remittances.[23] From this perspective, examining migrants' sustained connections to family and community in their origin country are central to understanding their remittances. Even though they leave their families behind in the origin country, migrants remain members of their families when they go abroad; they maintain this membership via remittances. In doing so, however, migrants' perspectives about remittances are often secondary in importance to structural and cultural factors. In this chapter, I focus on the migrants' perspectives and thereby shed light on their agency in relation to remittances. This study is based on my dissertation fieldwork among Bangladeshi immigrants in Los Angeles over four years of ethnographic fieldwork between 2011 and 2015 and in-depth interviews with forty-three migrants who engaged in sending remittances. I also revisited the field and followed up with some of the key informants on several occasions during 2016 and 2019. Based on my findings, I present an account of their transnationalism by looking at remittances.

What follows is a brief discussion of migrant remittances in scholarly literature, an examination of migration and remittances in Bangladesh, an account of the migrant group studied in the United States and their transnationalism via remittances, and a conclusion that summarizes the findings and offers recommendations for future studies.

Migrant Remittances as a Scholarly Topic

We live in "the age of migration,"[24] whereby more than 272 million people, or about 3.5 percent of the total world population, are living outside their countries of origin.[25] These migrants sent home more than $508 billion in remittances in 2020.[26] At the macro level, remittances constitute more than 10 percent of the GDP of some twenty-five developing countries, allowing for increasing investments in health, education, and small businesses in various communities. At the micro level, remittances appear to be the largest source of income for millions of families in their struggle to make ends meet in an era when state support of public services continues to decline. Remittances are continuously growing, in absolute numbers as well as in comparison with ODA and other external financial flows. Therefore, when the flow dwindled as a result of the global economic recession in 2009, experts suggested various measures to encourage savings and investment in migrants' origin countries.[27] Since the high cost of remittance-transferring services is a barrier toward promotion of development, an international movement is now underway to improve the system; the United Nations' Sustainable Development Goal No.10 calls for the cost of migrants' remittance transfer to be slashed to 3 percent by 2030.

While migrants have been sending remittances to their homes in origin countries for a long time,[28] the contemporary excitement about remittances is a result of four major changes: first, remittances from international migrants have grown rapidly compared to ODA and foreign direct investment (FDI). This growth has been significant, mainly in poor and lower middle-income countries despite considerable restrictions on international migration.[29] Second, remittance flows exceed

ODA and FDI for many developing countries and represent a large percentage of their GDP. Third, considerable improvements in remittance statistics have increased governments' awareness of the potential of international remittance to alleviate poverty and contribute to economic growth and development.[30] Finally, the gradual decline in the flows of ODA encourages poor and developing countries to look for alternative sources of development-related finance.[31] Consequently, remittances from international migrants stand out as an important new source of development funds for many countries in the developing world. Scholars have documented a strong positive impact of migrants' remittances on poverty reduction in their origin countries.[32]

Furthermore, unlike ODA and FDI, which come with a variety of strings attached and involve governments and a number of other intermediaries before reaching the grassroots, migrants' remittances reach their recipients directly. Moreover, as Germano and Rodriguez observe,[33] remittances perform functions strikingly similar to those of state welfare spending, a fact that has encouraged several governments in developing countries to adopt sending migrants abroad as a de facto social welfare policy. As a result, migrants' remittances have been recognized in both academic and policy circles as a new source of development funding, especially for the origin countries of international migration in the Global South.

Migration scholars, however, demonstrate shifting positions from development-related optimism in the 1950s and 1960s to neo-Marxist pessimism over the 1970s and 1980s, toward more optimistic views in the 1990s and 2000s.[34] In fact, there was an "international buzz" in the early 2000s, when policymakers and academics working on migration and development began exploring the productive links that could be forged around the notion of a "migration-development nexus."[35] This notion captures the twin problems of growing levels of migration and the failures of development strategies increasingly apparent in the post–cold war era. These were problems that could be best tackled—it seemed—by harnessing the economic benefits brought about by migration to international development.

The massive increase in the value of remittance transfers from high-income to lower- and middle-income countries in recent years,[36] and the possibility of migrants returning home with additional skills and capital to invest in their local economies, together generated a vision of migrants as potential transnational agents of development.[37] Subsequently, international think-tanks and policy groups such as the Global Commission on International Migration (GCIM) and the Global Forum on Migration and Development (GFMD) were set up to investigate the best ways to facilitate, encourage, and manage these trends, hoping to produce "triple wins" for migrant-sending countries, migrant-receiving countries, and migrants themselves.[38] This involved facilitating remittance transfers—as a form of capital—to compensate for the "brain drain" from developing to developed countries, as well as capitalizing on "brain gain" by incorporating migrant diasporas into development strategies.

But it is important to ask whether the current exuberant focus on remittances actually promotes a distorted view of the link between migration and development. This is especially the case since the origin countries of migrants do not actually show the expected level of development, even after decades of receiving substantial amounts of remittances.[39] Moreover, the experts rarely ask migrants for what purpose they send money home.[40] In fact, migrants' motivations to send remittances home are being inferred from how these funds are spent in the origin countries, often in their absence.[41] By examining migrants' perspectives of their remittances, this chapter both offers a more nuanced explanation about why migrants send remittances and recognizes the role of contextual factors in the migrants' origin and destination countries shaping their transnational practices, including remittances.

Bangladeshi Immigration to the United States

According to the International Organization for Migration (IOM), there are approximately seven million Bangladeshis currently living abroad, making it the sixth largest origin country of international migration.[42] While the majority of these Bangladeshis include temporary migrants in the Middle East and Southeast Asia, a significant number have permanently settled in the UK, the United States, Australia, and Canada, constituting a growing Bangladeshi diaspora. The total number of Bangladeshis in the United States was 208,000 in 2019, according to a Pew Research Center estimate,[43] dwarfed only by the number of Bangladeshis in the UK. Despite their relatively small numbers, Bangladeshis in the United States send the third-largest amounts of remittances home compared to Bangladeshi migrants elsewhere in the world, perhaps due to their better economic standing.[44]

Economic migration has been recognized as a survival strategy for families experiencing resource constraints and uncertain economic prospects.[45] There is a long history of research on household coping strategies in the Global South, especially in the context of population growth, rural development, and social change in agrarian societies.[46] Since the mid-1970s, Bangladesh has been undergoing massive social changes characterized by rapid population growth and an increase of development actors including the multilateral and bilateral organizations as well as development NGOs. As Bangladesh is one of the most densely populated countries in the world, rural households cannot find agricultural employment for all members and consequently turn to informal economic activity and migration to the cities and towns.[47] The drivers of emigration from Bangladesh have continuously strengthened with the worsening and adverse impacts of climate change.[48]

Arriving at the Land of Dreams

After the independence of Bangladesh in 1971, a small number of educated middle-class Bangladeshis traveled abroad to study and took employment in developed countries, including the United States. The Bangladeshi migration to the United States was relatively small until the introduction of the Diversity Visa (DV1) lottery in the early 1990s, when Bangladeshis began migrating to the United States in the thousands. The statistical yearbooks for the US Immigration and Naturalization Service documented only 154 Bangladeshis in 1973 and 787 in 1983. In 1990, the introduction of the OP1 visa lottery (the predecessor of the DV-1 visa lottery) resulted in the admission of 10,676 immigrants from Bangladesh,[49] vastly outnumbering those entering the United States by other means. Each year, several thousand Bangladeshis entered the United States through the diversity visa lottery, until they reached the numerical threshold that excluded Bangladesh from the program in 2012.

Despite this exclusion from the government-sponsored DV-1 visa lottery program, immigration from Bangladesh to the United States continued to grow, thanks to the family unification policy of US immigration: Those with family members and close relatives who are US citizens can still enter the United States as immigrants. According to the US Department of State statistics, 14,946 Bangladeshis entered the United States on immigration visas in 2018. Almost all (14,818, or 99 percent) of these immigrants received their visas through the sponsorship of immediate family members or close relatives. The Department of State statistics show that, from 2012 to 2018, the total number of annual immigrants from Bangladesh remained at more than 12,000. Vaughan and Huennekens observe that for the 2000–2016 period,[50] the Bangladesh chain migration multiplier was 4.44, higher than the most recent worldwide average chain migration multiplier of 3.45.

The US policy toward foreign students offers another avenue for Bangladeshis to enter the United States. The US ambassador to Bangladesh reported that there were 7,143 Bangladeshi students in the United States at the graduate level in 2018, making Bangladesh ninth among the top twenty-five student-sending countries.[51] Between 2012 and 2017, the number of Bangladeshi students in the United States increased by 53.5 percent, with a 9.7 percent increase in 2017 compared to the previous year, while the international average increased by only 3.4 percent.[52] After graduation, these students usually find professional employment and acquire permanent residency and citizenship,[53] thereby facilitating further migration of their close relatives through the family unification policy. Members of the Bangladeshi diaspora community are more likely to have a university degree than the average population of the United States, and their members have a higher household income than the US median.[54]

Finally, unlike in Europe, where undocumented Bangladeshis are among the biggest groups of "illegal" migrants entering Europe across the Mediterranean Sea,[55] Bangladeshis are very rarely among the undocumented migrants in the United States. Perhaps this is due to the vast geographical distance between the two countries and the absence of transnational underground networks like those serving other well-known migrant groups. There is, however, a small but significant number of undocumented Bangladeshi migrants in the United States, many of whom overstayed their visas after legally entering the United States as tourists and visitors. The majority of them manage to legalize their stay through marriage and applying for political asylum, while a few remain undocumented.

Bangladeshis in Los Angeles

Although the Pew Research Center reports 9,000 Bangladeshis in Los Angeles, making it the fourth-largest concentration of Bangladeshi immigrants in the United States, the actual number is much higher. A clerk at the Bangladesh consulate in Los Angeles reported that the number of Bangladeshis exceeded 20,000 in Los Angeles and was about 50,000 in California overall.[56]

The Bangladeshi immigrants in my study exhibit many of the typical characteristics celebrated by scholars of transnationalism. For instance, they make full use of communication technologies to establish strong cross-border interactions and to sustain social relations in multiple places, which corroborates the notion of transmigrants transcending the borders of nation-states. They have been successful in getting official recognition for their ethnic neighborhood, named "the little Bangladesh," where they have reproduced many of the social and cultural attributes of their origin communities back home. Little Bangladesh is marked by six restaurants and ethnic stores,[57] two video shops, two liquor stores, a secondhand store, two 99-cent stores, a mosque, and a community center that hosts two after-school prep centers. On any given day, women in brightly colored traditional dresses can be seen walking along the tree-lined residential streets, often pushing babies in strollers or accompanied by young children. On the weekends, they are joined by men. In addition to selling groceries and other necessary ethnic goods, these stores serve as socializing places for almost all types of Bangladeshi migrants in Southern California.

These Bangladeshi-owned businesses symbolize the ease with which Bangladeshis permanently settle and create their own social spaces in the United States. The signboards of restaurants are written in bold Bangla, followed by smaller English letters. A strong spicy smell of cooked food wafts out the open door to whet the appetite of passersby for authentic Bangladeshi cuisine. When somebody enters the restaurant, a smiling salesperson greets them with Bangla words. Together with the ethnic goods on display, the constant presence of a few Bangladeshi customers

inside, and the ongoing Bangla programs on the TV transform the restaurant into a unique and exquisite Bangladeshi social space. It is so
ethnically representative that Bangladeshis feel at home in this place,
whereas a non-Bangladeshi immediately feels out of place. For instance,
a non-Bangladeshi commented on the Yelp webpage about one of these
restaurants:

> As soon as I walked in, I swear I was in Bangladesh, lol. There's raw meat,
> flies, and Bangladeshi people. . . . The food was pretty good. I had the
> curry goat. I can definitely assure it tastes very ethnic.[58]

The ambience in these ethnic stores and restaurants is so homelike
that they attract all types of Bangladeshi immigrants. Especially for single immigrants, these stores facilitate interactions that they used to have
in extended families and friendship circles in Bangladesh. Those settled
with family in the valley areas far away from the neighborhood also visit
these stores on weekends.

I conducted in-depth and unstructured interviews with forty-three
(38 male and 5 female) Bangladeshi migrants, all representing family
breadwinners. To maximize the diversity of perspectives, I selected interviewees in professional careers and casual work, those with families
or single, documented or undocumented, having migrated recently or
long ago, and living in an ethnic neighborhood or outside it. I identified research participants at various locations in the neighborhood,
including five ethnic stores and two mosques. I also contacted many
participants at community gatherings and social events such as "the
Bangladesh Day Parade," the Bangla New Year's celebration, etc. As I
deliberately minimized my intervention in the conversations, the interviews varied in terms of length and emphasis, lasting between 25 and 90
minutes, with most averaging around 50 minutes.

Transnationalism through Remittances

Los Angeles is home to the second largest Bangladeshi immigrant community in the United States, well over 50,000 migrants, who exhibit
most forms of transnational practices, including being a major hub of
transnational communications with their communities back home, as

well as a major source of remittances. Migrants in my study perceived their transnationalism through remittances in one of three ways—family support, aiming at upward mobility, and maintaining connection to their "roots."

Supporting the Family

Migrant remittance is transnational and characteristically involves transnational relations and practices. As Viviana Zelizer states, remittances "maintain long-distance household ties between the emigrants and people back home."[59] Moreover, remittances are often intended to ensure the welfare of family members left behind in the origin country, so much so that scholars recognize it as a "currency of care."[60] Migrants endure immense physical and mental challenges in order to earn and send remittances for their families in the origin country.[61]

Regardless of their socioeconomic status in the United States, nearly all Bangladeshis in my study reportedly sent remittances to their families and relatives in Bangladesh. A small-scale purposive survey I conducted with a sample of 350 Bangladeshis in Los Angeles revealed that they sent remittances for their parental family's budget, including education and health expenses for their parents and younger siblings. Of all remittances, these migrants sent the largest amounts of money most frequently and consistently to support their family's subsistence. As Rahman (31 years in the United States, with a wife and son) told me:

> Bangladeshis send money religiously. Since their arrival in America, they are determined that they will work in gas station or whatever work they find and send $500 or $1,000 to the family at the end of the month. They set this program in their mind from the very beginning. All those I know who have their families in Bangladesh send money every month.

In fact, the idea of sharing financial responsibility to help their families is almost universal among Bangladeshi migrants.[62] This can be explained in terms of the origin culture in Bangladesh, where sons are expected to share responsibility for their family once they grow up and begin to earn,[63] which was corroborated by my informants who shared their family's expectation of financial assistance. These migrants acknowledged their parents' contribution to their education, employment, and even migration, which reinforces the migrants' moral obligation to pay back by sending money home. Hence, they explained remittances in terms of their responsibility to financially support the family and their moral obligation to reciprocate the assistance they received from the family. In other words, these migrants perceived their remittances in terms of a moral economy, highlighting moral rather than economic motivations in sending remittances.[64]

Bangladeshi migrants' shared sense of family responsibility meant that they regularly sent home remittances as monthly allowances for their families' subsistence. However, this would change with the fragmentation of the parental family and migrants establishing their own nuclear families, leading to consequential reduction in remittance. If a migrant's parents, spouse, and children were in Bangladesh, they would send remittances regularly for the family members' subsistence. But if the migrant's own immediate family and parents lived in the United States, it would not be necessary to send remittances toward subsistence in Bangladesh. Scholars studying migrants in other contexts also recognize transnational family—members living in different countries constituting a family unit—as the most common recipient of migrants' remittances.[65]

Transnational family relationships tend to weaken and eventually dissipate over time, whether due to the fragmentation of the parental family or the movement of a migrant's entire family and close relatives (e.g., the siblings) to the United States through chain migration. While this substantially reduced these migrants' strongest motivation for sending remittances, they rarely stop sending remittances altogether. After migrants settle permanently in the United States with their family and relatives, their sociocultural motivation to send remittances to Bangladesh for family support declines. But these immigrants continue to send remittances for newly recognized motivations out of their own economic interests.

Remittances for Upward Mobility

Migration has been pursued as a strategic move by families in Bangladesh to acquire additional resources to maintain their middle- and upper-class positions,[66] or to achieve upward social mobility.[67] As the days went by in their new home in the United States, my informants—especially those working-class migrants—would realize that they had settled in a marginal life with casual jobs at the bottom of the local labor market, which gave them low incomes and small savings, and little if any social prestige. However, they recognized that their small savings translated into big enough amounts to invest in assets in Bangladesh that would bring them both income and prestige—for instance, as owners of rental homes and apartments. The amounts required to invest in Bangladesh were small compared to those in the United States. For instance, a typical monthly installment on an average-sized apartment in Dhaka city would range from USD300 to USD500.

My informants reported a range of investment initiatives, including purchasing land and apartments, depositing money in savings accounts, investing in the share market, lending at high interest, and so forth. The most common investment project was purchasing residential land and apartments in Dhaka city, followed by purchasing agricultural land in the village, and depositing savings in their own bank account. The primary motivation for purchasing land or depositing savings in a bank was economic benefit: These immigrants could not afford real estate in Los Angeles, but they could spend small amounts in monthly installments to buy land and apartments in Bangladesh. Moreover, the price of real estate was rapidly increasing in Bangladesh—almost doubling in five to eight years. Again, interest on bank savings in America was nearly zero, whereas banks in Bangladesh would pay more than 10 percent.

While the economic benefit of sending remittances to invest in income-generating projects in Bangladesh was obvious, the social gain from the newly acquired property was much higher. Despite living in poverty-stricken neighborhoods in LA and working in casual jobs, the immigrants could feel accomplished as homeowners in Dhaka. Most of my informants acknowledged that they invested in Bangladesh not only for financial reasons, but also for social recognition as homeowners or business owners, a status that was inaccessible to them in Los Angeles. Migration scholars identify similar investment patterns among other immigrant groups of low socioeconomic standing in the United States, whereby immigrants find gratification by using a transnational comparative optic to elevate their own status in their origin communities.[68]

Moreover, communities with long-standing migration flows develop a sense of migration as a necessary event in the life of young male members, who would go abroad to earn and then return with money to improve their personal as well as their family's economic lot.[69]

According to more than half of my interviewees, investing in profitable real estate in cities, particularly in Dhaka, or agricultural lands in their villages often involved collaborative initiative for the migrants, their siblings, and parents. Generally, remittances meant expectations of financial gains along with increased family status and influence.[70] However, relationships among siblings would eventually deteriorate due to a growing sense of belonging to their respective nuclear families, independent of the parental family, leading to inevitable "friction" in their sense of family membership,[71] and complicating the distribution of financial gains. Anis (21 years in Los Angeles, with a wife and three children) demonstrated this fact from his experience. Anis sent money to his family for nine years. His family bought 140 decimals of agricultural land in the village, purchased a housing plot in Dhaka, and renovated the family household premises. Anis returned to Bangladesh to get married and to claim his share of his inheritance/family property after his two younger brothers grew up, got married, and formed their own separate nuclear families. Anis found that the homestead and agricultural lands had already been given to his brothers; only the housing plot in Dhaka remained to be distributed among the three brothers. Anis was thoroughly disappointed. Most of my informants shared their experience involving worsening consequences of joint investment with parents and siblings using remittances. Consequently, they limited their contribution to such projects. In fact, all of my informants, who reportedly invested in joint projects with their brothers and sisters, asserted that they did so within the first few years only. None continued after they had lived in the United States for eight years, showing the gradual decline in this kind of remittances, as a result of the growing distance among siblings and the diminution of their collective belonging to the parental family.

Despite the corrosion of family unity and diminishing association among the siblings due to disputes over financial matters, the sheer economic profit encouraged these migrants to invest in their own projects in Bangladesh: purchasing land, depositing money in a savings account, investing in stocks and bonds, lending at high interest, etc. My informants commonly discussed two motivations for remittances related to personal investment—enhancing social status as the owner of a house in an expensive residential area of Dhaka city, and a plan to return to the origin community. Historically, land ownership in Bangladeshi society has been connected to upper-class status.[72] Like Chinese and Vietnamese migrants in the United States,[73] my informants, particularly those in the lower-middle and working classes, approached overcoming the structural barriers to accessing a respectable middle-class status in the United States by sending remittances to invest in Bangladesh and gain economic benefits as well as social status. Given their ability to sponsor siblings' migration—most of whom eventually arrived in the United States—my informants reported their awareness that their family might not be able to enjoy the properties and profits they accumulated in Bangladesh. Nevertheless, most of them said they would continue investing in Bangladesh due to their return plan.

Remittances to Maintain Connections to the "Roots"

As migrant Bangladeshi families settled, the expenses slowly but steadily grew, with growing commitments to children and social obligations in LA as well as back in the origin community. Shortly after migrant families arrived and settled in the United States, many realized the need to maintain their connections with the origin country as they would not be able to depend on their children like their parents and grandparents did. They talked about imminent separation of their children once they grow up, and attributed this to the culture of individualism in America. They perceived this as a threat to their old-age sustenance, which they planned to mitigate against by moving back to Bangladesh to live in one of their apartments and to use their savings and income from other sources.

Almost all of my informants with teenage and adult children spoke about their concern for their own life after retirement. This would encourage them to purchase property and establish income-generating sources in Bangladesh through frequent home visits, with the support of their relatives and friends who had stayed behind. Many—particularly in the working class—shared their plans to return to Bangladesh to enjoy life after retiring from the backbreaking work in the United States. Those few who were from wealthy families did not worry about establishing income sources in Bangladesh, having inherited enough from their wealthy parents as well as being equipped with considerable savings in the United States. This explains why migrants from wealthy families were less likely to send remittances to invest in projects in Bangladesh. However, they as well as their low-income compatriots mentioned nostalgia and lack of a sense of belonging to the United States in explaining their desire to return to Bangladesh.

Like various transnational scholars,[74] I observed a deep longing for the origin culture among the first-generation migrants, expressed in their continued sense of belonging to Bangladesh. I observed a group of four taxi drivers in front of Deshi [a Bangladeshi restaurant-cum-grocery store], who were debating ongoing political issues in Bangladesh. I asked them, "Why do you talk so much about Bangladeshi politics? You have got US passports, and you are not going back, are you?" They all stopped and then spoke at once, saying that they would certainly return to Bangladesh. I asked, "People from all over the world are coming to America; why don't you want to stay here?" One of them explained, "America is heaven for immigrants. Everyone perseveres and enjoys their earnings here. But it is not our country. We always miss our childhood, our adolescence. No matter how much worse the situation is in Bangladesh, we like that place." Regardless of class, occupation, and income, all of my respondents expressed their loneliness in the United States and a desire to return to Bangladesh. I recognized this social isolation most vividly among the professional and middle-class migrants.

Despite having all or most of their siblings and close relatives in the United States, the middle- and upper-middle-class migrants would often turn to distant kin in the origin village or town. Almost all of my informants in the professional and business class reportedly sent money to build and/or renovate schools, mosques, and other charitable projects in their origin communities. They also increased the amount and frequency of monetary help to distant kin and former neighbors in Bangladesh. Moreover, they would actively look for their childhood friends in Bangladesh and reconnect. For instance, one of my informants spoke about his initiative to create a Facebook group with his childhood friends in Bangladesh and in different countries abroad, and their plan to develop a gated housing community with modern facilities, where he would stay a few months every year. These professionals sent substantial amounts of remittances to Bangladesh to realize their dream of returning to their roots.

Conclusion

The transnationalism perspective is said to have liberated migration studies from the ideological debates between the functionalism and structuralist approaches by reorienting the researchers from spatially bounded nation-states to a global field consisting of social relations, cultural connections, political practices, and economic activities across time, space, and national boundaries. Conceiving migrants' origin and destination as dispersed places within various nation-states has allowed this perspective to overcome the problem of methodological nationalism.[75] It introduces the term "transmigrant," which brings transnational practices from the actor's perspective at the center of analysis. Hence, it allows for capturing the migrants' perspective regarding their remittances, and thereby taking their agency into account in scholarly studies of remittances with the possibility to overcome the limitations in the dominant economic approaches to remittances.

Contrary to the idea of migrants' constant struggle against the state control of their lives, these migrants were able to effectively utilize the rights they achieved from the state in the forms of citizenship and legal residence to permanently settle in the United States and create a space of their own. Furthermore, the legal status facilitated their access to various kinds of support from the state that not only helped them get settled with jobs, inexpensive housing, school, and healthcare, but also enhanced their capacity to engage in transnational practices, including remittances. This challenges the assimilationist assumption about migrants' integration at the destination and eventual erosion of ties to the origin. Emanating from a structural-functionalist view, the assimilationist approach highlights the decisive role of the destination state in migrants' remittances by deploying legal mechanisms regulating the migrants' separation from their families and their return home at the end of their employment.[76] Later studies also confirmed the destination state's role in shaping a migrant's propensity to send remittances through immigration policies regarding entry, period of stay, and the migrants' labor market participation in the destination country.[77] Arguably, migrants might not choose to send remittances if destination states allowed them to stay longer and settle permanently with their families. But a transnational perspective recognizes simultaneity in migrants' transnational practices and goes beyond the zero-sum conception of migrants' belonging inherent in the assimilationist perspective.[78]

Central to the transnationalism perspective is the idea of migrants' simultaneous belonging to both the home (i.e., the country of origin) and destination (i.e., the country of settlement), as Meyer recognizes in her analysis of the remittance decay hypothesis. She observes that migrants' homes—to which they assign belonging and send remittances—"can be in multiple places at the same time."[79] This is particularly true in contemporary sociopolitical contexts characterized by racialization and marginalization of immigrants in most Western destination countries, resulting in migrants' growing sense of marginalization and exclusion in the destination[80] and then transnationalism, including sending remittances.[81] This confirms the idea that legal residence and citizenship do not automatically facilitate migrants' integration in the destination country. Thus, marginalization and structural exclusion by—for instance—racialized immigration policies and labor market and consequent challenges for migrants may create a structural necessity for migrants to look back to their origin country. Yet, this should not lead us to structural determinism by assuming that such inadequacies of integration are enough for migrants to engage in transnationalism including remittances. This may be just the necessary conditions, which require the migrants' willingness to respond by actively participating in transnationalism.

An emphasis on the migrants' life course—or, migration trajectory—allows for recognizing their agency in aspiring to a better life, desire for connection to the family and relatives, and decision-making based on their own evaluation of their life spanning across borders reveals how Bangladeshi migrants in Los Angeles engage in transnationalism. Instead of acting in response to the structural problems in the home country (e.g., the push factors) and opportunities in the destination country (e.g., the pull factors), these migrants simultaneously engage with both origin and destination societies and choose to engage with one over the other based on their own priorities. This helps overcome the inability of the NELM approach in explaining changes in migrant remittances over time, including remittances' decay. Moreover, it recognizes the possibility that migrants may begin to engage in transnationalism at any stage in their life. Given the limited scope of the study, this chapter cannot explore why some migrants are less likely than others to engage in sending remittances, or whether those intending to return to their home country actually do so. But a transnational approach with a focus on migrants' life course has the potential to advance our knowledge of transnationalism by looking at the interactions between the contextual/structural conditions and the migrants' agential capacity in shaping their actual practices.

NOTES

1 Gilbert F. Houngbo, President of the International Fund for Agricultural Development, stated on the International Day of Family Remittance, UN News, June 16, 2016, https://news.un.org.

2 Hein de Haas, "Migration and Development: A Theoretical Perspective," *International Migration Review* 44, no. 1 (2010): 227–264; Robert E. B. Lucas and Oded Stark, "Motivations to Remit: Evidence from Botswana," *Journal of Political Economy* 93, no. 5 (1985): 901–918.

3 See Payal Banerjee's chapter in this volume.

4 F. Ponsot, B. Vásquez, D. Terry, and P. de Vasconcelos, "Sending Money Home: Contributing to the SDGs, One Family at a Time," International Fund for Agricultural Development (IFAD), 2007, www.ifad.org.

5 In this chapter, I address financial remittances only and do not engage with what Peggy Levitt calls "social remittances"—ideas, behaviors, identities, and social capital flowing from receiving- to sending-country communities. See Peggy Levitt, "Social Remittances: Migration Driven Local-Level Forms of Cultural Diffusion," *International Migration Review* 32, no. 4 (1998): 926–948.

6 The World Bank, "COVID-19: Remittance Flows to Shrink 14% by 2021," October 29, 2020, www.worldbank.org.

7 Devesh Kapur, "Remittances: The New Development Mantra?" *G-24 Discussion Paper* no. 29, World Bank, 2004, https://unctad.org.

8 Maurizio Carbone, *The European Union and International Development: The Politics of Foreign Aid* (New York: Routledge, 2007); Raymond F. Hopkins, "Political Economy of Foreign Aid," in *Foreign Aid and Development: Lessons Learnt and Directions for the Future*, ed. Finn Tarp (London: Routledge, 2000), 423–449.

9 Matt Bakker, "Discursive Representations and Policy Mobility: How Migrant Remittances became a 'Development Tool,'" *Global Networks* 15 (2015): 21–42; Stuart S. Brown, "Can Remittances Spur Development? A Critical Survey," *International Studies Review* 8 (2006): 55–75.

10 See Banerjee's chapter in this volume.

11 UNHCR, "Migrant Definition," *Emergency Handbook*, https://emergency.unhcr
.org.

12 For a detailed discussion, Claire Alexander, "Contested Memories: The Shahid
Minar and the Struggle for Diasporic Space," *Ethnic and Racial Studies* 36, no. 13
(2013): 590–610; Katy Gardner, *Global Migrants, Local Lives: Travel and Transformation in Rural Bangladesh* (Oxford: Oxford University Press, 1995); Katy
Gardner and Kanwal Mand, "'My Away Is Here': Place, Emplacement and Mobility amongst British Bengali Children," *Journal of Ethnic and Migration Studies* 38,
no. 66 (2012): 969–986; Kanwal Mand, "I've Got Two Houses. One in Bangladesh
and One in London . . . Everybody Has': Home, Locality and Belonging(s),"
Childhood 17, no. 2 (2010): 273–287; Fatema Jahan, "Women's Agency and
Citizenship across Transnational Identities: A Case Study of the Bangladeshi
Diaspora in the UK," *Gender & Development* 19, no. 3 (2011): 371–381; Nazli Kibria, *Muslims in Motion: Islam and National Identity in the Bangladeshi Diaspora*
(New Brunswick, NJ: Rutgers University Press, 2011); Benjamin Zeitlyn, "Main-
taining Transnational Social Fields: The Role of Visits to Bangladesh for British
Bangladeshi Children," *Journal of Ethnic and Migration Studies* 38, no. 6 (2012):
953–968.

13 Kibria, *Muslims in Motion*.

14 Nicholas Demaria Harney, "Transnationalism and Entrepreneurial Migrancy in
Naples, Italy," *Journal of Ethnic and Migration Studies* 33, no. 2 (2007): 219–232;
Mohammad Morad and Francesco Della Puppa, "Bangladeshi Migrant Associa-
tions in Italy: Transnational Engagement, Community Formation and Regional
Unity," *Ethnic and Racial Studies* 42, no. 10 (2019): 1788–1807.

15 Petra Dannecker, "Transnational Migration and the Transformation of Gender
Relations: The Case of Bangladeshi Labour Migrants," *Current Sociology* 53, no. 4
(2005): 655–674; Nayeem Sultana, *The Bangladeshi Diaspora in Malaysia: Organizational Structure, Survival Strategies and Networks* (Münster: LitVerlag, 2009).

16 José Manuel Fraga Mapril, "The Patron and the Madman: Migration, Success and
the (In)visibility of Failure Among Bangladeshis in Portugal," *Social Anthropology*
19, no. 3 (2011): 288–296; José Mapril, "The Dreams of Middle Class: Consumption, Life-Course and Migration Between Bangladesh and Portugal," *Modern
Asian Studies* 48, no. 3 (2014): 693–719.

17 World Bank Group and Knomad, "Phase II: COVID-19 Crisis through a Migration Lens," *The World Bank Migration and Development Brief* 33, October 2020,
www.knomad.org.

18 Government of Bangladesh, Bureau of Manpower, Employment and Training
(BMET), "Statistical Reports," 2020, www.old.bmet.gov.bd.

19 Government of Bangladesh, "Statistical Reports."

20 Danièle Bélanger and Hong-Zen Wang, "Transnationalism from Below: Evidence
from Vietnam-Taiwan Cross-Border Marriages," *Asian and Pacific Migration
Journal* 21, no. 3 (2012): 291–316; Michael Peter Smith and Luis Eduardo Guarnizo,

eds., *Transnationalism from Below* (New Brunswick, NJ: Transactions Publishers, 1998).

21 Hasan Mahmud, "From Individual Motivations to Social Determinants: Towards a Sociology of Migrants' Remittances," *International Social Science Journal* 70, nos. 237–238 (2020): 175–188.

22 Z. U. Abdin and M. B. Erdal, "Remittance-Sending among Pakistani Taxi-Drivers in Barcelona and Oslo: Implications of Migration-Trajectories and the Protracted Electricity Crisis in Pakistan," *Migration and Development* 5, no. 3 (2016): 378–393; Leisy Abrego, *Sacrificing Families: Navigating Laws, Labor, and Love Across Borders* (Stanford, CA: Stanford University Press, 2014); Lisa Åkesson, "Remittances and Relationships: Exchange in Cape Verdean Transnational Families," *Ethnos* 76, no. 3 (2011): 326–347; Jørgen Carling, "The Human Dynamics of Migrant Transnationalism," *Ethnic and Racial Studies* 31, no. 8 (2008): 1452–1477; Joanna Dreby, *Divided by Borders: Mexican Migrants and Their Children* (Berkeley: University of California Press, 2010); Phyllis J. Johnson and Kathrin Stoll, "Remittance Patterns of Southern Sudanese Refugee Men: Enacting the Global Breadwinner Role," *Family Relations* 57, no. 4 (2008): 431–443; Patricia Landolt, "Salvadoran Economic Transnationalism: Embedded Strategies for Household Maintenance, Immigrant Incorporation, and Entrepreneurial Expansion," *Global Networks* 1, no. 3 (2001): 217–241; Sandra Lavenex and Rahel Kunz, "The Migration–Development Nexus in EU External Relations," *Journal of European Integration* 30, no. 3 (2008): 439–457; Peggy Levitt, *The Transnational Villagers* (Berkeley: University of California Press, 2001); Anna Lindley, "The Early-Morning Phonecall: Remittances from a Refugee Diaspora Perspective," *Journal of Ethnic and Migration Studies* 35, no. 8 (2009): 1315–1334; Hasan Mahmud, "'It's My Money': Social Class and the Perception of Remittance among Bangladeshi Migrants in Japan," *Current Sociology* 62, no. 3 (2014): 418–430; David Spener, *Clandestine Crossings: Migrants and Coyotes on the Texas-Mexico Border* (Ithaca, NY: Cornell University Press, 2009); Hung Cam Thai, *Insufficient Funds: The Culture of Money in Low-Wage Transnational Families* (Stanford, CA: Stanford University Press, 2014).

23 See Silvia Pedraza's chapter in this volume.

24 Hein de Haas, Stephen Castles, and Mark J. Miller, *The Age of Migration: International Population Movements in the Modern World* (5th edition) (New York: Guilford Press, 2014).

25 International Organization for Migration (IOM), *World Migration Report* (Geneva: IOM Publishing, 2020).

26 World Bank, "Phase II."

27 Manuel Orozco, "Understanding the Continuing Effect of the Economic Crisis on Remittances to Latin America and the Caribbean," Inter-American Development Bank, August 10, 2009, https://publications.iadb.org.

28 The most widely recognized study of transnationalism is William I. Thomas and Florian W. Znaniecki, *The Polish Peasant in Europe and America: A Classic Work*

in Immigration History (Champaign: University of Illinois Press, 1995). The work had a substantial focus on migrants' remittances.

29 Michael Fix et al., "Migration and the Global Recession," Migration Policy Institute, 2019, www.migrationpolicy.org.

30 Bakker, "Discursive Representations and Policy Mobility."

31 Mamoun Benmamoun and Kevin Lehnert, "Financing Growth: Comparing the Effects of FDI, ODA, and International Remittances," *Journal of Economic Development* 38, no. 2 (2013): 43–65; P. Gammeltoft, "Remittances and Other Financial Flows to Developing Countries," *International Migration* 40, no. 5 (2002): 181–211.

32 Naoyuki Yoshino, Farhad Taghizadeh-Hesary, and Miyu Otsuka, "International Remittances and Poverty Reduction: Evidence from Asian Developing Countries," Asian Development Bank Institute *ADBI Working Paper* no. 759 (July 2017), www.adb.org.

33 Robyn Magalit Rodriguez, *Migrants for Export: How the Philippine State Brokers Labor to the World* (Minneapolis: University of Minnesota Press, 2010).

34 Hein de Haas, "Migration and Development: A Theoretical Perspective," *International Migration Review* 44, no. 1 (2010): 227–264.

35 Bakker, "Discursive Representations and Policy Mobility"; Ida Marie Vammen and Birgitte Mossin Brønden, "Donor-Country Responses to the Migration–Development Buzz: From Ambiguous Concepts to Ambitious Policies," *International Migration* 50, no. 3 (2012): 26–42.

36 Hein de Haas, "The Migration and Development Pendulum: A Critical View on Research and Policy," *International Migration* 50, no. 3 (2012): 8–25.

37 Kavita Datta, "Risky Migrants?: Low-Paid Migrant Workers Coping with Financial Exclusion in London," *European Urban and Regional Studies* 16, no. 4 (2009): 331–344; Levitt, *The Transnational Villagers*; Birgitte Mossin Brønden, "Migration and Development: The Flavour of the 2000s," *International Migration* 50, no. 3 (2012): 2–7.

38 Stephen Castle et al., "Circular Migration: Triple Win, or a New Label for Temporary Migration?" in *Global and Asian Perspectives on International Migration*, ed. Graziano Battistella (Cham, Switzerland: Springer, 2014), 27–49; Lavenex and Kunz, "The Migration–Development Nexus."

39 Adolfo Barajas et al., "Do Workers' Remittances Promote Economic Growth?" *IMF Working Paper*, 09/153; Gregory Randolph, "Labor Migration and Inclusive Growth: Toward Creating Employment in Origin Communities," Solidarity Center, 2015, www.solidaritycenter.org.

40 Kavita Datta et al., "Work and Survival Strategies among Low-Paid Migrants in London," Working Paper 3, Queen Mary, University of London.

41 Richard H. Adams Jr., "The Determinants of International Remittances in Developing Countries," *World Development* 37, no. 1 (2009): 93–103.

42 IOM, *World Migration Report*, 2020, 26.

43 Abby Budiman, "Bangladeshis in the U.S. Fact Sheet," Pew Research Center, www.pewresearch.org.

44 Government of Bangladesh, "Statistical Reports."

45 Fouad N. Ibrahim and Helmut Ruppert, "The Role of Rural-Rural Migration as a Survival Strategy in the Sahelian Zone of the Sudan—A Case-Study in Burush, N Darfur," *GeoJournal* 25, no.1 (1991): 31–38; Adama Konseiga, "Household Migration Decision as Survival Strategy: The Case of Burkina Faso," *Journal of African Economies* 16, no. 2 (2007): 198–223; Syeda Rozana Rashid, *Uncertain Tomorrows: Livelihoods, Capital and Risk in Labour Migration from Bangladesh* (Dhaka: The University Press Limited, 2016); Mohammad Jalal Uddin Sikder, Vaughan Higgins, and Peter Harry Ballis, *Remittance Income and Social Resilience among Migrant Households in Rural Bangladesh* (New York: Palgrave Macmillan, 2017).

46 D. B. Grigg, *Population Growth and Agrarian Change: An Historical Perspective* (Cambridge: Cambridge University Press, 1981); Philip Guest, *Labor Allocation and Rural Development: Migration in Four Javanese Villages* (Boulder, CO: Westview, 1989); Charles H. Wood, "Structural Changes and Household Strategies: A Conceptual Framework for the Study of Rural Migration," *Human Organization* 40, no. 4 (1981): 338–344.

47 Rafiqul Huda Chaudhury and George C. Curlin, "Dynamics of Migration in a Rural Area of Bangladesh," *The Bangladesh Development Studies* 3, no. 2 (1975): 181–230.

48 Amelie Bernzen, J. Craig Jenkins, and Boris Braun, "Climate Change–Induced Migration in Coastal Bangladesh? A Critical Assessment of Migration Drivers in Rural Households under Economic and Environmental Stress," *Geosciences* 9, no. 1 (2019): 51; Amanda R. Carrico and Katharine Donato, "Extreme Weather and Migration: Evidence from Bangladesh," *Population & Environment* 41 (2019): 1–31; M. Rezaul Islam, "Climate Change, Natural Disasters and Socioeconomic Livelihood Vulnerabilities: Migration Decision Among the Char Land People in Bangladesh," *Social Indicators Research* 136 (2018): 575–593.

49 Barbara C. Aswad and Barbara Bilge, *Family and Gender among American Muslims* (Philadelphia, PA: Temple University Press, 1996), 159.

50 Jessica Vaughan and Preston Huennekens, "Bangladesh: A Case Study in Chain Migration," Center for Immigration Studies, 2018, https://cis.org.

51 Mohiuddin Alamgir, "Bangladeshi Students Heading for Univs Abroad on Rise," *The Daily New Age*, August 31, 2018, www.newagebd.net.

52 US Department of State, "Open Doors 2017 Executive Summary," Institute of International Education, www.iie.org.

53 See in this volume chapter 6 by Mishra and chapter 9 by Bhatti.

54 "The Bangladeshi Diaspora in the United States," Migration Policy Institute, July 2014, www.migrationpolicy.org.

55 Nayma Qayum, "Chasing the Dubai Dream in Italy: Bangladeshi Migration to Europe," Migration Policy Institute, October 5, 2017, www.migrationpolicy.org.

56 Personal correspondence, February 2021.

57 Stores primarily cater to migrant populations with goods and services imported from origin countries and often work as spaces for socializing among the coethnic immigrants.

58 A customer's comment on Yelp, www.yelp.com.

59 Viviana Zelizer, *The Purchase of Intimacy* (Princeton, NJ: Princeton University Press, 2005), 222.

60 Supriya Singh, Shanthi Robertson, and Anuja Cabraal, "Transnational Family Money: Remittances, Gifts and Inheritance," *Journal of Intercultural Studies* 33, no. 5 (2012): 475–492.

61 Abrego, *Sacrificing Families*; Karsten Paerregaard, "The Resilience of Migrant Money: How Gender, Generation and Class Shape Family Remittances in Peruvian Migration," *Global Networks* 15, no. 4 (2015): 503–518; Rhacel Salazar Parreñas, *Servants of Globalization: Migration and Domestic Work* (Stanford, CA: Stanford University Press, 2001).

62 A.K.M. Ahsan Ullah, "Dynamics of Remittance Practices and Development: Bangladeshi Overseas Migrants," *Development in Practice* 21, no. 8 (2011): 1153–1167; Mahmud, "It's My Money"; Natacha Stevanovic-Fenn, "Remittances and the Moral Economies of Bangladeshi New York Immigrants in Light of the Economic Crisis" (PhD diss., Department of Anthropology, Columbia University, New York, 2012).

63 D. M. Indra and N. Buchignani, "Rural Landlessness, Extended Entitlements and Inter-household Relations in South Asia: A Bangladesh Case," *The Journal of Peasant Studies* 24, no. 3 (1997): 25–64; Zarina Nahar Kabir, Marta Szebehely, and Carol Tishelman, "Support in Old Age in the Changing Society of Bangladesh," *Ageing and Society* 22, no. 5 (2002): 615–636.

64 Carling, "Migrant Transnationalism"; Hasan Mahmud, "Beyond Economics: The Family, Belonging and Remittances among the Bangladeshi Migrants in Los Angeles," *International Migration* (2021); Paerregaard, "Migrant Money."

65 Abrego, "Sacrificing Family"; Paerregaard, "Migrant Money."

66 Gardner, "Global Migrants"; Mahmud, "It's My Money."

67 Syed Ali, "Go West Young Man: The Culture of Migration among Muslims in Hyderabad, India," *Journal of Ethnic and Migration Studies* 33, no. 1 (2007): 37–58.

68 Thai, *Insufficient Funds*; Min Zhou and Xiangyi Li, "Remittances for Collective Consumption and Social Status Compensation: Variations on Transnational Practices among Chinese International Migrants," *International Migration Review* 52, no. 1 (2018): 4–42.

69 Ali, "Go West Young Man"; Gardner, "Global Migrants"; Alessandro Monsutti, "Migration as a Rite of Passage: Young Afghans Building Masculinity and Adulthood in Iran," *Iranian Studies* 40, no. 2 (2007): 167–185.

70 Ali, "Go West Young Man"; Mahmud, "Perception of Remittance."

71 Marta Bivand Erdal, "Theorizing Interactions of Migrant Transnationalism and Integration through a Multiscalar Approach," *Comparative Migration Studies* 8 (2020): 1–16.

72 Katy Gardner, "Keeping Connected: Security, Place, and Social Capital in a 'Londoni' Village in Sylhet," *Journal of the Royal Anthropological Institute* 14, no. 3 (2008): 477–495.

73 Zhou and Li, "Remittances for Collective Consumption"; Thai, *Insufficient Funds*.

74 Linda Basch, Nina Glick Schiller, and Cristina Szanton Blanc, *Nations Unbound: Transnational Projects, Postcolonial Predicaments and Deterritorialized Nation-States* (London: Routledge, 1994); Kibria, *Muslims in Motion*; Levitt, *The Transnational Villagers*; Robert Courtney Smith, *Mexican New York: Transnational Lives of New Immigrants* (Berkeley: University of California Press, 2006).

75 For details, see Andreas Wimmer and Nina Glick Schiller, "Methodological Nationalism, the Social Sciences, and the Study of Migration: An Essay in Historical Epistemology," *The International Migration Review* 37, no. 3 (2003): 576–610; Andreas Wimmer and Nina Glick Schiller, "Methodological Nationalism and Beyond: Nation–State Building, Migration and the Social Sciences," *Global Networks* 2, no. 4 (2002): 301–334.

76 Michael Burawoy, "The Functions and Reproduction of Migrant Labor: Comparative Material from Southern Africa and the United States," *American Journal of Sociology* 81, no. 5 (1976): 1050–1087.

77 Hasan Mahmud, "Impact of the Destination State on Migrants' Remittances: A Study of Remitting among Bangladeshi Migrants in the USA, the UAE and Japan," *Migration and Development* 5, no.1 (2016): 79–98.

78 Adrian Favel, *Immigration, Integration and Mobility: New Agendas in Migration Studies* (Colchester, UK: ECPR Press, 2014).

79 Silke Meyer, "'Home is Where I Spend My Money': Testing the Remittance Decay Hypothesis with Ethnographic Data from an Austrian-Turkish Community," *Social Inclusion* 8, no. 1 (2020): 275.

80 Gillian Creese, "'Where Are You From?' Racialization, Belonging and Identity among Second-Generation African-Canadians," *Ethnic and Racial Studies* 42, no. 9 (2019): 1476–1494; Umut Erel, "Complex Belongings: Racialization and migration in a Small English City," *Ethnic and Racial Studies* 34, no. 12 (2011): 2048–2068; Anna C. Korteweg, "The Failures of 'Immigrant Integration': The Gendered Racialized Production of Non-Belonging," *Migration Studies* 5, no. 3 (2017): 428–444; Elizabeth A. Onasch, "Lessons on the Boundaries of Belonging: Racialization and Symbolic Boundary Drawing in the French Civic Integration Program," *Social Problems* 64, no. 4 (2017): 577–593; Laurence Ossipow, Anne-Laure Counilh, and Milena Chimienti, "Racialization in Switzerland: Experiences of Children of Refugees from Kurdish, Tamil and Vietnamese Backgrounds," *Comparative Migration Studies* 7 (2019).

81 Mahmud, "Perception of Remittance"; Mahmud, "Social Determinants of Remitting Practices."

ACKNOWLEDGMENTS

This edited volume was completed during the worst global pandemic in human history. The COVID-19 pandemic has caused lockdowns, forced border closings, and physical distancing, making it tremendously challenging for collaborative research of this kind. We are immensely grateful for the resilience, dedication, and exceptional efforts from all individuals involved.

First and foremost, the book is the result of a collaborative project spearheaded and supported by the Center for International and Regional Studies (CIRS) at Georgetown University in Qatar. CIRS has been committed to promoting greater knowledge of the political, economic, social, and cultural dynamics of the Persian Gulf and the Middle East for over a decade, having conducted more than forty research initiatives and published numerous books and special issues of scholarly journals. One of CIRS's core areas of research has been in the migration to the Middle East, focusing particularly on migrant labor in the Persian Gulf, Arab migration to and within the Gulf Cooperation Council (GCC) countries, and forced migration and displacement in the greater Middle East. Building on the success of this area of research, CIRS has expanded its scope beyond the region to study migration dynamics from a broader and comparative lens. On February 15–16, 2020, just days before the CO-VID-19 pandemic lockdowns, CIRS organized a research roundtable on economic migration to the United States and invited a group of distinguished social scientists of migration studies to convene in Washington, DC. The main goal of the roundtable was to identify significant gaps in the established literature on international migration, brainstorm ways of addressing these gaps, and exchange ideas that would lead to an original contribution to the existing body of migration scholarship. The initial roundtable discussion was extremely intellectually stimulating and productive and led to the formation of a working group for the current book. Members of the working group were then invited to develop their respective chapters to be discussed and reviewed by peers in another workshop, hosted by CIRS virtually (originally planned as an in-person event in Doha, Qatar) on October 19–20, 2020. This book is the culmination of the discussions held in these two workshops and several rounds of chapter revisions.

We are, therefore, deeply indebted to the CIRS leadership and its extraordinarily capable and supportive staff. We are particularly thankful to Dr. Ahmad Dallal, former Dean of Georgetown University in Qatar, Dr. Mehran Kamrava, former Director of CIRS, and Zahra Babar, Associate Director for Research at CIRS, for entrusting us to lead the book project as coeditors and for offering their unwavering support, guidance, and resources. We thank them for doing all the groundwork for the project, including initial conceptualization, planning, and organization of the workshops, inviting the contributors, and summarizing peer comments and providing feedback to contributors for their chapter revisions. CIRS has also provided us with excellent staff support. Specially mentioned is Dr. Suzi Mirgani, Assistant Director for Publications at CIRS. Suzi has worked tirelessly behind the scenes, providing not only careful reading and meticulous copyediting of the entire manuscript but also critical comments and thorough editorial feedback that helped enhance the quality and readability of the work, as well as impeccable coordination among contributors in a timely and efficient manner. We much appreciate the administrative support of Misba Bhatti, CIRS Research Analyst, and Maram Al-Qershi, CIRS Coordinator, and we are especially grateful to Elizabeth Wanucha, CIRS Operations Manager, who assisted contributors with travel and numerous other logistic arrangements related to the project.

This book is the product of amazing teamwork. We would like to thank all our contributors for their active participation by presenting their own studies and engaging in intellectually stimulating and critical discussions of others' works, for their keen sociological imagination in theoretical framing and rigorous analysis, and for their seamless collaboration across geographic boundaries, always attentive to our countless requests and queries, while braving the global pandemic. The synergy generated out of our contributors' professional expertise and multidisciplinary approaches has greatly augmented the scholarly worth of this book. The collaboration has cemented our friendship as well.

We are incredibly fortunate to have received the attention of Jennifer Hammer, senior editor at New York University Press. Jennifer has been very responsive and enthusiastic about our book manuscript and has pushed it through the review process in record time. We are also thankful to the two anonymous reviewers whose thoughtful and critical feedback contributed to improving the final manuscript.

Last but not least, our deepest gratitude goes to our families, whose love and support are always heartfelt, no matter where we are on earth. Min owes every single piece of her professional accomplishment to her loving husband Sam, her soulmate, best friend, biggest fan, and love of 40 years. Min also thanks her younger sister Jenny, who shouldered the responsibility of taking care of their frail, elderly parents in China until the very end of their lives (Min's dad passed away with Jenny at his bedside in China on February 27, 2020, less than two weeks after Min became involved in this book project). Hasan would like to thank his lovely wife Sumiya and daughter Afreen for their continuous encouragement and support while working on this book, which took away much of the time he would otherwise have spent with them.

Min Zhou, Los Angeles, USA
Hasan Mahmud, Doha, Qatar
November 11, 2021

ABOUT THE EDITORS

MIN ZHOU is Distinguished Professor of Sociology and Asian American Studies, Walter and Shirley Wang Endowed Chair in US-China Relations and Communications, and Director of the Asia Pacific Center at the University of California, Los Angeles (UCLA). She is a member of the American Academy of Arts and Sciences. She received her PhD in sociology from State University of New York at Albany. Her main research areas are in migration and development, race and ethnicity, education and the new second generation, Chinese diaspora, and the sociology of Asia and Asian America. She has published widely in these areas, including an award-winning book *The Asian American Achievement Paradox* (with Lee), *The Rise of the New Second Generation* (with Bankston), and *Contemporary Chinese Diasporas* (editor). She is the recipient of the 2017 Distinguished Career Award of the American Sociological Association (ASA) Section on International Migration and the 2020 Contribution to the Field Award of the ASA Section on Asia and Asian America.

HASAN MAHMUD is Assistant Professor of Sociology at Northwestern University in Qatar. He received his PhD in sociology from the University of California, Los Angeles. His research interests include migration, development, globalization, and ethnography. He studies Bangladeshi migration to the United States, Japan, and the Middle East. His most recent publications outline a sociology of migrants' remittances. His articles appeared in *Current Sociology, Sociological Perspectives, International Migration, International Social Science Journal,* and *Migration and Development* journal. He coedited a special issue titled "Migration in a Turbulent Time: Perspectives from Global South" for *Migration and Development.* He teaches sociological theories, globalization, sociology of development, and international migration. He serves on the Research

Committee on Social Transformation and Sociology of Development of the International Sociological Association, and Sociology of Development Section of the Canadian Sociological Association.

ABOUT THE CONTRIBUTORS

CATALINA AMUEDO-DORANTES is Professor of Economics at the University of California, Merced. She received her PhD in applied economics from Western Michigan University. Her areas of interest include labor economics, international migration, and remittances. She has published on contingent work contracts, the informal work sector, international remittances, as well as on immigrant assimilation and the impact of immigration policies on migrants and the communities where they reside. Her work has been funded by the Banco Bilbao Vizcaya Argentaria, the Hewlett Foundation, the National Institutes of Health, the Robert Wood Johnson Foundation, and the Upjohn Institute for Employment Research, among other agencies. She was the Border Fulbright García-Robles Scholar, Chair of the Department of Economics at San Diego State University, and President of the American Society of Hispanic Economists, and has held visiting positions at the Upjohn Institute for Employment Research, the Center for Human Resource at Ohio State University, the Institute for Research on Poverty at the University of Wisconsin, Madison, and at the Public Policy Institute of California.

PAYAL BANERJEE is Associate Professor and Chair of Sociology at Smith College. She received her PhD in sociology from Syracuse University. Her research focuses on globalization, the political economy of migration, and the centrality of state policies in structuring labor incorporation and immigrant experiences. Her work on Indian immigrant IT workers in the United States has appeared in *Critical Sociology*; *Race, Gender, and Class*; and *International Feminist Journal of Politics*, among other journals and books. Her research on Chinese minorities in India and India-China relations has been published in *Huaqiao Huaren Lishi Yanjiu* (*Overseas Chinese History Studies*, in Chinese); *Security and Peace, China Report; Asian Journal of Comparative Politics*, and in the book *Doing Time with Nehru*. As a member of the Border Studies Group, she co-published *India China: Rethinking Borders and Security*. Her work on hydroelectric power projects and privatization in India appeared in *Perceptions* and as a UNRISD Occasional Paper. She has been a research fellow at the BRICS Policy Center in Rio de Janeiro, Brazil, and she has taught as visiting faculty at The New School in New York City, Sikkim University in Gangtok, India, and FLAME in Pune.

MISBA BHATTI is Research Analyst at the Center for International and Regional Studies, Georgetown University in Qatar. She received her Master's degree in international relations from the London School of Economics. Her research thesis was on the use of private military companies in war by states. Her current research interests include international relations of the Gulf states and security studies. She supports the Director and Associate Director in carrying out research for the center and identifies critical gaps in the scholarship where CIRS can engage in new research. She is also responsible for maintaining CIRS research presence online, as well as generating background research output for the center's projects. She previously worked as the Administrative Coordinator at the center.

KATHARINE M. DONATO is Donald G. Herzberg Professor of International Migration and Director of the Institute for the Study of International Migration at Georgetown University. She received her PhD in sociology from State University of New York at Stony Brook. Her research interests include migration in the Americas, environmental drivers of outmigration in Bangladesh, global governance, child migration, and gender. Her recent publications include a special issue of the *ANNALS of the American Academy of Political and Social Science* on "Refugee and Immigrant Integration: Unpacking the Research, Translating into Policy" (with Ferris), an issue of the *RSF: The Russell Sage Foundation Journal of the Social Sciences* on "The Legal Landscape of U.S. Immigration in the Twenty-First Century," and two books, *Refugees, Migration and Global Governance: Negotiating the Global Compacts* (with Ferris) and *Gender and International Migration: From the Slavery Era to the Global Age* (with Gabaccia).

B. LINDSAY LOWELL is Adjunct Research Professor in Georgetown University's School of Foreign Service and Senior Affiliate at the

Institute for the Study of International Migration (ISIM). He received his PhD in demography from Brown University. He was previously Director of Research at the congressionally appointed Commission on Immigration Reform, where he was also Assistant Director for the Mexico–US Binational Study on Migration. He has been Research Director of the Pew Hispanic Center at the University of Southern California, a Labor Analyst at the Department of Labor; and he taught at Princeton University and the University of Texas, Austin. Dr. Lowell has written more than 150 articles and reports. He has published in journals such as *Demography, American Economic Review, Population and Development Review, Industrial Relations*, and *Work and Occupations*. His research interests include immigration policy, labor force, economic development, Mexico–US migration, education, and the global mobility of the highly skilled.

SANGAY K. MISHRA is Associate Professor of Political Science at Drew University. He specializes in immigrant political incorporation, global immigration, and racial and ethnic politics. He received his PhD in political science from the University of Southern California. Before joining Drew, he was a Mellon Postdoctoral Fellow at Lehigh University in Pennsylvania. He teaches courses in American politics and political theory, including race and politics; immigration; cultural diversity and the law; Muslims and the West; and Latino politics and citizenship. His research interests focus on Indian, Pakistani, and Bangladeshi American communities. His book *Desis Divided: The Political Lives of South Asian Americans* analyzed features such as class, religion, nation of origin, language, caste, gender, and sexuality in mobilization and showed how these internal characteristics lead to multiple paths of political inclusion, defying a unified group experience. The book received the 2017 Best Book Award on Asian America of the American Sociological Association Section on Asia and Asian America. He served as co-chair of the Asian and Pacific American Caucus of the American Political Science Association.

SILVIA PEDRAZA is Professor of Sociology and American Culture at the University of Michigan, Ann Arbor. She received her PhD in sociology from the University of Chicago. Her research interests include the sociology of immigration, race and ethnicity in America, and the sociology of Cuba's revolution and exodus with a focus on comparative studies, both historical and contemporary. She has published widely in these areas, including *Political Disaffection in Cuba's Revolution and Exodus* and *Revolutions in Cuba and Venezuela: One Hope, Two Realities* (with Carlos A. Romero). She was elected to the American Sociological Association's (ASA) Council as well as its Nominations Committee, and was also elected Chair of several ASA sections, including the Latina/o Sociology, Racial and Ethnic Minorities, and International Migration. She also served on the editorial board of its journal, the *American Sociological Review*. She was also elected to the Social Science History Association's (SSHA) Executive Committee and served on the Distinguished Book Award Committee. She is now on the editorial board of its journal, *Social Science History*. She was also elected President of the Association for the Study of the Cuban Economy and society (ASCE) and served on the editorial board of the *Cuban Studies* journal.

KEVIN J. A. THOMAS is Professor of African and African Diaspora Studies at the University of Texas at Austin. He obtained his PhD in demography from the University of Pennsylvania, served as a post-doctoral fellow at both the Harvard Center for Population and Development Studies and the Harvard Initiative for Global Health, and was a faculty member at the Pennsylvania State University. His research focuses on international migration, global health, racial and ethnic inequality, children and families, and development and social change in Africa. He is the author of *Diverse Pathways: Race and the Socioeconomic Incorporation of Black, White, and Arab-origin Africans in the US*; *Contract Workers, Risk, and the War in Iraq: Sierra Leonean Labor Migrants at US Military Bases*; and *Global Epidemics, Local Implications: African Immigrants and the Ebola Crisis in Dallas*. He is the recipient of the Ray Lombra Award for Distinction in the Social Sciences of the Pennsylvania State University and the Outstanding Book Award of the American Sociological Association Section on Peace, War, and Social Conflict.

TERRY WOTHERSPOON is Professor of Sociology at the University of Saskatchewan, Canada. He received his PhD in sociology from Simon Fraser University. He has published extensively in areas related to his research on education, social policy, Indigenous-settler relations, and social inclusion, exclusion, and inequality in Canada. Current research projects include Indigenous education and reconciliation, educational policy, and labor market participation in Canada; and issues of social inclusion, exclusion, and diversity in settler colonial nation-states. He has received recognition for significant scholarly contributions to both sociology (the Outstanding Contribution Award from the Canadian Sociological Association) and education (the Canadian Education Association's Whitworth Award for Educational Research). An early edition of his book, *The Sociology of Education in Canada: Critical Perspectives* (now in its fifth edition), was recognized with a book award from the Canadian Association for Foundations of Education. In addition to several terms as the head of his department, he served as President of the Canadian Sociological Association and Managing Editor of the *Canadian Review of Sociology*.

RENÉ ZENTENO is Professor of Demography at the University of Texas at San Antonio (UTSA). He obtained his PhD in sociology and demography from University of Texas at Austin. He has published widely in the areas of social and demographic change, immigration, and social inequality, with a focus on Mexico-US relations and Latin America. He was Vice Provost for International Initiatives at UTSA and concurrently the Executive Director of ConTex, a joint initiative of the University of Texas System and Mexico's National Council of Science and Technology. He served as Under Secretary in the Ministry of the Interior in Mexico, the Executive Director for the Center for US-Mexican Studies at the University of California, San Diego, and Provost at *El Colegio de la Frontera Norte*. He has received several professional honors, including President of the Mexican Society of Demography and membership in the National Academy of Science of Mexico.

INDEX

Page numbers in italics indicate Figures and Tables.

Haiti, 325
Handlin, Oscar, 302
Harris, Kamala, 315, 327
Hart-Celler Act, US, 11, 12, 13, 63, 85, 86,
    95; numerical restrictions, 99; skilled
    immigrants and, 187
Harvey, David, 8
Hawaii, 86, 90–91, 93
HDI. *See* Human Development Index
headscarf (*hijab*), 313
healthcare occupations, 40, 56n11, 298n64;
    barriers in, 283–84; filling, 292
hierarchies, 37, 53
high immigrant selectivity, 18, 34n77
highly skilled labor, 25, 213, 214, 224,
    227–33, 235–36
high-skilled visas, 131, 133, *134*, 146
High-Tech Housewives (Bhatt), 202
hijab (headscarf), 313
hiring: data-driven, 47; preferential, 155,
    156–59, 177, 180n8; queues, 155, 156, 157
history, 37, 54n2, 310; African immigrants,
    247–50; East Asian immigration,
    86–93
Hollifield, James, 14
Hollinger, David, 318, 325
Hollywood, 314
Homeland Security, US, 38, 78, 130, 177
hometown associations, 21
honorary white, 106
Houngbo, Gilbert F., 337
house-job training, 286, 299n70
Howe, Irving, 307
human capital, 70, 74, 217; African im-
    migrants, 246, 265; endowments,
    247; income and, 248; international
    students and, 233–37
Human Development Index (HDI), 139,
    140, 145, 147, 154n68
human rights violations, 67
hybrid identity, 303, 318, 327
hyperglobalization, 1
hyperinegalitarian society, 43

hyperselectivity, immigrant, 11–12, 18,
    31n47, 34n77, 73, 105
hypo-selectivity, immigrant, 18, 34n77

ICT. *See* information and communication
    technology
identity: Asian American, 110, 111–12;
    assimilation and, 313; ethnic, 109–10;
    free-floating, 319; hybrid, 303, 318, 327;
    Puerto Rican, 321
IDFR. *See* International Day of Family
    Remittance
Illegal Immigration Reform and Immi-
    grant Responsibility Act, US, 120
illegal migration, legal *versus*, 51–52
ILO. *See* International Labor
    Organization
IMF. *See* International Monetary Fund
IMGs. *See* International Medical
    Graduates
Immediate Relative visa, 299n83
Immigrant Nominee Programs, Canada,
    237
immigrants: contemporary, 1–2, 3; desir-
    able *versus* undesirable, 281; economic
    incorporation of, 15–18, 74–75, 80; as
    individuals, 37; nation-states defining,
    10; SES, 2; social-historical processes,
    53–54; transnationalism, 19–21. *See also*
    specific immigrants
immigrant visas. *See* visas, immigrant
immigration: perceived categories of,
    53, 55n4; racialized control of, 12–14,
    41, 78; restrictive, 13–14; technologi-
    cal control of, 45, 48, 50–51. *See also*
    specific topics
Immigration Act, US (1924), 12, 17
Immigration Act, US (1990), 13, 23, 118,
    119, 121–22, 159–60, 220
Immigration and Nationality Act, US
    (1952), 189
Immigration and Nationality Act, US
    (1965). *See* Hart-Celler Act, US

Johnson, Lyndon B., 324
Johnson-Reed Act, US, 11, 89
justice, temporal, 205, 208
Justice and Development Party, Turkey,
326
J visa, 187, 209n3

Kanaiaupuni, Shawn Malia, 309
Kennedy, John F., 119
knowledge: as power, 279–80; workers,
277
Korean immigration, 85, 93, 94, 115n49;
demographic trends, 98, 99; economic
influences on, 96; 1940s–2018, *100*;
push factors for, 96–97; socioeconomic
characteristics of, 101
Korean War, 95

labor: demand, 65; flexibility, 41, 195, 196;
globalization impacting, 42; highly
skilled, 25, 213, 214, 224, 227–33, 235–36;
immigrant, 3, 27–28; regulations, 16;
shortages, 175, 181n23; surplus, 3–4;
temporary contract, 16, 44, 156–59, 192;
transience, 4
Labor Department, US, 150n12, 164,
181n23, 183n41
laborers, Chinese immigrant, 87, 88–89
labor markets: de-skilling in, 289;
disadvantage, 15; dual, 4, 15–16, 157;
education and, 218, 219; international
students and changing, 219–23
labor participation, 39, 42; geopolitical economy and, 41; percentages by
occupation, 40
labor-rich, 43, 44
Laguerre, Michel, 325
language, 15, 16, 232, 252, 255
Latino immigrants, 62–63, 81n6; aging
and longevity of, 67–68; changing profiles for, 65–69, *66*; changing trends in,
64–65, 78–79; demographics and SES,
66, 67; education, 70–71, *71*, 72, 73–74,

80; legal status of, *76*, *77*; 1970–219, *64*;
status and enforcement of, *76*
laws, anti-miscegenation, 91
Lee, Everett, 302
Lee, Jennifer, 18, 247
legal migration, illegal *versus*, 51–52
legislative reform, for visa policies,
148–49, 159–60
letters, 317
Levitt, Peggy, 356n5
liberal paradox, 14
liberation, 279
licenses, 277, 285, 288
Light, Ivan, 15
linear transnationalism, 328
Little Bangladesh, Los Angeles, 346–47
lived experiences, 20–21, 330
livelihoods, 22
loans, 320
lobbies, ethnic, 322–23
Lofstrom, Magnus, 180n1, 183n38
longevity, Latino immigrants, 67–68
long-term residents, Latino immigrants
as, 68
López-Obrador, Andrés Manuel, 323
Los Angeles, California, 346–48
lost decade, 248
Lowell, B. Lindsay, 24, 126, 220
low-skilled employment, 65
low-skilled immigrants, 73, 128
low-skilled visas, 131, 133, *133*, 143, 147
loyalty, dual, 318
Luce-Celler Act, US, 274
L visa, 187, 209n3

macroeconomics: dual labor market theory
of, 4; world system theory of, 4–5
Madonna, 306
Mahalingam, Ramaswami, 329
Mahmud, Hasan, 27
mainstream, 313–14
major multinational corporations
(MNC), 8

patron saints, 306

patterns: African immigrants occupational, 250; East Asian immigration resettlement, 94; gender, 309; SES, 41; of social mobility, 85, 104–5; of transnationalism, 316

Pearce, Susan, 308

Pearl River Delta region, China, 86

Pedraza, Silvia, 26, 311

penalty, wage, 259, 264

Pentecostalism, 328

permanent residency (PR), 101, 102, 160, 173, 180, 188, 300n94; H-1B conversion to, 190, 197; international study and, 215, 217–19

Pessar, Patricia, 308–9

Petersen, William, 106

pharmacist, 285

PhDs, 216, 217, 228

Physical Medicine and Rehabilitation (PM and R), 291

"picture brides," 92, 114n31

Piketty, Thomas, 43

PM and R. See Physical Medicine and Rehabilitation

policies. See visa policies, US

political migrations, 2

political value, of durational time, 205

politics: Bangladeshi, 353; party, 323–24. See also transnationalism, political

poor, working, 16

population: census, 69; climate change shifting, 28; movements, 1; problem, 45; US Asian, 98–99, 99, 112n1

portability, visa, 178

Portes, Alejandro, 303, 315, 320

positionality: East Asian immigration and, 106–8; social, 37

positive immigrant selectivity, 17, 18

poverty, 69

power: bargaining, 156, 157, 177, 185n73; knowledge as, 279–80

PR. See permanent residency

precarity, 24, 187; during COVID-19, 203; of skilled immigrants, 188, 198, 202–3, 208

preference categories, immigrant, 200, 201

preferential demand, 24

preferential hiring, 155, 156–59, 177, 180n8

presidential administrations, US, 140, 142–43, 145, 146, 147

pressure, to assimilate, 108–9

prestige, 350

prevailing wage, 163, 179, 182n24

pride, ethnic, 314

problem populations, 45

productivity, 175

profiles, Latino immigrant, 65–69, 66

proliferation, of temporary foreign workers, 195–98

Protestantism, 306

proxy H-1B visas, 162

Puerto Rican migrants, 318, 321

pure H-1B visas, 193

PWiC. See Pakistani Women in Computing

queues: hiring, 155, 156, 157; visa, 130, 204, 207–8

quotas, immigrant, 11, 13, 17, 189; adjusting, 239; nationality-based, 200

race discourses, 214

racialization, 22, 23, 85, 177, 189, 311–12; of African immigrants, 250; of Chinese immigration, 88; of East Asian immigration, 106, 108–10, 197; of immigration, 12–14, 41, 78; of Indian immigrants, 198–203; of Japanese immigration, 91; of visa quotas, 207–8

racial profiling, 229

racism, 12, 80, 110, 111, 222, 312, 313

railroads, 87, 88, 104

RAISE Act. See Reforming American Immigration for Strong Employment Act

Ramírez, Daniel, 327–28

standards, of living, 96
state: credential evaluations by, 277; migration, 14; nation-states, 9, 10, 21, 346
Statistical Yearbook, 275
statistics, descriptive, of college graduates, *254*
status, immigration, 63, *76*, 77, 251, 308
STEM. *See* science, technology, engineering, and mathematics
stereotypes, 267; "forever foreigner," 112; of international students, 221; "model minority," 80, 106, 109, 111–12
Still the Golden Door (Reimers), 316
structural adjustment programs (SAPs), 8–9
structural assimilation, 310
structure, agency and, 308
students, international, 25, 96, 102–3, 116n68, 127; advantages, 232–33; attracting, 214, 226, 236; Bangladeshi, 345; changing labor markets and, 219–23; from China, 227–28; COVID-19 pandemic impacting, 230–31; enrollment rates, 223, *224*; fields of study, 231–32, *232*; gender inequality for, 234–35, *235*; human capital and, 233–37; PR and, 217–19; as prospective workers and citizens, 237–38; settlement pathways, 215–17, 239; in US, *225*, 230
student visas, 127, 134, *135*
subcontractors, 47, 192
subordination, 38
Suny, Ronald, 322–23
surplus labor, 3–4
surveillance, 22, 38, 39, 42, 51, 54; bio-analytics of, 49–50; scholarship on, 58n20; Zuboff on, 48
survival jobs, 282
Sustainable Development Goals, UN, 341
symbolic ethnicity, 111

Ta, Vincent, 149n1
Taiwan, 89, 90

talent, global, 213, 217, 228, 236
Tandon, Reena, 308
Tarrow, Sidney, 323
technology, 17, 213; AI, 46–47, 216–17; algorithms, 42, 46, 47; bio-analytics, 49–50; communication, 315, 317, 346; data, 46–47, 48, 49–51, 53, 61n43; digital, 39, 42; immigration controlled by, 45, 48, 50–51, 53; specialized, 216–17; transnationalism and modern, 316–17. *See also* information technology
telecommunications, 286
television, 317
Telles, Edward, 312
temporal justice, 205, 208
temporary contract labor, 16, 44, 156–59, 192
temporary foreign workers, 40, 56n9, 155, 156–59, 178, 180, 182n33; emergence of, 189–95; exploitation of, 190, 193, 194–95; proliferation of, 195–98. *See also* H-1B visas
Temporary Protective Status (TPS), 120
terrorism, 229, 274
Texas, 321
theft, wage, 195
Thomas, Kevin J. A., 25–26, 126, 177, 234
three-D jobs, 4
Tichenor, Daniel, 13
time: measurements, 203–4; use decisions, 128; wait, 188–89
time, durational, 25, 203, 208, 209; Cohen on, 204–6; political value of, 205
TN. *See* NAFTA professional visa
TPS. *See* Temporary Protective Status
trailing spouses, 272, 288
transcultural parenting, 130
transculturation, 310
transferable education, 249–50
transferable skills, 228
transfers, remittance, 341, 343
transformation: of culture, 311; of immigrants, 38

visa policies, US, 10–12, 23–24, 50, 145–46, 220, 230, 246; as conflicted, 179; discrimination in, 274; executive actions on, 119–20; female Pakistani immigrants and, 276; inequality, 148; Ishikawa on, 185n68; merit-based, 292–93; overview of, 119–24; prior studies on, 124–30; reform of, 118, 147, 148–49, 159–60, 178; streamlining, 239; student, 102, 116n68

visas, immigrant, 118, 146, 147, 196; auction system for, 126; cancellation of removals for, 136, *138*; DV, 122–23, 130, 136, *138*, 248, 344; EB, 122, 136, *137*, 191–92, 201; family-sponsored, 121, 122, 124–25, 136, *137*; fixed-effects panel data, 139–40, *141*; fixed-effects panel data by type, *144*; 1997–2018 trends, 131, *132*; SIV and SIJ, 123–24; 2017 counts, *123*, 124; 2002–2017 trends by type, 134, 136, *136*

visas, nonimmigrant, 130, 146, 196; categories of, 121; exchange, 134, *135*; fixed-effects panel data, 139–40, *141*; fixed-effects panel data by type, *142–43*; high-skilled, 131, 133, *134*; low-skilled, 131, 133, *133*, 143, 147; 1997–2018 trends, 131, *132*; 1997–2018 trends by type, 131, *132*; student, 127, 134, *135*; 2017 counts, *123*, 124; VW program, 120, 149n10. *See also* H-1B visas

Visa Waiver (VW), 120, 149n10

voluntary immigrants, 316

volunteers, women, 324–25

vulnerability, 176, 192

VW. *See* Visa Waiver

wage, 157, 161; abuses, 151n24; determination, 182n27; family sponsored visas and growth of, 124–25; H-1B visas and, 125–26; penalty, 259, 264; prevailing, 163, 179, 182n24; STEM jobs, 126–27; theft, 195

Wage and Hourly Division, US Labor Department, 150n12

wait times, green card, 199–200, 201, 209, 210n5; as democratic deficit, 203–8; durational, 203

Waldinger, Roger, 21, 318

war: Cold War, 90, 95; Korean War, 95; Russo-Japanese War, 91; World War II, 94–95

War Brides Act, US, 89, 95

Washington Post, 207

wastage, skill, 278

weekly earnings, income, 251, 253, 263–64

Weinberg, Sydney, 307

Welcoming America, 237–38

welfare, 342

well-being, psychological, 249, 329

WhatsApp, 317

White House Taskforce on New Americans, 292, 300n91

workers: domestic, 163, 178; international students as prospective, 237–38; knowledge, 277. *See also* temporary foreign workers

work experience, 255

working poor, 16, 44

workplace abuse, 176–77

World Bank, 8, 9, 319, 338

The World of Our Fathers (Howe), 307

The World of Our Mothers (Weinberg), 307

world system theory, macroeconomic, 4–5

World Trade Organization (WTO), 8

World War II, 10, 89, 93–95, 119, 306

Wotherspoon, Terry, 25, 158–59

WTO. *See* World Trade Organization

Y2K moment, 190

"yellow peril," 88, 95, 109

Zelizer, Viviana, 348

Zenteno, René, 22

Zhan, Shaohua, 188

Zhou, Min, 18, 21, 23, 188, 313, 315

Zuboff, Shoshana, 48